BTEC
Level 2

excel
learning, changing lives

PUBLIC
SERVICES
LEVEL 2

BTEC First

Debra Gray | Tracey Lilley
Lizzie Toms | John Vause

A PEARSON COMPANY

Published by Pearson Education Limited, a company incorporated in England and Wales, having its registered office at Edinburgh Gate, Harlow, Essex, CM20 2JE. Registered company number: 872828

www.pearsonschoolsandfecolleges.co.uk

Edexcel is a registered trademark of Edexcel Limited

Text © Pearson Education Limited 2010

First published 2010

14 13
10 9 8 7 6 5 4 3 2

British Library Cataloguing in Publication Data
A catalogue record for this book is available from the British Library.

ISBN 978 1 846907 21 0

Designed by Wooden Ark
Typeset by Tek-Art
Original illustrations © Tek-Art
Cover design by Visual Philosophy, created by CMC Design
Cover photo © Derek Berwin/Getty Images
Back cover photos © Photodisc/Photolink/D Falconer, Agita Leimane/iStockphoto
Printed in Spain by Graficas

Disclaimer
This material has been published on behalf of Edexcel and offers high-quality support for the delivery of Edexcel qualifications.
This does not mean that the material is essential to achieve any Edexcel qualification, nor does it mean that it is the only suitable material available to support any Edexcel qualification. Edexcel material will not be used verbatim in setting any Edexcel examination or assessment. Any resource lists produced by Edexcel shall include this and other appropriate resources.

Copies of official specifications for all Edexcel qualifications may be found on the Edexcel website: www.edexcel.com

Contents

About your **BTEC Level 2 First Public Services** iv

About the authors

Debra Gray has taught public services in the Further Education sector for 13 years. She has a degree in Criminology and master's degrees in Criminal Justice and Education Management. She has written numerous publications for both learners and tutors on public services and other issues, such as the new diplomas. Debra also served as an Edexcel External Verifier for three years.

Tracey Lilley has worked as an Edexcel Senior Verifier and External Verifier for Edexcel and is involved in the writing of new BTEC Public Services specifications. She served as a special constable and, more recently, as a teacher and lecturer delivering and assessing programmes from level 1 to level 6. A member of the Institute of Educational Assessors and the Institute for Learning, Tracey is also a Senior Assessment Associate for the Principal Learning Public Services.

Lizzie Toms has recently been appointed as the Edexcel Principal Standards Verifier for Public and Security Services for QCF qualifications and has been a Senior Verifier for Edexcel. She has master's degrees in Education and Organisational Consultancy and is an experienced teacher with covering levels 1 to 7. She has worked closely with the Magistrates' Courts, the Probation and HM Prison Services. Lizzie has also written a range of Public Services materials including BTEC publications.

John Vause has taught public services for the past 10 years. He studied Philosophy after his career in the West Yorkshire and then the South Yorkshire Police. During this period he was involved in planning, organising and taking part in numerous outdoor activities and exhibitions while training Police Cadets. He has also attended several major incidents, including multiple-vehicle road traffic collisions and fire incidents. As a detective in the Criminal Investigation Department John investigated hundreds of crimes, including murder.

About your BTEC Level 2 First Public Services

Choosing to study for a BTEC Level 2 First Public Services qualification is a great decision to make for lots of reasons. Public Services can lead you into a whole range of professions and sectors and allows you to explore your skills in many different ways.

Your BTEC Level 2 First in Public Services is a **vocational** or **work-related** qualification. This doesn't mean that it will give you *all* the skills you need to do a job, but it does mean that you'll have the opportunity to gain specific knowledge, understanding and skills that are relevant to your chosen subject or area of work.

What will you be doing?

The qualification is structured into different types of units, some of which you must complete and others that are optional. To see the full requirements for your course you must check the specification (see www.edexcel.com).

- BTEC Level 2 First **Certificate** in Public Services: one mandatory unit and one optional unit that provide a combined total of 15 credits
- BTEC Level 2 first **Extended Certificate** in Public Services: one mandatory unit and optional units that provide a total of 30 credits
- BTEC Level 2 First **Diploma** in Public Services: three mandatory units, one of two specialist units and optional units that provide a total of 60 credits

The table below shows which units in your qualification are included in this book and whether they are mandatory (M), specialist (S) or optional (O).

Unit number	Credit value	Unit name	Cert	Ex Cert	Diploma
1	10	Public service skills	M	M	M
2	5	Employment in the uniformed public services	O	O	S*
3	5	Employment in the non-uniformed public services	O	O	S*
4	5	Career planning for the public services	O	O	M
5	10	Improving health and fitness for entry to the uniformed public services		O	M
6	10	Citizenship, the individual and society		O	O
9	10	Sport and recreation in the public services		O	O
11	10	Law and its impact on the individual in public services		O	O
12	10	Crime and its effects on society			O
13	10	Community and cultural awareness		O	O
15	10	Expedition skills in public services		O	O
17	10	Attending emergency incidents in public services			O
20	10	Volunteering in public services		O	O

- Learners must choose between units marked with an asterisk; they may do either unit, but not both.

How to use this book

This book is designed to help you through your BTEC Level 2 First Public Services course. It is divided into 13 units to reflect the units in the specification. This book contains many features that will help you use your skills and knowledge in work-related situations and assist you in getting the most from your course.

Introduction

These introductions give you a snapshot of what to expect from each unit – and what you should be aiming for by the time you finish it!

Assessment and grading criteria

This table explains what you must do in order to achieve each of the assessment criteria for each unit. For each assessment criterion, shown by the grade button **P1**, there is an assessment activity.

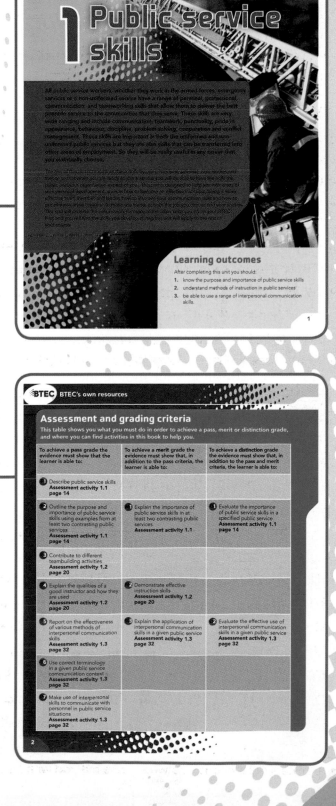

Assessment

Your tutor will set assignments throughout your course for you to complete. These may take the form of projects where you research, plan, prepare, and make a piece of practical work, case studies and presentations. The important thing is that you evidence your skills and knowledge to date.

Stuck for ideas? Daunted by your first assignment? These students have all been through it before...

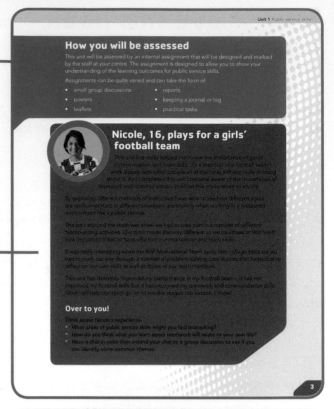

Activities

There are different types of activities for you to do: assessment activities are suggestions for tasks that you might do as part of your assignment and will help you develop your knowledge, skills and understanding. Each of these has grading tips that clearly explain what you need to do in order to achieve a pass, merit or distinction grade.

There are also suggestions for activities that will give you a broader grasp of the Public Services, stretch your understanding and deepen your skills.

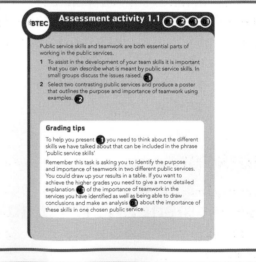

Personal, learning and thinking skills

Throughout your BTEC Level 2 First Public Services course, there are lots of opportunities to develop your personal, learning and thinking skills. Look out for these as you progress.

Functional skills

It's important that you have good English, maths and ICT skills – you never know when you'll need them, and employers will be looking for evidence that you've got these skills too.

Key terms

Technical words and phrases are easy to spot, and definitions are included. The terms and definitions are also in the glossary at the back of the book.

WorkSpace

Case studies provide snapshots of real workplace issues, and show how the skills and knowledge you develop during your course can help you in your career.

Just checking

When you see this sort of activity, take stock! These quick activities and questions are there to check your knowledge. You can use them to see how much progress you've made.

Edexcel's assignment tips

At the end of each unit, you'll find hints and tips to help you get the best mark you can, such as the best websites to go to, checklists to help you remember processes and really useful facts and figures.

Link

In the margin, alongside a topic in the main text, you will find cross references that guide you to other parts of the book where the topic is covered in more detail or where you will be able to find relevant information.

Hotlinks

There are links to relevant websites in this book. In order to ensure that the links are up to date, that the links work, and that the sites are not inadvertently linked to sites that could be considered offensive, we have made the links available on the Pearson website at www.pearsonschoolsandfecolleges.co.uk/hotlinks.

When you access the site, search for either the express code (7210V), title (*BTEC Level 2 First Public Services Student Book*) or ISBN (9781846907210).

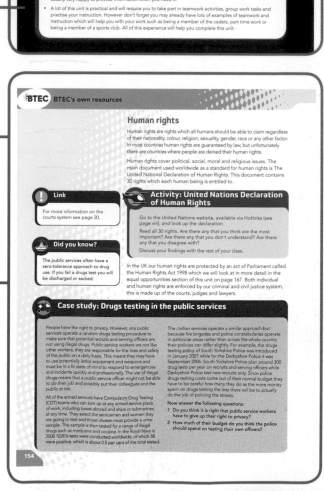

Don't miss out on these resources to help you!

Have you read your *BTEC Level 2 First Study Skills Guide*? It's full of advice on study skills, putting your assignments together and making the most of being a BTEC Public Services learner.

Your book is just part of the exciting resources from Edexcel to help you succeed in your BTEC course.
Visit www.edexcel.com/BTEC or www.pearsonfe.co.uk/BTEC2010 for more details.

1 Public service skills

All public service workers, whether they work in the armed forces, emergency services or a non-uniformed service have a range of personal, professional, communication and teamworking skills that allow them to deliver the best possible service to the communities that they serve. These skills are very wide ranging and include communication, teamwork, punctuality, pride in appearance, behaviour, discipline, problem solving, cooperation and conflict management. These skills are important in both the uniformed and non-uniformed public services but they are also skills that can be transferred into other areas of employment. So they will be really useful in any career that you eventually choose.

The aim of this unit is to explore these skills by using hands-on activities, case studies and theory, so that when you are ready to join a service you will be able to have the skills the public and your organisation expect of you. This unit is designed to help you with areas of your personal development, such as how to become an effective instructor, being a more effective team member and leader, how to improve your communication skills and how to put all these areas together to make you better at both the job you choose and your studies. This unit will provide the groundwork for many of the other units you do on your BTEC First and you will find the skills you develop during this unit will apply to the rest of your course.

Learning outcomes

After completing this unit you should:

1. know the purpose and importance of public service skills
2. understand methods of instruction in public services
3. be able to use a range of interpersonal communication skills.

1

Assessment and grading criteria

This table shows you what you must do in order to achieve a pass, merit or distinction grade, and where you can find activities in this book to help you.

To achieve a **pass** grade the evidence must show that the learner is able to:	To achieve a **merit** grade the evidence must show that, in addition to the pass criteria, the learner is able to:	To achieve a **distinction** grade the evidence must show that, in addition to the pass and merit criteria, the learner is able to:
P1 Describe public service skills **Assessment activity 1.1 page 16**		
P2 Outline the purpose and importance of public service skills using examples from at least two contrasting public services **Assessment activity 1.1 page 16**	**M1** Explain the importance of public service skills in at least two contrasting public services **Assessment activity 1.1 page 16**	**D1** Evaluate the importance of public service skills in a specified public service **Assessment activity 1.1 page 16**
P3 Contribute to different teambuilding activities **Assessment activity 1.2 page 21**		
P4 Explain the qualities of a good instructor and how they are used **Assessment activity 1.2 page 21**	**M2** Demonstrate effective instruction skills **Assessment activity 1.2 page 21**	
P5 Report on the effectiveness of various methods of interpersonal communication skills **Assessment activity 1.3 page 34**	**M3** Explain the application of interpersonal communication skills in a given public service **Assessment activity 1.3 page 34**	**D2** Evaluate the effective use of interpersonal communication skills in a given public service **Assessment activity 1.3 page 34**
P6 Use correct terminology in a given public service communication context **Assessment activity 1.3 page 34**		
P7 Make use of interpersonal skills to communicate with personnel in public service situations **Assessment activity 1.3 page 34**		

How you will be assessed

This unit will be assessed by an internal assignment that will be designed and marked by the staff at your centre. The assignment is designed to allow you to show your understanding of the learning outcomes for public service skills.

Assignments can be quite varied and can take the form of:

- small group discussions
- posters
- leaflets
- reports
- keeping a journal or log
- practical tasks.

Nicole, 16, plays for a girls' football team

This unit has really helped me to see the importance of good communication and team skills. As a member of a football team I work closely with other people all of the time, without really thinking about it. As I completed this unit I became aware of the importance of teamwork and communication and how this could relate to my life.

By exploring different methods of instruction I was able to see how different styles are really important in different situations, particularly when working in a pressured environment like a public service.

The bit I enjoyed the most was when we had to take part in a number of different teambuilding activities. Our tutor made this very different so we could see at first hand how important it was to have effective communication and team skills.

It was really interesting when the RAF Motivational Team came into college because we had to work our way through a number of problem-solving case studies that helped us to reflect on our own skills as well as those of our team members.

This unit has definitely improved my performance in my football team – it has not improved my football skills but it has improved my teamwork and communication skills which will help our team go on to win the league this season, I hope!

Over to you!

Think about Nicole's experience.

- What areas of public service skills might you find interesting?
- How do you think what you learn about teamwork will relate to your own life?
- Have a chat in pairs then extend your chat to a group discussion to see if you can identify some common themes.

1 The purpose and importance of public service skills

Are you in a team?

Think of what you do in your free time. Are you a member of a sports team? social club? Or is it just you and your friends? Think about your team or friends and how they work together.

Write down five factors (qualities) that you think are important to you and your team. You might consider: communication, combining individual skills or achieving aims and objectives.

Discuss your findings in small groups and compare the factors you have identified with those of the other groups.

From this, are you able to identify a list of the five most important factors a team should consider?

Key term

Public service skills – a general term given to a wide range of personal, professional and communications skills that employees of the public services develop and improve during their careers.

1.1 Public service skills

What do we mean by **public service skills** and why are they important? Are these special skills? Or are they skills that you could transfer during your working career? Public service skills are a set of core skills that an individual will need to possess and develop to be effective in the public services but are also skills that any individual would find useful during their working life.

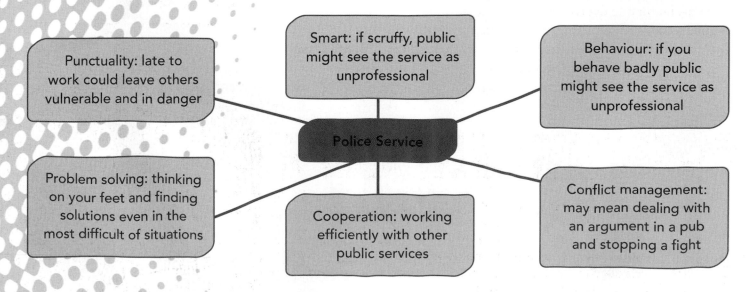

Figure 1.1: These are examples of public service skills applied to the Police Service. How can these skills be applied to the Prison Service?

Communication

Good communication skills are vital for working in the uniformed public services. You are taught these skills from the moment you start basic training. Communication can take place in a number of ways, such as: **non-verbal communication**, **verbal communication** and **visual communication**.

Professional and personal skills

This includes a number of skills that an individual may have initially but that can also be developed during your career and your BTEC First to improve your skills not only for the public services but for the wider employment market. Just a few of these skills are listed below and shown in Figure 1.2.

Punctuality/timekeeping

- Be on time, don't be late
- Factor in extra time into your journey for unforeseen circumstances
- Punctuality is a basic skill and your life (or the life of others) could be at stake.

Pride of appearance

- First impressions are very important
- Polish your shoes
- Iron your clothes
- Wash your hair, have a bath and a shave
- For example, a smart uniform shows that you are proud of your job and your position in society.

Behaviour

- Speak to people appropriately
- Show respect to everyone
- Consider your behaviour and its impact on others
- For example, if the public lose faith in a service they may lose respect for them and the work they do.

Key terms

Non-verbal communication – this includes your body language, gestures and facial expressions.

Verbal communication – this involves providing communication, instructions or orders to others, which can be done in different ways, such as in person, in groups, at meetings, even via radio communication. Verbal communication also includes factors such as tone of voice, choice of language and clarity of speech.

Visual communication – this includes writing or drawing pictures.

Did you know?

From 1285 there existed a system of parish constables who were local law enforcement officers, but because of the low status and pay of police work, parish constables tended to be illiterate and unskilled – they were effectively poorly paid watchmen. The system of parish constables disappeared in the late 1700s and was replaced with the beginnings of the modern and highly skilled Police Service we know today.

Activity: Your skills

Have you ever worked with the public either in a part-time job, on work experience or as a volunteer? What skills do you need to be able to work well with the public? Make a list and then grade yourself on a scale of 1–5 (with 1 being excellent and 5 being poor). Which skills are your strongest? Which skills are your weakest and what could you do to improve them?

Sarasa Dev is a police community support officer. Why is it important that she takes pride in her appearance and behaves appropriately?

Key terms

Team – a group of people who are working together towards a common goal or purpose.

Teamwork – a way of getting different people to work together to achieve the task the team was set up to complete.

Leadership – the setting of goals or targets for a team to achieve. It is an ongoing process where a leader directs the human and physical resources they have to reach a goal such as putting out a fire, winning a conflict or reducing crime. It is about the ability to influence the behaviour of groups of people in your command.

Discipline – a system of rules of conduct or method of practice.

Activity: Public service skills

Working in pairs

Make a list of the public service skills outlined above. Look at different public services such as the police/fire/army/prison and list which skills you think would be important for each service. Would some skills be more important than others in different public services?

Working individually

Choosing one public service from above produce a spider diagram showing how these skills will benefit the uniformed public service.

Discipline

- Make sure you don't let your emotions control you in pressured situations
- Always obey instructions
- Work as a **team** (success depends on **teamwork** and successful **leadership**)
- Self-discipline (self-control is the best form of **discipline**)
- Respect and trust your colleagues
- For example, discipline and self-discipline equip you with the skills to be able to deal with difficult decisions.

Problem solving

- Solve problems as quickly as possible
- Work efficiently
- Consider all solutions and agree on the solutions as a team
- For example, if there is a disagreement within the team over a task it is important to mediate, discuss the problem and seek a solution that both sides can agree on.

Cooperation

- Work together to achieve a common goal
- Support each other in achieving that goal
- Cooperate with each other physically and mentally in order to complete goal
- For example team members have to cooperate with each other physically and mentally in order to complete a task quickly, particularly if someone's life depends on it.

Conflict management

- Deal with the dispute quickly
- Utilise your listening skills
- Calm the situation down using a variety of communication skills
- Use force when all other techniques have failed
- Consider public safety and protect evidence
- For example, when police officers are required to arrest a violent offender they too will use listening and speaking skills. If calming a situation down by trying various communication skills does not work, uniformed service staff are trained to use necessary force to restrain people to stop aggressive behaviour. This is used as a last resort if other techniques have been unsuccessful.

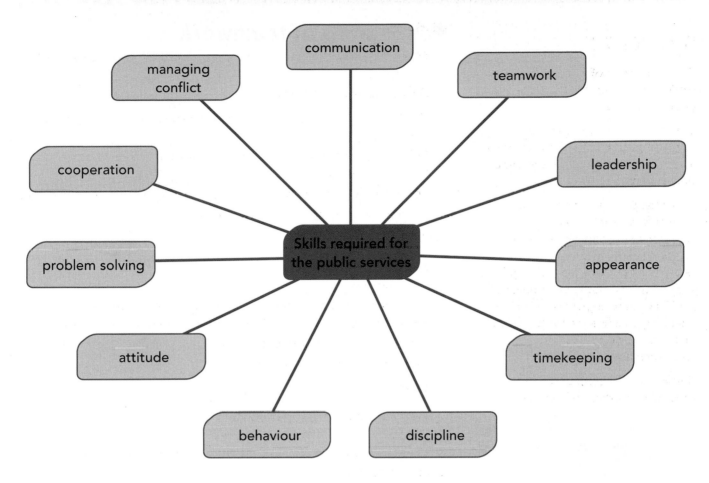

Figure 1.2: You could add patience, respect for diversity, honesty and a sense of humour to this diagram. What other examples can you think of?

1.2 Teamwork and different types of public service teams

The main aim of teamwork is to achieve the task the team was initially set up to achieve, for the police this might be crime reduction, for the fire service it might be extinguishing a fire and for the coastguard conducting a successful rescue. Most people in organisations work in teams and this is certainly the case with the public services. Public service teams can have many different names such as departments, sections, watches, shifts, units, crews, regiments, task forces and offices. Although their names may be different, their main purpose is the same – to work together as a team towards an agreed common goal or purpose.

For a team to succeed it has to have:

- good communication
- positive leadership
- motivation
- discipline.

Advantages of teamwork

The main purpose of a team in any organisation is to do a job, quickly, efficiently, cost-effectively, and to achieve the best possible results. If a team works well together it can bring with it some major advantages, particularly in the public services. Some of those advantages are:

- completing the task efficiently (to meet deadlines and to a high standard)
- ensuring a safe environment (as colleagues will look out for and protect one another)
- saving money (if people are working efficiently then they can be more productive and save on costs)
- raising confidence and courage within the team (in public services this is known as **morale**. Good teamwork helps to make people feel good about themselves and the work they do).

Value of teamwork

In the armed services for example, teamwork is valued very highly because:

- Teams are more efficient as you combine the efforts of more than one person to achieve a common goal.
- You are dependent on the person next to you and each person's actions and performance has a direct impact on the safety, well-being and goals of the team.
- It boosts morale, which can be particularly important in stressful and hostile situations. Having colleagues to rely on and share the burden of duty can relieve stress and therefore make the team as a whole more efficient and effective.
- Teamwork can bring job satisfaction, which means that people enjoy their work more and have increased respect for their team members.
- Some tasks in the services are simply too large to be achieved by one person, for example getting a jet aircraft ready for combat or

Key term

Morale – the confidence within a team, the team spirit, the willingness to succeed and support each other in working towards a common goal.

Look at the image above of a team activity. Describe what they are doing. What kind of team skills would be needed to achieve this activity?

Activity: Is teamwork important?

Think about the Police Service/Fire Service/Army/RAF/Navy/Prison Service and write down a list of reasons why you think teamwork might be important in these public services.

Share your findings with the rest of the class. Did you come up with the same reasons or were they different? Why do you think this is?

From this, are you able to identify a list of the five most important factors a team should consider?

the maintenance of an aircraft carrier. These things cannot be done by one person alone, they require extensive teams who know how to work together and cooperate to get the job done.

- Teamwork promotes flexibility as you can create teams to do specific tasks at very short notice and disband them when they are no longer required.

Types of teams

There are many different types of teams that exist in the public services. Some types of teams include:

- **Crew.** A crew can describe a number of different types of teams. From the perspective of the public services the most suitable definition is – a team of men and women who operate or maintain a piece of equipment such as a fire engine, ship or aircraft.

- **Shift/watch.** Shifts and watches can occur in a variety of jobs which require people to work to maintain a service continually over a 24-hour period, such as some manufacturing work, retail and transportation. It involves a work pattern that means enough people are working at any given time to deal with the demand of the public. An example of this is a police officer on duty at a police station that needs to be staffed 24 hours a day. For example, in the Police Service your shift pattern could be 2 days (consisting of an 8-hour shift) followed by 2 nights (consisting of a 2-day shift) followed by 4 rest days (days off). This pattern is then repeated.

- **Brigade.** A brigade is a military unit within the armed services that is made up of a variable numbers of battalions, commanded by a colonel. A brigade can be broken into two categories (1) the administrative unit which is responsible for non-operational management of battalions (such as human resources, training and strategic reserve) and (2) a deployable combat arm varying from a battalion to a regiment. The size of a modern combat regiment can range from a few hundred to 5000 soldiers.

Activity: Public service teams

Research the public service you want to join. Find out what names they give the types of team in that service and select three different teams to write a brief description about.

Share your findings with the class to see how many different teams you have been able to find in your service. Because your class will have people who want to join a variety of different public services this is a really good way to find out about and get an overview of the teams in many services.

- **Multi-agency team.** A multi-agency team describes the coming together of different teams from the public services working to achieve the same goal, objective or aim. They train together to become experienced as a team. For example, the police, local council, schools and Neighbourhood Watch working together to deal with anti-social behaviour on an estate is a multi-agency team.

- **Specialist team.** These teams are set up for a particular purpose and have special knowledge, training and skills. Other teams within the organisation do not usually possess these abilities, attributes and skills. For example, the Firearms Unit (SO19) within the Police Service.

- **Project team (for implementing new policies).** These teams are often government led and consist of individuals from a variety of public services who are working together on a specific project. These project teams may be used to assist in the implementation of new policies that could be applied across different public services.

1.3 The importance of teamwork

You can see from images like this that every single person in a team is important. There will never be a single person working in isolation dealing with an incident. It might be a team of two or three police officers who are dealing with a road traffic incident alongside colleagues from the Ambulance Service and Fire and Rescue Service. Working closely and efficiently with other public services means that the job gets done quickly and efficiently, and most importantly helps save lives and property.

Achieving organisational objectives

Every organisation has a purpose, a goal, an objective or a mission statement. This is the purpose of the organisation and what it sets out to achieve. The role of the armed forces is to defend the territories of the United Kingdom and to strengthen international peace and security. The role of the Fire Service is primarily to fight fire and take part in other rescue missions, as well as to promote fire safety to members of

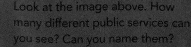

Look at the image above. How many different public services can you see? Can you name them?

the community. Each of the different Fire Services across the country will have a slightly different mission statement but they are all working towards a common goal.

Merseyside Fire and Rescue Service state that they wish to work in partnership to provide an excellent, affordable service that will:

– reduce risk throughout the community by protective community safety services
– respond quickly to emergencies with skilful staff who reflect all the diverse communities we serve
– restore and maintain quality of life in our communities.

It is clear from this mission statement that the core organisational objectives are part of the everyday work and training of the Fire Service.

In order to work together as an effective team and to achieve results, it is vital that everyone knows and understands the aims and objectives of their own organisation. If colleagues are not aware of these there is a danger that members of the team may be 'off task' and this could affect progress towards the aims and objectives as well as put the lives of other team members and the public at risk. It is vital that if you and your team are working in dangerous situations you all know what you are there to achieve and that you all feel suitably trained to perform efficiently and effectively. Many incidents that you might deal with in your public service career will involve life-threatening situations for you, your colleagues and the public. It is important, therefore, that your team is working together in an effective way. Achieving objectives and working together makes people feel a sense of pride, loyalty, **camaraderie** and part of something bigger.

Teamwork within an organisational structure

Teams exist in every organisation. For example, in the Police Service every police officer belongs to at least one team, usually more. Police teams are often quite specialist in their roles but they also do 'core' police work. For example, a police officer will be a member of:

- the police force they work for
- the division/area they work in
- the station they report to
- the shift they are working on.

Police teams do not work alone, they are advised and guided by senior officers who are in management teams and who themselves are guided by their senior officers. In all teams and organisations there is an organisational structure. If you look at the organisational chart in Figure 1.3 you can see these links more clearly.

Working within a structure can be necessary to ensure that teams do not come into conflict with each other in terms of their goals. By having a clear structure you can make sure that all of your goals within an organisation have teams working on them, rather than a disorganised system which may mean that multiple teams work on the same goal without coordinating their efforts.

Did you know?

You can check out Merseyside Fire and Rescue Service available via Hotlinks (see page viii).

Key term

Camaraderie – the feeling of closeness and bonding when people work closely together, and in particular when they face dangerous situations.

Activity: Objectives

Why do you think it is important for public service employees to know and understand the objectives of their organisation? Discuss as a class and agree a clear reason.

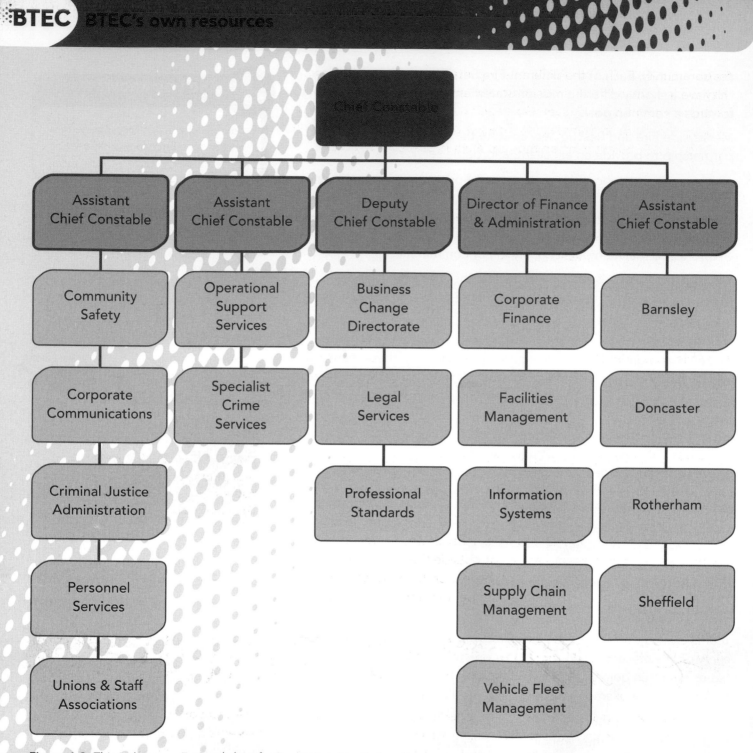

Figure 1.3: This is the organisational chart for South Yorkshire Police. Have you seen an organisational chart?

It is also worth pointing out that sometimes teams can work well without a formal structure if they have clear roles and a clear goal. Teams in the services can also be formed briefly and for specialist purposes, for example during a major incident teams are formed at Bronze, Silver and Gold level to deal with the incident. The members of the teams may not have met before that point and may never meet again, but they know what they are supposed to do and they do it extremely well.

You can see from this the structure within South Yorkshire Police Force that the senior officers are at the top of the tree and the operational teams are below. This means that as important decisions are made they are fed down the chain of command until they are undertaken by the officers at ground level. Operational knowledge can also feed back up the chain so that senior officers understand the picture on the ground. This is essential when they are making strategic decisions.

Command and control

Command and control is the coordination of a range of functions used by a senior officer in the achievement of a goal or the accomplishment of a mission. Some of these functions might be:

- deployment of personnel
- deployment of equipment
- communications
- facilities
- service procedures.

Command and control are essential in the work of the public services. The military in particular rely heavily on command and control structures. Modern military conflicts are very complex and usually involve **coalitions** of allied forces working together to achieve a common goal. Without command and control measures in place it would be impossible to coordinate the efforts of different nations.

Often in the public services the work you are required to undertake is physically and mentally demanding as well as dangerous. To be an effective team it is important to have a leader who is able to communicate within the team as well as outside the team. In most public services the higher the rank of the leader the more commands they have to give, usually to a larger number of people or teams.

Key term

Coalition – this is when different groups of people, organisations or nations work together to achieve a common goal.

Case study: British Forces in Afghanistan

There are a number of British forces operating in Afghanistan. In charge of these forces there is a Commander-in-Chief. He has a senior role in having an overview of what is going on at ground level and is responsible for managing and commanding the troops. To be able to do this job effectively he relies on a variety of information sources provided for him by other colleagues. He may take the opinion of staff who are of lower ranks but who have the various skills and knowledge from working at ground level that are essential to the planning and success of carrying out any future operations. This reliance on information provided by other staff is how the Commander-in-Chief will then begin to control the situation. As information is gathered he is then able to read and understand the current situation. In order to keep the situation in control he may well need to give out different commands or orders as factors change. The skills and knowledge from everyone in the chain of command are important in planning and carrying out a successful operation.

Now answer the following questions:

1 Referring back to Figure 1.2 on page 7, identify how the Commander-in-Chief uses professional and personal skills.

2 Are there any skills not used, or additional skills not listed? Discuss with a partner.

Case study: London bombings of 7/7

Four suicide bombers struck in central London on Thursday 7 July 2005, killing 52 people and injuring more than 770. The coordinated attacks hit the transport system as the morning rush hour drew to a close.

Three bombs went off at or around 8:50 a.m. on underground trains just outside Liverpool Street and Edgware Road stations, and on another travelling between King's Cross and Russell Square. The final explosion was around an hour later on a double-decker bus in Tavistock Square, not far from King's Cross.

In the aftermath of this major incident the emergency services all had to rely on teamwork and training to save lives.

Now discuss the following in groups:

1 How did effective teamwork enable the services to respond to such a major incident?

2 What types of team would have been involved in the emergency service response to this incident?

3 Why was teamwork particularly important in this incident? Do you think that working as a team in a situation like this is important? Explain your answer.

Did you know?

The Dare Devils Team of the Indian Army Signal Corps achieved a motorcycle pyramid consisting of 251 men balanced on 11 motorcycles on 11 June 2008 at Gowri Shankar Parade Ground, Jabalpur, India. The pyramid travelled a distance of 240 m. This is an amazing example of teamwork!

Activity:Team qualities

Your class will need to form teams

Scatter objects around your classroom. Blindfold one member of your team and then guide that person around the obstacles using only verbal instructions from the team. You could do this in two teams and see which team can get their person across the room the quickest with the least number of obstacle bumps.

1.4 Qualities needed for effective teamwork

For a team to be effective a variety of skills are important to ensure the team is operating efficiently and effectively. These are often skills that each person in the team holds to a greater or lesser extent but when the team comes together these skills are strengthened and help hold the team together and also help to support all members of the team. The main qualities that are important for an effective team are listed here.

Leadership

This is more than just being the senior rank and giving orders. An effective leader must be able to lead the team to achieve goals in an effective and motivating way. Most people have the potential to be leaders. It sometimes comes naturally or it may have to be taught. To be an effective leader you should:

- remember that you are part of the team too and that you need every single person
- be approachable and encourage your team
- be confident in your abilities and those of your team
- look after your team, ensure they receive the correct training and their welfare is looked after
- learn how to communicate effectively and try to create a sense of identify for the team
- reflect on the progress of the team and make changes if appropriate
- be inspiring so others may follow your lead through example and loyalty.

Combining individual skills

It is important that every team member plays a part and that the individual skills they bring to the team are used effectively to make the team a success. For instance, in the Fire Service an officer may have additional specialised skills that can be used in an incident such as the collapse of a building, or in the Police Service an officer may have undertaken additional medical training that could be used in an incident with large numbers of casualties.

Achieving aims

All teams are usually set aims, objectives and goals. To ensure your team is effective it is important that every member of the team is aware of what these are so that everyone is working towards a common theme. This then makes achieving the aims much easier. Remember that the whole point of having a team is to achieve a task.

Working with others

Your team will be made up of a number of individuals, all of whom will be different. They may have come from different cultures, different countries or different public services but they will all share a common goal. It is important for the success of teams that people are able to put aside any personal differences and work together efficiently and effectively to get the job done.

What teamwork and leadership skills could a football team bring to working in the public services?

Case study: Robert undertakes a career interview

Your best friend Robert is only 16 and is considering a career in the army. As someone who is already a member of the Army Cadet Force you are aware that to be a good soldier he will need to develop his personal, social and communication skills. Robert is fairly confident that this is the right career for him and has been to the Army Careers Office and completed his BARB (British Army Recruit Battery) test. His interview is next week. To help him with this you have decided to do a little research and write some notes that will assist him at interview. Look at the Army website, available via Hotlinks (see page viii), for help with this.

Now answer the following questions:

1   What are the main public service skills that Robert will develop during his army career?

2   Describe three types of teams that Robert may come across during his career in the Army.

3   Discuss three of the main qualities that Robert can develop to make him more effective as a team player?

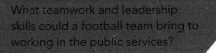
Activity: Team skills

Work as a whole class

Write your own name on a label. Your tutor will mix up the labels from the class and put one on the back of you (and each learner) without you seeing the name on the label. You must ask different yes/no questions to try to find out who you have become. Mingle with the whole class as much as you need to.

PLTS

By thinking of different scenarios where public service skills and teamwork are needed you will be improving your creative thinking skills.

Functional skills

This assignment may also help you to develop your functional skills in ICT if you word process your posters and include images or tables.

PLTS

As a team member you will contribute to different teambuilding activities.

Remember

In order for a teambuilding activity to be successful it is important that all members of the team are involved in the decision-making process as well as putting into action the agreed plan or solution to your exercise.

BTEC **Assessment activity 1.1** P1 P2 M1 D1

Public service skills and teamwork are both essential parts of working in the public services.

1 To assist in the development of your team skills it is important that you can *describe* what is meant by public service skills. In small groups discuss the issues raised. **P1**

2 Select two contrasting public services and produce a poster that *outlines* the purpose and importance of public service skills using examples. **P2**

Grading tips

To help you present **P1** you need to think about the different skills we have talked about that can be included in the phrase 'public service skills'.

Remember this task is asking you to identify the purpose and importance of teamwork in two different public services. You could draw up your results in a table. If you want to achieve the higher grades you need to give a more detailed explanation **M1** of the importance of teamwork in the services you have identified as well as being able to draw conclusions and make an analysis **D1** about the importance of these skills in one chosen public service.

1.5 Teambuilding

In order for you to develop your teamworking skills it is important that you practise through teambuilding activities. Teambuilding activities are used by the public services as well as many other organisations to help train new recruits and improve teamwork skills.

A teambuilding activity usually starts with a group of people who have not worked together being given a shared task to complete. The purpose of this is to force them to work together, cooperate and communicate so they can begin to work as members of a team. Teambuilding activities often require a problem-solving task which enables all members of the team to participate in the activity with the shared goal of solving the problem.

Characteristics within teams

There are often a number of characteristics that teams share. These characteristics should develop as the team works together and aims to be successful.

Table 1.1: Teambuilding activities develop these characteristics.

Characteristic	Explanation
Team culture	This means the members of the team share the same values with regards to the team and the tasks set.
Team identity	This is what makes each team different, it helps give a sense of pride to the team members and is often displayed through the team strip, a uniform or badges, for example.
Mutual support	In the armed forces, this might consist of physical back-up when under attack or that everyone does their fair share of heavy and boring work, such as loading trucks. Mutual support of a different kind may be given in a close-knit team when dealing with shocking or stressful events.
Trust	This means knowing that you and your team members are going to do the right thing in a difficult situation. High levels of trust are needed in dangerous working conditions such as warfare or disasters. Trust is linked to knowledge and skill, and ordinary qualities such as punctuality and reliability.
Commitment to aims/objectives/mission	This means determination to succeed within the team and effective teams show commitment under difficult or dangerous situations such as an emergency call-out.
Recognition of effort	This means team members respect each other and offer praise for good work and leaders value their team's work and make this apparent.

Activities: Teambuilding

In order to pass this unit, it is important that you participate in a number of team activities that will allow you to develop your own team skills.

Here are a few examples of teambuilding activities:

1 Work in teams of six to thirty

Your tutor will find a large open space and make a line across the centre to divide it into two areas. Half the class should move to one side of the line and the other half to the opposite side. No team should cross the line. Your tutor will give each team a bag of marshmallows. On the signal 'go' the members of each team try to eliminate the members of the opposite team by hitting them with marshmallows. If a marshmallow is thrown at you and you are hit, you must go to the sideline and form a line with any other members of your team who have been hit. When a member of your team catches a marshmallow that was thrown by a member of the other team, the first person in line may return to the game. The object is to eliminate the other team entirely!

2 Work as a whole class

Sit in a circle with 10 wrapped sweets each (you cannot eat the sweets until the end of the game). Taking it in turns a learner must tell the team/class something unique they have done or experienced. Anyone who has NOT done the same thing must give one sweet to the leaner speaking. Continue like this until everyone has had a turn. You can eat the sweets you have collected at the end of the game.

3 Your class will need to form teams

Take a list of 10 things to collect (scavenge hunt) and spend 20 minutes on collecting all the items on the list. The winning team is the one that manages to get most or all of the items. If there is a draw, the winners are those who complete the task in the quickest time.

2 Methods of instruction in public services

Instruction is the passing on of practical skills, it differs from teaching in that its primary focus is on getting an individual to do a task correctly rather than teaching them how or why they must do the task. Sometimes teaching and instruction work together, but sometimes they are separate functions. Methods of instruction can vary and can sometimes be aimed at a large group of learners or be on a one-to-one basis. It is vital in the public services that employees are able to give instruction in a variety of ways that best fit the situation. It is important to have good communication skills as an **instructor** so that your instruction is clear and concise and your learners are able to understand what is required of them easily and without confusion.

2.1 Instruction

The first step when instructing is to select the topic carefully to ensure that it is relevant to the people you are going to instruct. You also need to plan carefully what you are going to do. The best way to plan your session is to use a lesson plan. This is a document where you can make detailed plans on why you are doing the lesson (objective), who you will be instructing (audience), how long you have to teach them (timing).

It is good practice to include a variety of instructional techniques in your lesson to keep your audience interested. This could be:

Asking the audience to demonstrate something. For example, if you are trying to teach someone how to make a cup of tea then it is easiest for them to learn by copying you and showing you, step by step, what they would do and the equipment they might use for the task.

Discussing a topic you have raised. For example, as the instructor you could lead a discussion on a subject related to what you are going to teach in order to see the level of knowledge your audience has prior to the instruction. This can then be expanded and developed as a longer more detailed discussion to embed the learning further.

Looking at some case studies to apply the learning. For example, if you were going to show your audience how different teams work together you could give them a number of case studies to read through and identify examples within them where teamwork has occurred.

Role playing. This is the opportunity to give your audience the chance to 'practise' something you have taught them. For example, if you were trying to teach your audience how to resolve a conflict you could set up a role play of two people who are arguing and a third person, using the skills they have learned on conflict management, to show how they would resolve the situation.

By using varied methods of instruction, everyone in your audience will have learned something.

2.2 Qualities of a good instructor

It is important in the public service that those personnel given the task of instructing others do this job well. In many cases people's lives may depend on instructions made in very difficult circumstances when everyone is under enormous pressure. In these situations it is even more important that the person giving out the instructions has the confidence and suitable skills to do the job efficiently. What are some of the qualities of a good instructor?

Activity: Model tutors

Think about the time you were at school. Without naming a specific person, recall a tutor who you really liked and who was good at teaching.

1   What makes this tutor so good at what they did? Try to work out how they kept you engaged and motivated.

2   Discuss with a partner. Did you both identify similar characteristics and techniques?

3   Discuss as a class what this might mean for a tutor.

Being a confident instructor means that you understand what you are talking about and you can communicate in a clear and effective way. This means talking clearly and freely, perhaps changing your voice by varying the tone or speed. It also includes standing and facing the group, making eye contact, using positive body language, moving around the room to make all those listening feel included. Appropriate dress is also important, for example if you are giving instruction on how to put up a tent outside, you would need to be wearing outdoor shoes and clothing appropriate to what you are teaching. If you are in a classroom, a suit or formal clothing is more suitable.

A good instructor also needs to be sympathetic to their audience. You need to treat your listeners fairly and equally while still taking into account the individual needs of the audience (for example, some people may need a more thorough explanation of something than others). An instructor should be firm, fair and friendly and this way model the behaviour they expect in return. It is important to be hard-working and conscientious when you are giving out instructions as well as respecting any confidential information you might receive about your audience.

It is important that an instructor is both knowledgeable and enthusiastic about their subject. Enthusiasm and a passion for a subject will often spill out and inspire those you are teaching and assist their learning. An instructor needs to enjoy teaching and motivating their audience through praise and regular assessment. This also helps the audience keep on track with their learning.

Look at the image. Can you identify the type of instruction involved here?

Key term

2.3 Facts/skills for instruction

We can see there are a number of qualities that are important for a good instructor but these alone cannot make a good instruction or lesson. For the lesson to work, a number of processes need to be completed and these will assist learners about 'what' and 'why' as they learn something new. We have touched on these processes already with the lesson plan, but it is important to go through them in a little more detail.

- **Time** – how long have you got? You need to consider this when you are planning your lesson so you know how much you can teach. You do not want to overload the lesson and have to rush through quickly so that at the end no one can remember anything!

- **Parts and content** – do you know what you are teaching? Are you sure of the content, do you need to check anything or refresh your own knowledge before you teach the lesson?

- **Notes** – are these allowed? Notes can be used, especially if you are teaching a very technical subject as you can use your notes to assist you with this. However, sometimes notes are not practicable, for instance, if you are demonstrating a combat exercise.

- **Objectives** – the reasons why. It is important to tell your learners your objectives, what you expect they should learn by the end of the lesson. This is important for you as well so you don't go off track and forget what you are meant to be teaching.

- **Beginning/introduction** – what should you start with? Always introduce your lesson with a quick run through of what you will be doing. This is like providing a 'taster' for the learner and should make them look forward to what is coming next.

- **Incentives** – not every lesson will come with **incentives**. In some situations if you complete a course of study and gain a qualification you might be entitled to a promotion, which could bring extra pay.

- **Middle teaching points** – the middle of the lesson. As an instructor you have to be careful that you do not concentrate on the beginning and the end of the lesson and forget about the middle. The way you use this part of your lesson will depend on the time available. It is always good practice to swap styles of delivery in the middle part of a lesson. For example, 10 minutes of practical activity, 10 minutes of a slideshow, then 10 minutes of discussion.

- **Explain, Demonstrate, Imitate, Practice (EDIP)** – a way to assist learners to gain a deeper understanding of the topic. By following this cycle where you **e**xplain and **d**emonstrate, followed by the learners **i**mitating (copying) what you have done then **p**ractising their skill, their knowledge of the subject will grow. For example, if you wanted to teach someone to ride a bicycle you would explain and demonstrate how to do it, they would copy what you did with your support and then practise until they could ride the bike without your help.

- **End of lesson** – summary. After each lesson or instruction it is important to summarise what you have taught and ensure some learning. This could be as simple as asking questions about the lesson to make sure learners have listened, understood and gained some knowledge about the subject.

- **Handouts** – if you have handouts you must make sure you give them out at the appropriate time. This may be during the lesson for the learners to undertake an activity or at the end of the lesson to help learners retain the knowledge.

Case study: A training session

You work as a supervisor in a police canteen at weekends and in the evenings. Mike, your colleague, has just been promoted. This means that he will now be assisting you in the training of new staff on the basic health and safety that employees need to use. To try to assist Mike you have decided to put together a short guide to methods of instruction to help him with his first training session.

Try to include the following in your guide for Mike:

1 The importance of a lesson plan and its main elements
2 The qualities of a good instructor
3 Some basic hints and tips to help him with his instruction
4 An explanation of EDIP

Remember

To be a good instructor it is important to be organised, have a clear lesson plan, know your subject, keep cool and most of all don't panic!

BTEC Assessment activity 1.2 (P3) (M2) (P4)

To develop your public service skills it is important that you practise these skills on a regular basis and learn from them. An interesting and fun way to achieve this is by taking part in different team activities. To assist with achieving (P3) you need to:

1 *Contribute* to different teambuilding activities. (P3) Keep a log of these activities and then reflect on your performance so you can see your own areas of improvement.

2 For at least one of these activities you could *take the role* of the leader, which will allow you to demonstrate effective instruction skills to the rest of your team as well as your tutor. This evidence could then be used to contribute towards achieving (M2).

3 *Explain* the qualities of a good instructor and how they are used. (P4)

PLTS

Identifying the qualities of a good instructor and identifying skills or qualities you have or need to improve will help develop your reflective learning skills.

Grading tips

To make (P3) easier you should keep a log of your participation in the teambuilding activities along with the notes and lesson plan from when you undertook the role of the leader. You should easily be able to write a report that includes:

- Confidence and manner
- Attitude
- Enthusiasm and interest.

In order to achieve (M2) criteria you will need to arrange with your tutor which lesson you are going to lead so you can prepare the relevant paperwork, such as a lesson plan to help you present this information. You need to think about the different skills we have talked about that can be included in the phrase 'public service skills'.

To help you with achieving (P4) think about someone who you feel is a good instructor. What do they do? What skills and qualities do they have that helps them to be a good instructor? Make a list of the skills you have identified and use this to help you complete. (P4)

Functional skills

This assignment may also help you to develop your functional skills in ICT if you word process a lesson plan when you are demonstrating effective communicational skills.

21

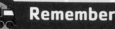

Key term

Interpersonal communication skills – these include reading and writing skills as well as listening and speaking skills plus all forms of non-verbal communication.

Remember

Learn the difference between **skimming**, **scanning** and **reading**.

Activity: Book group

Working in threes

You will compare the different types of reading.

1 One of you will use skim reading to assess how important Unit 17 (pages 323–356) is to someone interested in the Fire Service.

2 One of you will use scan reading to find out the history of the British Army from Unit 2 (pages 47–48).

3 One of you will use detailed reading to find out about the public service skills used by Phill Teye-Otum (page 35).

4 Explain what you learned to the rest of the group and see how the reading technique affected your understanding.

3 Interpersonal communication skills

Interpersonal communication skills are incredibly important as a public service employee. Being able to develop these skills and improve them will help you to progress your career within any organisation.

3.1 Reading

As you would expect, the public services want their staff to be able to read to an acceptable standard. For example, a police recruit or trainee prison officer will be expected to have high reading levels as their role involves digesting a large amount of written materials.

There are generally three different ways of reading a document, these are:

- skim reading
- scan reading
- detailed reading.

All of these reading skills are important for the public services particularly if you work in the police, courts and probation services as you will deal with a large volume of paperwork that you will need to process quickly.

Skimming. This is when you look through something quickly to see what it contains. We often do this when we buy a newspaper or magazine. In the public services people will skim a document to decide on its importance and prioritise their reading from this. You may have received a letter in the post, skimmed it to decide in its importance, and from there decided to read it or throw it away.

Scanning. This is when you are looking for a particular piece of information in a document. People often scan books, reports and documents. In many cases you are looking for a specific piece of information, key words and/or phrases and do not have the time to read the whole document in full. Again, this is another key way of reading in the public services but it is important that you do not miss a vital piece of evidence or information. You will need to be 100 per cent sure that you have taken all the information you need from a document after scanning it.

Detailed reading. This is about reading something carefully, in full, and taking in all the information held within the document. In the public services there will be many times when you will need to read something in detail so that you are aware of all the information it contains. For example, if you are working as a police officer you would read a witness statement in detail to make sure you have all the relevant information. Detailed reading will also help you understand the information and pick up on any hidden meanings or inconsistencies that there may be between documents that you read.

It might be that there are some detailed and precise instructions that you need to follow so you need to understand them fully to know exactly what you are meant to do. Reading in detail is important and you may need to find some quiet time where you can concentrate your efforts on the task at hand.

Barriers to effective reading. Reading is often difficult, this may be because you do not feel the topic is interesting, you find the language and words that are used difficult to understand or you do not feel in the mood to read. Some of the most common barriers are often categorised into three areas (1) personal barriers, such as being tired, not in the mood, lack of concentration, being bored and so on, (2) barriers to the text, such as long complicated words or language, poor layout or grammar, and (3) environmental barriers, such as distractions like noise, other people, bad light, uncomfortable chair and so forth.

3.2 Writing

An ability to write is needed in most employment, not least as a public service employee. The quality of your writing is of utmost importance, particularly if the written work you have completed could be crucial in a court case. All written work should be '**fit for purpose**'.

The amount of written work undertaken in the public services can and does vary. For example, at constable rank in the Police Service you will be required to undertake a wide range of written work, such as writing personal and witness statements, completing various documents while on duty such as search reports, vehicle defect forms and so on, as well as completing reports and preparing files to go to court. At management level in the Police Service you will have a larger volume of written work to complete that includes much of the written work completed at operative level as well as management and government reports. The same is true of the armed services, for example an infantry private may not have to write much, but a corporal will have to write more and a sergeant will have to write a significant amount.

Within the public services there are often rules regarding the format of written documents that you are required to follow. This is so that the service has a '**uniform approach**' to written material.

Letters. In the public services letters are usually fairly formal and are typed. They may be polite and friendly but still have a business-like tone to them. If you know the person you are writing to you should write a semi-formal letter where you can end with 'yours sincerely'. If you know nothing about the person you are writing to your letter will be formal and you will begin with 'Dear Sir or Madam' and end with 'Yours faithfully'. For example, you might write a formal letter if you were requesting an application pack for a job vacancy in a public service.

> ## Key term
>
> **Fit for purpose** – this means it is in a suitable format, is written clearly and accurately and is relevant to the situation.

> ## Key term
>
> **Uniform approach** – this means everyone using the same approach. The phrase is taken from the fact that people who wear a uniform are dressed in the same way, so a uniform approach to writing means the same style of writing.

Activity: Writing a semi-formal letter

Your tutor wants to take your class to visit the local police station. They know that the person in charge of these visits is called Mr Braithwaite because they have arranged class visits before. As your tutor knows the person they are writing to they need to compile a semi-formal letter.

Your task is to write a semi-formal letter to Mr Braithwaite about the proposed visit to include:

1 the station you would like to visit
2 the number of pupils in your class
3 some proposed dates for the visit.

Your tutor will provide you with the basic information but it is up to you to produce a letter in an appropriate format.

Internal memorandums. These are sent within public service organisations and generally give out information or instructions to people. They are very informal and are usually sent through the internal postal system of the organisation. For example, as a police officer you might receive an internal memorandum informing you of a change to your shift pattern. Many organisations do not use internal memorandums anymore as they have been replaced by emails, which can be delivered more quickly.

Report writing. Longer documents may be called briefs, submissions or reports. In general they are long and often split into sections, which are used to outline a situation, give information about it and suggest what ought to be done. An example could be a report from a PCSO (Police Community Support Officer) to other police officers from his/her station who has been dealing with criminal damage on the estate they all patrol. The PCSO could be informing the other officers of the issues that have risen and what he/she is proposing as a solution to the problem for the officers to consider. Some reports can be hundreds of pages long and include research about a particular problem. Generally reports follow the same format and include:

- title of the report, who wrote it, when it was written and who will read it
- content of the report, usually a list of the sections and page numbers
- a brief introduction to the report, what it is about
- the main findings of the report, what has been discovered
- conclusion, what the writer thinks
- recommendations, what should be done about it.

Note-taking. Notes need to be quick and easy to understand. Often people take notes (minutes) at meetings to keep a record of what has been said and decisions that have been made. One of the most important things about notes is that they are readable: they are useless if after taking them you cannot read what you have written. For example, as a police officer you may well need to take notes while talking to a witness or a suspect and these must be legible as they can be admissible as evidence. NCOs (non-commissioned officers) carry notebooks for writing down instructions in leadership tasks.

Email. Email is widely used now for both internal and external communications. Email might be used internally to get information out

Did you know?

Defence writing, which is used by command and leadership staff in defence management, is a form of uniform writing. For more information about defence writing look at the Defence Academy website, available via Hotlinks (see page viii).

What skills do you think you need in order to communicate effectively through writing?

quickly to different offices, branches or externally to other public service organisations both in the UK and across the world. The ability to send information through a computer quickly to anywhere in the world is hugely powerful in communicating urgent information. The format of emails can vary but generally they are fairly brief and concise containing only the relevant information. It is also important to think about what you are sending via email and consider the issue of confidentiality.

3.3 Verbal communication

They way we use our voice, its tone and how we emphasise words make it a very powerful tool. Verbal communication is the use of sound, words, language and speech to create sense and meaning between people. It is very important in the public services because it is the most usual form of communication and, therefore vital to execute correctly. For example at a road traffic collision if a person is trapped in a car and you are unable to reach them it is vital to be able to communicate with them effectively through your voice. You may well need to calm the casualty down and reassure them, as well as give concise and accurate information about the incident to the Fire Service to allow them to free the casualty, as well as describe the scene to a paramedic so they are able to give basic first aid advice to you in order for you to treat the casualty the best possible way. This may be in addition to giving verbal instructions to colleagues to close roads, take statements and so on.

Types of verbal communication

One-way communication. This usually takes the form of a briefing, a lecture, a speech, a presentation or instruction. In these situations one person is speaking and the other person/people are listening. There is usually an opportunity for questions to be asked at the end of the session.

Two-way communication. This can cover a wide range of situations such as discussions, debates, arguments, conversations, meetings, chats and so on. It is by far the most common use of verbal communication used at work and in our daily lives. Some types of two-way communication are formal and others are not.

Remember

The best way to introduce an abbreviation into a piece of writing is to spell out the words the first time you introduce the abbreviated form. For example, the FRA (Fire and Rescue Authorities) are made up of…

Remember

Get into the habit of carrying a notebook with you. You never know when you might need to record information.

Link

The techniques and qualities of a good instructor are examples of one-way communication. See page 19.

Activity: Two-way communication

Working in pairs

Discuss the different types of two-way communication identified above and complete the table opposite.

Try to see if you can identify which of these are formal and informal. Think about the situations where you might use these different types of communication during the day and give and example for each type.

Type	Brief description	Formal or informal?
Discussions		
Debates		
Arguments		
Conversations		
Meetings		
Chats		

Questioning skills. Good questioning skills are very important in the public services. For example, as a fire officer attending a house fire you will need to be able to ask effective questions that can be understood and answered easily, such as 'Is there anyone inside the house?'. How often you will use questioning will depend on the public service that you are considering joining. For example, as a police officer you will use questioning skills on a daily basis through speaking to the public and dealing with their complaints and questions. There are generally two types of questions and these are known as open questions and closed questions.

Closed questions. You would expect a short answer from a closed question. They usually begin with a verb like 'Did', 'Are', 'Have' or 'Do' and may be easier to answer. For example, 'Have you eaten today?' These questions take less time to ask and answer and do have a place in the public services, usually in surveys or questionnaires where statistics are going to be compiled.

Open questions. You would expect these to begin with verbs like 'Where', 'What', 'Why', 'Who' and encourage the person who is answering to speak at length. It is usually a more open-ended question and more difficult to give a simple 'yes' or 'no' reply. For example, 'Why did you run away when the policeman stopped you?' These types of questions are very important in all public services. In the police force, it allows officers to establish what has happened at an incident and if anyone is to blame. For a paramedic, it enables them to find out what injuries a person may have sustained, what their medical history is and if they are taking any medication.

Remember to tailor your presentation to the audience. How can you do this?

! Link

Personal discipline and its importance as a public service skill is discussed on page 6.

Speaking

The way in which we speak can contribute meaning to what we are saying. The tone of our voice and the way we emphasise words can make the sentences and words we speak mean different things. Even the same sentence said in a different way can take on a different meaning. By varying the volume of what we say we can communicate emotions and feelings. We can shout, whisper, talk gently or sternly and give insight into how we are feeling, which could be anger, excitement, sadness or impatience, for example.

Audience

When we speak we often change how we speak according to who is listening. You may use a different tone and style of language to speak to your friends compared to how you might speak to a stranger or a person in authority. Depending on the audience or who we are speaking to, we might use different words or phrases, speak more formally or informally, or even change our volume or tone. Other factors that influence the way we speak might be the age of the listener, the subject matter, or the situation that we are in. For example, if you were attending an interview you would ensure that you spoke politely, avoiding any **jargon** or **slang**. The tone you use would be more formal while calm to try to show your prospective employers that you can stay calm under pressure. In contrast to this, when you are back with your friends telling them how the interview went your tone and language would probably be quite different because you are in a more relaxed atmosphere.

When we speak we frequently use jargon, slang and **abbreviations**. This is fine when we are speaking with friends but in other situations it would be more appropriate to use formal language. Not everyone can understand jargon or slang and so in some situations using these may get in the way of good and effective communication. For example, at the scene of a fire it is very important that the fire chief who is taking charge of the incident does not use language and jargon that staff from other public services are not familiar with. This could affect the performance of the team as a whole as officers from the police or paramedics may not fully understand the instructions and what is required of them.

Speaking in a group

Another type of verbal communication is participation in group discussions. Group discussion is a vital part of many organisations. It allows all personnel to be involved and express their thoughts and opinions. To do this effectively it is important to be able to organise your thoughts logically so that you can share your views and opinions with others efficiently. Some people find that making notes prior to a group discussion helps them to put their points across better without forgetting anything. It is important when participating in a group discussion for only one person to speak at a time.

In many situations in life and in a career in the public services you may be required to do a verbal presentation. A verbal presentation is more than reading straight from a written document. It is a non-written way of conveying information to an audience. You need to remember to speak clearly, concisely and slowly. It is always good to have a short introduction and a short conclusion. It is very important to keep your audience's attention. Before you give a verbal presentation think about factors such as:

- can everyone see and hear you?
- how big is the audience?
- have you planned your presentation fully?
- have you got all the **visual aids** you need?
- who are the audience?

Are they colleagues, friends or management? All of these factors need to be considered when you prepare and present verbally, to ensure that you and your intended audience get the best out of your presentation.

Key terms

Jargon – this means key words, phrases or acronyms that are used specifically within the organisation. Such as 'refs' which means breaktime for the police or 'ablutions' which means bathroom in the army.

Slang – this means words that we use informally, including swear words that are inappropriate for use in a more formal setting. For example in rhyming slang 'apples and pears' means stairs and 'deep sea diver' means a fiver (£5).

Abbreviations – these are shortened forms of a word or phrase such as 'don't' instead of 'do not'. Other examples are 'aren't' instead of 'are not' or 'they're' instead of 'they are'. Abbreviations are also shortened forms of names of organisations such as BBC, which is the British Broadcasting Corporation.

! Link

For skills and qualities that are important in verbal presentations see page 20.

Key term

Visual aids – this refers to things that you might use in your presentation to show the audience what you are discussing as well as speaking on the topic. For example, if you are speaking about how a new mobile phone works you would have examples to hand out to your audience so they could see, at first hand, what you are referring to.

Barriers to verbal communication

There can be a number of things that stand in your way when you communicate verbally. These can generally be categorised into three areas:

- problems with you as the speaker
- problems with your audience (the listener)
- problems with the environment (where you are).

Activity: Overcoming barriers

Try to identify four barriers to verbal communication from each area. There is an example from each to get you started. Now try to complete a table like the one below:

Problems with the speaker	Problems with the listener	Problems with the environment
Not loud enough – very quiet voice so listener cannot hear what is being said	Bored and distracted because not interested in what speaker has to say	Other people are talking therefore it's too noisy to hear what is being said

Working in pairs

Think about these barriers – can you suggest ways that they can be avoided? Write your answers down and share them with the rest of the class.

What barriers to verbal communication might you find in a culturally diverse community?

Barriers like the ones described above can exist in both operation and non-operational situations. Operational situations would depend upon the public service involved. For example, an operational situation for the Police Service might be attending a car crash and for the army it might be a unit in Afghanistan involved in a skirmish with the Taliban. An example of a non-operational situation might be when a police officer attends a briefing.

Activity: Operational and non-operational communication

Working in pairs

Think about the operational and non-operational situations above. Which barriers to communication would be involved in a police officer attending a car crash or the case of a soldier on active duty in Afghanistan?

- Problems with the speaker?
- Problems with the listener?
- Problems with the environment?

Which barriers to communication would be involved in a police officer attending a briefing?

How do the barriers you have identified differ in operational and non-operational situations?

Make a few notes that you can use in a group discussion.

3.4 Listening

Listening skills are very important in daily life and especially in the public services. You will need to have good listening skills, for example when attending a briefing, a meeting, answering questions or dealing with a complaint or request. It is a definite skill to be able to listen to someone and absorb the information they tell you and remember the details. In many situations taking notes is vital to ensure that you do not forget anything or make a mistake with what you have heard. When looking at listening skills there are a number of things to consider:

Effective listening skills. Vital information can be picked up at any time through a conversation, therefore it is important that you pay attention to what is being said. Do not let your mind wander away and do not talk over the person you are listening to. This helps them stay calm and encourages them to open up to you.

Information collation. As you are listening, if there is a lot of information to take in, do not be afraid to take notes. Ask the person you are listening to if this is all right and then you can keep a record of the information you are receiving accurately. You want to avoid having to keep asking the person speaking to repeat what they are saying over and over as this could make you look inefficient. Also, it may make the person you are listening to feel vulnerable or worried that you are not taking things seriously. Using this technique allows you to ensure that you have collected the correct information. Once this is done, you can then collate the information. This means collecting up the information and putting it into an appropriate order so you can then make comparisons between the notes you have taken. For example, if you made notes from two witnesses at a road traffic accident you could then compare the notes to see if they can confirm a similar sequence of events that occurred and which vehicle might have been at fault and so on.

Look at the image. Why is it important to write down what you see at the scene?

Case study: Neil works as a Crew Manager

'I have been in the Fire and Rescue Services for over 18 years now. My role as Crew Manager involves using lots of communication skills, both verbal and written, on a day-to-day basis. On a broader level, I have to work with the community to organise school visits, fire safety talks and installing smoke detectors. I have to liaise with the Police Service and other agencies including the local council. I am also the link between the firefighters and the Watch Manager.

When we go to a fire my first job is to assess the type of fire it is and how best to approach it. I then communicate this to the team. It is my responsibility to monitor the situation and to make decisions if the fire is getting worse. I keep an overall eye on health and safety issues to make sure the firefighters are safe at all times. I deal with members of the public to get witness statements and to make sure they are kept safe. Once we have finished an operation, it is my responsibility to write up a report on every incident.

In my job, I need excellent verbal as well as written communication skills. I also have to take a leadership role and a decision-making role. My job is really varied and very interesting.'

Now answer these questions:

1 What communication skills do you think you would need to have to be a firefighter?

2 How do you think the communication skills you have learned about in this unit will relate to your own life?

3 Do you think you have strong communication skills? What communication skills do you think you could improve?

PLTS

By working in a team and communicating effectively you will develop your teamworking skills.

BTEC Assessment activity 1.3 **P5 P6 P7 M3 D2**

In order for you to report on and demonstrate your interpersonal communication skills you will need to undertake a number of practical assessments. These can be linked to the teambuilding activities that you have undertaken in Assessment Activity 1.2. You are required to:

1 *Use* correct terminology in a given public service communication context. **P6**

2 Demonstrate and *make use* of interpersonal skills to communicate with personnel in a given situation. **P7**

Once you have demonstrated these skills you are then required to produce a booklet that:

3 *Reports* on the effectiveness of various methods of interpersonal communication skills. **P5**

Grading tip

To achieve the higher grades you must include in your booklet a more detailed explanation **M3** of the application of interpersonal communication skills in a given public service as well as being able to draw conclusions and evaluate **D2** the effective use of interpersonal communication skills in a given public service.

Functional skills

Practising communication through verbal and written means will help you improve your functional English.

Phill Teye-Otum
Firefighter

I work on Red Watch at A2 Station North Hull. I have been in the job for 8 months now and I am really loving it. Today is my first day duty of this tour of 4 shifts (2 days and 2 nights). I always make sure I get to work in plenty of time to get ready for the start of the shift. I need to be in my fire kit and ready for roll call at 9.00 a.m. At roll call we are given our riding positions on the fire appliance (pump) and detailed our duties for the day. Once roll call is over we then check every piece of equipment on the pump is in working order and that our breathing apparatus sets (BA) work correctly. There are 12 personnel on Red Watch who man two fire appliances. As you can imagine, we have become a very close team as we work together at all times during out tour of 4 shifts.

A typical day

Our first call out (shout!) was to a sheltered housing complex where a resident had forgotten to remove a pan from the cooker and the smoke had set off the alarm. As soon as we arrived our training came into play.

Two colleagues had to wear their BA and go in, turn off the heat, remove the pan and ventilate the flat. The rest of the team (including me) had to make sure all the residents were accounted for and reassure them that everything was all right. It is nice to be able to put someone's mind at ease, however small the job might be. Once back at the station the team have to clean and service out the BA and then get on with our station work duties, which include ensuring every piece of equipment is tested regularly to ensure it is on tip-top condition ready for use.

After team break we got our second call which was a road traffic collision (RTC) between a lorry and a car. We had to release two people from the car so they could be taken to hospital. It takes good teamwork between us, the police, the paramedics, and the local council highways department to deal with an incident like this and to ensure that the casualties are taken to hospital as soon as possible as well as making sure the police can investigate the cause of the accident and keep the rest of the traffic flowing. Once back at the station we have to service the equipment we just used before we can have our lunch.

After lunch we are having a training session to set up and test procedures and practices at a simulated fire.

The best thing about the job

You never stop learning in this job, even long-serving firefighters are involved in this training because it is important that the team are able to work together effectively at all times. This is particularly important when individuals within the team might change from time to time. Once our training is finished I get some time to do private study. Before we leave at 6.00 p.m. we have to make sure that everything is clean and ready for the night watch to take over from us.

Think about it!

1. What areas have you covered in this unit that provide you with the knowledge and skills needed to become a firefighter? Think about the public service skills you have learned about, demonstrated and evaluated. Write a list and discuss it with your peers.

2. What further skills might you need to develop? For example, you might consider here how you would continue developing your interpersonal communication skills or teamwork skills. You might like to consider the specific skills required by the service of your choice. Write a list and discuss in small groups.

Just checking

1. List two advantages of working in teams.
2. Explain two types of teams that may exist in the public services.
3. Discuss two of the qualities needed for good teamwork.
4. Lesson plans are important when giving instructions, explain why.
5. Explain three qualities of a good instructor.
6. Name three skills that instructors need to consider when delivering a lesson.
7. Explain two types of verbal communication skills.
8. Explain two types of written communication skills.
9. What is NVC? Give two examples.

edexcel

Assignment tips

- The service you want to join may be different from those outlined in this unit or even those of your fellow classmates. Don't be hesitant about approaching the service of your choice directly for information, after all you will be approaching them soon for a job anyway so it won't hurt to make a positive first impression by showing an interest in the job they do and the conditions of service you will be working under.

- This unit requires a lot of research into the non-uniformed public services so making sure you use the right sources of research will be essential. Your local council is a great source of information and they are usually very happy to provide information when you need it.

- A lot of this unit is practical and will require you to take part in teamwork activities, group work tasks and practise your instruction. However don't forget you may already have lots of examples of teamwork and instruction which will help you with your work such as being a member of the cadets, part-time work or being a member of a sports club. All of this experience will help you complete this unit.

Credit value: 5

2 Employment in the uniformed public services

Many young people want to join a service because they see it as an exciting and glamorous career opportunity. In many ways this is correct, but service life is not without its difficulties and dangers and it is important that if you are considering a uniformed service career you are informed about the roles and responsibilities the services undertake and the conditions under which they operate.

This unit covers the roles and responsibilities of a variety of contrasting public services enabling you to make an informed decision about the service you would like to make a career in. It covers the positive and negative aspects of working in the services on both a personal and professional level and discusses the conditions you have to accept when being recruited.

Learning outcomes

After completing this unit you should:

1. know the main roles of different uniformed public services
2. understand the main responsibilities of different uniformed public services
3. understand the different employment opportunities available in the uniformed public services
4. know the conditions of service for different public service jobs.

37

Assessment and grading criteria

This table shows you what you must do in order to achieve a pass, merit or distinction grade, and where you can find activities in this book to help you.

To achieve a **pass** grade the evidence must show that the learner is able to:	To achieve a **merit** grade the evidence must show that, in addition to the pass criteria, the learner is able to:	To achieve a **distinction** grade the evidence must show that, in addition to the pass and merit criteria, the learner is able to:
P1 outline the main purpose and roles of two contrasting uniformed public services **Assessment activity 2.1 page 53**		
P2 discuss the main responsibilities of two contrasting uniformed public services **Assessment activity 2.1 page 53**	**M1** explain the role, purpose and responsibilities of contrasting uniformed public services **Assessment activity 2.1 page 53**	**D1** evaluate the role, purpose and responsibilities of a chosen uniformed public service **Assessment activity 2.1 page 53**
P3 outline the different employment opportunities available to the uniformed public services **Assessment activity 2.2 page 60**	**M2** explain the work of a chosen job in the uniformed services **Assessment activity 2.2 page 60**	
P4 describe the current conditions of service for a given job within a uniformed public service **Assessment activity 2.3 page 62**		

How you will be assessed

This unit will be assessed by an internal assignment that will be designed and marked by the staff at your centre. The assignment is designed to allow you to show your understanding of the learning outcomes for exploring careers in the uniformed public services. These relate to what you should be able to do after completing this unit. Your assessments might include some of the following:

- portfolios of evidence
- learning journals
- blog entries
- video diaries
- action plans
- skills audits
- presentations
- leaflets
- reports.

Nick, 16, meets uniformed public service workers

This unit was quite interesting, we got to look at a variety of different services and find out what they did and then we had the opportunity to focus down on the service we eventually want to join. This was an advantage for me because I thought I knew a fair bit about the service I want to join, but having compared it with some other services it's made me reconsider what I want to do.

All the services are different even though sometimes they do similar jobs and have similar roles. It's given me the opportunity to go out and meet people from different services and ask them about what they like best in their job and how the job is different from what they thought it was.

Most of my information was from television programmes like *The Bill*, but the police I've spoken to say its nothing like that, there is a lot of routine work and a big paperwork burden which I hadn't considered. It has also made me consider part-time work in the services until I've finished my qualifications so I'm in the process of applying to the Territorial Army which will help me develop my public service skills and provide me with excellent service experience.

The good thing about this unit is you get to find out about what the job is really like, the good bits and the bad bits so you can make sensible choices about what you want to do.

Over to you!

- What areas of exploring your potential career might you find interesting?
- Have you considered what career you would like?
- What preparation could you do to get ready for your assessments?

1, 2 The main roles and responsibilities of different uniformed public services

Talk up

About your preparation

Looking at your skills and abilities honestly can be a challenge for some people. Write down a list of your strengths and your weaknesses and think about how they would affect your ability to join a service.

Come up with at least three possible ways to overcome any weaknesses you have identified.

Key terms

Purpose – this is the reason a service was created in the first place. It is its reason for existing.

Role – this is the overarching job of the service, their main function.

Responsibility – these are all the things a service may be responsible for while fulfilling their role.

Although the uniformed public services work closely together and often work in similar situations the jobs they do are different. This section of the unit will look at the **purpose**, **role** and **responsibilities** of a variety of uniformed public services.

You will often find the services use words like roles, responsibilities and purpose interchangeably. This can make it a challenge for you to tell the difference between them when you are researching the public services.

Find all the different words that can be used in place of 'role', 'responsibility' and 'purpose'. List these words and add brief definitions. Use the key terms given here, a book of synonyms or an online synonym finder to help you.

Generally speaking the uniformed services fall into three categories which are outlined in Table 2.1.

Table 2.1: The categories of the uniformed public services.

Emergency services	Armed forces	Other services
The Police Service	The British Army	The Prison Service
The Fire and Rescue Service	The Royal Air Force	HM Revenue and Customs
The Ambulance Service	The Royal Navy	HM Coastguard

Activity: The Ambulance Service

Conduct some research on the roles and responsibilities of the Ambulance Service. Find out as much as you can about what they do and how they do it. Use the information you find to make a poster which shows the role of the ambulance service.

There is lots of information you can use at the NHS Careers website, available via Hotlinks (see page viii).

1, 2.1 The emergency services

The emergency services are those which respond to civilian emergencies via a 999 call. These services are usually the Police Service, the Fire Service and the Ambulance Service, although in some areas emergency services may also include the Coastguard and Mountain Rescue.

The purpose, role and responsibilities of the Police Service

The origins of modern law enforcement in the UK can be traced back to the thirteenth century, to the locally appointed magistrates and petty constables whose job was to maintain the peace and deal with those who broke the law. However, the modern Police Service in England and Wales was not formed until 1829, by the then Home Secretary, Sir Robert Peel, who created the Metropolitan Police Act. Police Services in counties outside of the London metropolitan area were created by the County Police Act 1839.

There are 43 Police Services in England and Wales, all of them sharing a common purpose and common values. These are to:

* uphold the law fairly and firmly
* pursue and bring to justice those who break the law
* keep the Queen's peace
* protect, help and reassure the community
* operate with integrity, common sense and sound judgement.

These are the roles and responsibilities the police are required to fulfil, however many Police Services also set local priorities which largely depend on the needs of their particular area. For example, the Police Service in rural areas may have a very different set of problems from Police Services in urban areas, so it makes sense that as well as these overall roles they can also adapt to deal with local needs.

It is important that the emergency services respond quickly to 999 calls. Which services do you think are involved in the Selby Train Crash? See page 343 to find out more.

Did you know?

That the name Robert is often shortened to Bobby – this is why police officers are sometimes referred to as 'Bobbies', after their founder Sir Robert Peel.

Activity: Urban and rural policing

Can you think of the different types of crime that the Police Service might have to deal with in urban and rural areas? Conduct some research and see what you find out.

Most Police Services also have individual mission statements, which are summaries of the aims of their particular constabulary, and each will also have individual organisational objectives that tell the public and government how well a particular Police Service is performing.

Case study: Police mission statements

West Yorkshire Police mission statement

The purpose of West Yorkshire Police is to uphold the law fairly and firmly: to prevent crime; to pursue and bring to justice those who break the law; to keep the Queen's peace; to protect, help and reassure the community: and to be seen to do all this with integrity, common sense and sound judgement.

We must be compassionate, courteous and patient, acting without fear or favour or prejudice to the rights of others. We need to be professional, calm and restrained in the face of violence and apply only that force which is necessary to accomplish our lawful duty.

We must strive to reduce the fears of the public and, so far as we can, to reflect their priorities in the action we take. We must respond to well-founded criticism with a willingness to change.

Now answer the following questions:

1 What do you understand this mission statement to mean?

2 Would you add anything else to this mission statement?

3 Police mission statements differ, find another three police mission statements and look at the similarities and differences between them and record these in a chart.

Most Police Services have mission statements and organisational objectives on their websites. You can access this information to find out more about which particular Police Service you would like to join. You can also use information like this to make comparisons between Police Service areas.

Performance indicators

Many of these sites will also contain performance indicators. All services have to set performance indicators, which are targets they have to meet within a certain timescale. Examples of performance indicators for the emergency services might be?

- 999 response targets
- ethnic minority recruitment targets
- reduction of crime targets
- staff development targets.

Performance indicators can be a good thing as they mean the government and the public can monitor how successful a service has been. However sometimes meeting the target becomes more important than the actual job and this can have a negative impact on the work of the services. For example, if the Police Service in a certain area had a target to increase arrest rates by 5 per cent then they might simply target groups that are easy to arrest, such as prostitutes, at the expense of other crimes.

What do the police do?

The police do a great deal more work than we are often aware of. Most of us think of police work as responding to emergency calls and the investigation of crime. This is true, but there are an enormous number of other responsibilities that the police take care of every day:

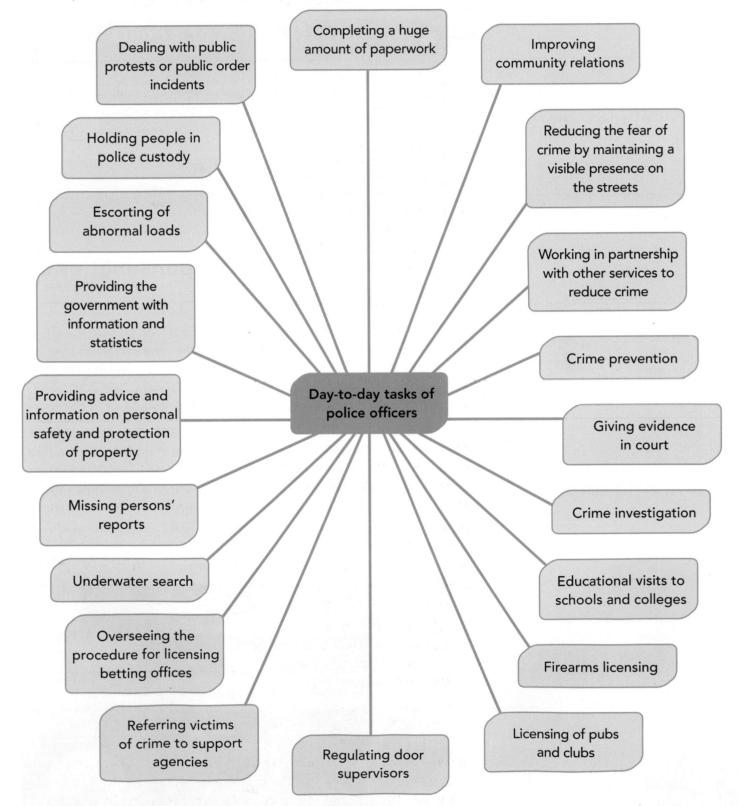

Figure 2.1: Have you considered the day-to-day tasks of the police?

The police are accountable for their performance to the government who monitor their performance and inspect them regularly. They are also accountable to the public who can make complaints against the Police Service to the Independent Police Complaints Commission (IPCC), which have to be investigated.

Activity: The work of a Police Officer

You are a police recruitment officer who is giving a talk to a local college about opportunities in the Police Service. The students ask you the following questions, and you must answer them as fully as you can.

1   What is the purpose of the police?
2   What kind of priorities do the police set?
3   What kind of work do they do?

The purpose, role and responsibilities of the Fire Service

The history of the Fire Service in the UK can be traced back to the Great Fire of London in 1666. This fire blazed for three days and made over 100,000 people homeless. As a result, London was divided into quarters and each quarter was allocated firefighting equipment. This was one of the first organised attempts to prevent fire.

The first formal fire brigade did not exist until 1824, when 80 men were recruited for the specific purpose of fighting fire in Edinburgh. The Fire Services Act 1947 is the legal basis for the existence of the Fire Service, although laws have been passed since then which have modified the role and responsibilities of the Fire Service, such as the 2004 Fire and Rescue Services Act. Today there are about 50 separate fire brigades in England and Wales employing around 33,400 full-time firefighters and around 12,000 retained (part-time) firefighters.

Find out the vision and mission statement for your local fire brigade.

Merseyside Fire and Rescue Service

VISION

To make Merseyside a safer, stronger, healthier community

MISSION

To work in partnership to provide an excellent, affordable service that will:

- reduce risk throughout the community by protective community safety services
- respond quickly to emergencies with skilful staff who reflect all the diverse communities we serve
- restore and maintain quality of life in our communities.

CORPORATE AIMS

Reduce risk

We will reduce the risk of fire and other emergencies in all communities of Merseyside through a combination of prevention and protection, working in partnership with other service providers.

Respond

We will respond to all emergency calls for assistance with a level of response appropriate to the risk and deal with all emergencies efficiently and effectively.

Restore

We will work with partners to help individuals, businesses and communities recover from the impact of emergencies and help the return to normality.

Organisation

We will operate efficient and effective organisational functions that will support the core functions of the Authority in a way that provides value for money for the communities of Merseyside.

Like the Police Service, the Fire Service is required to set aims, objectives and priorities. Since there is no national Fire Service to which you can go to find what these are, you must research individual fire brigades for their priorities and mission statements. The example opposite gives an indication of what some brigades are doing.

Although these targets give an indication of what the Fire Service does at an organisational level they do not specify the tasks and roles the Fire Service performs. Some of these are detailed on page 46.

Activity: The Fire Service

Look at Figure 2.2.

Does the Fire Service have more roles and responsibilities than you thought? What do you think are the five most important roles they have? How did the 2004 Fire and Rescue Services Act change the operation of the service?

What does the Fire Service do?
Apart from responding to emergency calls in the case of fire or serious road traffic incidents, there are other roles the Fire Service is required to do, such as:

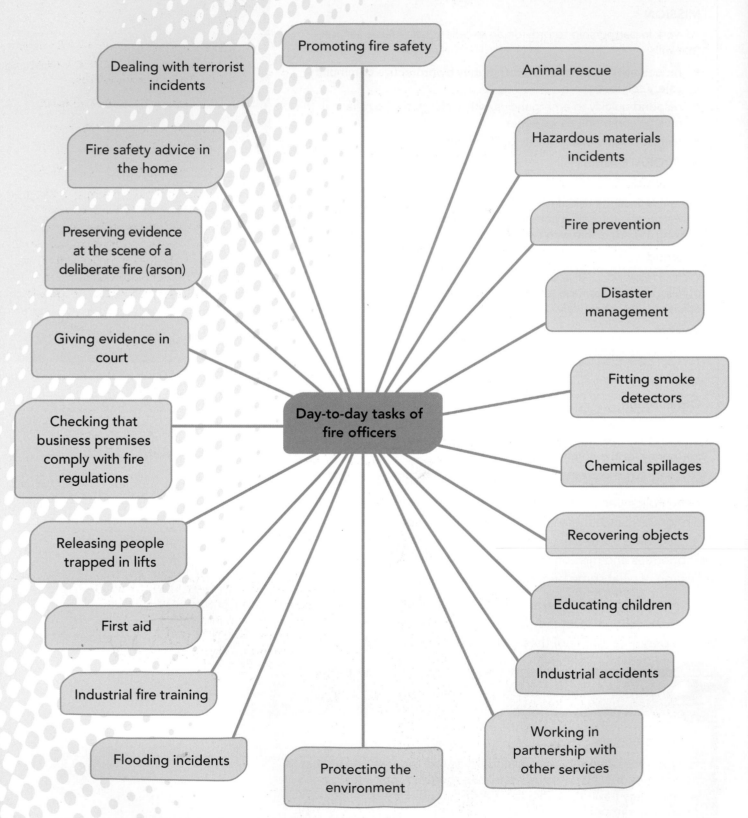

Figure 2.2: Have you considered the day-to-day tasks of a fire officer?

All of the emergency and armed services are accountable to the relevant government department such as the Ministry of Defence, the Ministry of Justice, the Department of Health and the Department of Communities and Local Government. They are monitored via inspectorates who inspect the quality of service that is provided to the public.

1, 2.2 The armed forces

These are the services that respond to external threats made either to our nation directly or to our civilians and financial interests abroad. They are collectively responsible for the defence of our nation and its resources.

The purpose, role and responsibilities of the armed services

The roles and responsibilities of the armed services are set out by the Ministry of Defence which is the government department responsible for the defence of our nation. All of the armed services have a similar role although how they put that role into practice may differ.

The roles of all the armed services includes:

- defence of the UK and its interests abroad
- building international peace and security
- conflict resolution
- responding to emergencies
- working with international partners.
- peacekeeping.

The purpose, role and responsibilities of the British Army

The British Army has a long and distinguished history having been formed by Royal Warrant on 26 January 1661. It is one of the few modern armies to be based on the 'regimental system'. This makes it difficult to discuss the army's history as a whole because each regiment has its own history and traditions. A soldier or an officer will normally serve in the same regiment throughout their career.

> **Did you know?**
>
> The purpose of the UK armed forces is to deliver the UK Defence Vision. This can be summarised as:
>
> - Defend the UK and its interests.
> - Strengthen international peace and stability.
> - Be a force for good in the world.
>
> You can find out more by accessing the Ministry of Defence website and then discover the variations within the armed forces by looking at the websites for the RAF, RN and the Army. All these websites are available via Hotlinks (see page viii).

This system has the advantage of creating pride and loyalty for the regiment, which boosts fighting spirit and leads to a committed and motivated fighting force.

Development of the British Army

Some regiments were established much earlier than others, for instance the Honourable Artillery Company was founded in 1537, the Royal Monmouthshire Royal Engineers in 1539, and the Coldstream Guards in 1650 to name just a few. These regiments are all older than the British Army itself, which has faced many major reforms since 1661, particularly in the 19th and 20th centuries. After the Crimean War against the Russians there were major calls for army reform as many soldiers had died from disease, neglect and poor administration. Although the Crimean War was a successful endeavour for the British Army, the loss of so many soldiers to non-battle conditions was disturbing and triggered the Cardwell Reforms which improved conditions for those in the army and changed the rules for commissioning officers. In 1907 the Haldane Reforms created the Territorial Army.

Other conflicts which changed the way the British Army operated included the Boer War at the end of the 19th century, which caused a major rethink in army tactics and strategy as the army was not used to dealing with fast moving militia groups like the Boers. As a result, the army that fought with the Germans in the First World War of 1914–18 was the best trained and equipped army that Britain had ever produced.

Some of the legislation which sets out the parameters under which the British Army must work are set out in the Army Act of 1955 and the Armed Forces Discipline Act of 2000. The army is currently under-strength in several areas, but has a total of around 100,000.

What does the British Army do?

The variety of individual roles within the army is tremendously large. What the average soldier or officer may encounter within their job will vary depending upon which regiment they are part of. The main elements of the army are described opposite in Figure 2.3, along with the roles they are likely to fulfil.

Activity: The Armed Services

Conduct some research to find out the roles and responsibilities of:

- the Royal Navy
- the Royal Air Force
- the Royal Marines.

Write up your findings in an information leaflet. You can find out more by accessing the relevant forces websites, available via Hotlinks (see page viii).

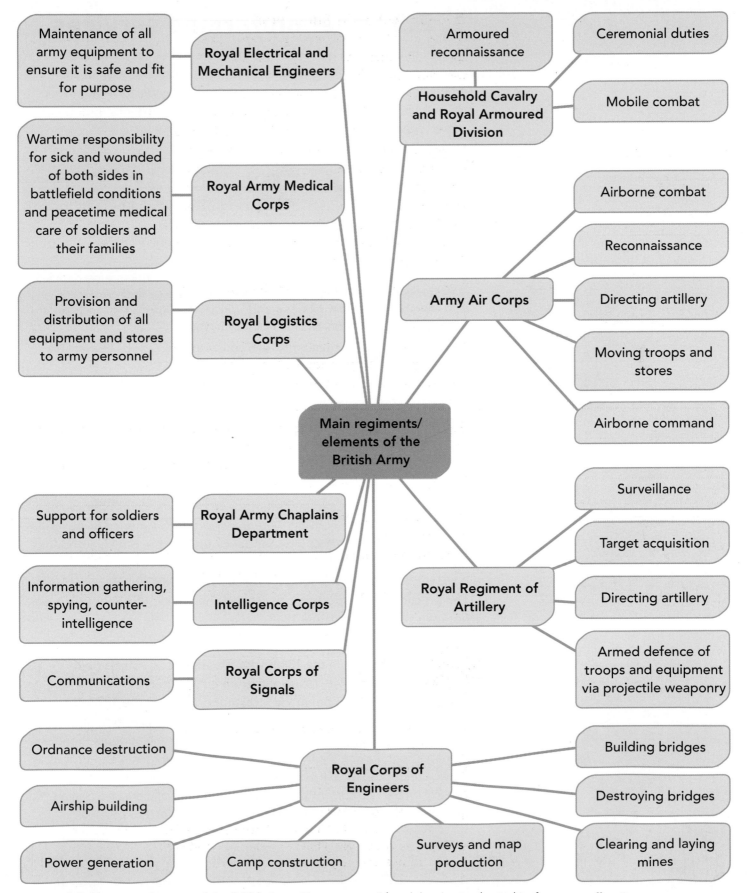

Figure 2.3: The main elements of the British Army. Have you considered the day-to-day tasks of an army officer?

1, 2.3 Other uniformed services

These are uniformed public services that are not usually involved in emergency response or the defence of the nation (although in an emergency they could be involved in either). They perform vital work for our nation yet are not as high profile as the emergency and armed services.

Activity: HM Coastguard

HM Coastguard is part of the government Maritime and Coastguard Agency (MCA).

It has responsibility for responding to civilian maritime emergencies around the coast of the UK. Research the service and produce a five-minute presentation on the work of the Coastguard and the main roles and responsibilities they have.

You will find information to help you at the MCA website available via Hotlinks (see page viii).

The purpose, role and responsibilities of HM Prison Service

Prisons have a very long history in the UK, but often other methods of punishment were used in preference to prison, such as hanging or transportation where convicts were transported to America or Australia. After the American War of Independence in 1776 the British authorities favoured Australia as the country for transportation of convicts, however the journey was long and arduous taking eight months by sea. The practice of transporting convicts was halted in 1857 although it was not officially abolished until 1868.

These changes in the treatment of prisoners led to a rapid prison building programme in the 1840s with 54 new prisons being built between 1842 and 1848. Many of them are still in service today. The Prison Service used to be run by local authorities, but the 1877 Prison Act brought all prisons under the control of central government, as they are to this day. The prison service is part of the National Offender Management Service (NOMS) which combines the Prison and Probation Service under the Ministry of Justice to try to help reduce re-offending. The Prison Service currently employs over 40,000 officers and civilian staff who deal with approximately 84,000 inmates in over 120 prisons.

Roles and responsibilities of HM Prison Service

The roles and responsibilities of the Prison Service are stated very clearly in their mission statement and strategic objectives outlined below.

HM Prison Service

STATEMENT OF PURPOSE

Her Majesty's Prison Service serves the public by keeping in custody those committed by the courts. Our duty is to look after them with humanity and help them lead law-abiding and useful lives in custody and after release.

VISION

To provide the very best prison services so that we are the provider of choice.

To work towards this vision by securing the following key objectives.

OBJECTIVES

To protect the public and provide what commissioners want to purchase by:

- holding prisoners securely
- reducing the risk of prisoners re-offending
- providing safe and well-ordered establishments in which we treat prisoners humanely, decently and lawfully.

In securing these objectives we adhere to the following principles.

PRINCIPLES

In carrying out our work we:

- work in close partnership with our commissioners and others in the Criminal Justice System to achieve common objectives
- obtain best value from the resources available using research to ensure effective correctional practice
- promote diversity, equality of opportunity and combat unlawful discrimination
- ensure our staff have the right leadership, organisation, support and preparation to carry out their work effectively.

These are the aims of the Prison Service overall, but what are the usual roles and responsibilities of an individual prison officer? Figure 2.4 highlights the tasks that a prison officer may have to fulfil in the course of their duties.

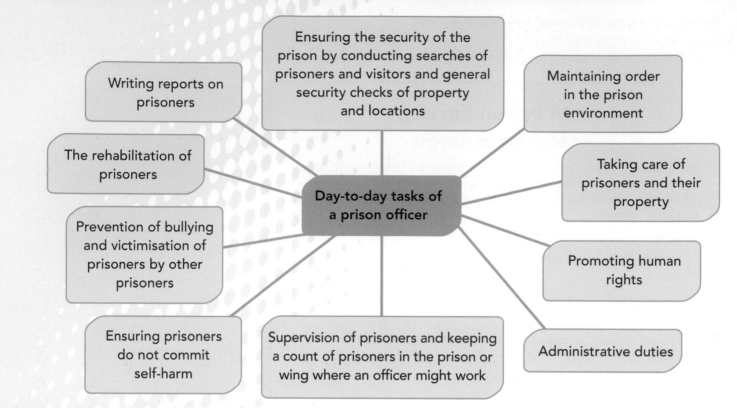

Figure 2.4: The duties of a prison officer. What other tasks might a prison officer do?

Activity: Would you make a good prison officer?

HM Prison Service has a set of points they ask you to consider before applying to become a prison officer. Look at the points below and consider whether you are suited for a career in the Prison Service.

1 The majority of prison officers are required to work to a shift pattern, which may include early starts, late finishes, night shifts, weekend and Bank Holiday working.

2 Although prisons are usually calm and controlled environments, very occasionally some prisoners can be volatile and prison officers need to be able to deal with conflict in an appropriate manner.

3 Prison officers need to work with a wide variety of people with diverse backgrounds and experiences.

4 When working as a prison officer, it is important not to judge people on the basis of the crimes they may have committed, but to treat everyone in the same fair and objective manner.

5 It is essential that prison officers have excellent interpersonal and communication skills, as these can be used to prevent and diffuse difficult situations and to create a positive prison environment.

6 Prison officers need to have the self-confidence to deal with all kinds of situations as and when they arise, sometimes in difficult circumstances.

7 Prison officers need to be patient in order to deal with prisoners when faced with challenging behaviour.

8 Prison officers work as a team and it is crucial that they cooperate and provide constant support to one another during every shift.

9 Security is of utmost importance in a prison and prison officers shoulder a great deal of responsibility for maintaining a secure and safe environment for everyone.

10 Prison officers have a duty of care for prisoners and are there to ensure that prisoners are in a safe environment, are treated with dignity and respect throughout their time in prison.

Are you able to accept these points? Are there any you would find difficult to do?

You can find out more at the Prison Service website, available via Hotlinks (see page viii).

Activity: HM Revenue and Customs

HM Revenue and Customs was created in 2005, following the merger of the Inland Revenue and HM Customs and Excise Departments. The Purpose of HMRC is as follows:

HMRC
STATEMENT OF PURPOSE

PURPOSE

We make sure that the money is available to fund the UK's public services. We also help families and individuals with targeted financial support.

VISION

We will close the tax gap, our customers will feel that the tax system is simple for them and even-handed, and we will be seen as a highly professional and efficient organisation.

WAY

- We understand our customers and their needs.

- We make it easy for our customers to get things right.

- We believe that most of our customers are honest and we treat everyone with respect.

- We are passionate in helping those who need it and relentless in pursuing those who bend or break the rules.

- We recognise that we have privileged access to information and we will protect it.

- We behave professionally and with integrity.

- We do our own jobs well and take pride in helping our colleagues to succeed.

- We develop the skills and tools we need to do our jobs well. We strive for continuous improvement in everything we do.

Conduct some research into the job HMRC officers actually do. What are their main duties? Where are they located? Why is HMRC so vitally important to the performance of the rest of the public services?

BTEC   Assessment activity 2.1

Understanding the roles and responsibilities of the services is really important if you are going to have enough knowledge to decide which career path you want to follow. Address the following tasks in the form of a presentation:

1   *Outline* the main purpose and roles of two contrasting uniformed public services. **P1**

2   *Discuss* the main responsibilities of two contrasting uniformed public services. **P2**

3   *Explain* the role, purpose and responsibilities of two contrasting uniformed public services. **M1**

4   *Evaluate* the role, purpose and responsibilities of a chosen uniformed public service. **D1**

Grading tips

P1 simply requires an outline of two different public services such as one emergency and one armed, and **P2** builds on this by asking for the responsibilities. To get **M1** you must explain in much more detail what you have already covered for **P1** and **P2** and **D1** requires you to choose one of the services you have looked at and consider the positive and negative aspects of its role, purpose and responsibilities.

3 The different employment opportunities available in the public services

The public services have to fulfil a variety of roles in their day-to-day operations. These roles vary across the services as you will have already seen in the first learning outcome for this unit, but they can include any or all of the types of work shown in Table 2.2.

Table 2.2: Roles of the public services.

Type of work	Description
Emergency work	This work involves 999 response or response to emergencies on conflict situations overseas. It might include dealing with casualties, fires, crime or terrorist incidents.
Routine work	The public services also do a great deal of routine work, such as the care and maintenance of equipment, educational visits, people management and intelligence gathering.
Administrative work	All the public services are required to complete the administration for the jobs they do, such as arrest reports, equality and diversity reports and routine paperwork.
Working with other services	Working with other services is also known as multi-agency work and is essential in all the public services. The emergency services must work together as they are often attending the same incident and they must coordinate their roles. The same is true of the armed services which must support and reinforce each other in areas of conflict.
Community work	The services are public servants, this means that they work in the best interests of the British public. In order to do this they often interact with the community directly by attending events, going to schools and colleges and improving their profile with the public.
Peacekeeping	The armed services are often involved in peacekeeping work abroad, usually with the support of the United Nations (UN) or the North Atlantic Treaty Organization (NATO). This involves monitoring ceasefires in conflict areas and protecting civilians.
Humanitarian work	In emergency situations overseas the public services can be deployed to assist with humanitarian work such as search and rescue, evacuation, distribution of food and shelter and the protection of vulnerable civilian groups such as women and children. British public services have responded with assistance in recent events such as the Asian tsunami in 2004 and the Pakistani earthquake in 2005, where emergency aid had to be delivered, search and rescue undertaken and reconstruction started.
Major incidents	In response to a major incident all of the public services can be called upon to support each other in dealing with casualties, environmental clean up, search and rescue, decontamination, establishing cordons, reducing risk to the public and evidence collection. A recent example of this occurred in 2007 where floods hit several parts of the UK very badly, such as South Yorkshire and Humberside.
Conflicts	The police and the armed services deal with conflicts at home and abroad. They must ensure they resolve the conflict as quickly as possible to minimise casualties.
Armed conflict	For a variety of reasons the armed forces may be called upon to become involved in armed conflict abroad. Here they will carry out the objectives set by the government as effectively as possible, while minimising their own casualties and harm to non-combatants.

3.1 Working in the services

Working in the public services is not for everyone. The variety of roles they do and the stresses of the jobs mean that you must be very committed and capable if you are going to make a good recruit. There are lots of advantages and disadvantages to working in the services on both a personal and professional level. If we look at the four services we examined in detail earlier in this unit we can compare the positive and negative aspects of working in a service and the implications for you personally.

Table 2.3: Comparison of advantages and disadvantages of working in various public services.

The Police Service	
Positive	**Negative**
• Interesting and varied work	• Unsocial hours/shift work interfering with personal and family life
• Plenty of opportunities for career development and progression	• Risk to personal safety
• Work as part of a team and make friends	• Unpleasant nature of some of the work, such as dealing with child abuse cases
• Meet different people every day	• Public attitudes towards the police are not always positive
• Opportunity to change job roles throughout career	• More than a 9–5 job as required to uphold the standards of the Police Service in off-duty hours too
• Good rates of pay compared with other services	• Responsibility for people's safety (can't afford a day below par)
• Excellent pension and benefits	
• Retirement at 60	
• Secure employment	
• Ongoing training	

The Fire Service	
Positive	**Negative**
• Secure employment	• Unsocial hours/shift work
• Variety of work	• Dangerous nature of the work
• Retirement at 60	• Poor pay in relation to some other services
• Opportunity for progression and promotion	• Disturbing nature of some of the work, particularly when deaths are involved
• Ongoing training	• Declining recruitment due to reduction in the number of fires
• Saving lives	

The Armed Forces	
Positive	**Negative**
• Varied and interesting roles	• Very disciplined environment
• Wide variety of job opportunities	• Lack of freedom to do as you please
• Opportunities for advancement and promotion	• Dangerous nature of work
• Stable and secure employment	• Poor starting pay in enlisted ranks compared with other services
• Opportunities for travel and living abroad	• Postings abroad can harm personal relationships
• Sense of belonging/ camaraderie	• Promotion is difficult to get without a good education
• Early retirement	
• Ongoing training	
• Opportunities for sports or developing new skills	
• Food and lodgings provided	
• Make many friends	

The Prison Service	
Positive	**Negative**
• Retirement at 60	• Poor salary in comparison with other services
• Stable and secure employment	• Shift work
• Good opportunities for promotion	• Confined working environment
• Graduate fast-track scheme	• Lack of opportunity to work outdoors
• Rewarding job which is a service to the community	• Prison can be a tense and intimidating environment
• Large variety of roles	• No guarantee of a posting of your choice
• Fast-track entry for experienced managers	• Can be a dangerous environment
• Opportunities for professional development and innovation	
• Opportunities to develop teamwork skills	

Activity: Your service

If you are considering joining a different service from the ones described in Table 2.3 draw up your own table of the positive and negative aspects of working in that service. What would the implications for your personal life be?

Roles within the public services

Each public service has a variety of job roles within it that you could fulfil. Not all people who work for the Police Service are police officers and not all people who work for the army are soldiers. You might not have considered some of the options available to you as shown in Figure 2.5.

Figure 2.5: Have you considered the variety of roles in the public services?

Some parts of public service roles are contracted out to private companies such as hospital cleaning and provision of meals in the NHS and the operation of private prisons.

How does the work of the community support officer differ from the role of the police?

Looking in detail at a chosen role: police constable

All police officers must spend two years completing a probation period as a constable before they can specialise in a particular area of police work. Many police officers choose to stay as constables for the whole of their career. The role of a police constable involves many of the following tasks:

Foot patrol. This involves the walking of a specific route (or beat) to act as a visible uniformed presence. This acts as a deterrent to criminals who are in the area and reduces fear of crime in the general public. Although it is rare that a beat officer will come across a crime in progress, the general public often express their opinion in polls that they would like to see more officers on the beat.

Working in schools to talk about safety and crime. Patrol constables may often be called upon by local schools to talk to children about issues as diverse as personal safety, making hoax 999 calls, drug awareness and paedophiles in internet chat rooms. This means that they must be well informed about such issues and confident enough to speak about them. This kind of role can help build police–community relations in younger generations and is therefore very important.

Activity: Your career

Have you considered any of the alternative public service career paths in Figure 2.5? Choose one that might be of interest to you and find out how you would be recruited for that role.

Assisting in the event of accidents, fights and fires. Patrol constables are often called to attend unexpected incidents in which they might be called upon to intervene in a public order incident, such as a pub fight or a domestic violence incident. They may also have to attend a local accident where a person has been injured and possibly administer first aid until assistance arrives.

Road safety initiatives. Patrol constables may often be called upon to participate in road safety initiatives, this may include visiting schools to educate children on the dangers of traffic, or it might be taking part in initiatives such as exhaust emissions testing, documents checks, or roadside car safety checks such as tyre tread depth.

House-to-house enquiries. During the investigation of serious crimes such as murder or abductions police constables are often called upon to go door to door in a particular district to gather information that householders may have about a particular crime in their area. This can be a time-consuming but necessary job and is a valuable investigation technique.

Policing major public events. Police constables are often asked to ensure public safety at events, such as football matches, or public demonstrations, such as political rallies. When large crowds gather together there is always the possibility of fights breaking out or people being hurt in crushes. Police officers plan for such events to make sure they are safe for everyone.

Giving evidence in court. Since police constables are often first at the scene of a crime or an incident they may have information which is relevant to the case and which may affect the outcome of a magistrates or crown court trial.

Crime reduction operations. Police constables take part in these operations which target crimes such as underage drinking or youth nuisance which may be causing problems in a particular area. They also offer crime reduction information on protecting your property and Neighbourhood Watch.

The role of a police constable can take many forms if after serving the two years probation period they decide to apply for a specific role other than patrol officer. Some of these roles are described in Table 2.4.

Table 2.4: Possible roles of a police constable.

Roles of Police Constable	Brief job description
Dog Handler	Dog Handlers and their dogs work as a team. The dogs assist with catching criminals, searching buildings and policing large crowds, such as those at football matches. They are often trained to find drugs or explosives.
Traffic Police	All forces have officers deployed on road policing. Part of their duties involves tackling vehicle crime. They ensure road safety by enforcing traffic laws such as those relating to speeding and drink driving. They also deal with road accidents and help road users.
Criminal Investigation Department (CID)	Officers engaged in detective work account for about 1 in 8 of all police staff. They receive intensive training to enable them to work effectively in this field. The day-to-day work of detectives is busy and demanding. Their core role is to investigate serious crime and to act upon intelligence which can lead to the arrest and prosecution of hardened or 'career' criminals.
Special Branch	Special Branch Officers combat terrorism. They work at airports and seaports, providing armed bodyguards for politicians and public figures and investigating firearms and explosives offences that may be connected to national security matters.
Firearms Unit	Firearms Unit Officers form specialist teams trained in the use of firearms to assist with dangerous operations.
Drugs Squad	The growth in the misuse of drugs in the UK is a major cause for concern. The specialist officers from the Drugs Squad work with operational officers and other agencies to target drug dealers and tackle the drugs problem. They play a very important role in combating this area of organised crime.
Fraud Squad	We all bear the cost of fraud in our insurance premiums or in the higher cost of products. The Police Service has a specialised Fraud Squad, run jointly by the Metropolitan Police and the City of London Police. Other forces also have Fraud Squads and they assist each other in investigating fraud. Fraud Squad officers also work with the Serious Fraud Office, a government department set up to investigate large-scale fraud.
Mounted Unit	Police horses work under the guidance of officers from the Mounted Unit who are very skilled riders. Together they work as a team and play a vital role at events where there are large crowds, such as football matches, race meetings and demonstrations. They are also used to provide high visibility policing at a local level, often in parkland and open spaces.

Assessment activity 2.2

P3 M2

It is important that you know all you can about your chosen public services career before you make an application. Address the following tasks by producing an information sheet which will help you and your colleagues improve your knowledge.

1 *Outline* different employment opportunities available to the uniformed public services. **P3**

2 *Explain* the work of a chosen job in the public services. **M2**

Grading tips

For **P3** chose a public service role and produce a job description for it. You could look for an official job description on your chosen services recruitment website to help you. For **M2** explain the work of that particular job role in detail.

4 The conditions of service for different public service jobs

Conditions of service cover the information you need to make a reasoned career choice about which service would suit you best. Conditions of service are illustrated in Figure 2.6 and described in Table 2.5.

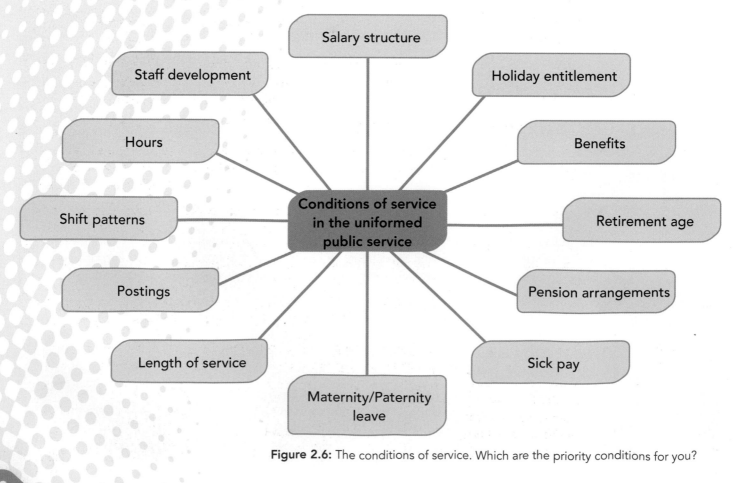

Figure 2.6: The conditions of service. Which are the priority conditions for you?

Table 2.5: Conditions of service for different public service roles.

	Police Service Constable	Fire Service Firefighter	Prison Service Prison Officer	British Army Soldier
Salary structure	Around £20,000 depending on the force area rising to £35,000 or so after 10 years	Around £20,000 rising to £26,500 or so when fully trained and competent	Ranges from around £17,744 to £27,530 or so	Starting salary of £13,377 rising to £25,887 for rank of Private
Holiday entitlement	Minimum of 23 days	30 days	22–25 days	30 days
Benefits	Flexible working Paid overtime	Flexible working	Season Ticket travel Childcare vouchers Flexible working	Free medical and dental care Accommodation provided Resettlement package on leaving the service
Retirement age	60 years up to rank of Chief Inspector	Normally 60 years	Normally 60 years	55 years
Pension	National Police Pension Scheme, 9.5% of salary paid in and full pension after 35 years	Local Government pension scheme and Firefighters pension scheme depending on role	Two civil service pensions schemes available	Armed Forces Pension Scheme available
Sick pay	Paid sick leave available	Paid sick leave available	Paid sick leave available	Paid sick leave available
Maternity/Paternity	Paid maternity and paternity leave provided	Paid maternity and paternity leave provided	Paid maternity and paternity leave provided	Paid maternity and paternity leave provided
Length of service	No fixed length	No fixed length	No fixed length	Variable
Postings	Anywhere within the force area	Anywhere within the brigade area	Any prison in England and Wales	Anywhere in the world depending on operational needs
Shift patterns	Varies from force to force. May be 2 days, 2 evenings, 2 nights and 4 days off or similar	Varies from brigade to brigade, may be 2 days, 2 nights and 4 days off or similar	Shifts in operation, including days, evening and nights to provide 24-hour cover	Varies depending on operational needs
Hours	40 hours	42 hours	39 hours	Varies depending on operational needs
Staff development	Training allowance given in some forces to fund training relevant to role. Ongoing internal police training available throughout career	Ongoing training provided throughout career	Ongoing training throughout career	Ongoing training throughout career

The conditions of service can vary across the public services and they might influence the decision you take about your future career path. Also, conditions of service may vary slightly within a service. These can be a difference between uniformed and non-uniformed roles, and differences between enlisted and commissioned ranks.

It is important to remember that not only is each service different, but each fire brigade or Police Service area might be different as well. Therefore, although Table 2.5 provides a guide you should check directly with the service you want to join regarding specific terms and conditions of employment.

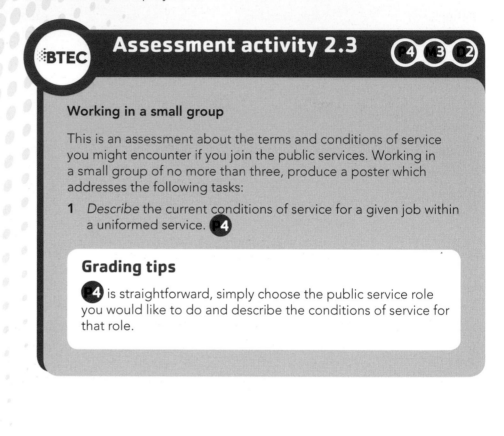

BTEC **Assessment activity 2.3** P4 M3 D2

Working in a small group

This is an assessment about the terms and conditions of service you might encounter if you join the public services. Working in a small group of no more than three, produce a poster which addresses the following tasks:

1 *Describe* the current conditions of service for a given job within a uniformed service. P4

Grading tips

P4 is straightforward, simply choose the public service role you would like to do and describe the conditions of service for that role.

Lance Corporal Kelly Stevens

Territorial Army

I work as part of 38 Signal Regiment, which is a TA regiment with responsibility for providing Information Communication Systems to the emergency services and local government in an emergency. As well as this several of our members are actively deployed overseas with regular soldiers. We can be called up on for a variety of things, for example our Brigade has been involved in dealing with firefighter strikes, foot and mouth disease and responding to severe flooding.

A typical day

There is no such thing as a typical day in the TA. When we are on camp we may be doing a variety of activities from battle simulations to working with other NATO forces from different countries, to training and equipment maintenance. The TA is required as an essential support to the regular soldiers and we have to make sure we are ready and prepared to be deployed if we are called upon.

The best thing about the job

I love my job with the TA. Not only is it radically different from my day job, but I get the opportunity to contribute to the safety and security of our nation which is a tremendous responsibility. The teamwork and camaraderie in the unit is excellent and I have met people from all walks of life who share the same goals as I do. I'm proud to be part of the TA and I would recommend it to anyone.

Think about it!

1. What topics have you covered in this unit that might give you the background to be a TA soldier?
2. What knowledge and skills do you think you need to develop further if you want to be involved in the British Army in the future?

Just checking

1. What does a police officer do?
2. What is the role of HM Prison Service?
3. What are the positive and negative aspects of working for the Fire Service?
4. What are the benefits of joining the British Army?
5. What are the conditions of service in the Fire Service?

edexcel

Assignment tips

- What are the conditions of service in the Fire Service? This unit requires research into the public services, so making sure you use the right sources of research will be essential. Your school or college should order in journals and publications about the services such as *Police Review* or *Soldier* magazine. These often contain issues arising from change in the services that you will need to be aware of if you are going to get the best grades in your assignment work. If your centre doesn't stock them, speak with your tutor or librarian about getting them in.

- The service you want to join may be different from those outlined in this unit or even those of your fellow learners. Don't be hesitant about approaching the service of your choice directly for information, after all you will be approaching them soon for a job anyway so it won't hurt to make a positive first impression by showing an interest in the work they do and the conditions of service you would be working under.

3 Employment in the non-uniformed public services

The **public sector** is the largest employer in the UK with over 6 million employees. This does not only include the highly visible uniformed services but also the hidden army of non-uniformed public services, such as education, social services, healthcare and local government, who offer vital structure and support for our society and our communities.

This unit provides you with the opportunity to explore careers in a wide range of non-uniformed public services and understand the purpose, roles and responsibilities of those services and how they work with and complement the uniformed sector.

You will also examine pay and conditions in the non-uniformed services so you will be able to make informed judgements about which career path you would like to take.

Learning outcomes

After completing this unit you should:
1. know the main roles of different public services
2. understand the main responsibilities of different non-uniformed public services
3. understand the different employment opportunities available in the non-uniformed public services
4. know the conditions of service for public sector jobs.

Assessment and grading criteria

This table shows you what you must do in order to achieve a pass, merit or distinction grade, and where you can find activities in this book to help you.

To achieve a **pass** grade the evidence must show that the learner is able to:	To achieve a **merit** grade the evidence must show that, in addition to the pass criteria, the learner is able to:	To achieve a **distinction** grade the evidence must show that, in addition to the pass and merit criteria, the learner is able to:
P1 outline the main roles of two different public services **Assessment activity 3.1 page 74**		
P2 discuss the main responsibilities of two different non-uniformed public services **Assessment activity 3.1 page 74**	**M1** explain the role, purpose and responsibilities of two different non-uniformed public services **Assessment activity 3.1 page 74**	**D1** evaluate the role, purpose and responsibilities of a chosen non-uniformed public service **Assessment activity 3.1 page 74**
P3 explain the different non-uniformed employment opportunities available in the public services **Assessment activity 3.2 page 79**	**M2** explain the work of a chosen non-uniformed public service job **Assessment activity 3.2 page 79**	
P4 describe the current conditions of service for two non-uniformed public service job roles **Assessment activity 3.3 page 80**		

Key terms

Public sector – the part of the economy that is controlled by the government or state.

Private sector – the part of the economy that is not directly controlled by the government or state.

Voluntary sector – the part of the economy that includes charitable and voluntary organisations.

How you will be assessed

This unit will be assessed by an internal assignment that will be designed and marked by the staff at your centre. The assignment is designed to allow you to show your understanding of the learning outcomes for exploring careers in the non-uniformed public services. These relate to what you should be able to do after completing this unit. Your assessments might include some of the following:

- portfolios of evidence
- learning journals
- blog entries
- video diaries.
- action plans
- skill audits
- presentations
- leaflets
- reports.

Ali, 16, finds out about the non-uniformed public services

I wasn't really interested in this unit at the start as I wanted to be a police officer so the non-uniformed services were a bit of a mystery to me. I hadn't realised how essential the non-uniformed services were and how the work they do supports society just as much as the uniformed services.

It's made me consider my options a bit more. All of the services have to work together anyway and some of the jobs they do are quite similar. This unit has given me the opportunity to compare a really wide range of jobs so I can make an informed choice about what career is best for me.

I appreciate the work of the non-uniformed public services a lot more now, sometimes they can seem a bit invisible when you compare them to the emergency or armed services, but they are every bit as necessary to society.

Over to you

- What areas of exploring careers might you find interesting?
- Have you considered what career you would like?
- What preparation could you do to get ready for your assessments?

1, 2 The main roles and responsibilities of different non-uniformed public services

Talk up

A public service for you

What do you know about the non-uniformed services? Which non-uniformed services appeal to you the most as a career? Look at the whole range of jobs available in this sector and choose two or three that you are most interested in.

Research these job roles and decide which might be the right one for you.

Key terms

Purpose – this is the reason a service was created in the first place. It is its reason for existing.

Role – this is the overarching job of the service, their main function.

Responsibility – these are all the things a service may be responsible for while fulfilling their role.

The non-uniformed public services are those front-line services that provide support for our society but often aren't as high profile as the emergency and armed services. They include:

- the Education Service
- the Health Service
- Social Services
- the Probation Service
- Housing Services
- the Highways Agency
- Sanitation Services
- Leisure and recreation
- Local council planning
- Environmental Health Services.

Without these services our society would be a very different and a much more difficult place to live in.

Activity: Life without non-uniformed services

Consider the list of the public services above. If they didn't exist what would be the impact on you, your family or your community? Many people feel that they owe their lives to the service provided by the National Health Service. What would happen if it wasn't there?

Look at each service and make notes on the possible impact on society if it didn't exist. Could the service be provided by private companies or the **voluntary sector**? Which non-uniformed services are the most essential in your opinion?

1, 2.1 Role, purpose and responsibilities of the Education Service

Education has been around for as long as there have been people who needed to learn new skills and abilities. Education doesn't only mean learning in schools and colleges, it also incorporates learning from any source such as books, parents, grandparents or employers. In the past the vast majority of people in the UK had no formal education at all, only the very wealthy could afford to educate their children and many of them chose not to do so as the types of society which existed in the past did not need a tremendous amount of academic learning in order to function well. The ability to farm or craft items was of far more use than the ability to read in a society where there were few books.

This began to change with the introduction of the Education Act 1870, which was the first step towards compulsory primary education and set out a framework for education for all 5–12-year-olds. However, attendance at schools did not become compulsory until 1880 (for children up to the age of ten). The reason education became so important at this time was that the government was concerned that Britain was failing to maintain its lead in industry and needed more skilled and educated workers to be able to compete.

The education system you are now in is a direct result of the 1870 Education Act and the many education **acts** which have been passed by Parliament.

Key term

Act – a piece of law which is created by the government and passed by Parliament. All of the public services are governed by acts that set out their roles, purpose and responsibilities.

Activity: Finding out about education

Research your local Education Service. What are its main roles and responsibilities?

Draw up an information leaflet with your findings.

1, 2.2 Roles and responsibilities of the Health Service

The origins of the National Health Service (NHS) began with the Beveridge Report 1942. William Beveridge created a series of proposals which were the starting point for many of the non-uniformed public services, including the NHS and social services. The NHS was created by the National Health Service Act 1946 but didn't become operational until July 1948. Before this time people had to pay for their medical treatment, which had real disadvantages for the poor who could not afford treatment.

Although we take the NHS for granted and some people complain about the standard of service they receive, it is one of the finest health care services in the world and is free at the point of use for British citizens. In some parts of the world your ability to pay can mean the difference between life and death, which is why many people value the NHS.

The NHS employs more than 1.5 million people, including:

- 120,000 hospital doctors
- 40,000 GPs
- 400,000 nurses
- 25,000 ambulance staff.

These are supported by managers and administrators who help the service to run smoothly. The annual budget of the NHS in 2007–2008 was over £100 billion and this will increase, on average, by about 4 per cent per year. The NHS is managed by the Department of Health who give responsibility for the NHS to 10 strategic health authorities who run all NHS services in particular areas of the country.

The original purpose of the NHS was to provide a health service which catered to all citizens regardless of their wealth and this is still true today. The NHS has a set of core principles which it uses to provide high quality healthcare to those who need it. In effect, these principles are its responsibilities.

NHS Core Principles

- The NHS will provide a comprehensive range of services – this includes: information, advice, hospital care, community care, disease prevention, health promotion, rehabilitation and aftercare.
- The NHS will shape its services around the needs and preferences of individual patients, their families and their carers.
- The NHS will respond to the different needs of different populations.
- The NHS will improve the quality of services and minimise errors.
- The NHS will support and value its staff.
- Public funds for healthcare will be devoted solely to NHS patients.
- The NHS will work with others to ensure a seamless service for patients.
- The NHS will help to keep people healthy and work to reduce health inequalities.
- The NHS will respect the confidentiality of individual patients and provide open access to information about services, treatment and performance.

What does the NHS do?

This is a very difficult question to answer since many parts of the NHS have different roles. The roles and responsibilities of a nurse are different from those of a physiotherapist, doctor or administrator. The role of a mental health unit will be vastly different from a special care baby unit, dentist's surgery or geriatric ward. What all of these parts of the NHS have in common is a commitment to patient care and the health and well-being of their patients and the population in general.

Performance indicators

As you will have seen outlined in Unit 2, all the public services have to set and abide by performance indicators. The non-uniformed services are in exactly the same position where they have to set indicators which are targets to meet within a certain timescale. Examples of performance indicators for the NHS might be:

- outpatient waiting times
- inpatient waiting times
- waiting times in Accident and Emergency departments
- standards of hospital cleanliness
- numbers of vaccinations delivered
- patient survival rates.

Performance indicators are a good thing as it means the government and the public can monitor how successful a service has been. Sometimes meeting the targets becomes more important than the purpose of the job and this can have a negative impact on the work of the services. For example, a hospital might have a high rate of deaths in premature babies, but this could be because it is the expert hospital in the area and takes on more critical cases than others, not because its service is failing.

The NHS and all health and social care provision in England is accountable to the Care Quality Commission (CQC). The commission acts as an independent inspectorate or regulator of standards in the health and social care sectors.

Activity: Roles of the NHS

Choose three different roles in the NHS and produce an information sheet about the day-to-day work of those undertaking the roles.

Activity: Accountability of the NHS

Research the Care Quality Commission and find out exactly how they monitor the activities of the NHS and hold them accountable for the standards of care they offer patients. Produce a five-minute presentation which details what you have found out.

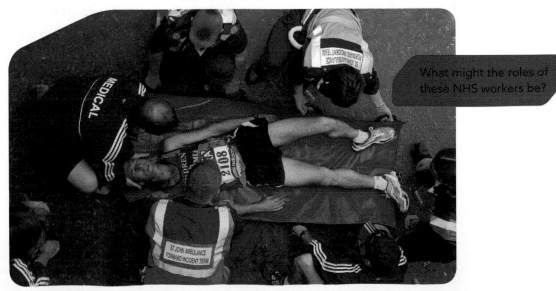

What might the roles of these NHS workers be?

1, 2.3 The role, purpose and responsibilities of the National Probation Service

The Probation Service has existed since 1907, when it was created by the Probation of Offenders Act. Its original role was to supervise offenders who were released into the community in the hope that regular contact and supervision with a recognised official would reduce the chances of them re-offending.

In 2004 the Probation Service joined with the Prison Service under the banner of the National Offender Management Service (NOMS) and the Ministry of Justice has responsibility for these services. The Probation Service today still performs a very similar role to the one it was introduced to do in 1907: it supervises offenders in the community. This includes individuals who have received community sentences and those who have been released early from prison.

Case study: Jason's early release

I've been in and out of trouble since I was 12 years old. Lots of people in my position will blame anyone for their trouble but themselves, but getting in trouble with the police has always been my choice and my responsibility. I'm 28 now and have two young kids, the last spell I did in prison nearly killed me. I missed my kids desperately and I didn't want them to see me in here or, God forbid, grow up to follow in my footsteps.

I knew it was time for a change but crime had been a way of life for so long I had no idea how to change or what to do. My probation officer was brilliant. Normally they've heard stories like mine a million times and when you say you want to change you can see in their eyes they've heard it before, but she took me seriously and helped me pick up some voluntary work and start some construction courses at a local college.

I can't say my life is all rosy now, but I'm learning a trade, doing work I can be proud of and I haven't been in trouble for over a year. If my probation officer hadn't helped me out I would have been back inside within 6 months and my kids would be without their dad again.

Now answer the following questions:

1   How can probation officers help prisoners who have an early release?

2   Why is supervision of offenders so important?

3   How does the National Probation Service link to the Prison Service?

The National Probation Service employs about 21,000 staff and operates in 42 geographical areas. It has the following responsibilities:

- protecting the public
- reducing re-offending
- the proper punishment of offenders in the community
- ensuring offenders' awareness of the effects of crime on victims and communities
- the rehabilitation of offenders.

What do the Probation Service do?

Personnel in the Probation Service undertake the following roles:

- supervise offenders in the community
- write pre-sentence reports and bail reports
- deal with premises that house prisoners who have been released on licence
- work with victims
- work with other criminal justice partners such as the Prison Service and police
- liaise with employers and councils to find sources of community work for those sentenced to community service
- **risk** assess offenders.

As with all public services the National Probation Service is accountable to both the public and the government for its performance. This is monitored by Her Majesty's Inspectorate of Probation, which evaluates the effectiveness of work with individual offenders, children and young people aimed at reducing re-offending and protecting the public and reports back to the Ministry of Justice.

1, 2.4 Roles, purpose and responsibilities of Social Services

Social Services are provided to communities by their local councils. The services include:

- helping children in need of protection
- adults and children with disabilities or mental health problems
- residential care for children and the elderly
- fostering and adoption
- young offenders
- supporting carers
- meals on wheels (mainly for the elderly)
- day centres
- care in the home
- occupational therapy
- equipment and adaptations to homes.

The purpose of Social Services is to help all people regardless of background, age or disability to reach their full potential. Unfortunately, there are many people in society who suffer from significant problems which may require outside intervention in order to be solved. These may be a child suffering abuse or a young person with learning difficulties who wants to attend a mainstream school. Social Care Services assess the needs of vulnerable people such as this and assist in providing a care package which ensures individuals are safe, protected and have their needs met.

> **Key term**
>
> **Risk** – a risk is the chance that a hazard may cause harm to someone.

> **Remember**
>
> As with all public services, Social Services can only do as much as their staffing and budgets allow and, unfortunately, they cannot meet the needs of every vulnerable person in society. They often take a great deal of criticism for this with high profile failures such as the case of Baby P (who died in 2007 aged 17 months) dominating the media. What you don't often hear are the stories of the thousands of people whose lives might have been very different if they had not been helped by Social Services.

Like the NHS, Social Care Services are inspected and regulated by the CQC who ensure that all Social Services in the country are fit for purpose and report back to the government on their findings.

Activity: Local councils

One of the largest providers of non-uniformed public services is your local council, which manages services such as refuse collection and disposal, housing, planning and leisure services. Go to the website of your local council and find out what non-uniformed services it provides. Produce a poster showing how the council manages its services.

Activity: The Highways Agency

The Highways Agency is a non-uniformed public service which reports to the Department for Transport. It is responsible for operating, maintaining and improving the strategic road network in England.

Go to its website available via Hotlinks (see page viii) and find out about its roles and responsibilities. Consider how it differs from other non-uniformed public services and how essential its work is for the operation of the other services.

1, 2.5 Dealing with diversity

Like their uniformed colleagues the non-uniformed public services must deal with a diverse society in order to provide the best services to the community. This includes a range of measures such as:

- leaflets and information in a range of languages
- minority recruitment so the workforce reflect the wider population
- translators and interpreters
- religious and cultural training for all staff.

Diversity in social care is not just about people from differing ethnic backgrounds, it also includes dealing with people of all ages, sexualities and genders. It also includes individuals with a wide range of disabilities and mental health problems. Working in the social care sector is not easy, but improving the lives of the most vulnerable members of our society is very rewarding.

BTEC Assessment activity 3.1

Understanding the roles, purpose and responsibilities of the services is really important if you are going to have enough knowledge to decide which career path you want to follow. Address the following tasks in the form of a presentation:

1 *Outline* the main roles of two different public services. **P1**

2 *Discuss* the main responsibilities of different non-uniformed public services. **P2**

3 *Explain* the role, purpose and responsibilities of two different non-uniformed public services. **M1**

4 *Evaluate* the role, purpose and responsibilities of a chosen non-uniformed public service. **D1**

Grading tips

P1 simply requires an outline of two different public services, **P2** builds on this by asking for the responsibilities. To get **M1** you must explain in much more detail what you have already covered for **P1** and **P2**. **D1** requires you to choose one of the services you have looked at and consider the positive and negative aspects of its role, purpose and responsibilities.

3 The different employment opportunities available in the non-uniformed public services

The non-uniformed public services have to fulfil a variety of roles in their day-to-day operations. These roles vary across the services as you will have already seen in the first learning outcome for the unit, but they can include any or all of those shown in Table 3.1. Some jobs have, for example, a high proportion of routine work and will scarcely ever involve emergencies, others will be the opposite.

Table 3.1: The roles of those employed in the non-uniformed public services.

Type of work	Description
Emergency work	The non-uniformed public services do not respond to 999 calls in the way that the uniformed services do, but in the event of an emergency social services and the NHS are often called upon to respond. For example if there is a major incident all the local hospitals will be put on alert and will take part in dealing with multiple casualties. Social Services often respond to domestic incidents where they are notified by the police that children need to be removed from the home and placed in temporary foster care.
Routine work	Routine work occurs in all services whether uniformed or non-uniformed. It might include the writing of reports, dealing with non-emergency medical matters, keeping in contact with offenders or making assessment visits to people's homes. It makes up the bulk of what the services do.
Administrative work	All the public services are required to complete administration for the jobs they do, such as reports on offenders, vulnerable children and adults and patient records.
Working with other services	Working with other services is also known as multi-agency work and is essential in all the services. One service cannot solve a community's problems on its own, it must liaise with others to draw upon a wide base of expertise, for example a drug addicted offender will need supervision from the Probation Service as well as addiction treatment from the NHS, and if they have children with them Social Services and the Education Service may also be involved in their monitoring.
Community work	The vast majority of non-uniformed work is conducted in the heart of the community at GP surgeries, in people's homes or in the local environment. The services provided by the non-uniformed services help bind us together as a community.

3.1 Working in the services

Working in the public services is not for everyone. The variety of roles they do and the stresses of the jobs mean that you must be very committed and capable if you are going to make a good employee. There are lots of advantages and disadvantages to working in the services on both a personal and professional level. If we look at some of the services we have examined above we can compare the positive and negative aspects of working in a service and the implications for you personally (see Table 3.2).

Table 3.2: The positive and the negative aspects of working in some of the public services.

The Education Service	
Positive	**Negative**
• Relatively well paid • Good holidays • Stable employment • No shift work • High level of qualifications required • You make a difference • Lots of opportunity for training	• Constantly changing profession • Often not respected by service users • Under-funded in some areas • Often used as a political tennis ball

The Probation Service	
Positive	**Negative**
• Secure employment • Opportunity for progression and promotion • Ongoing training • Variety of work • Protecting communities • Supporting individuals • No shift work	• Interacting with offenders every day can influence your view of society • Despite your best efforts offenders will often re-offend • Often unappreciated by society

The NHS	
Positive	**Negative**
• Varied and interesting role • Wide variety of job opportunities • Opportunities for advancement and promotion • Stable and secure employment • Ongoing training • Saving lives • Well regarded by the public • Some roles are well paid • Teamwork	• Some jobs are poorly paid • Shift work • Difficult nature of some of the work • Stressful and physically demanding at times

Social Services	
Positive	**Negative**
• Some roles are well paid • Secure employment • Opportunities for ongoing training • Varied work • Satisfaction of helping people • May save lives • You are protecting those who need it most	• Under-funding is a problem in some areas • Some staff have workloads beyond their level of experience • Media scrutiny of failures • Some roles are very poorly paid • Some councils contract out social care and have less control over quality • Stressful • Not well respected at times by the public

3.2 Roles within the non-uniformed public services

Each public service has a variety of job roles you could fulfil within it. Not all people who work for the education service are teachers and not all people who work for the social services are social workers. You might consider some other options available as shown in Figure 3.1.

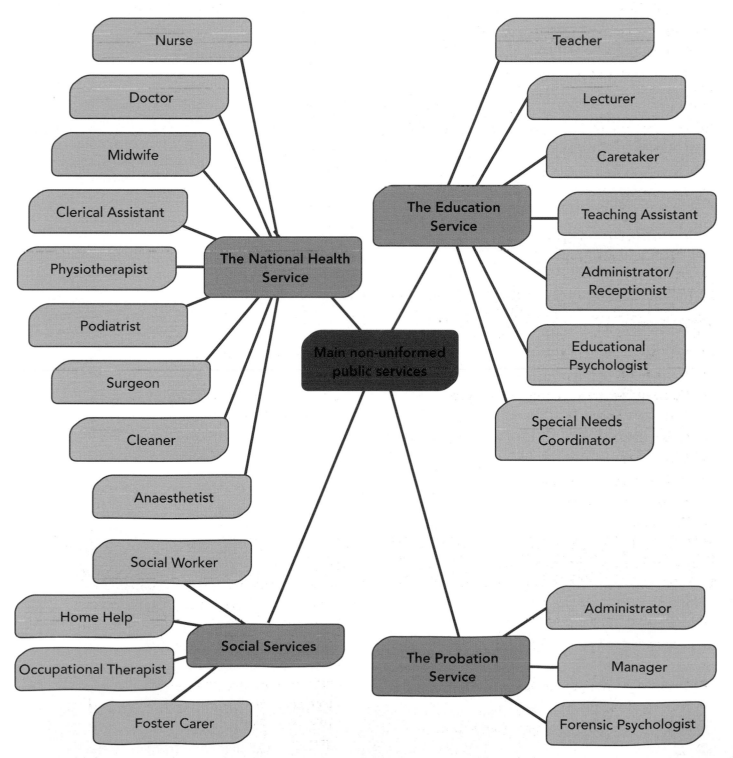

Figure 3.1: Roles in different non-uniformed services.

Looking in detail at a chosen job – probation officer

A fully qualified probation officer must hold a Diploma in Probation Studies. The diploma is made up of two parts a BS (Hons) degree in community justice and an NVQ level 4 in community justice. The diploma is therefore a mix of academic work and practical work. It should be clear to you that probation officers are highly trained and professional. They deal with some of the country's most dangerous and difficult people and as a result of this they must have a firm and disciplined approach without losing sight of the fact they are there to help offenders as well as protect the community. In this respect they have a lot in common with some of the uniformed services such as the police.

Risk assessment. Probation officers draw up risk assessment reports which advise the courts and other agencies of the risks posed by individual offenders. These risk assessments can be crucial information in deciding on the length of a sentence given or whether an offender is released from prison early. The consequences of getting a risk assessment wrong could be catastrophic if the offender continues to offend or increases the severity of their crimes such as murder, rape or child abuse.

Manage and enforce community orders. Probation officers have a duty to ensure that the sentence imposed by the courts is carried out. This might include finding work for someone who has to do community service, making sure offenders attend for drug or alcohol treatment or attending group sessions such as anger management or counselling. The purpose of all of these programmes is to reduce offending behaviour and make the community a safer place.

Assisting with the resettlement of offenders. Probation officers work with offenders who are about to be released to ensure that they do not re-offend when they return to the community. This might include giving housing or education advice.

Challenge offending behaviour. Probation officers work closely with other agencies to challenge the behaviour and attitudes of offenders and address the causes of their criminal behaviour.

Managing hostels. Some probation officers manage hostels where offenders are released on license. These hostels provide a halfway point between prison and release so that offenders can integrate back into society while still under supervision.

Minimising the impact on victims. Probation officers may contact victims of serious crime to advise them of the release date of offenders or listen to their concerns.

BTEC | **Assessment activity 3.2** | P3 M2

It is important that you know all you can about your chosen non-uniformed public services career before you make an application. Address the following tasks by producing an information sheet which will help you and your colleagues improve your knowledge.

1. *Explain* the different non-uniformed employment opportunities available in the public services. **P3**

2. *Explain* the work of a chosen non-uniformed public service job. **M2**

Grading tips

For **P3** choose a public service role and produce a job description for it. You could look for an official job description on your chosen services recruitment website to help you. For **M2** explain the work of that particular job role in detail.

4 The conditions of service for different public service jobs

Conditions of service cover the information you need to make a reasoned career choice about which service would suit you best. Possible factors to consider are outlined in Figure 3.2.

The conditions of service can vary across the non-uniformed public services and they might influence the decision you take about your future career path. Table 3.3 shows some of the possible conditions of service you might encounter.

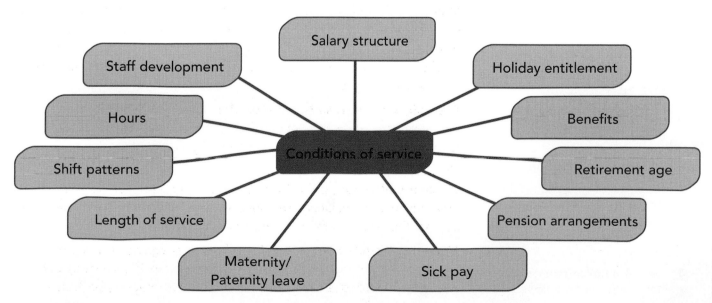

Figure 3.2: Factors in conditions of service

Table 3.3: Possible conditions of service in the non-uniformed public services.

	Education Service Teacher	Social Services Social Worker	Probation Service Probation Officer	The NHS Nurse
Salary structure	Starting salary of around £21,000	Average starting salary of £20,000	Trainees start around £17,000, rising to £26,000 once qualified	Starting salary of around £20,700
Holiday entitlement	Varies, can be up to 45 days	At least 27 days	32 days	At least 27 days
Retirement age	65	65	65	65
Pension	Teachers pension scheme	Local government pension scheme available		NHS Pension Scheme
Sick pay	Paid sick leave available	Paid sick leave available	Paid sick leave available	Paid sick leave available
Maternity / Paternity	Paid maternity and paternity leave provided	Paid maternity and paternity leave provided	Paid maternity and paternity leave provided	Paid maternity and paternity leave provided
Length of service	No fixed length	No fixed length	No fixed length	No fixed length
Shift patterns	No shift work	Shifts for residential social workers	No shift work, but irregular hours can be worked	Shift system in operation
Hours	Normally 36 hours, but many teachers work more	Normally 37 hours, but can vary if you are a residential social worker	Average of 37.5 hours	37.5 hours
Staff development	Ongoing training provided throughout career	Ongoing training provided throughout career	Ongoing training throughout career	Ongoing training throughout career

The non-uniformed services can vary greatly in their terms and conditions because some of this essential work is conducted by agencies who are contracted by local government to provide the services in question. These agencies can have terms and conditions which bear little relationship to their government-organised counterparts and this can make trying to find details about working in the sector very confusing.

BTEC ## Assessment activity 3.3

Working in a small group

This is an assessment about the terms and conditions of service you might encounter if you join the public services. Working in a small group of no more than three, produce a poster in which you address the following task:

1 Describe the current conditions of service for two non-uniformed public service job roles. **P4**

Grading tips

P4 is straightforward, simply choose the public service role you would like to do and describe the conditions of service for that role.

Annie Gupta
Teacher

I work as a junior school teacher in an inner city area. My job is to make sure that the children I teach reach their full potential and enjoy a safe and healthy learning environment. I am required to teach to the National Curriculum for the Key Stage my class is at and make sure they progress towards their targets.

A typical day

A typical day for me involves being at work for around 8:00 a.m. to ensure my classroom is set up with the things I need for the day, to deal with any administration that has cropped up and to see parents who have concerns. Classroom work normally begins at 9:00 a.m. but can vary if there is an assembly or other event on. I'll teach the group until about 3:30 p.m. and we will cover a variety of topics. At 3:30 p.m. I usually see more parents and at around 4:00 p.m. I'll start marking the day's work and preparing for the next day. I often take work home and sometimes don't finish until late into the evening.

The best thing about the job

The best thing about the job is seeing children interested and engaged with the world around them. It's an amazing feeling to know you might have set a child on a journey to a career they love as adults. Although the working hours can be very long and you often don't receive any thanks, watching a child make a connection because of the information you have given them is all the reward you need.

Think about it!

1. What topics have you covered in this unit that might give you the background to become a teacher?
2. What knowledge and skills do you think you need to develop further if you want to be involved in education in the future?

Just checking

1. What does a probation officer do?
2. What is the role of Social Services?
3. What are the positive and negative aspects of working for the Education Service?
4. What is the average starting pay for a nurse?
5. What pension plan can teachers join?

edexcel

Assignment tips

- This unit requires research into the non-uniformed public services, so making sure you use the right sources of research will be essential. Your local council is a great source of information and they are usually very happy to provide information when you need it.

- The service you want to join may be different from those outlined in this unit or even those of your fellow learners. Don't be hesitant about approaching the service of your choice directly for information, after all you may be approaching them soon for a job, so it won't hurt to make a positive first impression by showing an interest in the job they do and the conditions of service you will be working under.

- The non-uniformed services can be contracted out to agencies. Make sure when you are researching that you also draw comparisons between agency workers and government-employed non-uniformed public service workers.

4 Career planning for the public services

The public services take their recruitment of new officers very seriously. If they don't choose the right people for the right jobs they will not be able to serve the public as well as they would like. The nature of the public services means that any recruits are likely to be put under pressure, face stressful situations and engage in potentially dangerous activities. Not everyone is suited for these roles, it takes special skills and abilities to work confidently in the public services and be able to deal with their day-to-day duties.

In order to be ready to join a public service you must be ready to learn about your strengths and weaknesses and what you can do to improve them. You must also be ready to do a significant amount of research on your chosen service so you are as well prepared as you can be for the recruitment process.

This unit covers all of the key recruitment areas you will need to know about before you join a service and will help you improve you skills and qualities to make you someone the services would be proud to have representing them.

Learning outcomes

After completing this unit you should:

1. know the application and selection process for public service employment
2. know the skills and qualities required for a job in the public services
3. be able to complete an application for a role in a chosen public service.

Assessment and grading criteria

This table shows you what you must do in order to achieve a pass, merit or distinction grade, and where you can find activities in this book to help you.

To achieve a **pass** grade the evidence must show that the learner is able to:	To achieve a **merit** grade the evidence must show that, in addition to the pass criteria, the learner is able to:	To achieve a **distinction** grade the evidence must show that, in addition to the pass and merit criteria, the learner is able to:
P1 describe the current entry requirements for two public service jobs **Assessment activity 4.1 page 88**		
P2 describe the application and selection process for two public service jobs **Assessment activity 4.2 page 95**		
P3 identify the different skills and qualities required for a given public service role **Assessment activity 4.3 page 96**		
P4 carry out a personal skills audit for a given public service role **Assessment activity 4.4 page 100**	**M1** analyse your skills against a given public service role **Assessment activity 4.4 page 100**	**D1** evaluate your skills against a given public service role **Assessment activity 4.4 page 100**
P5 complete an application for a role in a specific public service **Assessment activity 4.5 page 102**		

How you will be assessed

This unit will be assessed by an internal assignment that will be designed and marked by the staff at your centre. The assignment is designed to allow you to show your understanding of the learning outcomes for career planning in the public services. These relate to what you should be able to do after completing this unit. Your assessments might include some of the following:

- portfolios of evidence
- learning journals
- blog entries
- video diaries
- action plans

- skills audits
- presentations
- leaflets
- reports.

Brynn, 16, prepares with an action plan

I really liked this unit, it made me look at myself in quite a different way than before. I was always very confident that I would just apply to a service and they would take me. I hadn't even considered how many people I might be up against and the fact that they might be better than me. I know now that wanting to join a service isn't the same as preparing to join a service. You can't just waltz into the recruiting office and they will take you, you have to show them how good you are and that's not always easy.

It was difficult for me to look at myself and see my weaknesses, it felt quite uncomfortable but I knew if I didn't identify my weaknesses and do something about them I would have no chance of joining the Fire Service.

The hardest thing was looking at my action plan and trying to come up with ways to improve my fitness and my teamwork skills. I don't like exercise that much, but my fitness was way below what it needed to be and I knew it would only get harder to address as the course went on so I started going regularly to the gym. I still don't like it but at least I know I'm doing it for a good reason.

The good thing about this unit is that you get to see exactly what you need to do to make yourself ready for a service. If you don't prepare properly then you have no one to blame but yourself if you don't get in.

Over to you!
- What areas of public service employment might you find interesting?
- Have you ever done a skills audit before?
- Do you have any fears or concerns about looking at your weaknesses?
- What preparation could you do to get ready for your assessments?

1 The application and selection process for a chosen career

If you are planning to apply to a public service you will need to know how to apply and how the services choose their recruits. Each service is very different in terms of the application and selection procedure of new recruits. The procedures can also change every few years, so it is worth speaking directly to a recruiting officer as well as using books and the internet to make sure the information you have for your service is as accurate and up to date as it can be.

Talk up

Preparing for your career

Looking at your skills and abilities honestly can be a challenge for some people. Write down a list of your strengths and your weaknesses and think about how they would affect your ability to join a service.

Come up with at least three possible ways to overcome any weaknesses you have identified.

Why do you think it important that the public services set entry requirements?

! Link

For more on entry requirements see Unit 20, page 357.

1.1 Entry requirements

Entry requirements specify the minimum personal and professional achievements that you should have before applying to a public service. These can be factors such as education, fitness and health. The more specialised and difficult the role, the more entry requirements will be asked for. If you do not meet the entry requirements for your chosen public service, you will have to consider what you can do to develop your skills and abilities to meet or even exceed the requirements.

Of course, in some cases it may just be a case of waiting until you are old enough to join, but even while you are waiting you could be doing things which make you more attractive to a public service, such as getting additional qualifications at college or taking up some voluntary work in the community.

Whenever you consider applying to a public service you should remember that there are many other people who want that particular job, these may be people with more experience and qualifications than you and you must compete with them for your chosen career. As you can imagine this can be difficult, but the key is good preparation. If you have researched your chosen career and you have made the most of the opportunities you have been given in your life so far, you will have a distinct advantage over the competition. Table 4.1 shows the general entry requirements for the Police Service.

Table 4.1: The entry requirements for an example of a job in the Police Service.

Police officer entry requirements	
Age	You must be 18 years old to apply. There is no maximum age limit, but the usual retirement age of police officers is 65 years.
Height	There are no height requirements for this service.
Health	You are required to undergo a physical examination, so you should be in a good physical and mental state of health. The Police Service may reject applicants who are obese, diabetic, asthmatic, have a history of mental health difficulties or who have any other condition which may affect your ability to perform the duties required of you. However, the service has to comply with the Disability Discrimination Act 1995, so many cases are examined on an individual basis.
Fitness	You do not need to be super-fit, but you will be expected to show a reasonable level of fitness and pass a test which includes strength and endurance. Police officers need to be physically and mentally fit to cope with the stressful elements of the job.
Qualifications	The Police Service does not require any formal qualifications, but you must demonstrate a good standard of English which will be tested during your application procedure. However, it is important to remember that although you may not need any formal qualifications to join, they will certainly help you appear more attractive as a potential new employee and help with your promotion prospects.
Eyesight	You will be required to have your eyes tested by an optician as part of the recruitment process. However you can wear glasses and contact lenses to correct your vision and bring it up to the required standards.
Nationality	You must be a British citizen, a member of the Commonwealth or European Union (EU) and have no restrictions placed on your residence in the UK.
Criminal convictions	You should declare all criminal convictions in your application. Having a criminal record will not necessarily prevent you from becoming a Police officer as many convictions are judged on an individual basis, but there are some offences which will automatically rule you out. These are offences such as: murder, manslaughter, rape, kidnapping, terrorism, hijacking and death by reckless driving. In general, you will be excluded if you have served a prison sentence or if you have committed crimes of violence.
Tattoos	You may be rejected if you have a tattoo that could cause offence or is particularly prominent and can't be covered up with a normal uniform.

Just because you meet these requirements it doesn't mean you will be a good police officer. In addition to these you need to possess the following skills and qualities:

- self-confidence
- interest in the community
- excellent communication skills
- tact and diplomacy
- teamwork skills
- ability to work on own initiative
- problem solving ability
- reliability
- punctuality
- honesty
- integrity
- commitment
- good attitude.

All of the services require very similar personal qualities in their officers.

Key terms

Conviction – a formal decision by a judge or jury that someone is guilty of a criminal offence.

Criminal record – a list of someone's crimes.

How would you prepare yourself for interview with the Police Service? Make a checklist.

PLTS

Researching the current entry requirements for your service will help develop your independent enquirer skills.

Key term

Paper sift – a paper sift is a way of getting rid of unsuitable applications and it is used by many public services as well as many other employees. It involves checking an application form through and weeding out any forms that are incomplete, do not show a reasonable standard of English or where the form demonstrates an individual is clearly unsuitable for the job or doesn't meet the entry requirements.

Assessment activity 4.1

BTEC **P1**

In order to get into the service of your choice the first thing you need to do is know the current entry requirements for your service. Produce an information leaflet which addresses the following tasks:

1 *Describe* the current entry requirements for two public service jobs. **P1**

Grading tips

To achieve **P1** choose two public service jobs of your choice and describe their current entry requirements. You can usually find these in the recruiting section of the website for the service.

1.2 Application forms

All of the public services will require you to complete an application form. This is a document where you record all the personal information the service asks of you and they use this information to make judgements about whether you would be suitable for the service. Application forms are normally available from the recruiting office of your chosen service and you can download many of them from the internet. Once you receive an application form you may have to answer a number of questions, some are outlined in Figure 4.1.

Completing the form takes time and effort. If you complete the form incorrectly or it shows you in a poor light, you will be weeded out in what is called a **paper sift**.

Remember

When completing an application form there are several things that you can do to make sure you give your application form the best chance of success:

• Read the form thoroughly and ensure you understand every question.
• Read the guidance notes thoroughly, they give you specific advice on what you need to do.
• Photocopy the form several times so that you can practise and get it checked through before you complete the original.
• Be honest. If you are not it will be found out and you will ruin your chances of the career you want.
• Be meticulous about your spelling and grammar.
• Ensure the things you write do not breach the principles of equality and diversity.
• Take guidance from your local careers office or your tutors on how best to present yourself.
• Use the appropriate style of writing, if it says black ink and block capitals then this is what you must do. In addition your handwriting should be clear and legible.

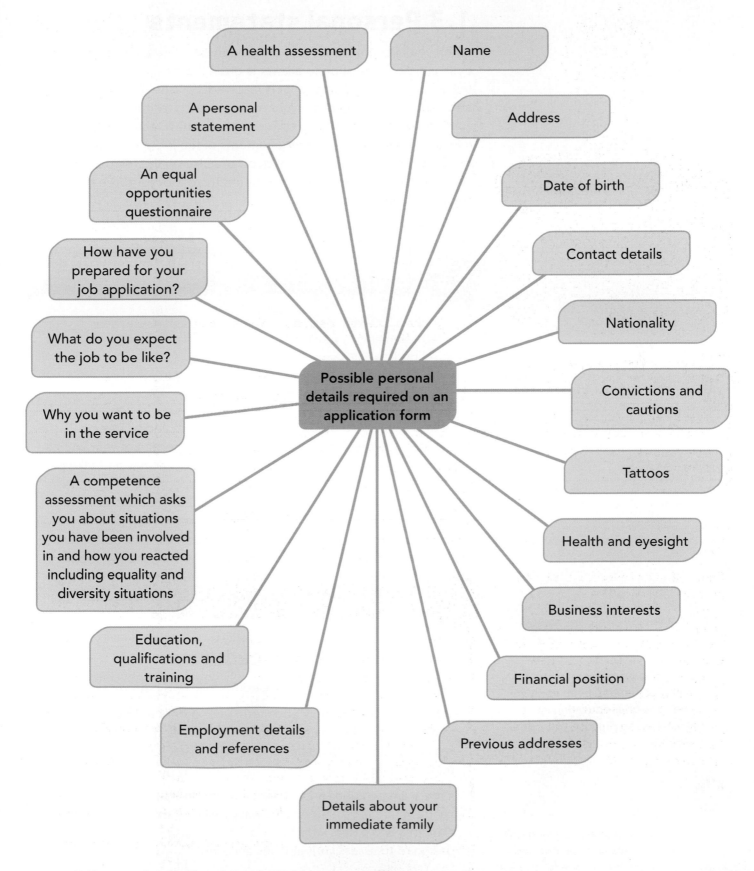

Figure 4.1 Have you thought about how you would answer any of these questions?

1.3 Personal statements

When you are completing your public service application form the most difficult type of question to answer is often the personal statement or the supporting information that is required. You should pay particular attention to this part, as it is your opportunity to tell the service of your choice why they should take you on as a new recruit. It should be relevant and specific to the requirements of the job you are applying for. There are often examples of good practice on the recruitment websites for the services and you should try to look for these before you complete your own.

Activity: Your personal statement

Write a 250-word personal statement that summarises your achievements in your life so far.

1.4 Selection process

Once you have completed your application form and all the paperwork, you need to send this to the public service of your choice. Subsequently, you may be invited to attend an interview and take part in a further selection procedure. This can include many different tests and activities, all of which are designed to assess your suitability for your chosen service. It might include psychometric tests (see Table 4.2), fitness tests, simulations, presentations, discussions, practical role plays, testing your knowledge of equal opportunities or your basic reading, writing and mathematics. The selection procedures of all the services are very different and you should check with the recruiting office for your service exactly what you will be expected to do.

Police selection procedure

Generally the police selection procedure follows a pattern:

- On receipt of a full application form your details will be checked to make sure you meet the entry requirements. If you meet the requirements your application form will have a competency-based questionnaire review.

- If there are no issues arising then you would attend an assessment centre where recruiting officers will watch you perform a series of exercises and assess what you do. You will also have an interview designed to assess your abilities and skills.

- After the assessment centre your references and background would be checked and you would undergo your medical and fitness assessments.

Did you know?

You will also have to complete a personal statement if you apply for further or higher education, so it makes sense to practise yours until it is perfect.

Did you know?

You can find lots of additional detail on Police Service applications and procedure at: the website for the police force, available via Hotlinks (see page viii).

1.5 Curriculum vitae (CV)

You may be asked to produce a CV at some point in your application procedure for any service and it is important that your CV is up to date and relevant to your application. It used to be the case that a CV was just a list of your personal information, but the presentation of CVs has moved on and you should be aware of this. The examples below show two CVs with identical information, the first one is an example of how not to do it, the second one is an example of good practice.

Name:	David Smith jnr
Address:	32 East Way Close, Botheringham, B32 7AJ
Telephone Number:	01742 112112
E-maoil:	daveyboy@lovemachine.co.uk
Date of Birth:	1/1/1992
Marital status:	Single, but have a girlfreind
Driving Lisense:	I do not drive, but I am taking lessons
School:	Botheringham Compreensive I passed 5 GCSE's
	Maths E • Endlish F • Geography C • PE B • French F
	I have also completed a Btec Fitst Diploma in Public services at Botheringham College
Work experiences:	I have woked in a pizza shop and done a paper round. I also do some roofing with my dad and help at a local youth club
References:	
David Smith Snr	Fat Garrys Piza shop
Botheringham Roofing Co	101 high Street
Botherningham	Botheringham

Figure 4.2: What would you do to improve this CV?

Activity: Checking a CV

Look carefully at the CV above. How many things can you find that are wrong with it? Make a list and compare your list with those of your classmates.

Compare this with the CV on page 92. What are the differences between the two examples. Why would an employer prefer the second CV?

Curriculum Vitae

David Smith

A hard working and energetic young man, well able to cope with working in a high-pressure environment under specific time constraints. Excellent interpersonal skills and a high level of experience in working with the public in a variety of situations. Excels in a variety of sports and has a high level of commitment to working with the community.

Contact Details:

Address: 32 East Way Close, Botheringham, B32 7AJ   Date of Birth: 1/1/92
Telephone: 01742 112112 (Home) 07967 11231123 (Mobile)   E-mail: d.smith@both-coll.ac.uk

Educational Achievements:

2003 – 2008 Botheringham Comprehensive School, Main Street, Botheringham, B23 4EW

Physical Education A   English F   Maths E
Geography C   French F

I also achieved 100% attendance certificates for every year I attended Botheringham Comprehensive and I won The Arthur Wenden Award for excellence in sporting achievement in 2005 and 2006.

2008 – 2009 Botheringham College of Further Education, Lower Vale, Botheringham, B45 4TY

BTEC First Diploma in Public Services
Public Services Employment   Distinction
Public Service Skills   Distinction
Exploring Careers in the Public Services   Distinction
Crime and Its Effects   Merit
Expedition Skills   Merit
Citizenship, the Individual and Society   Distinction

Career Achievements:

Sept 2006 – June 2007 Newspaper Delivery Operative

This position involved the delivery of early morning and evening newspapers on a set route. I developed my time-management skills and self-discipline fulfilling this role as I had to be very conscious of making sure I delivered all of the goods regardless of external conditions such as the weather.

July 2007 – May 2009 Pizza Chef

Working to fulfil food orders with speed and efficiency, I interacted with the public on an ongoing basis providing a friendly and reliable front-of-house service as well as observing health and hygiene regulations with diligence.

June 2009 – Sept 2009 Builders Labourer

In this position I worked as part of an interconnected team of roofers and builders adhering to strict deadlines and producing high-quality work. My teamwork skills were enhanced and I developed an appreciation of how people working together can achieve more than individuals working alone.

Sept 2009 – Present Volunteer Youth Worker

I volunteer three evenings a week to help at a youth club in my local area. This involves coordinating and running sporting events for young people aged 11–14, improving their sporting skills and ensuring that health and safety guidelines are followed. I enjoy this type of work very much and like to think that I act as a positive role model for the young people I train.

Additional Information

I have played football and cricket for the county under 18s teams and I enjoy a variety of other sporting and adventurous activities such as skiing, climbing and canoeing. I like to go to the cinema, particularly to see science fiction films and socialise with my friends. I have recently started to attend ju-jitsu classes and I hope this will enhance my physical coordination and sense of self-discipline even further. I am looking for a career opportunity where I can work with people in a community environment as I feel that this is what my skills and inclination best suit me for.

References

Ms Alison Court   Mr A J Singh
Lecturer in Public Services   Youth Services Manager
Botheringham College of FE   Botheringham Youth Club
Lower Vale   Murray Road
Botheringham B45 4TY   Botheringham B17 9LU

Figure 4.3 Would you organise your CV in this way?

Activity: Create your own CV

Using the example of good practice in Figure 4.3, work on producing your own CV.

1.6 Additional recruitment information

Table 4.2 highlights some common factors you might have to deal with during any public service application and selection procedure.

Table 4.2: Information for interviews and selection procedures.

Interview guide	
Psychometric tests	These are tests designed to assess your capabilities in maths, English, problem solving, spatial awareness and mental agility. Not all services use them but many do. They give the service in question a reasonably accurate picture of your abilities.
Fitness tests	These are self-explanatory and you will find several of them detailed in Unit 5 Improving health and fitness. They show the service of your choice that you are fit enough to complete the duties required of you.
Simulations	Role plays and simulations are becoming more common in public service selection as they give an idea of how people react when put in difficult situations. They can be used to assess the interpersonal skills and problem-solving ability of potential new recruits.
Presentations	Many services require you to give a presentation of around 10 minutes on a particular public service topic. It highlights your ability to speak in public and communicate information effectively to others, which as you can imagine, is a key skill in the public services.
Types of interview	There are many kinds of interview that you might be faced with when applying to a public service. These might include formal interviews, group interviews and panel interviews. It is your responsibility to find out what you are likely to face and prepare for it.
Dress code	Generally you should always be smart and professional at interview, unless you are attending for a fitness test or other task which requires specific dress. This means suits for both men and women.
Diversity	The services often have targets to ensure diversity among their new recruits and to test you during the application and selection procedure to see if you understand and support diversity.

1.7 Interview preparation

It is important that you prepare for your interview, you can bet that the people you will be up against will be preparing and you need to make sure you do not let yourself down. One of the key aspects in interview preparation is knowing the interview arrangements. Do you know:

- where the interview is?
- what time you should be there?
- what you need to take with you?
- what to wear?

Have you confirmed your attendance? Have you researched the organisation so you know what they do and how they do it?

Have you thought of some relevant questions you might ask at the interview?

It is amazing how many people do not prepare adequately for an interview and are then disappointed when they don't get the job they want. A burning desire to be a firefighter or a paramedic **isn't** enough! You must be able to prove that you are more suitable for the job than any of the other 100 applicants – this is a tall order! However there are many things you can do to maximise your chances.

- **Take care with personal appearance**. You must dress appropriately; this will usually mean a suit for both men and women. Jewellery and make-up must be subtle and discreet and you should be free from any facial piercing such as that through the eyebrow, nose or lips and men should consider removing earrings. Your clothing should be clean and pressed and you should get a friend or family member to check you over before you set off.

- **Be punctual**. There is no excuse for being late. It gives an impression that you are unreliable. Instead, aim to arrive around 10 minutes early. If necessary practise your journey beforehand to ensure you have your timings right.

- **Be polite to other candidates**. Part of the assessment process in public services interviews revolves around your interaction with others. If you are unpleasant or uncooperative to your competition it shows you do not have the interpersonal skills to work in a close-knit team or work with the public.

- **Do your research**. It does you no credit if you turn up to an interview without knowing the first thing about the public service in question. If you are completing a public service qualification you will have an advantage, but don't become complacent. Research your chosen public service, be familiar with its structure and principles, and ensure you have read its annual reports and its literature. If you want the job be prepared to learn everything you can about the local, national and international issues which affect it.

- **Be confident, not dominant**. If you try to dominate an interview it screams 'NOTICE ME!!' Your interviewer will notice you but for all the wrong reasons. You should project an image of a confident team player, not a dominant leader.

- **Be genuine**. Public service interviewers are usually officers of many years standing and they will have seen hundreds of hopeful candidates just like you. Don't think that flattery or humour will sway them in their choice and don't be tempted to exaggerate or lie about your skills and abilities. Recruiting officers read people very well and the last thing you want is to be considered false or fraudulent. It is appropriate to laugh politely at a joke made by your recruiter but inappropriate to roll about on the floor claiming it's the best joke you ever heard.

- **Don't get rattled**. Interviews are tremendously nerve-racking, make sure you stay calm and in control. This means not fidgeting, paying close attention to questions and making sure you understand the question before you answer. When people are nervous they tend to babble and may say inappropriate things – watch for this. The interviewer expects a certain amount of nervousness but someone who appears very edgy will give the impression of not coping well in stressful situations – clearly not a desirable quality in the public services.

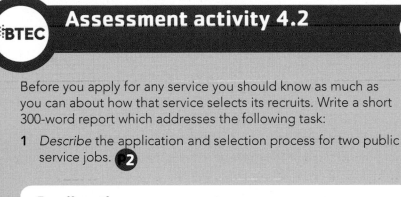

BTEC

Assessment activity 4.2   P2

Before you apply for any service you should know as much as you can about how that service selects its recruits. Write a short 300-word report which addresses the following task:

1   *Describe* the application and selection process for two public service jobs. P2

Grading tip

Research your chosen service and include in your report how you would apply to the service and what process you would go through if they were to select you.

2 Skills and qualities required for the public services

Individuals who work in the public services are required to do a variety of jobs which can change from minute to minute in response to rapidly changing circumstances. All of the services need a specific set of skills which they train you in after you have been accepted as a recruit, for example the navy will teach you shipboard firefighting skills, the Prison Service will teach you restraint techniques and the Ambulance Service will train you in the administration of medication. These are not skills you need to have already, they are skills you gain on the job.

However, the services require you to have a basic set of skills and qualities before they will accept you in to their employment and train you in any other skills. In actual fact all employers, not just the services, require you to have a basic set of skills before they will employ you.

Table 4.3 identifies some of the key skills you should have and considers how and when they might be used in public service life.

Table 4.3: Some of the key skills you should have and how and when they might be used in public service life.

Required skills	Use
Leadership	The ability to lead a team will be essential in some public service work, army officers and non-commissioned officers must be effective leaders when taking their unit into combat.
Cooperation	You must be able to work well with others to achieve a goal. Firefighters must cooperate when putting out a fire, paramedics must cooperate when dealing with multiple casualties.
Communication	Clear communication is essential, if you cannot be understood your orders cannot be followed or your information will not reach the people you need it to reach. All services need this particularly when using radios.
Problem solving	The public services come across many problems in their day-to-day duties. You must be able to think of a way to solve those problems. For example, if the army are moving towards a strategic position but have to cross a river – what could they do?
Achieving aims	The services set goals to achieve, e.g. numbers of arrests, 999 response times and recruitment diversity. You must be able to show that you have achieved the aims you have set. It doesn't look good to an employer if there are unfinished targets on your CV because you haven't been bothered to complete them. On the other hand, you can show you are on track and on schedule to achieve long-term targets.
Working with others	All of the services work together, particularly in case of a major incident or national emergency. You must show you have a good record of working well with others.
Reading	The public services produce many reports and circulars which have to be read and understood by all personnel such as new defence guidance, reports on the treatment of detainees and changes to the law. You must demonstrate that you can read and understand complex information.
Writing	In many of the services you will be required to produce reports and complete a lot of paperwork. Police officers have to complete paperwork for every suspect they arrest, and this paperwork is often the starting point for a prosecution, so if it is impossible to read or poorly written the suspect may go free. You must show your writing skills are of a high standard.
Speaking	Communicating with your colleagues and the public is an essential skill of the services. You may have to break bad news, interrogate a suspect, issue orders or coordinate a disaster response. The ability to speak clearly and confidently is essential to this.
Listening	If you don't listen you will miss vital information which may harm how you do your job or potentially even cost lives.
Body language	Body language includes things such as gestures, facial expressions, eye contact and posture. Being able to read body language can help the public services resolve conflict or get away from dangerous situations and understanding your own body language can help make the right impression on the people you deal with.

Assessment activity 4.3

BTEC — P3

If you are going to be successful in joining a service you will need to know the skills the uniformed services require, and when and how they could be used. Produce a PowerPoint presentation with your partner which addresses the following:

1 *Identify* the different skills and qualities required for a given public service role. **P3**

Grading tip

P3 is very straightforward, you should provide a short definition of each of the skills needed by the public services.

Skills are very useful things to have, but they are not the whole picture. Your interpersonal qualities are equally as important when the services are considering your application. If you are dishonest, can't be trusted, lazy or have a bad attitude then your chances of joining a service are extremely slim. Remember that the services do a thorough job of checking you out before they employ you, including asking for several references. If your behaviour or conduct has been negative, they will find out and it may harm your career chances.

Activity: Your skills

Look at Table 4.3. Write a list of those skills and give an example of when you have used that skill recently. If you can't come up with an example it might be an area of weakness for you.

Table 4.4: Important interpersonal qualities in job seeking.

Required qualities	Description
Honesty	The ability to be trusted is essential in the services, you deal with confidential information all the time and you must respect the trust that has been placed in you. You must also be a role model to the public so if you lie or are seen to be dishonest you shame the whole service.
Integrity	This is about having values and principles which support your organisation and the public of this country who pay you. It is about being fair, respectful and understanding that you do not become more important than everyone else because you wear a uniform.
Reliability	This is when you say you will do something or be somewhere at a certain time and you do it.
Punctuality	This is the ability to turn up on time. If you are late in the public services your colleagues and the public could be put at risk.
Commitment	You must be able to see a job through from start to end. Commitment is a promise you make to yourself, the communities you serve and your organisation.
Positive attitude	A positive attitude welcomes challenges and change and does not engage in complaining about things. If you have to do a job you should do it to the best of your ability, that is what the public pay you for.
Concern for others	The whole point of being in a public service is that you serve the public. If you are not concerned about this country and the communities in it you should not join.

3 Complete an application for a role in a chosen public service

Before you apply to a public service you need to make sure you are ready to join. This means that you have the skills and qualities they are looking for in a new recruit. The competition for public service jobs is fierce and you must make sure you have done everything you can to be ready.

It isn't enough in the public services to know what skills and qualities are required, you must be able to demonstrate that you know when they should be used and that you are confident to use them yourself. This means that you should put into practice the skills looked for by the uniformed public services. This could be done in a variety of ways, such as:

- on an activity day
- on a residential course
- linked with an expedition
- in class
- by observing you in your workplace
- a work placement report.

3.1 Identifying strong and weak areas

It is important to be able to identify your own strengths and weaknesses. If you don't know where you are strong you won't be able to make the most of those aspects of yourself in the application and interview. Equally, if you don't know where your weaknesses are how will you improve them?

SWOT analysis

A good way of seeing if you are ready to join a public service is to draw up a SWOT analysis. SWOT stands for:

Strengths
Weaknesses
Opportunities
Threats.

Case study: Kassim considers his career options

Kassim has just completed his First Diploma in Public Services with mainly merits and is considering his future career options.

Name: Kassim Hussain

Strengths	Weaknesses	Opportunities	Threats
Good academic record	Not old enough for the police	To complete the National Diploma in Public Services	Other candidates with more experience
Likes learning	Lack of work experience	To join the army straight away	Join a service too young and may regret it
Prepared to undergo further training	Lack of life experience	To do an IT course	
Supportive family		To take a year out to travel	
Confident		Work in a civilian job to get some experience	
Good communication skills			
Physically fit			
Good state of health			
No ties or commitments			
Bi-lingual			

Now answer the following questions:

1　Look at Kassim's SWOT analysis. Draw up a SWOT analysis for yourself.

2　What do the results show?

3　What are your strengths and weaknesses?

Skills audit

Another way to find out your strengths and weaknesses is a skills audit. A skills audit is a way of measuring and recording an individual's skills and abilities and comparing them to what they need for a certain job. There are many methods of evaluating your skills and abilities and you can find these both on the internet and in self-development books. Consider the audit below:

Activity: Are you ready yet?

Draw up a table like the one shown here. Answer the following questions as honestly as you can on the following scale by placing a tick in the appropriate box:

Public service skills	1	2	3	4	5
Confidence					
Public speaking					
Coping with new situations					
Making friends					
Talking to strangers					
Making eye contact with others					
Communication					
Vocabulary					
Clear speech					
Body language					
Respect for diversity					
Honesty and directness					
Teamwork					
Ability to work with others					
Ability to take orders					
Ability to listen and respond to others					
Respect for the opinions of others					
Ability to participate in discussions and offer suggestions					
Interpersonal skills					
Sensitivity to others					
Ability to cope with the distress of others					
Diplomacy					
Ability to be fair and impartial					
Able to read body language of others					
Conflict management					
Ability to keep your temper					
Ability to calm others					
Ability to resolve a situation without shouting or violence					
Confidence to step in to help others who are in conflict					
Ability to liase with all different kinds of people					

1 Very poor
2 Poor
3 Average
4 Good
5 Very good

Each section has a maximum of 25 points available. Copy the table below and fill in your results.

Skills	Points
Confidence	
Communication	
Teamwork	
Interpersonal skills	
Conflict management	

Which were your strongest and weakest areas? How essential are these areas to your chosen public service? Are there any areas you feel aren't covered in the test?

In areas where you have received less than 15 points you need to consider how you will address these areas of weakness so that you can improve the core skills needed for career development in the public services.

3.2 Improving weak areas

Once you have identified your weaknesses you need to do something to improve them. That's where an action plan can be very useful.

An action plan is a method used to help you turn areas of weaknesses into areas of strength and help you monitor the process so that you know how far you have progressed towards your goals. For example, if your area of weakness was a failure to resolve conflict, then your objective would be to become effective in that skill and the way of achieving this would be improving your methods by going on a training course, for example.

There are several points which ought to be listed in a personal development action plan, these are:

- identify the problem
- set an objective or several objectives to achieve
- detail how you intend to meet your objectives
- describe the support you need from others
- list any resources you might need access to
- set dates for review or completion.

Action plans can be used to improve and develop your skills in many different areas such as:

- education
- fitness
- communication.

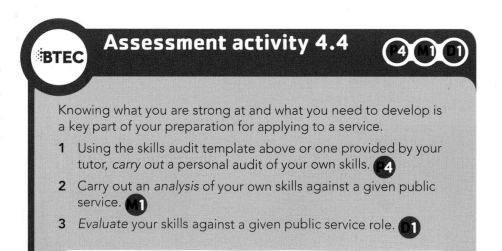

BTEC **Assessment activity 4.4** **P4 M1 D1**

Knowing what you are strong at and what you need to develop is a key part of your preparation for applying to a service.

1. Using the skills audit template above or one provided by your tutor, *carry out* a personal audit of your own skills. **P4**

2. Carry out an *analysis* of your own skills against a given public service. **M1**

3. *Evaluate* your skills against a given public service role. **D1**

Grading tip

For **P4** carry out the audit you are given as honestly as you can. To achieve **M1**, analyse the results of the audit and write a short report detailing how your strengths and weaknesses compare to the skills needed by the services. **D1** asks you for more detail and an evaluation and comparison of your skills with skills required for a public service role.

AREA/S FOR DEVELOPMENT:

My interpersonal communication skills are weak and I find myself misreading situations or not understanding what's going on because I don't have the confidence to ask. This has got me into trouble a couple of times when I've thought people were being mean to me or I haven't understood a tutor's instructions. This is going to be a big barrier in joining the Fire Service.

TARGETS TO ACHIEVE:

1. To improve my understanding of body language
2. To become more conscious of my own body language
3. To develop the confidence to ask for clarification in situations if I don't understand what is going on
4. To find out what interpersonal skills the Fire Service require in a potential recruit

Actions required by you:

- Ask a close friend to monitor my body language to see if I am communicating in a friendly manner or if I'm coming across as a bit hostile.
- Make a diary of body language that I see and use a good-quality body language book to see what it means.
- Consider going on a course on interpersonal communication to improve my skills.
- Research the interpersonal skills needed by the Fire Service.

Actions required by others:

- Friends to help me by monitoring my actions and giving me the benefit of their advice.
- Tutor to help me research Fire Service.

Resources

- College prospectus
- Fire Service application information
- Good-quality body language book

Dates for review / completion

I will review the situation every two weeks to see the progress I have made and change the action plan if needed. Dates: 30 Jan, 15 Feb, 1 Mar, 15 Mar

By the 15 March I should have achieved my targets completely.

Figure 4.4: Example of a personal action plan.

Case study: Josh's learning curve

We had to do a skills audit in class to see if we were well prepared for the service we wanted to join. I didn't think I had any weaknesses to be honest, I'm fit and healthy and joining the RAF has always been my goal.

I was really surprised at my results. I am really weak at conflict management and quite weak at teamwork. I'm not going to do well in the RAF if I struggle to work with people and can't solve conflicts when they happen. I had a chat with my tutor about it and he said that he can see why the skills audit came up with those weaknesses as I always want to be the leader and not a team player.

I'm going to have to think carefully about how I change my behaviour and learn these skills because the services won't take me without them.

Now answer these questions:

1 What could Josh do to improve his teamwork?

2 What could Josh do to improve his conflict management?

3 Why would a service be reluctant to take him without these skills?

Each person is individual and just because one of your colleagues is good at something, it doesn't mean that you will be. You may be better at the things they are weak at. People develop at their own pace and in their own way. If you are not ready to join a service yet there are lots of things you can do while you work on your skills and qualities which will make you a better recruit in the long term, such as progressing onto a higher level course, doing a job with training or doing some voluntary work while you study.

Assessment activity 4.5 (P5)

When you have found any weaknesses you can aim to improve them. An action plan will help you and contribute to your overall preparation when applying for a job.

1 This assessment requires you to *complete* an application when applying for a role in a public service. P5

Using the template in Figure 4.4 or one provided by your tutor, produce an action plan which prepares you to join the service of your choice.

Grading tip

For P5 you will need to complete your application by identifying any strong and weak skills you may have. You will then need to set out your aims and a way to achieve them before applying for your chosen role in the public services.

Jackie Knowles
Police Recruiting Officer

I work as part of the recruiting team for a Police Constabulary. We deal with all of the administration and processing of applicants and once they have been through the application process we deal with their selection. It is my job to make sure that all applicants are given the right information and paperwork and I'm also part of the team who paper sifts the application forms to weed out the applicants who aren't suitable.

A typical day

A typical day for me involves dealing with administration and responding to all the many applicants who want to be police officers and PCSOs. I usually spend some of the day going through application forms and organising an assessment centre day as well. It isn't just the candidates we have to coordinate it's also all the police officers who help out at the assessment centres and provide their professional opinion on whether someone is suitable.

The best thing about the job

The best thing about the job for me is knowing I have a say in who serves our community and who doesn't. We have a really clear idea of the kinds of skills and qualities we look for in a police officer and I wouldn't want anyone policing the streets who wasn't fit to be there. I know I have a role in making my county a safer place because of the officers I help choose.

Think about it!

1. What topics have you covered in this unit that might give you the background to be a Recruiting Officer?

2. What knowledge and skills do you think you need to develop further if you want to be involved in recruiting in the future?

Just checking

1. What are entry requirements?
2. Can you think of any common interview questions?
3. What are psychometric tests?
4. What is a paper sift?
5. What personal qualities do the services look for in new recruits?

edexcel

Assignment tips

- Producing action plans and skills audits as part of your assessments may seem initially quite easy, but they often need to be reviewed over time so you can see if you have made any improvements and are better prepared for your service. This means for an action plan you may need to *review* it several times and for a skills audit you may need to repeat it two or three times across the year. It is really important that you don't lose your original otherwise you won't have anything to compare your latest results against and you won't know if you have improved.

- Primary research is when you go out and find the information yourself rather than relying on summaries of information or second-hand information. You can do this by sourcing information produced by the service itself. Recruiting information changes regularly across the services and sometimes recruiting information can be different even for the same service if they operate in different parts of the country.

- Going out to, or calling, a recruiting office is a good way to get accurate information which will help with your assessments and your career preparation. Talking to someone who is in touch with the available jobs can be the best way forward.

Credit value: 10

5 Improving health and fitness for entry to the uniformed public services

The uniformed public services are very active professions and there will be times when they need to respond physically to an incident or situation. This means in order to be a good public service officer you will need to be physically fit and healthy enough to do the job.

In this unit you will look at a variety of factors associated with health and fitness including: the major body systems and how they are affected by diet and exercise; the key components of nutrition and diet and the fitness tests you need to undertake and pass if you are going to be successful in being recruited to the uniformed public services.

Learning outcomes

After completing this unit you should:

1. know the major body systems associated with a healthy lifestyle
2. understand the effect of basic nutrition and lifestyle factors on public service fitness
3. be able to take part in fitness tests in order to appreciate the requirements of the uniformed public services
4. be able to participate in a personal health improvement programme for uniformed public services.

105

Assessment and grading criteria

This table shows you what you must do in order to achieve a pass, merit or distinction grade, and where you can find activities in this book to help you.

To achieve a pass grade the evidence must show that the learner is able to:	To achieve a merit grade the evidence must show that, in addition to the pass criteria, the learner is able to:	To achieve a distinction grade the evidence must show that, in addition to the pass and merit criteria, the learner is able to:
P1 define key terms associated with a healthy lifestyle **Assessment activity 5.1 page 109**		
P2 describe the effects of exercise on the body systems associated with health **Assessment activity 5.2 page 121**	**M1** explain the impact of regular exercise on body systems associated with health **Assessment activity 5.2 page 121**	**D1** evaluate the short- and long-term effects of regular exercise on body systems associated with health **Assessment activity 5.2 page 121**
P3 outline the benefits of exercise **Assessment activity 5.3 page 121**		
P4 keep a personal food and lifestyle diary **Assessment activity 5.4 page 128**	**M2** review the effect of basic nutrition and lifestyle factors on fitness taking account of your personal food and fitness diary **Assessment activity 5.4 page 128**	**D2** evaluate the effect of a personal food and lifestyle diary suggesting areas for improvement **Assessment activity 5.4 page 128**
P5 describe the effect of basic nutrition and lifestyle factors on fitness **Assessment activity 5.4 page 128**		
P6 identify components of and testing methods for fitness **Assessment activity 5.5 page 133**	**M3** demonstrate improvements in performance in a fitness test used by a uniformed public service **Assessment activity 5.5 page 133**	
P7 perform fitness tests used by the uniformed public services **Assessment activity 5.5 page 133**		
P8 plan a personal health improvement programme **Assessment activity 5.6 page 138**	**M4** participate in a personal health improvement programme **Assessment activity 5.6 page 138**	**D3** create an action plan for further improvement in health **Assessment activity 5.6 page 138**

How you will be assessed

This unit will be assessed by an internal assignment that will be designed and marked by the staff at your centre. The assignment is designed to allow you to show your understanding of the learning outcomes for health and fitness. These relate to what you should be able to do after completing this unit. Assessments can be quite varied and can take the form of:

- reports
- leaflets
- presentations
- posters
- practical tasks

- case studies
- diaries
- fitness records
- action plans.

Kiera, 17, aims to improve her lifestyle

This unit was great for me because I'm not very fit and I eat lots of junk food. By completing this unit I was able to see what the effects of this kind of lifestyle were on my health and what I would have to do to improve before I apply to join a public service.

One of the things I enjoyed most was looking at body systems. I hadn't really done much biology before but I feel I now have a really good understanding of how my body systems work and how they are affected by the lifestyle choices I make, such as smoking or eating too much of the wrong foods. Also I was really interested in looking at my own food and lifestyle diary, although I was a bit shocked at how poor my diet is. I'm not overweight so I always assumed that my diet must be alright, but I didn't have any fresh fruit or vegetables at all in my diary for over a week! The fat content of what I was eating means I might be storing up health trouble for myself in later life. Now I know I can, at least, do something about it. Another thing my lifestyle diary showed me was that I was very irregular with my exercise. I do play netball sometimes, but unless it's arranged for me I tend not to bother. I need to put some exercise time into my schedule!

The good thing about this unit is that there are lots of opportunities for physical activity in fitness practicals. It makes a change to get out of the classroom and get some fresh air. After I had done any exercise I didn't want to spoil it by going to the college canteen and having a plate of chips and gravy for dinner. So this unit had a big effect on me really.

Over to you!

- What areas of health and fitness might you find interesting?
- Have you ever kept a food and lifestyle diary before?
- Do you have any fears or concerns about your level of fitness? Will you have to make lifestyle changes?
- Are you currently fit enough to pass the fitness tests in the service of your choice?
- What preparation could you do to get ready for your assessments?

1 The major body systems associated with a healthy lifestyle

Talk up

Thinking about fitness

Consider the fitness requirements for the service of your choice. Will you have to make any lifestyle changes in order to pass the tests? Is your diet currently healthy and nutritious?

Working individually, write down an honest assessment of your health and fitness and consider what steps you can take to improve them.

Share your findings with the rest of your class. Did you come up with the same list of changes or was each learner's assessment different? Why do you think this is?

This part of the unit looks at how your body works and how it responds to the effects of exercise, diet and lifestyle, but before we can examine those things you need to understand some of the key definitions used commonly in health and fitness.

1.1 Definitions

There are several key terms that you need to be aware of and understand before we look in detail at body systems (See Table 5.1). Being able to define and explain these terms will help you understand the rest of the unit.

Table 5.1: Key terms in health and fitness.

Key term	Definition
Fitness	Fitness is the ability of your muscles (including your heart, which is a muscle) to perform a particular task or set of tasks. The level of fitness required for particular tasks will vary. For example, if you sit at a desk all day your muscles do not have to work particularly hard to perform the task of sitting so only low level fitness is required. If you are fighting fires or chasing criminals, your muscles and systems will have to work harder to complete the task and so a higher level of fitness will be needed.
Health	Health is a state of physical and mental well-being where your body is free of disease and is working as it should.
Well-being	Well-being is a term which describes our happiness, confidence and general outlook on life.
Nutrition	Nutrition is a branch of science which studies the process by which all living organisms acquire the materials they need to live. For humans these materials are present in foods, such as fats, carbohydrates and proteins, vitamins and minerals. Nutrition also examines what happens to bodies which have too much or too little of some of these materials.
Lifestyle	Lifestyle is about the way you choose to live your life. It is about factors such as leisure activities, dress, diet and your personal relationships. The way you choose to live your life reflects your attitudes.

Assessment activity 5.1

BTEC **P1**

Understanding the key terms in health and fitness is essential if you are going to be successful in this unit. Create an information sheet which provides the following information:

1 *Define* key terms associated with a healthy lifestyle. **P1**

2 Give a full *explanation* of the terms. **P1**

Grading tip

This is very straightforward: on your information sheet define and explain terms such as fitness, health, well-being, nutrition and lifestyle.

PLTS

Completing this assessment will develop your independent enquirer skills.

1.2 Body systems

Although each individual is unique, the vast majority of people have an almost identical set of body systems. Each system is essential to health and well-being and has evolved specifically to perform a set of functions that no other body system can do. The major systems include:

- skeletal system
- muscular system
- respiratory system
- cardiovascular system.

Understanding your major body systems is essential in knowing how to improve your overall health, fitness and well-being.

Did you know?

There are many body systems in addition to the ones we will be looking at, such as the digestive system, the reproductive system and the nervous system.

The skeletal system – structure and function

The human adult skeleton consists of 206 bones, most of which are paired on the right and left part of the body. It is an internal skeleton (which means it sits inside the body, unlike some insects that have a skeleton on the outside of the body).

The skeleton can be divided into two parts:

- the axial skeleton, which consists of 80 bones concentrated in the upper central part of the body
- the appendicular skeleton, which consists of 126 bones concentrated at the extremities.

The structure of a human skeleton is shown in Figure 5.1.

Did you know?

The proper term for a skeleton inside the body is an endoskeleton and a skeleton outside the body, which some insects have, is called an exoskeleton.

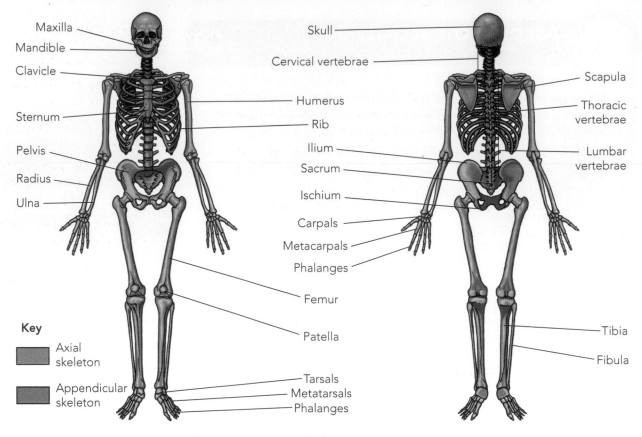

Figure 5.1: Can you distinguish between the axial and appendicular parts of the human skeleton?

The skeletal system is a network of bone, cartilage and joints. It provides several major functions and these are outlined in Table 5.2.

Table 5.2: Functions of the human skeleton.

Function	Detail
Support	The skeleton provides a shape for the body – a framework which takes the body's weight and supports body structures.
Protection	Bones help protect the body from injury, for example, the skull protects the brain and the sternum and ribs protect the heart.
Movement	Bones provide attachment points for muscles. The bones provide a structure for the muscles to work against. As muscles can only contract, the bones are used as levers against which one muscle contracts in order to extend another.
Storage	The bones serve as storage areas for minerals such as calcium and phosphorous which are used by your body.
Production of blood cells	Red blood cells, which carry oxygen around the body, and some white blood cells, which fight infection, are produced in the long bones.

Bone

A living bone consists of about 35 per cent organic tissue, such as blood vessels, and 65 per cent minerals, such as calcium compounds.

The bone illustrated in Figure 5.2 is called a long bone. It is covered by the **periosteum** which is like the skin of the bone. The periosteum contains the cells that make new bone. The bone itself is divided into two parts: the **epiphysis**, which is the two rounded end parts, and the **diaphysis**, which is the central, straight part of the bone. The end parts of the bone (epiphysis) are covered in a substance called **cartilage** which makes **joints** move together easily and the inside of the end parts of the bone and the straight parts of the bone are filled with **bone marrow**.

The different types of bones are described in Table 5.3.

Table 5.3: The different types of bones.

Type	Examples	Purpose
Long bones	Clavicle, humerus, radius, ulna, femur, tibia (collar bone, arm and leg bones)	To provide support and to act as levers for muscles
Short bones	Carpals, tarsals (finger and toe bones)	To provide movement, elasticity, flexibility and shock absorption
Flat bones	Ribs, sternum, scapula (chest and shoulder blade bones)	Protection, attachment sites for muscles
Irregular	Skull, pelvis, vertebrae	Protection, support, movement
Sesamoid	Patella (kneecap)	Protection of tendons, makes the joint more effective and more powerful

Joints

Joints occur at points in the body where bones come together. They are areas where flexible connective tissue holds bones together while still allowing freedom of movement. Since the skeleton is not naturally flexible, joints are essential for movement and are a key part of the skeletal system.

Activity: Joints

Working in small groups

What problems would damaged joints pose for a member of the public services? How would their day-to-day activities have to change? Why are joints so important to the skeletal system and what would happen if we had no joints? Discuss these issues.

Key terms

Periosteum – the skin of a bone.

Epiphysis – the rounded, end part of the long bone.

Diaphysis – the straight, middle part of the bone.

Cartilage – a body tissue which acts like a cushion between joints.

Joint – an area of the body where bones move against each other to allow freedom of movement.

Bone marrow – a soft substance in the bones which help make blood cells.

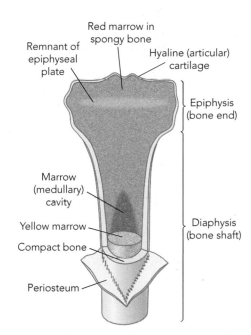

Figure 5.2: Diagram of a cross-section of a long bone. How many long bones in humans?

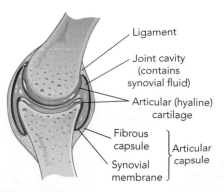

Figure 5.3: What happens at a joint?

The muscular system – structure and function

Key term

Filament – a thread-like fibre of muscle cells that form bundles of muscle tissue.

Muscles are bundles of protein **filaments** that work together to produce motion in the body.

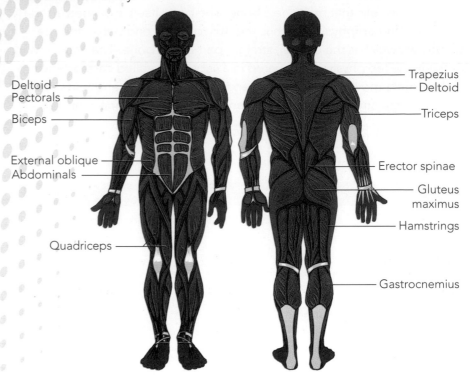

Deltoid
Pectorals
Biceps
External oblique
Abdominals
Quadriceps

Trapezius
Deltoid
Triceps
Erector spinae
Gluteus maximus
Hamstrings
Gastrocnemius

Figure 5.4: Muscle systems of the human body.

The main functions of muscles are shown in Table 5.4.

Table 5.4: Functions of muscles.

Function	Detail
Provide movement	The actions of muscles allow you to change position and move around.
Maintain posture	Believe it or not, standing upright is a very difficult thing for the body to do because gravity is always pulling you down. The reason you don't fall to the ground is due to the actions of your muscles.
Produce heat	The action of muscles produces heat and this is why you get hot when you are doing physical activity. If you are cold and inactive your muscles will start to rhythmically contract in an effort to keep you warm – this is called shivering.
Regulate blood flow	Your heart is a muscle which pumps blood around your body in accordance with your needs. If you need more oxygen to get to the muscles to enable them to work harder, your heart rate will increase.
Aid digestion and waste removal	The digestive system moves food through the body and eliminates waste due to muscle action. Equally, the bladder holds on to your urine until you relax the muscles that allow it to be eliminated.
Support the skeleton	Muscles act as a way to tie the skeleton together. There are muscle attachment points at all joints and this ensures the bones stay in position.

Muscle tissue typically composes 40–50 per cent of your body weight and the human body contains well over 600 muscles, which usually work in pairs. These pairs consist of the agonist, which is the prime mover and the antagonist which works against it. For example, your arm moves by the bicep muscle (agonist) working against the triceps muscle (the antagonist).

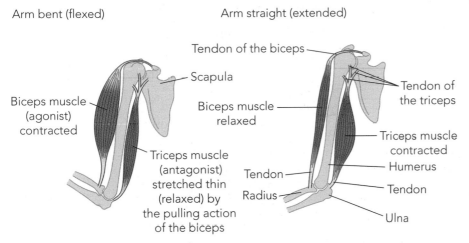

Arm bent (flexed)

Arm straight (extended)

- Tendon of the biceps
- Scapula
- Biceps muscle (agonist) contracted
- Biceps muscle relaxed
- Triceps muscle (antagonist) stretched thin (relaxed) by the pulling action of the biceps
- Tendon of the triceps
- Triceps muscle contracted
- Humerus
- Tendon
- Tendon
- Radius
- Ulna

Figure 5.5: Muscle action usually occurs in pairs. Can you think of other pairs of muscles?

Muscles can only pull, they cannot push. This is why they usually work in pairs. One muscle pulls a limb into the required position and the other muscle pulls it back when required. Muscle action can be **voluntary** or **involuntary**.

Types of muscle

The body must be equipped to deal with a variety of tasks and we have three types of muscle to carry out these tasks. These are described in Table 5.5.

Key terms

Voluntary – these muscles are controlled by the individual themselves, such as the biceps and triceps in the arm. You can usually move these muscles whenever you like.

Involuntary – some muscles in the body are automatically controlled by the brain, such as the heart, diaphragm and intestines. This means that they operate without you thinking about it.

Activity: Muscles

Working in groups

Why is it important to have cardiac muscle which resists fatigue? What would happen if your heart muscle got tired and didn't work efficiently?

Write your answers and then discuss with the group.

Table 5.5: The main types of muscle tissue.

Type of muscle	Explanation
Cardiac muscle	This is found only in the heart and makes up the walls of the heart or myocardium. It acts as a single sheet of muscle that operates on an involuntary basis and has its own blood supply. Unlike many muscles in the body the cardiac muscle is not attached to bone and resists fatigue well.
Smooth muscle	Smooth muscle makes up a large part of our internal organs such as the bladder, veins and digestive tract. It is involuntary which means that it works without conscious thought on an automatic basis. Smooth muscle contracts very slowly and so it is able to resist fatigue. In addition, it can stay contracted for relatively long periods of time.
Skeletal muscle	This is the most common type of muscle found in the human body and can make up about 40 per cent of an adult male's body weight. It has stripe-like markings called striations and is composed of large cells bound together in bundles or sheets. The muscles are served by a system of nerves that connect them to the spinal cord and the brain which controls the activation of a muscle. Skeletal muscles are attached to bones by tendons and the majority of skeletal muscles are under your direct control and respond to what you want them to do.

The respiratory system

Cells continually use oxygen (O_2) in their reactions and release carbon dioxide (CO_2) as a waste product. The body therefore needs a system that provides O_2 for the body and gets rid of CO_2 before it builds up and causes damage. This system is the respiratory system. The exchange of O_2 and CO_2 is completed in three stages.

The respiratory system has several parts:

- nose
- pharynx
- larynx
- trachea
- bronchi
- bronchioles
- alveoli.

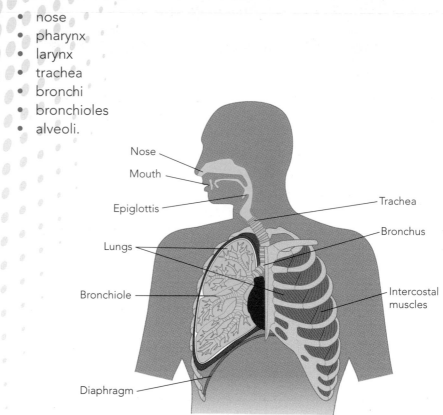

- Nose
- Mouth
- Epiglottis
- Trachea
- Bronchus
- Lungs
- Bronchiole
- Intercostal muscles
- Diaphragm

Figure 5.6: Can you name the gas we inspire and the gas we expire?

The main function of the respiratory system is to provide the body with enough oxygen to live and to get rid of carbon dioxide as waste. The way it does this is called breathing: the correct name for breathing in is 'inspiration' and the correct name for breathing out is 'expiration'. At rest a typical healthy adult will take 12 breaths per minute with each inspiration and expiration moving about half a litre of air.

The main parts of the respiratory system

Nose. Air usually enters through the nostrils and proceeds to open spaces within the nose called the nasal passages and nasal cavity. The air is filtered by small hairs and mucus in the nostrils and warmed before it reaches the lungs. The mucus also helps moisten the air. This is why it is better to breathe through the nose rather than the mouth.

Pharynx and larynx. Moving on from the nose, air travels through the pharynx (throat) and the larynx (voice box). Air vibrates the vocal chords, which are on either side of the larynx, enabling us to make sounds.

Trachea. The larynx connects with the trachea (windpipe), which is a tube approximately 12 cm in length and 2.5 cm wide in adults. It is held open by rings of cartilage and is covered with tiny hairs (cilia) and mucus which help filter the air and remove obstructions that have passed down the throat.

Bronchioles. The bronchial tubes further divide and spread becoming smaller and thinner tubes called bronchioles.

Alveoli. Each bronchiole ends in a tiny air chamber containing a cup-shaped cavity (alveolus). The tissue of an alveolus is very thin and this allows O_2 and CO_2 to be exchanged through its walls.

Did you know?

The impurities in the air which are filtered out by your nose hair and nose mucus become your bogeys.

The cardiovascular system – structure and function

The cardiovascular system consists of the heart, blood vessels and blood. Oxygen and waste products are carried to and from the tissues and cells by blood. The heart is the mechanism that allows this by pumping blood around the body through tubes called veins and arteries.

The heart pumps continually throughout your life to the tune of around 30 million beats per year. While you are asleep it pumps approximately 10 litres of blood a minute through the 60,000 miles of blood vessels which make up the transport system of your body. The cardiovascular system is one of the most important of all the body systems.

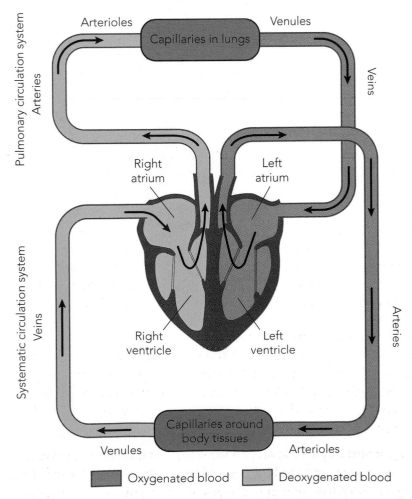

Figure 5.7: Can you name the main constituents of the cardiovascular system?

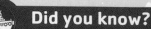

The heart

The heart is about the size of a clenched fist and is located in the chest between the lungs with its apex (pointed end) slightly tilted to the left. It is made up of cardiac muscle (myocardium) and is surrounded by the pericardium, which is a fluid filled bag which reduces friction when the heart beats.

The heart contains four chambers: the left and right atria, which are the upper chambers of the heart, and the left and right ventricles, which are the lower chambers. These form the basis for the two distinct transport circuits of the body, both of which begin and end at the heart.

The two blood transport circuits are:

- **The pulmonary circuit** – which carries blood to and from the surface of the lungs.
- **The systemic circuit** – which involves blood flow to the rest of the body.

Both of the blood flow circuits mentioned above rely not only on the heart but also on the blood and blood vessels.

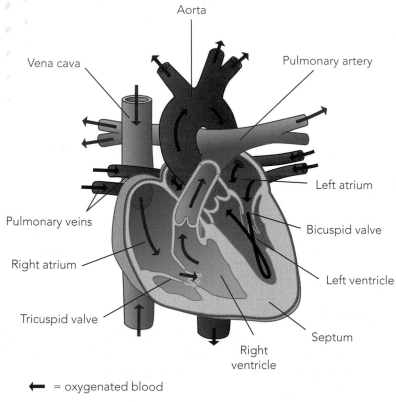

= oxygenated blood

= deoxygenated blood

Figure 5.8: The arrows show the direction of blood flow. Can you identify the different regions of the heart?

Blood vessels

The blood vessels are the transport network of the body. They allow blood to travel to every part of the body and return to the heart. The transport network consists of several types of vessels, as shown in Table 5.6.

Table 5.6: The vessels of the cardiovascular system.

Type of vessel	Description
Arteries	These are large vessels which usually carry oxygenated blood away from the heart to the rest of the body (the exception is the pulmonary artery). They subdivide to form smaller vessels called arterioles which then branch off again to form capillaries. These vessels are cylindrical and muscular and are able to contract and dilate in order to regulate blood flow.
Veins	These vessels are usually responsible for the movement of deoxygenated blood back towards the heart so that it can be sent on the pulmonary circuit once more, and back to the lungs. Vessels called venules connect the capillaries where the oxygen has just been deposited to the veins which then return it to the heart. The blood flow in the veins is under less pressure than the arteries and so they tend to be slightly less muscular.
Capillaries	These are the smallest blood transportation vessels in the body. They are incredibly thin which allows the exchange of gases through them. Organs and tissues which need a high amount of oxygen and nutrients, such as muscles and the brain, will have many capillaries.

Blood

Blood is a red fluid which carries oxygen, nutrients, hormones and disease fighting agents around the body. The typical human has around 5 litres of blood in their body. Blood is made up of several different substances:

- plasma
- red and white cells
- platelets.

Plasma. Plasma is what makes the blood a liquid. It transports the cells in the blood around the body. It is a pale yellow fluid made mostly from water and a small amount of protein.

Red blood cells. Red blood cells are the most numerous type of cell in the blood. They are disc shaped with a depression in the centre (see Figure 5.9). They are created by the marrow in the bones and have a life span of approximately 3 months. They carry a substance called haemoglobin which helps transport oxygen around the body. It is haemoglobin that gives the blood its red colour.

White blood cells. White blood cells are the soldiers of the body as they are the cells that fight off bacteria and viruses. They are much bigger than red blood cells and are irregular in shape. Without them we would not be able to fight off infection or disease.

Platelets. Platelets play an important role in the repair system of the body. They help restrict blood flow to a damaged part of the body, such as a graze or a cut. They stick together at the site of an injury to plug gaps in broken blood vessels and so reduce bleeding. Also, they help form scabs over wounds. The scab prevents foreign particles entering the bloodstream and stays in place until the tissue underneath is repaired. It falls off once the tissue is healed.

Red blood cell (side view shows depression in centre)

Red blood cell (biconcave in shape and no nucleus)

White blood cell (irregular in shape and containing nucleus)

Plasma (fluid part of blood)

Blood platelets (cell fragments involved in blood clotting)

Figure 5.9: What is the major difference between red and white blood cells?

1.3 Effects of exercise on the body systems

Exercise has many short-term and long-term effects across all the major body systems. Table 5.7 highlights the most important of these.

Table 5.7: The effects of exercise on the human body.

Short-term effects	Explanation
Blood flow	Blood flow around the body becomes faster and it is diverted away from areas such as the stomach, which are not essential to exercise and directed towards the heart, lungs and muscles. This is because the blood is required to carry more oxygen and take away more waste products.
Raised heart rate	The heart beats faster, fills up with more blood and moves blood around the body faster. Exercise increases not only heart rate but also blood pressure and stroke volume. Stroke volume is the amount of blood that can be moved with each beat of the heart.
Increased respiration	Respiration becomes faster and deeper as it responds to the need for more oxygen in the body. It also increases to remove a larger volume of carbon dioxide which is produced during exercise.
Long-term effects	**Explanation**
Muscle tone	Depending on the exercise, the muscles can become bigger and are more clearly defined.
Lowered heart rate	At resting state the heart is able to pump blood more efficiently, which means it needs to beat less to move the same volume of blood.
Blood pressure	Although the short-term impact of exercise is to raise blood pressure, the long-term effect is the opposite. Long-term exercise has the benefit of generally lowering overall blood pressure as the heart works more efficiently.
Strength	As muscles work hard during a programme of exercise they will become stronger. Again, this can depend on the type of exercise.
Stamina	Muscles are able to work for longer without becoming fatigued.
Weight	A long-term exercise plan can have a varying effect on weight. Some exercise will increase muscle mass and lead to a weight gain while other types of exercise will help reduce or maintain original weight.
Cholesterol	Cholesterol can be reduced by a long-term exercise plan.
Digestion	Although the short-term impact of exercise is to direct blood away from the digestive organs, the long-term effect is the opposite. Long-term regular exercise helps to strengthen the muscles of the abdomen and digestive organs and reduces sluggishness by stimulating the muscles to push digestive contents through your body.

1.4 Effect of lifestyle on the body systems

Each of us makes lifestyle choices that can affect our levels of health and fitness. Our lifestyle is the way we choose to conduct our lives from what we eat, to the jobs we do, to the types of relationships we choose to have. The following lifestyle choices impact upon our health and fitness.

Smoking

Smoking is a major danger to your health. It can cause heart disease, numerous types of cancer and bronchial disorders. Over 114,000 people in the UK die every year from smoking-related diseases. Smokers have double the heart attack risk of non-smokers and, linked with the contraceptive pill, in women the risk may even be higher.

The body becomes addicted to nicotine, which is a stimulant, making the heart beat faster and the blood vessels narrow, causing a strain on the cardiovascular system. In addition, the blood becomes more 'sticky' with fats and sugars leading to a 'furring up' of the arteries. Carbon monoxide in cigarette smoke can drastically reduce the capacity of the blood to carry O_2 to the tissues which again means that the heart must work harder. In the short term smoking can also increase the rise of an asthma attack which might compromise your job performance in any public service work.

Alcohol

Alcohol has an impact on all of the major body systems and abuse of alcohol can lead to death. Some of the main effects of excessive alcohol are: blackouts, liver cancer, liver disease, diarrhoea, heartburn, cancer of the oesophagus, malnutrition, high blood pressure, loss of libido, reduced fertility, impaired decision making and increased risk of accidents.

In terms of public service work, the abuse of alcohol can directly affect your working performance. Many public service jobs require the operation of complex equipment such as breathing apparatus, weapons and vehicles. The presence of alcohol in your system will impair your judgement, placing yourself and others at risk.

Drugs

The abuse of drugs will lead to a variety of effects on the short- and long-term health and fitness of an individual. These include:

- **Opiates (heroin)** – constipation, loss of libido, drowsiness, respiratory distress, an overdose is fatal. It is also linked to the spread of HIV and hepatitis through the sharing of contaminated needles
- **Amphetamines (speed, whizz)** – sleeplessness, anorexia
- **LSD** – sensory distortions, hallucinations, a feeling of panic or anxiety
- **Ecstasy** – hallucinations, heatstroke, dehydration, panic attacks and depression
- **Cocaine** – damage or loss of nasal septum, may cause paranoid psychosis.
- **Marijuana (cannabis, weed, pot)** – serious effects on short-term memory, and smoking it is harmful to the lungs

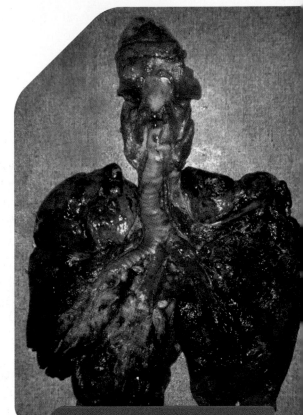

These are human lungs. What evidence of inhaling cigarette smoke can you see?

Did you know?

Alcohol is very high in calories and without proper exercise this will lead to weight gain. Carrying excess weight places an additional strain on the body, especially the cardiovascular and respiratory systems, which have to work harder to perform their functions.

Did you know?

Drug abuse may also lead to unwise sexual behaviour or involvement in crime.

In any sports or fitness-related area of study there is also the danger from use of performance-enhancing drugs such as anabolic steroids. Steroids are taken by some athletes and bodybuilders to increase their muscle mass and strength but these can have significant side effects such as:

- in men – shrunken testicles, baldness, higher voice, prominent breasts and infertility
- in women – a deeper voice, increased body hair and baldness.

Sleep

Lack of enough sleep can cause the body short- and long-term problems including:

- feeling of tiredness
- irritability
- lack of concentration
- sleeping at inappropriate moments, such as while driving
- a depressed immune system that leaves us vulnerable to disease and infection
- slowed reaction times.

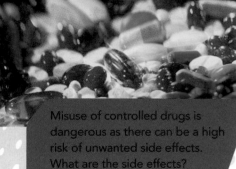

Misuse of controlled drugs is dangerous as there can be a high risk of unwanted side effects. What are the side effects?

Activity: Effects of lack of sleep

Consider the list of problems associated with not getting enough How would these affect the job performance of an army soldier? What might the consequences of this be to the whole unit? Discuss this with your group.

Key terms

Stress – the emotional and physical reaction our body shows to meet a challenge, this can be harmful and/or beneficial.

Fight or flight – an instinctive response of the whole body to a threatening situation which prepares you to resist or run.

Did you know?

Public service officers may also be at risk of post-traumatic stress disorder (PTSD) if they experience stressful or traumatic events during their working life, such as a major disaster or war conditions.

Stress

Stress is a constant part of our lives, whether it is worrying about getting assignments in on time or more serious worries such as divorce or bereavement. The kind of stress that is really damaging to your body is long-term stress, which can be caused by family problems, financial difficulties or being unhappy in your workplace.

- **Symptoms.** Stress can show itself physically and emotionally through signs such as indigestion, fatigue, insomnia, feeling irritable or headaches. These symptoms are caused by the increased activity of the nervous system as it responds to your stress and the production of hormones which trigger your **fight or flight** response. These hormones stimulate the heart to beat faster and to redirect blood to the brain, heart and muscles. This causes an increase in blood pressure, which can lead to the heart and blood vessels being placed under stress. If a blood vessel bursts in the brain it is called a 'stroke' and can have fatal consequences. In addition, the blood becomes 'sticky' with sugars and fats released from the liver in order to give the muscles more energy to power the fight or flight response. However, if you are sitting at a desk fuming at your boss, these fats and sugars are not utilised by the muscles and they can stick to artery walls clogging them up with fatty deposits which put you at greater risk of heart disease.

- **Reducing stress.** Stress has been linked with many other problems such as eczema, stomach ulcers and depression. The obvious way to deal with this problem is to tackle the cause of the stress so that it no longer exists or to change the way you react to stress. Techniques such as meditation and exercise can help an individual cope with stress more effectively.

BTEC **Assessment activity 5.2**

Working in pairs

Understanding how your body works and the effect regular exercise can have on it is your first step to improving your fitness to enable you to pass the fitness tests in the service of your choice. Produce a PowerPoint presentation together, which covers the following points:

1 *Description* of the effects of exercise on the body systems associated with health. **P2**
2 *Explanation* of the impact of regular exercise on body systems associated with health. **M1**
3 *Evaluation* of the short- and long-term effects of regular exercise on body systems associated with health. **D1**

Grading tip

These three criteria are very closely linked and require you to *describe, explain* and *evaluate* the effects of exercise on body systems such as the respiratory system, the cardiovascular system, the skeletal system and the muscular system.

1.5 Benefits of exercise

It is a well-known fact that individuals who exercise regularly, either as part of their job or in their leisure time, have fewer heart attacks than those who don't. Exercise builds up the strength of the heart, which means it can cope better if you put a sudden physical demand on it. Exercise will also:

- help reduce blood pressure
- keep weight in check
- slow down the bone deterioration in older people (particularly important for women)
- keep muscles strong and joints flexible
- help you deal with stress and depression in more productive ways
- decrease the amount of bad cholesterol in the blood helping keep the heart and blood vessels healthy
- promote psychological well-being and positive self-image
- give you an opportunity to meet and socialise with other people, perhaps in the gym or as part of a sports team.

> **! Link**
>
> In addition to the mental and social benefits of exercise you can see more on the physical benefits of exercise in Table 5.7 on page 118.

BTEC **Assessment activity 5.3** **P3**

Produce a leaflet which *outlines* the benefits of exercise. **P3**

Grading tip

Make sure you mention, physical, mental and social benefits.

2 The effect of basic nutrition and lifestyle factors on public service fitness

Nutrition is the study of the process of providing the body with the materials it needs to be healthy and function properly. Understanding nutrition will enable you to examine your own diet and make sure you are providing your body with all that it needs.

2.1 Nutrition and impact of poor nutrition

Nutrition is the study of how the body uses foods and nutrients vital to health in promoting growth, maintenance and reproduction of cells. In essence, it is how what we eat and drink affects our health.

An understanding of nutrition is important as it helps us understand how our body uses the food we eat. There are seven essential foodstuffs the body needs:

- protein
- carbohydrate (including simple carbohydrates in the form of sugars)
- fats
- water
- mineral salts
- vitamins
- fibre.

Remember

There are two types of amino acids:
- essential
- non-essential.

Non-essential amino acids are made for you by your body, they are essential to your health and well-being but are called non-essential because you don't need to get them from your food. Essential amino acids must be acquired through your food as your body does not make them for itself. So it is important to have a diet that contains adequate amounts of proteins that contain essential amino acids.

Protein

Protein is composed of chains of amino acids, which are the building block of cells. They provide cells with material with which to grow and maintain their structure.

The digestive system breaks down protein in the food we eat and allows it to be absorbed into the bloodstream where it is then utilised for growth. Protein is found naturally in most diets in foods such as fish, milk and bread, pulses and meat. Protein is also important as it is responsible for making haemoglobin which is responsible for the transportation of oxygen in the blood (see page 117). Protein is also a prime ingredient in the white blood cells that fight off infection and repair wounds.

Carbohydrates

Carbohydrates provide fuel for the body. The digestive system enables the absorption of the 'sugars' and 'starches' that make up carbohydrates and allows them to be carried in the bloodstream to every cell in the body where they are converted into a substance called adenosine triphosphate (ATP) which powers the functions of a cell.

Remember

Sugars such as glucose, fructose (found in fruit) and lactose (found in milk) are called simple carbohydrates as they are easily digested and enter the bloodstream quickly. There are also complex carbohydrates, which are commonly called starches. Complex carbohydrates occur when simple carbohydrates bond together to form a chain. Complex carbohydrates are found in food stuffs such as potatoes, wheat, corn, pasta and rice.

The digestive system breaks down the complex carbohydrates into their simple sugars and as a result they are released into the bloodstream at a much slower pace than simple sugars which can reach the bloodstream very quickly. Therefore complex carbohydrates keep you going for longer. If you have an excess of sugars in the bloodstream, such as glucose, they are stored by the body in the liver as a product called glycogen. If the amount of glycogen is high and will not fit into the liver then it is stored as fat. When you are exercising for short periods of time the glycogen in your liver will be used for energy, but if you exercise for a long time your body will begin to burn fat instead.

Fats

A high fat diet can lead to obesity, heart disease, heart attacks and strokes. However, fat is essential to the body in insulating its systems from the cold and cushioning our hardworking organs against jolts and knocks, it also helps process some vitamins and minerals and is the major source of energy storage In the body. At the simplest level there are three kinds of fat (see Table 5.8).

> **Did you know?**
>
> Fats are also called lipids. Trans fats are oils that have been transformed from their normal liquid state into solids, to make margarine for instance. The unsaturated oil is converted to a saturated fat and all the benefits of the oil are removed. An excess of trans fats in the diet raises the cholesterol level in the blood.

Table 5.8: The three kinds of fat.

Saturated fat	This is the most harmful type of fat to the body, it can cause clogged arteries leading to heart disease. Saturated fats are normally solid at room temperature, butter and lard are examples. They are found primarily in animal products such as meat, eggs and milk, but also in vegetable products such as coconut milk and palm oil. The excessive use of saturated fats in the diet has links with obesity, high levels of cholesterol, breast cancer, strokes and heart disease.
Polyunsaturated fat	This has fewer fatty acid molecules than saturated fat and is generally liquid at room temperature. It is thought to be less damaging to the body systems than saturated fats, examples are sunflower oil and corn oil. It is also found in oily fish.
Monounsaturated fat	This is considered to be the best of all three of the fats as it actively helps to lower cholesterol levels. Monounsaturated fats are generally found in food such as olive oil, rapeseed oil, nuts and seeds.

Fats that you eat in your food are broken down in the digestive system by an enzyme called 'lipase' which ensures they are ready for transport in the bloodstream. The fats are then either used in muscles as fuel for energy or stored for later in fat deposits on the body. It is important to remember that although some fats have a more damaging effect on our body systems than others, there is no difference in their calorie content. Eating too much monounsaturated fat will make you overweight just as quickly as saturated fat will.

Water

The human body is about 60 per cent water and constantly needs to be replaced as we lose a great deal through respiration, sweating and urine. At rest a person loses approximately one litre of water per day. Without water no system in the body could survive. Many people do not drink enough water to replace the losses that occur naturally in the body, this can lead to inattention, headaches and irritability.

Key term

Cholesterol – a fat-like substance that is essential for maintaining health but which cannot be made by the body, however, high concentrations in the blood increase the risk of heart disease.

Mineral salts

These are inorganic substances the body must have in order to regulate processes or manufacture specific molecules. They are involved in all body systems, some of the most well known are described in Table 5.9.

Table 5.9: Some of the minerals essential to the human body.

Mineral*	Function	Sources
Calcium	Formation of bone	Milk, dairy produce, green vegetables, nuts and seeds
Iron	Formation of red blood cells	Meat, cereals, vegetables
Iodine	Metabolism and body weight	Fish, seaweed, dairy produce
Magnesium	Bone support, activation of vitamins, production of cholesterol, relaxing effect on muscles	Cereals, green vegetables, potatoes, nuts and seeds
Manganese	Activation of vitamins and enzymes, neutralisation of poisons in blood, antioxidant	Cereals, nuts, fruit, vegetables
Phosphorus	Provision of strength to bones and teeth, transportation of fats, activation of vitamins, cell membranes	Dairy produce, bread, red meat and poultry
Potassium and sodium	Sodium/potassium pump, transmission of nerve impulses, control of body pH, control of blood pressure	Vegetables, fruit, sodium in table salt
Selenium	Activation of enzymes, recycling of iron from red blood cells, joint lubrication, bonding to hazardous heavy metals in the body to facilitate ease of elimination	Cereals, meat, fish, shellfish, brazil nuts
Zinc	Aid to calcium absorption, role in sexual maturity, helps in blood sugar regulation	Meat products, shellfish, bread, dairy products

*Other essential minerals include chloride, copper, chromium and fluorine.

Did you know?

Minerals are only required in very small amounts and slight variations can impact on the body:

- **high** levels can have a negative effect, for instance, too much sodium has been linked with high blood pressure.
- **low** levels can also have a negative effect, for instance too little iron leads to anaemia.

Vitamins

Vitamins are organic compounds, which can provide energy for the body and help assist chemical reactions within the cells of your body and help regulate metabolic processes, including converting the food you eat into energy. The human body needs 13 different vitamins including A, B, C and D (see Table 5.10).

Table 5.10: Vitamins play vital roles in the functioning of your body.

Vitamin	Description
Vitamin A (retinol)	plays a role in the health of the eye. Vitamin A enables nerve impulses to be sent from the eye to the brain which then interprets them. It is primarily stored in the liver, and people who have alcohol problems may experience problems with their vision, such as night blindness. Vitamin A is found in meat, but it can be easily made by the body from molecules that come from carrots, sweet potato and spinach. Vitamin A is also essential in the immune and reproductive systems.
Vitamin B (There is a whole family of vitamin Bs)	B_1 **thiamine** – plays a vital part in converting the carbohydrates, fats and proteins that you eat into energy. B_2 **riboflavin** – essential for repair and growth of body tissue and good digestion. It is also linked to the speed of your metabolism, that is the rate at which you burn the energy in the food you eat. B_3 **niacin** – used in the metabolism of fats, which helps provide enough energy for the body to perform its functions. B_5 **pantothenic acid** – as with other B vitamins, this helps in the conversion of food to energy, it also helps the adrenal glands work properly. This is important because the adrenal glands produce adrenaline which is an essential part of the body's response to **stress**. B_6 **pyridoxine** – crucial in the ability of cells to maintain sodium and potassium levels, which help the cells get rid of waste and collect nutrients. It is also important in the production of red blood cells, the production of energy from food and the nourishment of the brain and spinal cord. Pyridoxine can be found in liver, bananas, potatoes and sunflower seeds. A deficiency can lead to anaemia, dermatitis and confusion. B_{12} **cyanocobalamin** – has many of the qualities that are common to the vitamin B family, such as helping in metabolism and the production of red blood cells and the effective functioning of the nervous system. It is found in foods such as meat, fish, eggs and dairy produce. It is important that vegetarians and vegans get enough B_{12} since most of the sources are animal based.
Folic acid	plays a large role to play in the nervous system. It is used to produce serotonin and norepinephrine, which are neurotransmitters used by the brain to pass messages along the nervous system. It is particularly important in the development of the nervous system of unborn babies.
Vitamin C (ascorbic acid)	encourages the growth of collagen, which makes the skin appear younger and firmer. Collagen is also used in all fibrous tissue such as bone, cartilage and teeth, in essence it bonds the body together. It also helps the immune system fight off infection and viruses and helps your body repair itself when it is injured. Citrus fruits are very good sources of vitamin C as are potatoes and green vegetables.
Vitamin D (calciferol)	the main function is to help the body absorb calcium and phosphorous, both of which are needed in the production of healthy bones. You are able to manufacture vitamin D yourself by exposure to sunlight. The ultraviolet rays from the Sun penetrate the skin and cause a chemical reaction which leads to the production of vitamin D. You can also find vitamin D in foods such as oily fish, fortified margarines and egg yolk.

Fibre

Fibre is the indigestible part of the plants in our food that gets pushed through our digestive system and absorbs water making sure that the elimination of waste is straightforward and easy. Good sources of fibre include oats, beans, potatoes, wholegrain foods such as cereal, fruit and vegetables. Eating enough fibre doesn't only make elimination of waste easier but it can also protect you from high cholesterol, heart disease and cancer of the colon.

2.2 Diet

Your diet is the sum total of the food you eat over a certain period. People have many different types of diet such as:

- vegetarian diet – avoids the eating of meat or meat products
- vegan diet – avoids the eating of any animal products at all including milk, butter or eggs.

A well-balanced diet includes food from the five main food groups. These are:

- bread, cereal (including breakfast cereals) and potatoes (starchy foods)
- fruit (including fresh fruit juice) and vegetables
- meat and fish
- milk and dairy foods
- fat and sugar.

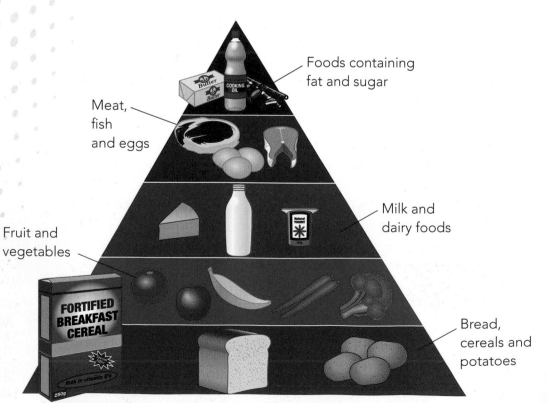

Figure 5.10: Does your diet include the five main food groups?

Figure 5.10 shows how a well-balanced and healthy diet would consist of enough of each of these components to satisfy the needs of the body. The portions outlined are only an indication the amount of food you should eat to stay healthy. The amount you should consume depends on your current weight, level of physical activity and current health. As a general guide, a woman should be aiming to eat around 2,000 kcals per day and a man around 2,500 kcals per day. If you eat more calories than you burn up you will put on weight. **Obesity** is a growing problem across the Western world.

A balanced diet can help to improve health and reduce the incidence of heart disease and cancer.

2.3 Lifestyle factors

Your diet should reflect your lifestyle. If you are very active you will need more calories than if you are not active. This can have a big impact on the uniformed public services which is why an average ration pack for the armed services contains food with an average of around 4000 Kcals.

Food and lifestyle diaries

A food diary is a record of what you eat and when. Sometimes it is also coupled with an exercise diary so you can see how active you are and get an overview of your lifestyle pattern. Elements to record in your food diary are:

- the type of food you eat
- when you eat it
- the amount you eat
- your feelings when you eat
- what exercise you take
- when you take it
- how strenuous it is
- how long you take it for
- how it makes you feel, both during and after.

Research has shown that if you monitor these elements you are more likely to lose weight and maintain a steady weight. A food and activity diary will encourage you to make sensible choices about what you eat and when – writing it down gives you the chance to think twice before you eat. This is one of the most useful things you can do to help you gain control of your weight and improve your sense of fitness and well-being.

Activity: Food and exercise diaries

Do you know how good your diet is and whether you take enough exercise? Keep a food and exercise diary for three days, writing down everything you eat and drink and the type of exercise you take. Make a note of how many calories there are in each item and add them up for a daily total. Are you getting a balanced diet? Are you taking enough exercise? Are you getting enough calories or are you eating too many?

Key term

Obesity – a state in which the weight of a person is at a level where it can seriously endanger their health. It is on the increase due to the availability of high fat and sugar foods and snacks and a decrease in the amount of exercise we take. Obesity increases the risk of heart disease and strokes.

Did you know?

A study by the National Audit Office published in February 2001 found that nearly two-thirds of adults in England are overweight. This costs the health services over £2.5 billion per year.

Did you know?

Surveys show that two-thirds of adults in the UK do not take enough exercise to keep themselves healthy. The list shows the effectiveness of some common activities. Regular exercise and a healthy diet helps reduce and maintain weight.

Exercise	Average energy expenditure (kJ per min)
Walking slowly	10–20
Walking quickly Cycling slowly Tennis Jogging	21–30
Cycling fast Football Swimming Squash	31–40

Activity: Food myths or food facts?

Listed below are some common things people say about food. What do you think of the statements? Do some research and find out whether they are true or false.

- Healthier foods are always far more expensive than other foods.
- The experts are always changing their minds about what healthy eating really is.
- If the label says 'low fat' or 'reduced fat' then the product will always be a healthy choice.
- If you want to have the healthier option it's best to choose a vegetarian dish.
- Margarine contains less fat than butter.
- Red meat is always very high in fat and poultry is always low in fat.
- Drinking ice-cold water uses up more calories and helps you lose weight.
- It's all right to skip breakfast.
- Most of the salt in our diet is added at the table.
- Fruit juice can be harmful to teeth.

BTEC Assessment activity 5.4 P4 P5 M2 D2

This assessment requires you to:

1 *Keep* a personal food and lifestyle diary. P4

2 *Describe* the effects of basic nutrition and lifestyle factors on fitness. P5

Grading tips

Keeping an accurate food and lifestyle diary will achieve P4, reviewing it will get you M2 and evaluating it and suggesting areas for improvement will get you D2. Describing and commenting on your diet and fitness programme will get you P5.

3 Take part in fitness tests in order to appreciate the requirements of the uniformed public services

All of the uniformed public services have some kind of fitness assessment that you must pass in order to be considered for employment. Fitness is really important to the public services as the nature of their work is very physically active. This outcome looks at the components of fitness, fitness tests and the reasons testing is done.

3.1 Components of fitness

Being fit is not just about how fast you can run or for how long. It isn't about how much weight you can lift or how many times you can lift it. Fitness is actually all of these things, and more. To be truly fit and able to live healthily and deal with the rigours of an active life, you need to be fit in several areas. It is these different areas, or components, that make up the sum total of physical fitness.

The components of physical fitness can be divided into two main areas:

- health-related components
- skill-related components.

Health-related components

Cardiovascular endurance

This is also known as aerobic endurance or stamina, which put simply is the ability to repeat an activity for a length of time without becoming tired. This is crucial to performance in many sports, whether it be a 90-minute football match or a 3-hour long distance run. Stamina depends on the efficiency of your cardiovascular system (heart, blood, blood vessels, lungs) in terms of how well they provide the muscles with oxygen. The armed services often have rely on this because they may have to march for miles to reach a combat zone or safe area in battle.

Strength

Strength can be defined as the maximum muscular force we can apply against resistance. There are many benefits to improving strength such as:

- Increased strength of tendons and ligaments, which may help prevent strains and sprains while taking part in physical activity. This increases strength in an individual's joints and this may also have the potential to help him or her become more flexible.

- Reduced body fat and increased lean muscle mass, which helps the body's metabolic system run more effectively and enables food to be utilised more efficiently.

- It may help to reduce blood pressure.

What kind of strength is required for this exercise?

Did you know?

The strength, or force we can apply against resistance, can be demonstrated in three ways:

- **Static strength.** This involves resistance against a stationary load. For example, pushing as hard as you can against a wall or pulling against an equal force as in a 'tug of war'.

- **Dynamic strength.** This uses muscle contractions to move heavy loads, for example, in weight training or power lifting.

- **Explosive strength.** The use of fast and powerful muscular reactions. An example of this would be the static long jump.

- It may help to reduce the amount of cholesterol in the body, offering some protection from the 'furring up' of arteries, which can lead to heart disease.

Muscular endurance

Muscular endurance (or stamina) is the ability to repeat an activity for a length of time (for example, press-ups or sit-ups) without becoming tired. Muscular endurance can be developed through resistance training or circuit training.

Flexibility

Suppleness and flexibility is defined as the range of movement possible at joints. Up until the age of 40, ligaments, tendons and muscles are relatively elastic but after this age, movement in muscles and joints that are not used frequently can be decreased and eventually lost. This can cause problems and injuries if the body is suddenly asked to do something it has not done for a while.

Skill–related components

Speed

Speed is the ability to move a part of the body or the whole body quickly. Speed can be crucial in many sports where the activity is timed or you may be required to outpace an opponent. Speed is not just important for athletes, a quick physical reaction time might help you avoid injury in public service work or perhaps chase and run down criminal suspects.

Reaction time

This is how quickly messages are transmitted around the body. The brain receives information from a range of receptors in the body including: eyes, ears, skin and nose. The brain then reacts to this information. Putting a hand in a flame results in a pain signal being sent to the brain – this reacts by telling the hand to move away from the flame. The length of time the messages travel from the hand to the brain and back again is the reaction time.

Agility

This is the ability to move with quick fluid grace and it is critical for improving sports performance. It involves rapid changes in speed and direction while maintaining balance and skill. Like skill it can be developed with practice and is improved by developing strength, stamina and suppleness. The ability to change speed and direction rapidly could be of great benefit to the armed services in combat situations.

Coordination

Being coordinated involves using different parts of the body at the same time. Some actions require hand–eye coordination, for example catching a ball. Again, coordination is strongly linked to agility and can be practised with agility drills. This is an essential skill in the public services, which may require many body parts to be used simultaneously in activities such as firefighting.

3.2 Testing methods for fitness

The methods the public services have for testing fitness and performance can range from service to service. Their purpose, however, is always the same – to see if you are physically fit enough to take on the role you are applying for. The main aim of public service performance assessments or fitness tests is to determine your stamina and strength. Table 5.11 shows some of the tests that might be encountered in the public services and how they relate to the components of fitness outlined above.

Reasons for testing methods

An employer may have many reasons to ask employees to undertake fitness tests as they:

- assess current levels of fitness
- provide a baseline of an initial fitness level against which future progress can be monitored and measured
- can be used to ascertain level of fitness loss after injury, illness or pregnancy
- allow medical practitioners to recognise and assess some specific health problems such as heart disease
- can motivate you to do better
- allow you to see if a particular fitness programme is working
- make sure you are as fit to do a job now as you were when you joined a public service. This is why some public services have an annual fitness test.

Table 5.11: Methods used for testing fitness.

Feature being tested	How
Cardiovascular endurance	The **multi-stage fitness test** involves continuous running between two markers 20 m apart and in time to a set of pre-recorded bleeps. (The MSFT is often called the **bleep test** for this reason.)
	The advantage of this test is that large numbers of people can be tested at the same time but the disadvantages are that you need to be highly motivated to run until you can't go any further.
	The armed services also use the combat fitness test (CFT) which is an extended run completed with backpack and weapon.
Strength	The **grip test** measures the strength of an individual's grip by use of a grip strength dynamometer. The dynamometer is set at zero and the handle adjusted to fit the size of the palm. Then the dynamometer is simply squeezed as hard as possible. The reading on the gauge tells you how strong your grip is. Most people find the hand that they use frequently is the stronger.
Muscular endurance	The **press-up test** is an assessment of the muscular endurance of the chest, shoulders and arms. The total number of press-ups completed in one minute is the score. The press-ups for males and females differ as men should be in contact with the ground at their hands and toes while women should be in contact with the ground at their hands and knees or on a slightly raised bar. The resting position is up with elbows locked.
	The **sit-ups test** is also an assessment of muscular endurance but this time the muscles involved are in the abdomen and hips. The test usually involves the number of sit-ups completed in one minute.
Flexibility	The **sit and reach test** is a flexibility and suppleness assessment. The individual sits down with their legs straight out in front of them and the soles of their feet flat against a box with a measuring device such as a ruler or distance gauge on top of it. They then reach forward with the fingertips to see how far past their toes they can reach. The movement should be smooth and continuous rather than lunging. The test is very easy to administer but it only assesses hamstring flexibility rather than the flexibility of the whole body. The test is usually measured in centimetres and as a rough guide females tend to be slightly more flexible than males.
Speed	The **sprint test** involves the individual running as fast as possible down a 60 m course/track. The results are recorded. For most people the race should take well under one minute and can be completed without breathing.
Reaction time	One of the more common ways of testing **reaction time** is by rigging up a system where the performer pushes a button when a light comes on. Variations are available on the internet, where instead of pushing a button the individual clicks the mouse button when the background changes. The time taken to react will be monitored.
Agility	The **Illinois agility run** is a reasonably simple test to carry out, using only a flat, non-slip 10 x 5 m course, a series of cones and a stopwatch. The individuals start at the start line, lying on their front, hands by shoulders. When instructed they leap up and run the course.
Coordination	The **alternate hand wall toss test** is used for hand–eye coordination. The individual stands at a set distance from a wall (for example, 3 m). A ball is thrown underarm at the wall and the aim is to catch the ball with the opposite hand. The test can be timed and the successful number of catches recorded.

Assessment activity 5.5 **P6** **P7** **M3**

It is important to know what the fitness requirements are for your service and it will be essential to gather as much information on the fitness test before you apply to join a service as you can. That way you will be able to practise so that you are physically ready for the service you have chosen.

1. *Identify* components of and testing methods for fitness. **P6**
2. *Perform* fitness tests used by the uniformed public services. **P7**
3. *Demonstrate* improvements in performance in a fitness test used by the uniformed public services. **M3**

Grading tips

Your tutor will set out some public service fitness tests for you to complete, such as the MSFT, CFT or battle swim test. Once you identify the main components and the tests for them you should achieve **P6**. If you complete them you should achieve **P7**. To achieve **M3** you need to show that you have made an improvement in your performance on a fitness test.

4 Participate in a personal health improvement programme for public services

4.1 Personal health improvement

Personal health improvement included assessing factors such as your nutrition, fitness and lifestyle to see if or where you need to make changes. A good way to do this is via an improvement action plan.

Target setting

When you start your programme (or anything, for that matter) you need to decide on your aims and goals. To do this you need to give yourself achievable targets, which should lead to your ultimate goal, for example becoming a police officer or a Royal Marine Commando. Goals can be short term, medium term and long term. For example:

• Short-term goal – complete a 3-mile circuit, alternating walking and running (walk to a lamp post, run to the next one, walk to the next one, etc.).
• Medium-term goal – run the 3-mile circuit (this should be achievable after walking and running the course three times a week for four weeks).
• Long-term goal – achieve level 5.4 on the bleep test (this should be achievable after running 3 miles three times a week for a month).

As you can see in the example, each step towards the ultimate long-term goal builds on what has gone before and uses a plan for success.

Activity: Health Improvement Action Plan

Draw up a personal improvement action plan which highlights where in your diet, fitness or lifestyle you need to make changes. Outline exactly how you are going to change over a defined timescale.

Activity: Targets

What short-term, medium-term and long-term goals could you set for meeting the fitness requirements of your service?

List them and then speak to your health and fitness tutor about how best to put them into practice.

In order to be successful with your goal setting, use the SMART technique. Goals should be:

S – specific to your ultimate goal (Is this going to help me join the public service of my choice?)

M – measurable, for example, run 3 miles (Can I see what I've done?)

A – achievable (Is the task possible?)

R – realistic/relevant (Is this really going to help? Is it what I should be aiming to do?)

T – time-related, for example, 3 times a week for a month (Will I know when to be moving on with my goals?)

You should try to stick to your goals as much as possible but sometimes life might get in the way or maybe your goals are too hard (or too easy). In this case, sit down and look at your plan; how can you change it to fit the problem?

It is also good practice to use a training diary. This can be used to log each session you have completed so that you can monitor your performance. This will motivate you when you see how you've progressed. You can also note how you felt you're you were training as this could have an impact on whether the programme should be changed (you won't do it if you don't like it). Ensure that your goals are outlined clearly – that way you can link performance to your progress in achieving your goals.

Training

Training can take many forms (see Table 5.12), but the most common types of training follow the FITT principles. FITT stands for:

- **Frequency** – this is how often you train. For example, if you want to develop your cardiovascular stamina you can run up to 5 times a week. Once you've built it to the required level, you can change to running 3 times a week to maintain that level and use the rest of the time to concentrate on upper body strength. In another example, you may have been undertaking a simple strength circuit twice a week for the last 12 weeks and now want to devote more time to increasing strength – you decide to go to the gym Monday, Wednesday and Friday, instead of just twice.

- **Intensity** – this is how hard you train. It can be used to adapt training in many ways.

- **Time** – this is how long your session is. If you have increased the intensity, you may need to train for a shorter time but you have a harder work-out. Or you may be running further and therefore need a longer session. This will depend upon how much time is available, of course.

- **Type** – this is the type of training (you can change this). For example, to develop cardiovascular fitness, your first programme was to run continuously for 30 minutes. To improve your performance you may try Fartlek training in order to improve your speed at completing your distance. In terms of strength, after completing a programme using a simple circuit of 12 exercises for 3 times a week, you may wish to develop more strength using **pyramid training**.

Have you set your targets for your fitness training?

Table 5.12: Types of training methods.

Types of training methods	Description
Resistance training	Resistance training develops strength. The muscles work against a resistance (weight) to develop size and strength). In addition to strengthening the muscles, all the other soft tissues in the area that is worked are strengthened too, i.e. the tendons and ligaments. It is dangerous to jump straight into strength training as it is easy to damage not only the muscles but also the surrounding tendons and ligaments. In order to avoid this, a lightly challenging programme should be put together that gets the body used to lifting weights. The resistance should be reasonably light and repeated about 10–12 times (reps); use a circuit of the gym and aim to work most of the body in between 8 and 10 exercises. Go around two or three times: this is a simple circuit.
Continuous training	This is running, walking, swimming, cycling, etc. at a steady continuous pace. For best gains this should be performed for at least 20–30 minutes and at least three times per week. Running is often seen as the most effective way of developing this kind of fitness although it does have a higher incidence of injuries than swimming or walking.
Circuit training	This involves going quickly from one exercise apparatus to another and doing a prescribed number of exercises or time on each apparatus. This ensures the pulse rate is kept high and promotes overall fitness by generally working all muscle groups as well as heart and lungs.
Cross training	This is a training method which combines different activities to improve overall performance. For example, a combination of running to improve cardiovascular endurance coupled with a weights programme for strength.

Key term

Pyramid training – this is just one way to lift weights or engage in any strength-building activity and involves changing your repetitions and added weights for each set of each exercise. In other words, you'll start light and end heavy or start heavy and end light.

Activity: Training methods

Ask your health and fitness tutor which type of training they recommend for you in order to reach your goals?

Programme design

Designing a programme can be challenging, however using the acronym SPORT will help you get your training programme right. SPORT stands for:

Specific. Your training must be specific to your ultimate goals. This might include improving strength for potential Firefighters or cardiovascular endurance for Royal Marine Commandos.

Progressive. Your training must be progressive, this means it must become more challenging over time. This might include doing more repetitions in the gym or lifting more weight each time.

Overload. You should overload the muscle to get it to grow larger and stronger. This means making the muscle do things it is not used to, such as carrying more weight or working harder.

Relevant. The activities must be relevant to your goals. Are you doing the right activities for your fitness preparation?

Time. You need to allow enough time to train properly. This includes periods of rest time to allow the body to recover naturally. Going all out on a training programme can lead to over-training which may harm your motivation and fitness.

Review

Once you have completed your programme you can start to review it. This is where it's useful to refer to your training diary and collect feedback from others about your performance. Feedback can be gained from the following sources:

- your tutor
- uniformed service personnel
- your peers and colleagues
- your action plan targets.

You should review the training programme and the results achieved, determining your strengths and areas for improvement in each (see Figure 5.11).

The final question to ask is:

To what extent did the training programme achieve your identified goals? Compare your original goals with the results of your review.

Evaluating the programme

Hopefully, your review will have more strengths than areas for improvement. However, even if it didn't all work out to plan, don't worry – you should now have a good idea why and be able to modify and improve the programme for future use. This is essential to see further improvement and ties in directly to the principles of training.

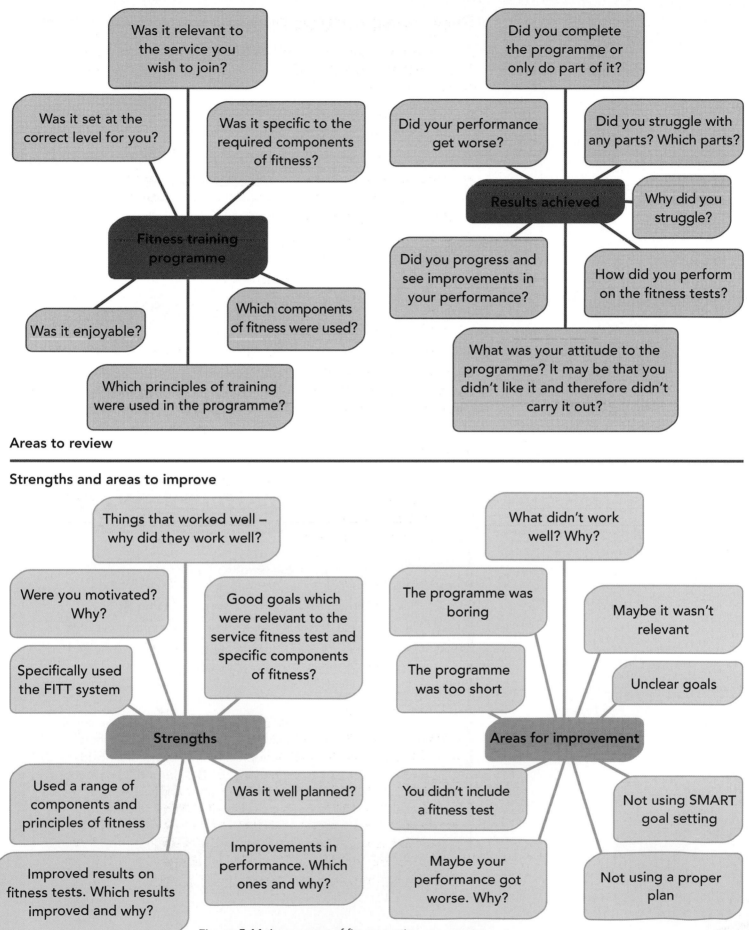

Areas to review

Strengths and areas to improve

Figure 5.11 Assessment of fitness testing programme

To evaluate the training programme, you need to look at the following:

- Use the areas for improvement to guide you.
- Do you need clearer goals?
- Was something missing? What was it?
- How can you make the programme more interesting to motivate you more?
- Can you make it more relevant?
- How can you change the programme so that you can carry on using it?
- Do you need to change the components you used?
- How about the principles of training?
- Frequency?
- Intensity?
- Type of training?
- Time spent training?

Goal setting, planning, completing, reviewing and evaluating your training programme should be a continual process. All professional athletes and coaches use this system to continue improving fitness and performance. After a while it should become second nature and you will certainly be reviewing and evaluating your techniques and performance without conscious effort. Make sure that you continue to use a training diary, though. It can be very easy to forget the results of performance and reviews.

Assessment activity 5.6 P8 M4 D3

This assessment requires you to work on your own personal health.

1 *Plan* a personal health improvement programme. P8
2 *Participate* in a personal health improvement programme. M4
3 *Create* an action plan for further improvement in health. D3

Grading tips

To achieve P8 you should produce your own unique personal health development programme, for M4 you need to show you have participated in your programme, this could include evidence such as a training diary. For D3 you should produce an action plan which evaluates your strengths and weaknesses and makes clear recommendations as to how you can further improve your health.

Corporal Dave Richards

Army Physical Training Instructor

My job is to ensure that the personnel in the army are fit and ready for combat. This includes a whole range of things from sporting activities to improve teamwork and coordination, to individual training to improve agility of endurance, to the preparation for the annual combat fitness test we have to do.

A typical day

A typical day for me could be spent in the gym instructing new recruits or supervising the health and safety of the personnel who use it. Or I could be delivering scheduled fitness sessions throughout the day.

The best thing about the job

It's great that other personnel come to me for advice on health and fitness issues. Without PTIs like myself there's a possibility the service men and women would not be fit for combat and that could cost lives. Army personnel need to be physically and mentally fit for duty and it's my job to make sure they are. I'm very proud of the work I do and I hope to progress further in physical training.

Think about it!

1 What topics have you covered in this unit that might give you the background to be a forces physical training instructor?

2 What knowledge and skills do you think you need to develop further if you want to be involved in fitness training in the future?

139

Just checking

1. What are the four chambers of the heart called?
2. What are the parts of the respiratory system?
3. What is the effect of a lack of sleep on physical performance?
4. What are the most common minerals found in food?
5. What are the FITT principles?

edexcel

Assignment tips

- The service you want to join may be different from other learners in your class but don't be concerned about this. Your training programme is likely to be very different from people who join other services. Don't be tempted to do the same as they do because it's easier than designing your own training programme. Remember, you are getting yourself ready for your service, following a training programme for police officer fitness standards won't be of much help if you want to be a Royal Marine.

- Health and safety is a key component of this unit. Remember to take care when training and if you have any medical problems or issues make sure you discuss them with your tutor and doctor. The training programme for your assesments should fit around your own personal needs.

- Keep a training diary throughout this unit. It will provide evidence for some of the criteria and help you monitor your progress towards your goals.

6 Citizenship, the individual and society

Most public service workers, whether they are police officers, firefighters or armed service personnel join a service because they want to make a difference in the lives of others or make society a better place to live in. Citizenship is a key part of this as it helps us understand the relationship between individuals and society and our rights and responsibilities. Public service workers must show good citizenship in their daily working lives and show an awareness of the communities they work with. If they did not demonstrate these good citizenship skills they would not be respected by the communities they serve and it would be very difficult for them to help change society for the better.

Being a good citizen means you respect the differences between people in your community and understanding that with the rights given to you by society come responsibilities to act appropriately towards others. The key to good citizenship is recognising that even one individual working alone can make a difference.

Learning outcomes

After completing this unit you should:

1. know what is meant by the terms citizen, citizenship, individual rights and human rights
2. understand the relationship between individuals, society and the public services
3. understand the importance of equal opportunities in society and the public services
4. be able to investigate the roles of statutory and non-statutory public services to the citizens and to a changing society.

Assessment and grading criteria

This table shows you what you must do in order to achieve a pass, merit or distinction grade, and where you can find activities in this book to help you.

To achieve a pass grade the evidence must show that the learner is able to:	To achieve a merit grade the evidence must show that, in addition to the pass criteria, the learner is able to:	To achieve a distinction grade the evidence must show that, in addition to the pass and merit criteria, the learner is able to:
P1 define the terms 'citizen', 'citizenship', 'individual rights', and 'human rights' **Assessment activity 6.2 page 156**	**M1** describe how citizens are protected by their individual and human rights **Assessment activity 6.2 page 156**	**D1** analyse how citizens are protected by their individual and human rights **Assessment activity 6.2 page 156**
P2 describe the qualities a good citizen requires to enter a public service **Assessment activity 6.1 page 153**	**M2** justify the requirements of good citizenship that are needed to enter a public service **Assessment activity 6.1 page 153**	
P3 explain how public services, citizens and society work together **Assessment activity 6.3 page 161**		
P4 explain why equal opportunities are important in society and the public services **Assessment activity 6.4 page 168**		
P5 illustrate how equal opportunities are enforced in the UK with reference to appropriate legislation **Assessment activity 6.4 page 168**	**M3** compare how two public services use legislation to address equal opportunities **Assessment activity 6.4 page 168**	**D2** evaluate the approaches used by public services to support society by addressing the main issues of equal opportunities **Assessment activity 6.4 page 168**
P6 explain the different ways in which public services have supported society **Assessment activity 6.5 page 171**	**M4** analyse the different ways in which public services have supported society **Assessment activity 6.5 page 171**	
P7 demonstrate the different ways in which public services have affected society **Assessment activity 6.6 page 172**		

How you will be assessed

This unit will be assessed by an internal assignment that will be designed and marked by the staff at your centre. The assignment is designed to allow you to show your understanding of the learning outcomes for citizenship. These relate to what you should be able to do after completing this unit. Assessments can be quite varied and can take the form of:

- reports
- leaflets
- presentations
- posters
- practical tasks
- case studies.

Sam, 16, widens her view on citizenship

This unit helped me to see that you have to be a good citizen if you want to work in the public services. You have to show care and commitment to the community around you and be aware of what is going on in the world if you are going to be successful in a service.

One of the things that I really enjoyed looking at was human rights. We looked at some case studies of where people had had their human rights infringed or taken away completely, and they were quite shocking. The most interesting thing for me was to realise that it isn't just poor countries where people's rights can be taken away, it can happen in rich countries like ours too. That's why you have to be a good citizen in the services, because they have a lot of power and influence over our lives, if they didn't behave to a high standard they could take away people's rights and abuse their power.

The good thing about this unit is that there are lots of opportunities for discussions in class, people have different views on rights and equality and it's really interesting to hear what other people think even if you don't agree with them sometimes. I know that when I join a service I will be able to use the information I learned in this unit to help me do my job better and be a better person.

Over to you!
Thinking about Sam's experience on the public services course shown above:
- What areas of citizenship might you find interesting?
- Could you start to read a daily newspaper or check a news website to keep up with current events?
- What preparation could you do for your assessments?

Table 6.1: Types of British citizenship.

Type	Detail
British citizens	People who gained British nationality because they are connected with the UK, for example: – being born in the UK – their parents were British citizens – they have registered to be a British citizen – they have applied to become a British citizen. This is the only group of people who have the right to live permanently in the UK and enjoy freedom of movement throughout the EU. This is called the ***Right of Abode***.
British dependent territories citizens (BDTC)	People who live in dependent British colonies, e.g.: – Gibraltar – British Virgin Islands These are territories which Britain still has responsibility for.
British overseas citizens (BOC)	These are groups of people who have a connection with the UK because they used to live in a former British colony which is now independent.
British nationals (overseas) (BNO)	People from Hong Kong were given the chance to acquire this status as many were unhappy at the thought of losing British nationality when Hong Kong was returned to China in 1997.
British protected persons (BPP)	Individuals who had a connection with a former British Protectorate. This is an overseas territory that Britain used to protect, such as the country of Brunei.
British subjects	Individuals who were British subjects under the 1948 British Nationality Act were allowed to keep their status under the 1981 Act. Applies mainly to citizens of Eire and India, which both had very strong links to the UK.

Case study: Gurkhas' right to live in the UK

The Gurkhas are Nepalese soldiers who are recruited into the British Army from their home country of Nepal. They have fought with the British Army for almost 200 years and are considered to be an elite fighting force having shown bravery, heroism and dedication to the UK in every conflict we have engaged in since Victorian times. They make up about 3 per cent of the British Army's total strength and 8 per cent of its infantry.

Gurkhas who retired before 1 July 1997 were not allowed to settle in the UK even if they had been wounded or disabled in battle. They had to resettle in Nepal regardless of how many years service they had given to the UK.

This was widely considered to be unfair and after a public campaign backed by several newspapers and celebrities the Home Secretary agreed to change the rules in May 2009 to allow retired Gurkhas and their families the right to live and settle in the UK as long as they had given at least 4 years service.

Now answer the following questions:

1 Why do you think the public considered it unfair that Gurkhas were not allowed to live in the UK after they retired?

2 Do you think Gurkhas show the qualities of a good citizen?

3 Do you think it is beneficial for the UK to have former Gurkhas living and working here? Explain your answer.

Gurkhas had to 'fight' for the right to live in the UK.

If you do not fall into any of the categories described in Table 6.1 then there are two main ways in which you can become a British citizen:

1 Registration. This is a way of becoming a British citizen if you already have some connection with the UK, such as being a British overseas citizen or a British protected person. You can also register if you gave up being a British citizen and went to live elsewhere and now you want your original citizenship back.

2 Naturalisation. This is where you can apply to become a British citizen if you have no connection to the UK at all. In order to qualify for naturalisation you must:

- have lived legally in the UK for five years
- be 18 years or over
- be of good character
- be of sound mind
- know a UK language such as English or Welsh
- want to stay connected with the UK.

You can also apply for naturalisation if you are married to a British citizen and have lived in the UK for three years or more. Some people think that it is too easy for people of other nationalities to become British, but the application process is very strict and many applicants are unsuccessful.

People who are successful in becoming British citizens have to take part in a citizenship ceremony. They are required to take an oath or an affirmation of allegiance and make a pledge of loyalty to the United Kingdom.

Oath of allegiance

I (name) swear by Almighty God that on becoming a British citizen, I will be faithful and bear true allegiance to Her Majesty Queen Elizabeth the Second, her Heirs and Successors, according to law.

Affirmation of allegiance (used when people do not want to swear by God)

I (name) do solemnly, sincerely and truly declare and affirm that on becoming a British citizen, I will be faithful and bear true allegiance to Her Majesty Queen Elizabeth the Second, her Heirs and Successors, according to law.

Pledge

I will give my loyalty to the United Kingdom and respect its rights and freedoms. I will uphold its democratic values. I will observe its laws faithfully and fulfil my duties and obligations as a British citizen.

A citizenship ceremony.

Moral citizen

The public services look for similar qualities of moral citizenship as the rest of society, usually this covers the following kinds of behaviour:

- **Community involvement**. This means being an active part of your community, perhaps in voluntary work or in local issues which matter to the community.

- **Taking responsibility for the safety of others**. This means making sure that you look after the people in your community, such as checking on elderly neighbours or driving safely where children are likely to be playing.

- **Taking responsibility for the safety of the environment**. This could mean joining groups like Neighbourhood Watch or reporting anything suspicious you see to the police.

- **A commitment to continually develop life skills**. This means you should want to make yourself a better person throughout your life by learning new things and undertaking new experiences.

- **A positive attitude which welcomes challenges**. The services will only employ people who are positive about their communities and have a commitment to making society a better place.

Activity: Visiting your armed services recruitment office

The armed services have lots of information on citizenship issues. Consider making an appointment to go to the local recruitment office and discuss their views of citizenship. You may find lots of useful information to help you with your assignments.

1.2 What is citizenship?

As you would expect, citizenship is all about being a citizen. It takes account of your legal and political status as well as your rights and responsibilities and how you behave in your community and wider society.

Citizenship can be looked at in two ways as we mentioned earlier when we looked at the term 'citizen'. It can mean a person's legal status and also their social and moral responsibilities.

Key factors in citizenship

Table 6.2: Key factors in citizenship.

Key factor	Explanation
Legal status	Your legal status is whether you are actually a legal citizen of a country, with the right to live in that country permanently and leave or return to the country whenever you like.
Political status	Your political status is whether you have a say in the political life of your community of your country. Will you be able to vote when you are old enough? If you can take part in the politics of a society you have more chance of changing it for the better.
Rights and responsibilities	As a citizen of the UK you are allowed certain rights and freedoms, such as the right to privacy or the right to free health care and the right to an education. With these rights come legal responsibilities, these are things you must be prepared to do in order to enjoy the rights you are given. Responsibilities can include things such as not breaking the law, paying your taxes and being prepared to fight for your country if necessary.
Responsibility to others	A citizen has the moral responsibility to do the best that they can for others. Society can only exist when we reach agreements and cooperate with each other. We have a responsibility to judge people fairly rather than discriminating against them and to treat others with consideration and respect.
Public life and affairs	A citizen should try to live their life as a role model for others, and they should be honest and trustworthy in their public life. This is particularly true of the public services.
Behaviour and actions	Your behaviour and actions can indicate what kind of citizen you are and demonstrate whether you care about your community. Do you drop litter in the street or do you care about your environment? Do you check on elderly neighbours or do you ignore them? Citizens can be judged on their behaviour and actions.

Did you know?

Citizenship is like a contract between you and the country you live in. You get to enjoy all the rights and protection which society gives you, but you must be prepared to pay for it by fulfilling your responsibilities. Responsibilities here covers legal responsibilities and moral responsibilities. You must fulfil legal responsibilities by law and you should fulfil moral responsibilities in order to be a good person.

Case study: MPs' expenses

In May 2009 the *Daily Telegraph* newspaper obtained a full list of the expenses claimed by Members of Parliament and released the information to the public over a period of a few weeks. The public were shocked and disgusted at the expense claims which included paying for mortgages which no longer existed, switching the property they were using as their main home to claim more money and refurbishing properties at the taxpayers' expense and then selling them for profit.

There were also allegations about MPs employing family members on high salaries for work which could not be evidenced and spending taxpayers money on items such as a duck house for a pond, clearing debris from a moat and cleaning a swimming pool at a country home.

After the scandal became public many MPs were forced to step down from their jobs or pay back significant amounts of money.

Now answer the following questions:

1   Why do you think the public were angry at the expenses scandal?

2   What harm do you think the scandal did to the reputations of MPs?

3   Why do public servants like MPs have to be careful about their public conduct?

4   Did the MPs display good citizenship? Explain your answer.

What makes a good citizen?

A good citizen is someone who takes their responsibilities to society seriously and maintains high standards of personal conduct in their public and private life.

Activity: Are you a good citizen?

Think about what qualities a good citizen might have and write down a list of as many as you can think of. Looking at your list consider how many of those qualities you have shown recently – are you a good citizen?

There are many possible qualities that a good citizen might possess, for example:

Self-discipline. Self-discipline is about being able to manage your own behaviour and conduct. It is essential to being a good citizen and is a quality the public services like to see in their new recruits and serving officers. If you have self-discipline you are likely to be reliable, see a job through to its end rather than get bored and leave it unfinished. Good citizens who work in the community or volunteer have to motivate themselves every day to do their jobs and not respond to people who may be negative or hostile about improving society.

Being a good neighbour. This can take many forms such as being an active member of your local neighbourhood watch, doing some shopping for a poorly neighbour or volunteering to baby-sit in your community. It is about keeping an eye out for people who might be in difficulties and seeing what you can do to help. A good citizen won't turn a blind eye if someone in their community is in distress, they will try to help out where they can.

Fairness. Good citizens are fair. They do not jump to conclusions and will listen to many sides of the same story rather than judging a situation before they know the full story. They treat people equally based on their skills and abilities rather than their colour or religion and they do not discriminate against other people who may be different from themselves.

Respect. Respect is about valuing each person's qualities and skills and understanding that society is made up of very different groups of people. The fact that some people may appear different from ourselves or may believe things we do not believe does not make them any better or worse than anyone else. A good citizen respects these differences and values the contributions made to society by all individuals.

Use of language. The language you use in your personal and public life is very important. If you use unpleasant terms for people, or call people names based on their race or sexuality you are not displaying the qualities the services might expect from a good citizen. Sometimes people don't even realise the terms they use could be considered offensive until someone points it out to them. You need to be aware that what you say and how you say it can have a huge impact on the willingness of the services to employ you.

Empathy. This is the ability to stand in another person's shoes and see how they feel about an issue. A good citizen will have the ability to see things from another perspective and feel how someone else might feel in those circumstances. This is an incredibly useful skill in the public services in terms of understanding why people behave the way they do and supporting vulnerable members of the community, such as victims of crime.

Authority. Good citizens are expected to deal with different levels of authority. Authority is the legitimate use of power over others. For example, a police officer has authority over the arrest of law breakers, a leading firefighter might have authority over her watch in how a fire is dealt with, parents have authority over their children. Good citizens will respect the authority of another or they themselves may have authority and should use it wisely to the benefit of the community they live in.

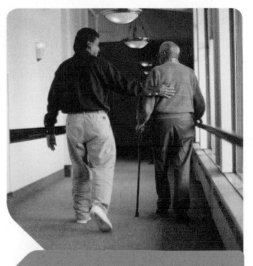

What everyday action can you take to be a good citizen?

Expectations. Having high expectations is the first stage in reaching them. A good citizen believes the best of people and genuinely believes change is possible. If you believe that nothing can change then nothing will change, it is only when you are motivated by expectations of something better that people are prepared to work together to achieve change.

Good citizenship and entry into the public services

These qualities of a good citizen are very similar to the qualities which are looked for in the public services. The public services value recruits who are disciplined, motivated, caring and involved in the community. By working towards being a good citizen you are improving your chances of being recruited into the public services.

Case study: The Fire Service

The firefighter giving orders is wearing the white hard hat while the rest of the team wear yellow.

The Fire and Rescue Service has a varied role including emergency response to fires, dealing with major incidents and safety inspections. The role of a firefighter is physically and emotionally challenging and good citizenship qualities are very important. The Fire Service looks for qualities such as:

- teamwork
- community involvement
- reliability
- ability to act quickly
- understanding
- flexibility.

Firefighters go to work every day knowing that they may have to put their own safety on the line in order to protect others. The real test of a good citizen is whether they are prepared to put their own safety on the line in order to protect their community.

Now answer the following questions:

1 Why do firefighters need good citizenship qualities?

2 What aspects of citizenship are important to the Fire Service?

3 Are you a good enough citizen to be a firefighter? Explain your answer.

Assessment activity 6.1

BTEC P2 M2

Good citizenship is an essential quality you need to be recruited into the public services and to perform well once you have been accepted. Produce an information sheet which covers the following tasks:

1 *Describe* the qualities a good citizen is required to have to enter a public service. P2

2 *Justify* the requirements of good citizenship that are needed to enter a public service. M2

Grading tips

For P2 you should make a list of good citizenship qualities and provide a brief description of each quality. For M2 you should say why citizenship qualities are needed in the services and why each quality is considered important and useful. Remember this task is asking you for an information sheet so you could include a table of qualities, images and pictures to inform the reader, also remember to check your spelling and grammar before you hand it in.

PLTS

This assignment may be useful for the reflective learner (RL) part of your PLTS course when you consider what qualities of good citizenship are needed in the services.

Functional skills

This assignment may also help you to develop your functional skills in ICT if you word process your information sheet and include images or tables.

Did you know?

Women's right to vote in the UK was formally taken away by the Reform Act of 1832 and the right was not returned to all women until the Equal Franchise Act of 1928.

1.3 Individual and human rights

Individual rights

Individual rights are a set of freedoms that an individual citizen can expect to have in a society. These rights can change from country to country and can also change over time. Rights are not always the same, they are given to individuals by the state or country they live in and can be removed or changed by a legal process whenever the state thinks it is appropriate to do so.

In the UK we do not have a written document that sets out all the rights a person is entitled to. A document that sets out rights is called a constitution and the USA has a very famous constitution which sets out the rights a US citizen is entitled to and the limits the government has to work to. A constitution protects citizens against governments that might want to take away their individual rights.

Although we don't have a constitution in the UK we do have rights which citizens are entitled to. These are found in:

- the Acts of Parliament
- common law
- customs and traditions.

Human rights

Human rights are rights which all humans should be able to claim regardless of their nationality, colour, religion, sexuality, gender, race or any other factor. In most countries human rights are guaranteed by law, but unfortunately there are countries where people are denied their human rights.

Human rights cover political, social, moral and religious issues. The main document used worldwide as a standard for human rights is The United National Declaration of Human Rights. This document contains 30 rights which each human being is entitled to.

Link

For more information on the courts system see page 220.

Did you know?

The public services often have a zero-tolerance approach to drug use. If you fail a drugs test you will be discharged or sacked.

Activity: United Nations Declaration of Human Rights

Go to the United Nations website, available via Hotlinks (see page viii), and look up the declaration.

Read all 30 rights. Are there any that you think are the most important? Are there any that you don't understand? Are there any that you disagree with?

Discuss your findings with the rest of your class.

In the UK our human rights are protected by an act of Parliament called the Human Rights Act 1998 which we will look at in more detail in the equal opportunities section of this unit on page 167. Both individual and human rights are enforced by our criminal and civil justice system, this is made up of the courts, judges and lawyers.

Case study: Drugs testing in the public services

People have the right to privacy. However, any public services operate a random drugs testing procedure to make sure that potential recruits and serving officers are not using illegal drugs. Public service workers are not like other workers, they are responsible for the lives and safety of the public on a daily basis. This means they may have to use potentially lethal equipment and weapons and must be in a fit state of mind to respond to emergencies and incidents quickly and professionally. The use of illegal drugs means that a public service officer might not be able to do their job and possibly put their colleagues and the public at risk.

All of the armed services have Compulsory Drug Testing (CDT) teams who can turn up at any armed service place of work, including bases abroad and ships or submarines, at any time. They select the servicemen and women they are going to test and those chosen must provide a urine sample. This sample is then tested for a range of illegal drugs such as marijuana and cocaine. In the Royal Navy in 2008 10,876 tests were conducted worldwide, of which 58 were positive, which is about 0.5 per cent of the total tested.

The civilian services operate a similar approach but because fire brigades and police constabularies operate in particular areas rather than across the whole country their policies can differ slightly. For example, the drugs testing policy of South Yorkshire Police was introduced in January 2007 while for the Derbyshire Police it was September 2006. South Yorkshire Police plan around 300 drug tests per year on recruits and serving officers while Derbyshire Police test new recruits only. Since police drugs testing costs come out of their normal budget they have to be careful how many they do as the more money spent on drugs testing the less there will be to actually do the job of policing the streets.

Now answer the following questions:

1 Do you think it is right that public service workers have to give up their right to privacy?

2 How much of their budget do you think the police should spend on testing their own officers?

1.4 Other rights

There are several other rights which are important to consider, these are described in Table 6.3.

Table 6.3: Rights in addition to human and individual rights.

Right	Explanation
Rights of service users and customers	When you use a public service, or indeed any service, you have a right to expect a minimum standard of service from them. This might include respect, following up your query or complaint in a timely manner, courtesy and efficiency. The public services try to provide services to the public that are as user-friendly as possible and are designed to help with their problems.
Rights of employees	Employees have many rights while in employment, these include: parental leave, the minimum wage, a safe and healthy environment, an environment free of discrimination, time limits on working hours and a contract of employment. The government website, which covers a range of public service issues, discusses each of these and more rights in lots of detail. You can find it via Hotlinks (see page viii).
Rights of employers	As with employees, employers have certain rights they should expect from employees, such as: a minimum notice period before an employee leaves, a satisfactory level of performance, the employee not bringing the company or organisation into disrepute.
Participation in democratic and electoral processes	If you are a citizen of a country there is an expectation that you will take part in its political life, this might mean voting in elections or standing for election yourself. In some countries you must vote by law, but in the UK it remains an individual choice. If you choose not to vote you are choosing not to have a say in how your country is run. We live in a democratic society, this means that all adults are entitled to have a say at election time about what the government should or should not be doing or whether we need a new government. Because we live in a democratic society you should respect everyone's right to have their views heard.

 ## Case study: Human rights

In June 2009 Debbie Purdy took a human rights issue to the House of Lords. Ms Purdy has a disease called multiple sclerosis, which may lead to a deterioration in her quality of life to such an extent that she would want to commit suicide. The nature of the disease means that if her disease progresses to a certain stage she will be unable to end her own life and will need help. In some countries, such as Switzerland, there are special clinics where people can go if they want to end their lives but if someone helps them go to the clinic they could be prosecuted and imprisoned.

Ms Purdy went to court to find out whether her husband would be prosecuted and sent to prison if he helped her travel to Switzerland to one of these special clinics. In the UK someone who helps another person commit suicide is guilty of a criminal offence and may spend several years in prison, Ms Purdy does not want this to happen to her husband.

The House of Lords does not support assisted suicide in the UK, but it did ask the Crown Prosecution Service, who are responsible for taking people to court in England and Wales, to issue guidance on what will happen to people who help other people travel abroad to die. This will help very ill people and their relatives make an informed decision about what will happen to loved ones if they help.

Now answer the following questions:

1 What's your view on assisted suicide?

2 Do you think relatives and loved ones should be imprisoned if they help a person who wants to die travel to a clinic in another country where it is legal?

3 Which human rights are affected by this case study?

BTEC Assessment activity 6.2

Being able to understand and explain the key terms in the citizenship unit is important. The public services consider a knowledge of citizenship very important and you should be able to define some key words and explain how individual and human rights work.

Working in small groups or pairs

As part of a pair or in a small group produce an A3 poster or wall display which covers the following tasks:

1   *Define* the terms 'citizen', 'citizenship', 'individual rights' and 'human rights'. **P1**

2   *Describe* how citizens are protected by their individual and human rights. **M1**

3   *Analyse* how citizens are protected by their individual and human rights. **D1**

Grading tips

P1 is a very straightforward task – research the definitions for all four terms and include the best ones on your poster.
M1 and **D1** are very similar tasks. For **M1** you have to provide a description of how citizens are protected by their rights – you could give some examples of human rights from the United Nations Declaration of Human Rights and describe how they protect people from violence or discrimination.
In **D1** you have to analyse how citizens are protected and this means going into more detail about how rights help protect people – you could provide a case study of a situation where rights have been protected. Remember that you have been asked to produce a poster, use plenty of images to make sure your poster is eye-catching and informative.

PLTS

Conducting research into different definitions and how rights protect people gives you the opportunity to develop your independent enquirer skills.

2 The relationship between individuals, society and the public services

There is a complicated relationship between individuals, society and the public services. They are interlinked with each other and it can be difficult to tell where one ends and another begins. They each have an effect on the others that can be both positive and negative.

2.1 The public services

The public services as a whole provide both individuals and society with a variety of functions and roles such as:

- defence
- protection
- emergency aid
- medical assistance
- victim support
- investigation
- crime prevention
- social welfare
- education
- peacekeeping
- public safety.

The individual public services can have very different roles and functions, these are covered in detail in earlier units (see page 83).

The public services exist to provide us with services that we could not necessarily provide ourselves with. They are provided by the state or country you live in, but paid for by individuals through the taxes they pay. This is one key aspect of the relationship between individuals, society and the services as you can see in Figure 6.1.

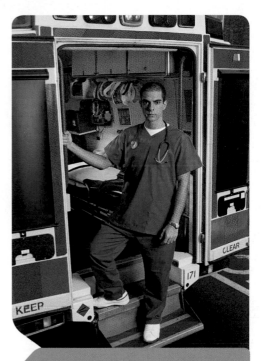

Medical assistance is one of the public services provided to individuals and society. How many others can you think of?

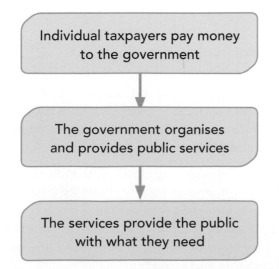

Individual taxpayers pay money to the government

↓

The government organises and provides public services

↓

The services provide the public with what they need

Figure 6.1: Relationship between individual, society and the services.

Although it is possible that if you were very rich you could afford to pay for your own fire service, police service, armed services, private health care, private education and your own local amenities, most of society is not quite so wealthy. It makes more sense for us all to pay a small proportion of our income to the government who organises these services on our behalf by pooling all our money together.

The public services serve our society and individuals in a number of ways. Public servants respond to the government and since the government is elected by individuals to represent their views, they are effectively carrying out the wishes of individuals in society. This is another part of the relationship between society, individuals and the public services as shown in Figure 6.2:

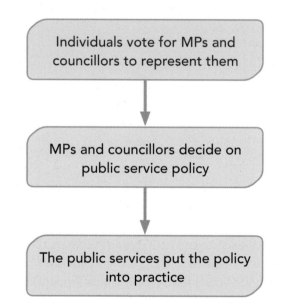

Figure 6.2: Relationship between individuals, society and the services in context of decisions and policy.

Not everyone is always happy with the role taken by our public services. Although the services can choose the best way to deal with particular situations such as fires and public order situations their main job is to implement government policy. They have a duty to obey orders even if they don't approve of them.

The public services also work very closely with individuals on a day-to-day basis. This might involve treating them for injuries or illnesses, dealing with prisoners, dealing with victims of crime or fire and working with young people at risk of crime. The whole nature of the public services is that they serve the needs of individuals and society ensuring that individuals are safe and cared for.

Activity: Training methods

If you are not happy with government policy you can take it up with your local MP or councillor.

Are there any other courses of action you could take if you were dissatisfied with the actions of a public service?

2.2 The individual

Individuals can choose the role they take in society and they can also choose how much they want to participate in society. They can participate in the following ways:

Locally, as a member of the local council or by participating in volunteer work in the area, or serving on local committees.

Nationally, by choosing to stand as a Member of Parliament and have a say on national issues or by joining a union that has a voice nationally, or a charity that lobbies the government.

Internationally, by taking part in the international community through voluntary work in less developed countries or by acting as a member of the armed service in peacekeeping or international aid missions to help those who are less fortunate.

It is important to remember that all of the public services are made up of different individuals and the role of each one of them is of vital importance to the performance of the service as a whole. In the services, individuals must rely on each other for their safety and security and there are many jobs which cannot be done by just one person; other individuals must team up to get the work done. The contribution of each individual member of the service is valued and respected.

The individual is very important in society, in fact without individuals there would be no society. The individuality of each citizen is protected with rights so that every person can choose how to express themselves, choose their religion, education, beliefs, decide where to live and how to live. Although society provides us with the services to help us in our day-to-day lives it does not aim to take away our freedoms, unless in doing so it believes it makes us all safer. The rights of individuals should be protected and only a poor government would seek to take them away. Individuals can also stand up and challenge government rules and have them changed. There are many examples of one person or a small group of people starting a movement which changed society and the public services.

The rights of each individual in our society is protected. What are some of the ways the public services protect the individual?

Activity: The importance of individuals

There are many individuals throughout history who have made a significant difference to society and the lives of their fellow citizens. Some examples are:

- Dr Martin Luther King Jr
- Mother Theresa
- Mahatma Gandhi
- Nelson Mandela
- Harvey Milk
- Florence Nightingale
- Keir Hardy
- William Wilberforce
- Elizabeth Fry
- Emmeline Pankhurst.

Research one or two of these individuals and find out what difference they made to society and what difference they made to their fellow individuals.

2.3 Society

A society is a group of individuals who bond together and become dependent upon each other for their daily needs. Individuals in a society may share common values, culture and institutions. Society works by providing the individuals with living conditions and services that they couldn't achieve if alone. In turn, each individual contributes and shares with the rest of society.

For example, a builder may provide homes for people, but while he is doing this someone needs to educate his children (a teacher), someone may take care of his elderly parents (a nurse) and someone needs to design the houses he builds (an architect). In this way we are all dependent on others.

Societies can have many structures which are often based around a political system such as **capitalism** or **communism**, or based around the primary means of survival such as agriculture. In a modern democracy society may be structured as shown in Figure 6.3.

Key terms

Capitalism – a system of running a country where wealth and the ways or producing wealth (such as factories or industry) are owned by private individuals.

Communism – a system of running a country where wealth and the ways of producing wealth are owned by the state on behalf of all its citizens.

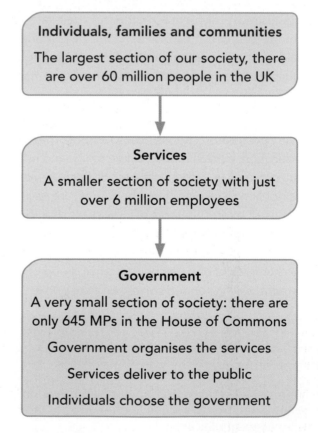

Individuals, families and communities

The largest section of our society, there are over 60 million people in the UK

Services

A smaller section of society with just over 6 million employees

Government

A very small section of society: there are only 645 MPs in the House of Commons

Government organises the services

Services deliver to the public

Individuals choose the government

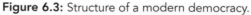

Figure 6.3: Structure of a modern democracy.

The UK is often called a representative democracy as all registered voters have the right to elect a representative who will take the views of a community to local or national government. The government can then choose to act upon those views or choose another course of action. In a democratic society all adults have an equal right to vote and have their voice heard.

In a sense the UK is a monarchy and not a true democracy at all as our head of state is Queen Elizabeth II. The Queen is also head of the government, Church of England and the armed services. Since she is unelected and gained her position through birth rather than through a democratic process. However, since political power is held by a democratically elected government, the UK is in fact a democracy. This sort of arrangement is called a constitutional monarchy. Other constitutional monarchies include the Netherlands and Japan.

It is also important to remember that our society is made up of many different groups of people with different languages, cultures and traditions who all find a home under the larger umbrella of British society. This is what it means to be **multi-cultural**. There are lots of countries like ours which are multi-cultural, the USA is a good example as is Australia.

Did you know?

Serving prisoners were banned from voting in elections in the UK. A landmark human rights case called Hirst v UK was taken to the European Court of Human Rights, which found that the UK was unlawful in not allowing prisoners to vote. What are your views on allowing those who have broken the law to have a say in how society is run?

Key term

Multi-cultural – describes a society where individuals and groups from different cultural or racial backgrounds can exist peacefully, side by side.

Activity: Diversity in your classroom

Groups of people are often more diverse than you might think. Your class may have 20 or 30 individuals in it who are all from a variety of cultural backgrounds.

Send a piece of paper round your class and ask each person to write down where their family originally comes from. Use the results to draw up a chart on the board or flipchart paper and discuss with your group how diverse you all are.

BTEC Assessment activity 6.3 P3

The relationship between the public services, citizens and society is very important and as a potential public service recruit it is vital you understand these relationships. Produce a leaflet that you could give to members of the public to explain these relationships. Make sure it covers the following task:

1 *Explain* how public services, citizens and society work together. P3

Grading tips

This is a straightforward task – in your leaflet you need to show the public the relationship between the services, individual citizens and society. You might find this easier to do by drawing some diagrams of the links between them and then adding some written explanation on the diagrams.

PLTS

By working on the relationships between different parts of society, you will be developing your independent enquirer skills.

3 The importance of equal opportunities in society and the public services

Equal opportunities are important for both society and the public services. Equality and equal opportunities are based around the ideas of fairness and respect. It is the idea that everyone ought to be able to take part in the political, social and cultural life of a society regardless of their personal traits and characteristics such as:

- gender
- religion
- sexuality
- race
- disability
- class.

3.1 Equal opportunities in society

This is important to society because if you exclude certain groups based on one or more of the above characteristics you lose the contribution they can make to society. For example at one time it was frowned upon for middle class married women to work. Then the needs of industry in the First World War and the Second World War, when women had to take over the bulk of jobs as the men were away fighting, changed this view. If women today were excluded from the jobs market then 50 per cent of the talent and skill in the country would be going to waste. This clearly does not benefit society, which needs a skilled and diverse workforce to compete against other countries.

The educational system in the UK is free and available to all children and young people up to the age of 18. After this point education is still offered but it has to be paid for either by the individual themselves or via a student loan system. Education can challenge our **prejudices** and make us rethink how we look at others. Why should any individual be worth less than any other just because they have a different colour skin or have a disability? Each individual may be very different from another, but that doesn't mean they are worth more or less than anyone else.

In the UK equal opportunities are enforced with Acts of Parliament which make it illegal to discriminate against others on grounds of race, sexual orientation, disability or religion in matters such as employment, education or providing public services. The main UK laws are described in Table 6.4.

Key term

Prejudice – a negative way of thinking about a person or group of people based on personal opinions rather than evidence.

Table 6.4: Equal opportunities legislation.

Equal opportunities legislation	Description
Sex Discrimination Act 1975	This is a law that makes it illegal to discriminate against someone on the grounds of their gender or marital status in the workplace, education, transport and the provision of goods and services. This could cover things such as job interviews, promotion, college courses and driving licences. It also covers issues such as sexual harassment. Although many people don't realise it, the act applies to men and women equally and a man could use the act to protect his rights just as easily as a woman.
Equal Pay Act 1970	This is an important piece of law as it stops employers paying people more based on their gender. If a man and a woman are doing the same job or work which is considered of equal status then they should receive the same pay. This act also applies to things like holiday pay, pensions and some kinds of bonuses.
Human Rights Act 1998	This act protects the rights of individuals in the UK from the government, public services or individuals who might want to take your rights away. It tells you what rights you are entitled to in law, these rights are: • the right to life • freedom from torture and degrading treatment • freedom from slavery and forced labour • the right to liberty • the right to a fair trial • the right not to be punished for something that wasn't a crime when you did it • the right to respect for private and family life • freedom of thought, conscience and religion, and freedom to express your beliefs • freedom of expression • freedom of assembly and association • the right to marry and to start a family • the right not to be discriminated against in respect of these rights and freedoms • the right to peaceful enjoyment of your property • the right to an education • the right to participate in free elections • the right not to be subjected to the death penalty. If any of these rights and freedoms are breached, you have a right to go to court and make a complaint, even if the breach was by someone in authority, such as a member of the public services.
Race Relations Act 1976	This act makes it illegal to discriminate against someone or harass them based on their nationality, colour, ethnic, racial or national group. This could mean employment conditions such as pensions, pay, promotions and so on.

Table 6.4: (contd) Equal opportunities legislation.

Disability Discrimination Act 1995	This act makes it illegal to discriminate against people based on a disability. It defined what a disability was and as with the Sex Discrimination Act and the Race Relations Act it banned discrimination in the workplace, education, transport and the provision of goods and services.
Freedom of Information Act 2000	This act made the public services and public sector in general more open with the information they have and collect. It made it possible for members of the public to request access to information held by the services, although these requests can be denied if the information might affect the rights of others to privacy or might affect issues of security.
Employment Equality Regulations 2003 and 2006	The 2003 regulations ban employers from discriminating against employees based on their **sexual orientation** or their religious beliefs. The 2006 regulations ban employers from discriminating against employees based on their age.

Key term

Sexual orientation – a term used to describe your sexual preference.

Many of these laws have been extended and clarified over the years by changes to the original acts called 'amendments'. These amendments don't normally change the original Act of Parliament but they can make the law clearer and extend it to cover different things. This is necessary as society changes over time.

3.2 Equal opportunities in the public services

Equal opportunities in the public services means exactly the same as it does in society. It is about respecting the contributions of all members of the organisation and serving all members of the public regardless of their ethnic background, gender or sexuality. However, there are some differences in how equal opportunities are implemented in the public services and how they are implemented in society.

Activity: Equal opportunities in the public services

In the armed services there are some job roles which are not open to women, such as serving in the infantry or as a submariner. This does not promote equal opportunities. Can you think why the armed services have reached this decision? Discuss the issue with your colleagues and make a list of possible answers.

Key term

Diversity – the differences between people or groups, such as gender, religion, ethnicity or social class.

Attitudes to equality have changed greatly in the public services over the last 30 years. It used to be the case that the British uniformed services, as a whole, were mainly made up of white males, but this is changing. The services now realise that they must reflect the communities they serve and must welcome more **diversity** in the form of more women or more ethnic minorities.

The impact of equality legislation on the services has been enormous, but the public services in general often have exemptions from some equality legislation in order to ensure they can remain operationally effective.

Case study: Armed service exemption from the Disability Discrimination Act 1995

The statement below was issued by Baroness Taylor of Bolton on behalf of the Ministry of Defence.

'The Armed Forces have an exemption from the employment provisions of the Disability Discrimination Act 1995 because all service personnel need to be combat effective in order to meet a worldwide liability to deploy. This means that everyone who joins the Armed Forces undergoes a rigorous selection and initial training process to ensure that they can withstand the hardship and challenges of military service.

The Armed Forces do not allow units to have a protected role or reduced commitment, which means that everyone is liable to deploy and to fight anywhere in the world, even if only in self-defence. Accordingly, the MoD has concluded that it is essential that exemptions from domestic and international disability legislation are retained. For this reason the Armed Forces' exemption from the DDA has been replicated in the Equality Bill. This is required to ensure the continued combat effectiveness of the Armed Forces, as decisions on operational effectiveness must be taken by MoD Ministers, accountable to Parliament and based on military advice, not by the courts. The Armed Forces must be able to determine and set their own standards, based on the tasks to be performed.

The Government do not expect the rationale for the exemption from the DDA to change, hence there are no plans to remove this exemption.

The Armed Forces perform a role which is fundamentally different from those of other organisations, such as the police and the fire services. All service personnel are weapons-trained and need to be able to respond to the uniquely harsh realities and complexities of warfare. This involves deployment overseas and prolonged working in stressful situations and arduous environments. Service in the police and the fire services is intrinsically different, not least because there is no requirement for everyone to be weapons-trained, or to serve overseas for prolonged periods.'

Now answer the following questions:

1 What are the Baroness's reasons for not allowing individuals with disabilities to join the armed services?

2 Do you agree with these reasons? Explain your answer.

3 What would the impact on the armed services be if they had to obey disability discrimination law?

Equality legislation has changed the way the public services operate, particularly in areas such as:

- recruitment
- training
- interaction with the public.

The Sex Discrimination Act 1975. This act had an impact on the fitness tests for the uniformed services as it is considered to be indirect discrimination when a higher proportion of one sex can meet fitness tests compared to the other. It also had an impact on recruitment with the police services in England and Wales recruiting more female officers. However, despite this law and its many amendments over the years the public services are still male dominated. The Home Office puts the figure for female police officers as 25.1 per cent in March 2009. This means that three quarters of police officers are male. Estimates in 2008 put the number of female firefighters at just 3 per cent. Although attitudes in the public services are changing, clearly more needs to be done in terms of encouraging females to apply and ensuring the opportunities they have are free from discrimination.

This act has also had an impact on how the public services deal with females in the community with many police initiatives to change the treatment received by rape victims and victims of domestic violence, who are usually female. This change has required officers to be trained to deal with these issues more sensitively.

The Race Relations Act 1976. This act made it illegal to discriminate against individuals based on their ethnic background. This has had significant effects on the services in terms of how officers are trained to deal with their own prejudices both in terms of recruiting ethnic minority officers and also in terms of how they deal with members of the public. However as with female recruitment, black and ethnic minority recruitment still has a long way to go in the services if they are going to represent the communities they serve. In March 2009 the percentage of ethnic minority police officers in England and Wales was 4.4 per cent, of ethnic minority firefighters in 2008 was 3 per cent and the RAF recorded just 2.6 per cent of ethnic minorities in 2008–9. The percentage of ethnic minorities in the population at the time of the 2001 census was 7.9 per cent.

Case study: Stephen Lawrence

A key issue which affected the approach of the public services to racial equality was the murder of a young black teenager called Stephen Lawrence in 1993. Stephen was an 18-year-old student who was stabbed multiple times by a gang of white youths while he was waiting at a bus stop. The murder was handled by the Metropolitan Police Service who failed to conduct the investigation in an appropriate manner by demonstrating a lack of respect for Stephen's family and black witnesses, a lack of urgency in dealing with aspects of the investigation and a refusal by many officers to accept that the crime was racially motivated. The Metropolitan Police Service were labelled as institutionally racist by the report into the murder conducted in 1999 by Sir William Macpherson.

'One of the things that I hope will come out of the Inquiry is for everyone to see that the things we have been saying for the past 5 years are true. I hope that this can be a step towards ensuring that when another tragedy is suffered by the black community the police act responsibly and investigate the crime properly. When a policeman puts his uniform on, he should forget all his prejudices. If he cannot do that, then he should not be doing the job because that means that one part of the population is not protected from the likes of those who murdered Stephen.'

Neville Lawrence, quoted in the Macpherson Report, 1999

Now answer the following questions:

1 Why was the investigation of the murder of Stephen Lawrence flawed?

2 Why did the media cover this story in detail?

3 Do you think the media has helped improve the situation for reporting racist incidents to the police?

The Race Relations (Amendment Act) 2000. This came about in response to the Stephen Lawrence inquiry. It made it law that the public services must promote racial equality, consult with communities, tackle racial discrimination and publish reports on how well they have done these things.

The Human Rights Act 1998. This provided all citizens with a set of rights (See Table 6.4). This piece of law has had a significant impact on the services, as all officers must be trained about the rights and freedoms the public are entitled to and make sure they do not break them as the service could be taken to court.

The public services must build equality legislation into their dealings with the public. Figures 6.4 and 6.5 show how the Royal Navy and the British Army have taken measures to address equal opportunities.

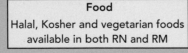

Recruitment
Campaign for increased recruitment of ethnic minority applicants at both officer and other ranks launched

Gender issues
75% of roles in RN are open to women (recruitment of women has doubled and 20% of officer entrants are female)

Religion
Adequate provision made for spiritual and moral needs
Commanding officers encourage religious observance by those under them
Sympathetic consideration is given to officially recognised non-Christian faiths

Dress
Sikh men may wear turbans for general service
Muslim women may wear long sleeves

Food
Halal, Kosher and vegetarian foods available in both RN and RM

Naval Swimming Test
Option for test to be carried out with female staff only attending

Figure 6.4: Equal opportunities in the Navy.

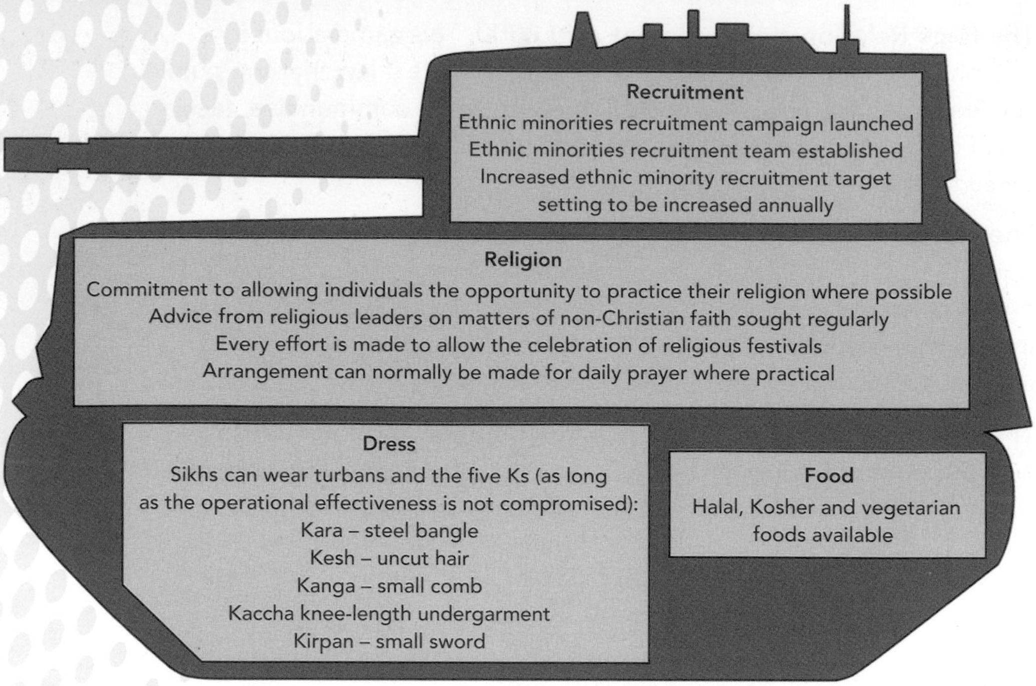

Recruitment
Ethnic minorities recruitment campaign launched
Ethnic minorities recruitment team established
Increased ethnic minority recruitment target
setting to be increased annually

Religion
Commitment to allowing individuals the opportunity to practice their religion where possible
Advice from religious leaders on matters of non-Christian faith sought regularly
Every effort is made to allow the celebration of religious festivals
Arrangement can normally be made for daily prayer where practical

Dress
Sikhs can wear turbans and the five Ks (as long
as the operational effectiveness is not compromised):
Kara – steel bangle
Kesh – uncut hair
Kanga – small comb
Kaccha knee-length undergarment
Kirpan – small sword

Food
Halal, Kosher and vegetarian
foods available

Figure 6.5: Equal opportunities in the Army.

Assessment activity 6.4 P4 P5 M3 D2

Equal opportunities are very important to the public services, you must demonstrate that you know enough about equality and diversity to be a valuable recruit. Working in pairs research and deliver a 10-minute PowerPoint presentation which covers the following tasks:

1 *Explain* why equal opportunities are important in society and the public services. P4

2 *Illustrate* how equal opportunities are enforced in the UK with reference to appropriate legislation. P5

3 *Compare* how two public services use legislation to address equal opportunities. M3

4 *Evaluate* the approaches used by public services to support fairness in society by addressing the main issues of equal opportunities. D2

Grading tips

For P4 you need to give examples of how equal opportunities has increased diversity in the public services and for P5 you need to look at a range of equal opportunities legislation such as the Disability Discrimination Act 1995 and explain how they make abiding by equal opportunities compulsory.

M3 requires you to choose two public services and compare how they have used the legislation to support equal opportunities – this might mean comparing how the Police Force have dealt with recruiting disabled officers or ethnic minority officers compared to the Royal Navy.

For D2 you have to evaluate how the services have supported fairness in society by dealing with equal opportunities issues – this means considering the good and bad points of what the services have done and coming to a conclusion about how well they have helped promote equality.

PLTS

Completing this assignment will give you the opportunity to develop your creative thinker skills.

4 Investigate the roles of statutory and non–statutory public services to the citizens and to a changing society

4.1 The public services

In general the public services fall into two main categories:

- statutory
- non-statutory.

Statutory public services are required to exist by law and are funded by the government, non-statutory public services are not required to exist by law and, although some do receive government money, many are charities or self-funded. Table 6.5 shows some examples of statutory and non-statutory public services.

Table 6.5 Statutory and non-statutory public services.

Statutory public services	Non-statutory public services
The Police Service	Victim Support
The Fire Service	Help the Aged
The National Health Service	Shelter
The Royal Air Force	The Samaritans
The Royal Navy	Church groups
The British Army	The NSPCC
The local council	The RSPCA

All of our public services have a very clear job to do, and many of these roles are covered earlier in the book (see page 89). However, there are other services that are equally important to the running of our country. The main ones are shown in Figure 6.6.

Did you know?

Help the Aged and Age Concern have plans to join forces and be known as Age UK. Look out for an announcement in the near future.

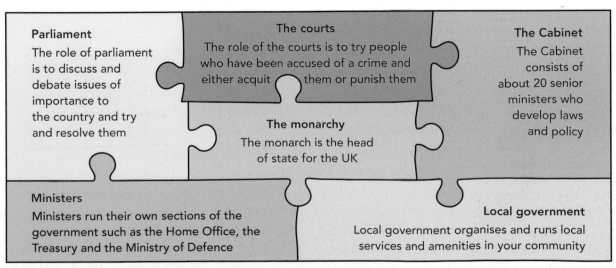

Parliament
The role of parliament is to discuss and debate issues of importance to the country and try and resolve them

The courts
The role of the courts is to try people who have been accused of a crime and either acquit them or punish them

The Cabinet
The Cabinet consists of about 20 senior ministers who develop laws and policy

The monarchy
The monarch is the head of state for the UK

Ministers
Ministers run their own sections of the government such as the Home Office, the Treasury and the Ministry of Defence

Local government
Local government organises and runs local services and amenities in your community

Figure 6.6: Public services that are important in running the country.

Link

For more on crime and its effects see page 234.

Key term

Secular society – a society where individuals can take part in public life whatever religion they follow and even if they have they don't have a religion.

Although the monarch is our head of state, the day-to-day running of the public services is in the hands of local and national government, who are themselves a public service.

4.2 Public services and changing society

The one thing you can always count on about society is that it is always changing. The society your grandparents grew up in was different from the one your parents grew up in and both of these are very different from the society you live in now. These changes can involve lots of different things such as:

- sexual behaviour
- crime
- education
- employment
- family circumstances
- religion
- technology
- prosperity
- politics.

This can be a source of conflict and arguments in society as older people struggle to understand the behaviour of younger people and younger people appear to show a lack of respect for older people. These conflicts are around different expectations of what is appropriate behaviour. For example, your parents may consider it very rude for you to use your mobile phone at the dinner table, but you might not see anything wrong with it.

The family has changed over the years, more and more children are raised by single parents, unmarried couples or homosexual couples. Fifty years ago this would have been seen as socially unacceptable but today these things are accepted as being normal. It is very common for children to split their time between two homes as parents divorce and remarry other partners.

Crime is constantly changing as new forms of crime become profitable and other forms of crime fall out of fashion. Internet and online crimes become more of a problem as technology becomes more popular, and anti-social behaviour is increasingly seen as a major threat to our society.

The influence of religion has declined in recent years, so that the majority of people in the UK are not regular churchgoers and do not follow a formal religion – this is described as a **secular society**. Some people have argued that the decline in religion is linked with poor public behaviour and if people were more religious then public behaviour would be better, but there is no real evidence to support this.

4.3 Impact of government action on individual lives

The government has a large impact on our day-to-day lives, some of the most important impacts are highlighted in Table 6.6.

Did you know?

At the time of publication government spending accounted for about 45 per cent of the Gross Domestic Product (GDP).

Table 6.6 Impact of government action.

Impact	Explanation
Taxation	Taxation is where the citizens of a society provide a proportion of their income to the government so that the government can provide services that we all need. The payment of the taxes allows the state to provide the public services that support us in preventing crime, making us well, fighting fires and defending the nation. There are many people who complain that the level of taxation is too high, but if you reduce tax you nearly always have to reduce the money you spend on public services. This would lead to poorer services for the community and the individual.
Housing	Most local authorities provide some form of social housing. This is housing for those people who either cannot afford to buy their own home of prefer not to. It is the responsibility of the local council (or any private housing agency who they give the responsibility to) to make sure that tenants have safe and secure housing. This kind of support is essential for the well-being of society.
Employment	The government employs over 6 million people in the public sector. This is clearly a great support to those 6 million people who are able to contribute to the economy and provide services, but it also means that they are supported by the rest of the population (in the form of wages and so on).
Voluntary services	Some voluntary services do receive money from the government but many do not, they have to rely on donations and volunteers for their work. Voluntary services support thousands of people every day through their services in areas such as victim support, prevention of cruelty to children and animals, specialist mental health services and the Citizens Advice Bureau.
Laws and regulations	Laws, rules of the road and regulations aim to provide a framework to allow people to live together peaceably and in an orderly manner.

BTEC Assessment activity 6.5

The reason the public services exist is to support society and help make our communities a better place to live. Write a 500-word report which covers the following questions.

1 *Explain* the different ways in which public services have supported society. **P6**
2 *Analyse* the different ways in which the public Services have supported society. **M4**

Grading tips

For **P6** write about the different ways the public services have helped or hindered society, in areas such as crime prevention, healthcare, defence, housing and so on.

If you want to get **M4** as well make your answer detailed and comprehensive, considering the support provided by the service from different angles.

PLTS

As you consider the support the services give us from different perspectives, you will be developing your reflective learning skills.

Functional skills

Your report may also contribute to your functional skills in written English.

4.4 How the public services can affect society

We mustn't forget that the public services are part of society. The statutory and non-statutory public services can have a great impact on society, for example:

- they support the community by doing the difficult and challenging tasks they are given
- they can act as a pressure group to bring about change
- they can campaign for more resources so they can support the public better but some believe this should not be the role of the public services
- they can influence and advise governments on changes to the law or new laws
- they can advise the government on social issues such as knife crime or domestic violence
- they can highlight issues which otherwise would be hidden from the public.

The media

The media is the collective term for the ways in which society or other individuals communicate information. It is made up of types of communication such as:

- newspapers
- magazines
- television
- radio
- internet
- books
- journal articles
- service magazines.

The public services use the media in a variety of ways such as appeals for information, safety warnings, disaster management and improving their image with the public. The media also has a huge impact on how the public services are seen by the public, if the media concentrate their coverage on negative aspects of policing, such as deaths in custody, then some sections of the public may feel hostility towards the police, equally if the news of soldier deaths in Afghanistan is treated sympathetically by the media then much of public opinion will rally round the role of the armed services.

Assessment activity 6.6 — P7

Create a web page which contains all the information you need to answer the following question:

1 *Demonstrate* the different ways in which the public services have affected society. **P7**

Grading tip

Include on your web page all the different things the public services have done that have affected society such as doing their jobs every day, advising the government, campaigning for more resources and acting as a pressure group.

Jez Machin

Citizens Advice Bureau volunteer

I work for the Citizens Advice Bureau as a volunteer adviser. I'm currently studying law and working for the CAB is a great way of putting into practice what I have learned and helping other people. The CAB tries to help people resolve their legal and money problems by providing free information and advice on their rights and responsibilities. I work two days a week and I am responsible for:

- interviewing clients
- helping them negotiate with creditors or service providers
- drafting letters for clients
- making telephone calls on behalf of clients
- representing them in court and at tribunals
- referring them to other agencies.

A typical day

There is really no such thing as a typical day at the CAB. Each person who comes looking for help and advice has a really unique set of problems. I might see a person who needs help with their debts and so spend a lot of time with them talking through their options, ringing round their creditors to try to make arrangements for them to pay or drafting letters they can send which explain their financial position and why they can't pay their debts. Immediately after that I might see someone who is having problems with an ex-husband or wife or is having problems with nuisance neighbours. We can't always deal with the client's problems, but if we can't then we always send them to an organisation that can, such as the local council or the police.

The best thing about the job

The variety is great, no two days are the same and I have the added bonus of really helping people who may not have had anywhere else to go. It's really rewarding seeing people feel empowered enough to sort out problems which may have been causing them upset and distress, and knowing you played a part in helping them solve their problems and disputes.

Think about it!

1. What topics have you covered in this unit that might provide you with the background knowledge you would need to work for the Citizens Advice Bureau? Write a list and discuss it with your colleagues.

2. What further skills might you need to develop for this kind of job role? Draw up a list and consider how you could improve your skills to make you ready to serve the public like Jez does.

Just checking

1. What is the difference between legal and moral citizenship?
2. What are human rights?
3. Why do we have public services?
4. What is society?
5. What is the difference between statutory and non-statutory public services?

edexcel

Assignment tips

Getting the most from your assignments and aiming for the highest grades is not always easy. The tips below will help you in moving towards those merit and distinction grades.

• Research and preparation

This may sound very basic, but make sure you have read your assignment thoroughly and you understand exactly what you are being asked to do. Once you are clear about this then you can move on to your research. Doing your research well and using good sources of evidence is essential. Lots of students rely too much on the internet and not enough on other sources of information such as books, newspapers and journals. The internet is not always a good source of information. It is very easy to use information from American or Australian websites without noticing – but your tutor will notice. Always double check the information you find, don't just accept it at face value. Good research and preparation is the key to getting those higher grades.

• Being socially aware

The citizenship unit really lends itself to being practical and discussion based. Your tutor will be asking for your opinions and views on a variety of issues so it is really important you are aware of what is going on in society around you. Try to read a quality newspaper at least once a week such as the *Guardian* or *The Times*. It might be easier for you to find time to check the BBC news website in your lunch hour or in your break between lessons. You can use the information from the news to bring to your group discussions and include in your assignments. This will really help with your grades.

9 Sport and recreation in the public services

Credit value: 10

Sport and recreation is a very big part of many public service organisations. It helps individuals and teams become mentally and physically fit, improves team coordination and fosters positive relationships. It can also help beat stress and provide relief from the day-to-day tension that many public service workers have to deal with in their job roles.

This unit looks at the importance of sport and recreation to the public services. This includes both team sports and individual ones as they can both offer different benefits to the services. It also examines the safety issues you will need to be aware of when organising sporting or recreational activities and how you would go about planning these activities to gain maximum benefit from your time.

It also encourages you to look at your own levels of participation and at the types of clubs and activities you could consider in order to improve your own career prospects.

Learning outcomes

After completing this unit you should:

1. know the importance of sport and recreation to the public services
2. understand the safety issues to be considered when organising sports and recreational activities
3. be able to plan a sport and recreational activity used by the public services
4. be able to participate regularly in a public services sport and recreational activities.

175

Assessment and grading criteria

This table shows you what you must do in order to achieve a pass, merit or distinction grade, and where you can find activities in this book to help you.

To achieve a **pass** grade the evidence must show that the learner is able to:	To achieve a **merit** grade the evidence must show that, in addition to the pass criteria, the learner is able to:	To achieve a **distinction** grade the evidence must show that, in addition to the pass and merit criteria, the learner is able to:
P1 identify different sports and recreational activities used by the public services **Assessment activity 9.1 page 183**		
P2 describe the importance of sports and recreational activities to the public services **Assessment activity 9.1 page 183**		
P3 explain the safety issues when organising sport or recreational activities **Assessment activity 9.2 page 186**		
P4 identify the responsibilities of the different people involved in sports and recreational activities **Assessment activity 9.2 page 186**		
P5 plan a sport or recreation activity **Assessment activity 9.3 page 190**	**M1** lead a sport or recreational activity **Assessment activity 9.3 page 190**	**D1** evaluate your sport or recreational activity **Assessment activity 9.3 page 190**
P6 participate regularly in sport and recreational activities in different venues **Assessment activity 9.4 page 192**	**M2** review your part in the participation of sports and recreational activities in different venues **Assessment activity 9.4 page 192**	
P7 report on the personal benefits of regular participation in sports and recreational activities **Assessment activity 9.4 page 192**		

How you will be assessed

This unit will be assessed by an internal assignment that will be designed and marked by the staff at your centre. The assignment is designed to allow you to show your understanding of the learning outcomes for sport and recreation in the public services. These relate to what you should be able to do after completing this unit. Assessments can be quite varied and can take the form of:

- reports
- leaflets
- presentations
- posters
- practical tasks
- case studies
- diaries
- activity records
- action plans.

Will, 16, experiences the benefits of team sports

I wasn't really keen on this unit to start with, I'm fit and healthy, but team sports aren't really my thing. I much prefer to do solo activities like going running or going to the gym. What really surprised me is the importance the public services put on sports and recreation, they see it as really important as it helps improve teamwork and can bond groups together.

This unit helped me make the shift from just doing solo activities to including team sports and activities as part of my fitness regime. I also liked the fact that it wasn't just all about sports, it was about the benefits of spending your leisure time doing hobbies, such as music, computer games and going out to socialise. It becomes really obvious if you think about it, that recreation and leisure will be just as important to the services as working hard. If you don't relax properly you probably won't deal with the stress of your job very well.

For me the best thing about the unit was getting an appreciation of the benefits that sport and recreation can bring to you on a short-term and long-term basis. I've joined the college's rugby team and I am seeing the effect that working and playing with others has had on my confidence.

Over to you

- What areas of sport and recreation might you find interesting?
- Do you have any fears or concerns about your level of fitness?
- Have you ever led a sporting activity before?
- What preparation could you do to get ready for your assessments?

1 The importance of sport and recreation to the public services

Thinking about sport and recreation

Consider the types of sport and recreational activities the services might use. How many can you list? Have you played any of them yourself? Do you know how to remain safe while taking part in sport and recreational activities?

Share your findings with the rest of your class. Did you come up with the same kind of things or was each person's list different? Why do you think this is?

Sport and recreation are important to the public services because they bring many benefits, such as:

- strengthening relationships
- building fitness
- promoting stress management
- improving team coordination
- cost-effective relaxation and teambuilding.

Sport and recreation combine these benefits with the fun and competitive element of physical activity at a low cost. Sport and recreation can be done as part of a team with other people or by yourself, both have benefits for your personal development.

Activity: Your sport and recreation

What sporting activities do you take part in? What are your main hobbies? How do your sports and recreation help make you more employable by the services?

Jot down some notes to these questions and share your findings with the rest of the class. How does your leisure time compare with theirs? Do you need to change your activities to make you more employable?

1.1 Sport and team games

Sport and team games are used frequently in the public services to promote strong working relationships and group cooperation and competition. Although all sporting activities have some value there are some team sports and games which are favoured by the services for the benefits they bring.

Team games

Team sports and games that are used by the services include:

- football
- netball
- basketball
- hockey
- rugby
- cricket.

These are sports which are competitive, active and skilful: all of which are characteristics which the services look to promote in their employees. They also encourage teamwork and cooperation, which are essential in any work where groups of people have to work together to achieve a common goal. The nature of public service work is that often many teams of people have to come together to achieve an objective, team sports help prepare people for this and show them that they cannot win alone, they must trust the skill and judgement of their teammates in order to be successful.

Did you know?

Team games have a long history with many of the most popular sports played today having hundreds of years of history behind them. However most of the team games we know today didn't have formal rules and regulation on how to play until the nineteenth century.

Case study: The Allfield Belles

I play for a ladies' football team in my area, which is based at a local recreation ground. We started the team up as a bit of a laugh to be honest, most of us used to go to the ground every Sunday to watch our dads, boyfriends and brothers who play for the men's team and we decided we wanted to have a go as well.

The ladies' teams who we play against are deadly serious about it and it wasn't long before we really started to take it seriously too. We train twice a week and play our matches on Sunday. The team spirit is amazing, we really support and back each other up as we know that we all need to work as a cooperative unit if we are going to beat the teams we go up against.

Although it started as a laugh and it's still a lot of fun, it's become much more than that. Not only has my fitness and stamina improved but my communication and teamwork skills have too. This has been a real benefit for me on my BTEC First course and I know it will help me when I decide to join the Fire Service in a few years time.

Now answer the following questions:

1 What benefits does playing football or any other active team sport bring?

2 Why do the services place so much value on team sports?

3 Do you play enough team sports? If not, how can you improve?

Table 9.1: Benefits of team games and sport.

Benefit	Explanation
Physical fitness	Your physical fitness will improve with team sport and brings a whole host of other health benefits with it, such as weight management, increased strength and increased stamina. All of which are required in the public services.
Mental fitness	Taking part in team sport can make you mentally tougher and more resilient which is important in many public service occupations due to the nature of the stress encountered and the difficulty of the job roles.
Fitness tests	Most services have a series of fitness tests you must pass in order to be successful. Taking part in regular sport activities will help you be ready to undertake these and give you a better chance of passing.
Communication	Playing team sports requires excellent communication skills as you have to be able to pass information between teammates in order to know how best to play against another team. Good communication skills are essential in any service career, so by developing these skills in sports you are giving yourself an advantage.
Team player	The services rely on teamwork in order to meet their objectives and do their jobs. Playing as part of a sports team will help you understand how to be a team player and ultimately help you in your chosen career.

Did you know?

The British Army support 'adventurous training' (AT) (such as climbing and sailing) and suggest it enhances an individual's ability to withstand the rigours of operations and rapid deployment. They also advocate the therapeutic use of sport in the rehabilitation of injured servicemen, especially in the Battle Back programme. You can find out more at the MOD website, available via Hotlinks (see page viii).

Individual sports

There are some individual sports and activities that the services use to develop their employees. These include:

- cross country running
- climbing
- skiing
- tennis
- badminton
- sailing.

Individual activities can have a whole range of personal development benefits some of which are similar and some of which differ from those of team sports and games, as shown in Table 9.2.

Table 9.2: Benefits of individual sports.

Benefit	Description
Increased fitness	Team sports increase fitness but individual sports and games give you the opportunity to customise your programme to suit the areas of your fitness that you want to develop. As long as you are as fit as everyone else in your team you will be able to pull your weight, but in individual sports you don't have the benchmark of colleagues to judge your fitness by so you may have to work harder.
Increased stamina	Team sports rely on a number of players who may or may not be active at any given point in a game, the workload is shared between the team. In individual sports you only have yourself to rely on and the pressure cannot be passed to another player. This means you are likely to have to improve your stamina as you alone will be the focus of the entire match.
Improved confidence	Taking on challenges and overcoming them as an individual builds confidence.
Self-reliance	Taking part in individual sports can build your self-reliance. You are able to trust yourself and your own performance and do not need to rely on others for support or back up. Although the public services value teamwork very highly they also value the ability of an individual to be self-reliant and work alone if required.
Initiative	Playing a sport where you and only you are responsible for winning and losing may make you think more strategically and use your initiative and intellect to outwit your opponent. Being able to think quickly on your feet is a key skill required in the public services.

1.2 Recreation

Recreation in this context means any activity which is designed to stimulate or refresh your body or mind. This could include any or all of the following:

- cinema
- theatre
- music
- hobbies
- socialising.

The health and fitness benefits of yoga are well reported. What form of recreation do you pursue?

Recreation is important to the public services in general for several reasons:

- **Health, fitness and well-being**. Recreation is designed to give your mind and body time away from the normal stresses and strains of the day. It is supposed to be fun and enjoyable as well as having a purpose. Depending on the activity, it can improve your mental and physical fitness and your overall sense of well-being.

- **Self-esteem**. Taking part in recreational activities can improve your self-esteem, this is the way you think and feel about yourself. Taking part in group or solo activities can help you think more positively about yourself and your skills and abilities.

- **Personal development**. Many recreational activities can be very challenging and even frightening at times, such as climbing or abseiling. Meeting these challenges helps you push your personal boundaries and develops your strengths and overcome your weaknesses making you a better overall employee in the public services.

- **Stress relief**. Public service jobs can be very stressful and involve dealing with enormous amounts of pressure in very difficult circumstances. It is essential that public services employees have an outlet for these stresses and strains, for some it might be a physical sport such as boxing or football, for others it may be letting off steam by socialising with friends or relaxing with a good book.

> ## ! Link
>
> There are many long- and short-term physical benefits to taking part in sport and recreation, you will find these discussed in detail in Unit 5 (page 105).

Case study: Jayne's recreational activity

I'm a police community support officer in a deprived inner city area. I really enjoy my job and I like being part of the community and making the area a safer place for businesses and residents.

My previous job was as a night security guard and I didn't experience any stress at all because I never really saw anyone. In this job, dealing with the public all day every day can leave you feeling really frustrated and angry with the bad attitude some people show. I have to remain professional at all times so I found I was bottling up my anger and this was causing me so much stress that it started to affect my personal life.

A friend suggested that if I had an outlet for my frustration at the end of each day I'd deal with the job much better so I started kickboxing. It's been fabulous for

me, I take all my frustrations out on a punch bag at the end of a working day and I'm able to go home feeling relaxed and calm. It has also had the added bonus of improving my physical fitness, my body shape and my confidence and well as the obvious self-defence benefits.

I'd recommend it to anyone feeling stress in their job.

Now answer the following questions:

1 Why is it important for public service workers to take part in recreational activities?

2 Why do public service workers sometimes face stress in their jobs?

3 What might happen if public service workers didn't use recreational activities in order to unwind?

1.3 Importance to the public services

As you will have already seen, the services consider sport and recreation very valuable in creating an effective workforce. The reasons why the public services look at sport and recreation this way are considered in Table 9.3.

Table 9.3: The importance of sport and recreation to the public services.

Reason	Explanation
Enhanced productivity	A workforce will be more productive if they are fit, active and able to relax. They will be able to work more efficiently and meet more of the goals they are set. This means that if an organisation invests in leisure time for its employees then it will reap the rewards in better and more effective staff.
Improved staff loyalty	Staff who are treated well and who take part in teambuilding activities will be more loyal to the organisation.
Reduced absenteeism	If staff are happy and healthy they will not take as much time off sick as others who are in a more difficult work environment. This means the organisation is more productive and can serve the public better.
Healthier workforce	Involvement in sport and some recreational activities leads to a definite improvement in your overall health. This can make you physically and mentally fitter to do your job and improve the overall performance of the organisation.
Team morale	One of the key issues that can affect public service teams is low morale. Morale is a sense of team spirit and happiness in your workplace. If this is lost then teams will not be very motivated to succeed and will fail to achieve their targets or give the public a poorer service than they deserve.

The uniformed services, in particular, value sport and recreation. Other public services also take part, as shown in Figure 9.1.

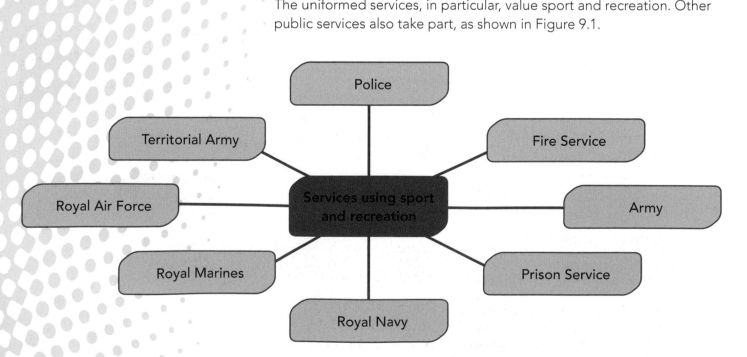

Figure 9.1: Have you any suggestions for other public services that would benefit from using sport and recreation?

BTEC **Assessment activity 9.1** **P1** **P2**

Working in pairs

Understanding the value of sport and recreation is essential if you want to join a uniformed public service in the future. Produce an A3 poster which addresses the following tasks:

1 *Identify* different sports and recreational activities used by the public services. **P1**

2 *Describe* the importance of sports and recreational activities to the public services. **P2**

Grading tips

Make a list and add a brief description of the sports and recreation activities used by the services **P1** and ensure your poster describes why sports and recreation are important to the services **P2**.

PLTS

As you identify different sports and recreational activities used by the public services you will develop your independent enquirer skills.

2 The safety issues to be considered when organising sports and recreational activities

All sports and some recreational activities have the potential for risk or injury. Many involve contact between opposing teams or between team members. It is really important that you try to minimise these risks as much as possible to avoid injury to yourself and others.

2.1 Safety

Safety is about being protected from harm. When you are playing team sports or participating in recreational activities there is always the chance that you may be injured or hurt. This in itself is not a reason to avoid the activities as the risk of injury can be drastically reduced and controlled with some very simple safety measures. The most common sporting injuries are sprains, strains and the effects of dehydration and these can very often be dealt with at the time without the need for medical help.

Did you know?

The accepted method of dealing with sprains and strains is the RICE method. RICE stands for:

- Rest
- Ice
- Compression
- Elevation.

Activity: Safety first

Consider the safety measures outlined in Table 9.4. Can you think of any other measures you might take? Do you think the public services value safety in sporting activities? What would be the impact on the public services if they didn't play sport safely?

There are occasions where injuries can be more severe and include consequences such as bruises, cuts, grazes, fractures, concussion, heart problems and spinal damage. One of the main things you can do to prevent injury is to prepare properly for your activity, this may include the following:

- warm ups
- suitable clothing
- protective equipment
- hydration and nutrition
- seeing medical guidance if you have a pre-existing condition
- assessing your own fitness and skills to see if you are ready for the activity
- doing the activity correctly
- making sure risk assessments are in place
- ensuring first aid is close by
- making sure your surroundings are suitable
- ensuring sufficient other people are nearby to help if required.

Case study: 'Spaces for Sport'

The Spaces for Sport survey in 2005 found that there are approximately 22 million sporting injuries each year and that each person who regularly participates in sport can expect to be injured an average of 1.65 times per year. Other major findings from the survey included:

- 25 per cent of those injured have been forced to quit sport
- A quarter (26 per cent) of respondents did not treat their injury
- Only 43 per cent of those injured asked a GP or physiotherapist for advice or treatment
- Football is the number one sport to cause an injury (32 per cent) with rugby second (13 per cent)
- People in eastern England spend the most on treatments (£165 per person)
- People in the north-east and London are most likely to take a sick day as a result of an injury (14 days taken off work each year per person)
- The number one sporting injury is a sprain or muscle pull (80 per cent)
- Men are over twice as likely (59 per cent) to blame third party involvement for their injury in comparison to women (22 per cent).

Now answer these questions:

1 Have you ever had a sporting injury, if so what was it and how did you treat it?

2 Why do you think football is the most common cause of sporting injuries?

3 Why do you think men are more likely to blame another for their injury than women are?

Table 9.4: Safety measures in detail.

Safety measure	Description
Warm ups	Warm ups help prepare your body for the activity you are about to do. This includes raising the heart rate and stretching the muscles so they are less likely to be injured. Cool downs at the end of a sporting session are also important.
Suitable clothing	There is no one set of clothing that is suitable for all sporting activities. Each sport normally has its own mode of dress and some sports insist on certain types of garment in order to comply with safety guidelines. For example a football kit may be comfortable and suitable on the pitch but would not be much use to a fencer who needs clothing that protects them from a fencing blade.
Protective equipment	Protective equipment is used in many sports and can include gum shields, gloves, pads, helmets and shin pads. The equipment is designed to protect a part of the body that is particularly vulnerable to injury in a particular sport, for instance in football shin pads are used as physical contact below the knee between players is commonplace; in sports such as boxing or martial arts gum shields are used as the face is often a target for injury and the teeth can be knocked out or the skin of the lips and tongue sliced or bitten.
Hydration and nutrition	It is crucial that before and during your sporting activity you have had sufficient food and water to fuel your body. Loss of water due to sweating should be replaced so it makes sense to have a bottle of water with you when performing any sport. Although you need to have sufficient food to fuel your body for sport, you should be sensible about when you eat it, playing a rugby match or sparring in a boxing ring after a full Sunday lunch is not ideal.
Medical guidance	If you have a pre-existing medical condition, such as asthma, or a long-standing injury or even if you are pregnant, you must seek medical advice from your doctor about what exercise you should and shouldn't do.
Assessing your own fitness	Many sporting activities will test your endurance and your stamina, if you are not fit enough to take part you should be careful about how much you do otherwise you will risk injury. Create a training programme which gets you fit gradually rather than trying to leap in at the deep end and play 90 minutes of football or spar for 5 lots of 3-minute rounds in boxing.
Doing the activity correctly	You must know how to do an activity correctly if you are going to be safe. Watch and learn from others how it is done and seek specialist tuition or coaching if required. Good sportsmen and women can often make things look far easier than they are, don't make the mistake of thinking you know how to perform an activity without guidance.
Risk assessments	You should evaluate the risk you face when performing an activity under the control measures that are in place to prevent problems or dangers. The risk assessment should cover the equipment you are using and your surroundings. Your school or college sports hall will have these in place for you to look at.
First aid	Injuries may still happen even when you take the best of care, risk assess the activity, wear the right clothing and use the correct protective equipment for the activity. The key is to make sure that there is a trained first aider who has access to a suitable first aid kit who can treat the injury or call for further help from the ambulance service of required. There should also be a suitable place close by to treat the injured.
Suitable surroundings	It is dangerous to make do with very poor facilities in which to play sport and play wherever you happen to be. If you decide to play football on the street you run the risk of injuries such as severe bruises and cuts from the road that a grass pitch wouldn't give you, there is also the problem of traffic danger or damage to surrounding property. Make sure your surroundings are suitable and you will increase your safety.
People nearby	Having people nearby means your chances or receiving help if you are hurt are very good. If you are injured, early treatment can improve your chances of making a full recovery.

2.2 Responsibility of different people

The responsibility for safety in sporting and recreational activities is split between the organisers of the activity and the participants. This is really important because the organiser can risk assess, provide equipment and first aid, but if the participants do not follow instructions or decide to behave foolishly then all the safety measures will count for nothing. Equally, the participant should be able to trust the organiser and that safety measures have been put into place.

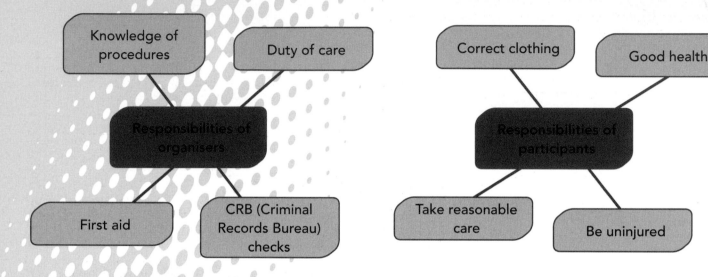

Figure 9.2: Are there any other areas for organisers to consider?

Figure 9.3: Are there any other factors for participants to consider?

As you can see from Figures 9.2 and 9.3 the responsibility for safety is not just one person's job, it is everyone's job.

PLTS

As you prepare for your information leaflet you will be developing your independent enquirer and creative thinker skills.

Assessment activity 9.2 (P3) (P4)

It is really important that you know how to keep yourself and others safe when taking part in sporting activities. Produce an information leaflet which could be given out in your school or college sports hall which addresses the following task:

1 *Explain* the safety issues when organising sport or recreational activities. (P3)

2 *Identify* the responsibilities of the different people involved in sports and recreational activities. (P4)

Grading tips

Table 9.4 identifies many of the issues you need to be aware of, use this information to build your own safety leaflet. (P3) (P4)

3 Plan a sport or recreational activity used by the public services

Sporting and recreational activities do not happen by magic. The public services put time into the planning and organising of the activities to ensure they run smoothly and people get the most from them.

3.1 Planning

There are many aspects that the public services must consider when planning and organising sports and recreational activities. These are outlined in Figure 9.4.

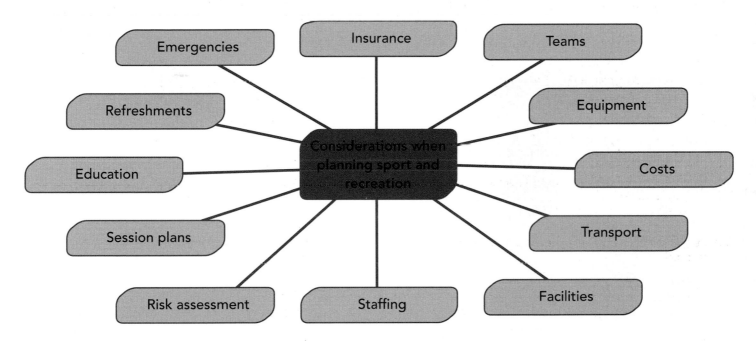

Figure 9.4: Are there any other factors to consider when planning sport and recreation?

⊕ Case study: Sports injury

In 2008 Ben Collett was awarded £4.5 million compensation for a sports injury he received while playing for Manchester United reserve team. Ben was on the receiving end of a reckless tackle from a Middlesbrough player that left his leg broken in two places and effectively ended his footballing career.

The judge in the case awarded £3.9 million for loss of future earnings, £460,000 for past earnings and about £40,000 as compensation for pain and suffering. This is in comparison to the estimated £16 million he could have earned as a premiership footballer if he had played consistently until the age of 35.

The compensation was paid by Middlesbrough Football Club's insurers.

Now answer these questions:

1 Who would have had to pay compensation if Middlesbrough had not been insured?

2 Was the amount awarded fair in your opinion?

3 What would be the impact on the public services if they had to pay out compensation like this without being insured?

Insurance

Before you conduct any sporting or recreational activity you must make sure you are covered by an insurance policy to do so. The insurance policy is there to help cover medical costs if someone is injured and legal costs in case an individual or organisation is sued by a participant. If you are not covered by insurance then you personally, or the organisation, will have to pay for any medical or legal expenses themselves. This could run into several thousands of pounds or more.

Teams

Part of effective planning includes making sure you have sufficient numbers of people to play and you have organised a team to play against. A cricket match with only one team playing is not much of an activity. Equally, if you arrive at a venue with less than the required number of players you will forfeit the match and the other team will win automatically.

Equipment

Effective planning includes ensuring you have the appropriate equipment that you need with you. If you don't have tennis racquets you can't play tennis. Without the proper equipment an activity cannot go ahead and will be a waste of everyone's time.

Costs

The cost of activities can be very high, both in terms of time and money. You will have to weigh up carefully whether you can afford to do the activities you want with the resources that you have at your disposal. It is no good taking 30 people to paintballing at a cost of £40 per head when it might eat up your entire sports and recreation budget for the whole year. You need to plan the spending of your budget by considering how much you have versus the activities you would like to do and be prepared to make compromises if required.

Transport

Transport is a key aspect of your planning, you must be able to get to venues safely and return from them. Your transport should be from an approved supplier who is covered by insurance in case of an incident and should be large enough to carry all your players and support members. Transport costs can be expensive so this is another aspect of transport planning you will have to consider.

Facilities and venue

You need to check your venue and that the facilities it offers are suitable for your activities. Consider issues such as cleanliness, staffing, safety and reputation. If the venue is unsafe and does not have the facilities you require you won't have planned very effectively. It might also be sensible to make sure that the venue has refreshments available or you will have to take your own with you as it is quite common to need a drink or a snack during activities.

Without the appropriate equipment an activity cannot go ahead. What actions can you take to ensure you transport all necessary equipment?

Did you know?

A minibus with more than eight passengers cannot be driven at all without passing a minibus test. Many local authorities insist on a clean driving licence for minibus drivers and some public service organisations sometimes require those driving minibuses to have passed a local minibus test.

Case study: Lyme Bay tragedy, 1993

Four young people lost their lives while on a supervised canoeing trip across Lyme Bay in 1993. This gave rise to a radical rethink about how activities should be managed and organised and led to the creation of the Adventure Activities Licensing Authority (AALA) and the Activity Centres (Young Persons Safety) Act 1995.

On 22 March 1993 a group of eight school pupils, their teacher and two instructors set off on a canoeing trip from an outdoor centre. The trip ran into trouble almost immediately with the teacher requiring assistance from one instructor and the rest of the party drifting away out of sight and further out into the bay. The waves became higher and the canoes quickly became swamped with water, this left all eight pupils and their instructor in the sea. Although they were supposed to be due back at lunchtime the emergency services were not called by the centre until 3.30 pm. The group were not located and rescued until after 5.30 pm, by which time it was too late for four members of the party.

The Devon County Council report into the tragedy states 'the immediate cause of the tragedy was, however, the lamentable failure of the St Alban's Centre to organise and supervise the canoeing activity, to employ suitable staff and to have prepared and operated sensible and pre-determined procedures when difficulties arose'. The owner of the outdoor company was convicted of corporate manslaughter in the trial that followed.

Now answer these questions:

1. How could the situation in Lyme Bay have been prevented?
2. What could the public services learn from this incident?
3. What can you learn from this incident when you are planning activities?

Staffing

Many activities have legal guidelines that require a certain staffing ratio, for example one instructor to ten participants. You need to make sure you include these ratios in your planning. Also, it is important you plan to take the right people for the activities: Do your instructors know what they are doing and are they qualified to do it? Have they been CRB checked to ensure safety? Will they be required to drive and do they have a licence and insurance? All of these things will be your responsibility to check and plan for.

Risk assessment

Any planned activity will require a risk assessment to estimate the risk of the activity and ensure that the appropriate safety measures are put in place.

Session plans

When planning and organising activities you should have a clear written plan of what you are aiming to do and why and how your timings and resources will work, this is called a session plan. A session plan enables you to set out clearly your aims and objectives, and ensures you have accounted for any safety or resourcing issues. Your plan can also be left with other people so they know what you are doing and where you are doing it, in case you fail to return or need assistance.

Link

Risk assessments and their importance are covered in detail in Unit 15 (page 310).

Education

Many activities also include an educational aspect. Either the task itself is designed to teach, such as effective teamwork or leadership, or learning how to complete the task properly provides the education, such as soccer skills or martial arts.

Emergency supplies

When planning for any activity make sure you have the equipment you need in case of emergency. This includes a first aid kit and a phone as a minimum, but may include other equipment such as life jackets, flares or rations depending on the activity.

Always carry a first aid kit to a sport or recreational activity. Have you been on a first aid course?

BTEC Assessment activity 9.3 · P5 · M1 · D1

The ability to take part in a sport or recreational activity will be an important aspect of your life in the services. Address the following tasks:

1 *Plan* a sport or recreational activity. P5

2 *Lead* a sport or recreational activity. M1

3 *Evaluate* your sport or recreational activity. D1

Grading tips

In order to get P5 show you have considered all of the key planning issues, perhaps by producing an action plan which shows how you have organised your activity. For M1 provide evidence that you have led an activity such as a witness statement, observation statement from your tutor or video evidence. For D1 evaluate how well your activity went and how you could improve it for next time.

4 Participate regularly in public service sport or recreational activities

Taking part in sport or recreation activities should not be a one-off event. The key to getting the most out of these activities is to take part in them regularly and over an extended period of time. For many people in the services taking part in sport and recreation activity is a key aspect of their job that begins while they undergo recruit training and only ends when they retire or leave the service.

4.1 Participation

Choosing where and how to participate in sport and recreation activities can be difficult. There are lots of possible activities you could choose and many places where you could do them. However the most common places to undertake sports and recreation activities are:

- **Sports clubs**. You can find sports clubs across the country and there are likely to be several in your immediate area and anything up to a dozen or more run by your school or college. These can include sports clubs, hobby clubs, special interest clubs or social clubs.

- **Activity centres**. You should always use a centre which is approved and ask for copies of registrations and up-to-date risk assessments. These centres offer a range of activities including caving, canoeing, climbing, abseiling, hiking, high ropes course, confidence course and survival courses.

- **Fitness centres**. Fitness centres and gyms can be found in most good schools and colleges, so you shouldn't have to travel far to find membership of a fitness centre at a low cost. It is better to use your school or college facilities as they will be far cheaper (or in many cases free) than commercial fitness centres.

4.2 Benefits

As we have discussed earlier in this unit there are many benefits to undertaking regular sport or recreation activities, as shown in Tables 9.1 and 9.2.

Did you know?

The Adventure Activity Licensing Authority (AALA) has a list of approved adventure activity centres on their website, available via Hotlinks (see page viii).

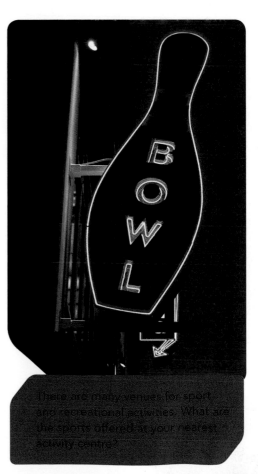

There are many venues for sport and recreational activities. What are the sports offered at your nearest activity centre?

BTEC Assessment activity 9.4

For this assessment you need to show you are participating in activities regularly. Keep a logbook of your time spent on sport and recreation in order to answer the following tasks:

1 *Participate* regularly in sport and recreational activities in different venues. **P6**

2 *Report* on the personal benefits of regular participation in sports and recreation. **P7**

3 *Review* your part in the participation of sports and recreational activities in different venues. **M2**

Grading tip

If your logbook includes a plan of what you are going to do and logs the activity you take part in, you should be able to pass these tasks.

Juan Peto
Student Activities Coordinator

My job is to provide sport and recreation activities for a large college in the Midlands. We have over 2500 full-time students aged between 16 and 60 and we have to cater for all of them. This could include organising social activities in local nightclubs, sports fixtures and special interest clubs like game design and drama.

A typical day

A typical day for me could be spent sorting out sports fixtures with other colleges, securing funding for clubs, booking transport and so on. I have to be really on the ball in terms of planning everything well and checking out insurance and staff qualifications, because we run the risk of being sued if anything goes wrong.

The best thing about the job

It's great to see that the college students have a variety of things to do at any time, they can play sports, go on trips abroad, go to the cinema or join outdoor clubs like running or climbing. It helps them make friends and settle into the college environment. This ultimately makes them want to stay at college and they become better educated and more able to get a job in the long term.

Think about it!

1. What topics have you covered in this unit that might give you the background to be an activities coordinator?

2. What knowledge and skills do you think you need to develop further if you want to be involved in sport and recreation in the future?

Just checking

1. Name several different team sports.
2. How important is sport and recreation to the public services?
3. What are the key issues to consider in planning an activity?
4. What are the benefits of sport and recreation to the public services?
5. Name some types of place where can you take part in sport and recreation?

edexcel :::

Assignment tips

- The service you want to join may be different from others in your class. Don't be concerned about this, the sports or activities you choose are likely to be very different from people who want other services. Don't be tempted to do the same as they do because it's easier than taking up activities on your own.

- Health and safety is a key component of this unit, remember to take care when planning activities and be meticulous about checking issues such as insurance and transport.

- Keep an activities log throughout this unit. It will provide evidence for some of the criteria and help you monitor your progress towards your goals.

11 Law and its impact on the individual in public services

Have you ever wondered how our complex legal system developed and how it operates today? Most of us give little consideration to the legal system until we come face to face with a crime or need the protection of the court.

This unit provides you with the opportunity to explore how the legal system of England and Wales has developed over time. The unit also looks at how crime is prosecuted in the courts, the purpose and powers of the police and other agencies involved in the justice system and the rights of those brought before the courts, including the right to a defence lawyer.

You will follow the legal process from when an offence is committed to the arrest of a **suspect**, charging of the suspect, the trial proceedings, the decision of the court, through to the conviction and subsequent sentencing of the offender.

Learning outcomes

After completing this unit you should:

1. understand the origins of common law and how criminal law has evolved
2. know the codes of practice set out by the Police and Criminal Evidence Act 1984 and subsequent amendments which apply to the rights of offenders throughout the judicial process
3. know the powers given and the points to prove to support a successful prosecution
4. understand the role of the prosecution, the defence and the courts.

Assessment and grading criteria

This table shows you what you must do in order to achieve a pass, merit or distinction grade, and where you can find activities in this book to help you.

To achieve a **pass** grade the evidence must show that the learner is able to:	To achieve a **merit** grade the evidence must show that, in addition to the pass criteria, the learner is able to:	To achieve a **distinction** grade the evidence must show that, in addition to the pass and merit criteria, the learner is able to:
P1 discuss how common law has evolved from community norms and customs to present day legislation **Assessment activity 11.1 page 203**		
P2 explain how decided cases and stated cases may give direction to current cases being tried in court **Assessment activity 11.2 page 204**		
P3 identify powers available to the police to deal with suspects **Assessment activity 11.3 page 209**	**M1** analyse the powers available to police dealing with a suspect **Assessment activity 11.3 page 209**	**D1** justify the use of police powers when dealing with suspects **Assessment activity 11.3 page 209**
P4 select a piece of legislation to identify the points to prove beyond all reasonable doubt **Assessment activity 11.4 page 218**		
P5 describe the rights afforded to a person held in police custody before and after charge **Assessment activity 11.3 page 209**	**M2** explain when bail can be refused after charge for both adult and juvenile offenders **Assessment activity 11.3 page 209**	
P6 explain the process of disclosure **Assessment activity 11.5 page 222**		
P7 explain the role of the Crown Prosecution Service, the defence and the courts **Assessment activity 11.5 page 222**	**M3** analyse the role of witnesses and their part in giving evidence in court **Assessment activity 11.5 page 222**	

How you will be assessed

This unit will be assessed by internal assignments that will be designed and marked by the staff at your centre. It may be subject to sampling by your centre's External Verifier as part of Edexcel's ongoing quality assurance procedures. The assignment is designed to allow you to show your understanding of the learning outcomes for law and its impact on the individual. These relate to what you should be able to do after completing this unit. Your assessment could be in the form of:

- role plays and scenarios
- presentations
- tutor observations
- case studies

- practical tasks
- leaflets
- posters
- written assignments.

Sarah, 16, investigates the legal system

This unit helped me to understand how complicated our legal system is and how many different people are involved in running the courts and bringing offenders to court. I also learned that different offences are tried in different courts and that the powers to sentence vary between these courts.

I found out a lot about the rights you have if arrested by the police and how the police have to uphold those rights and always follow the set procedures.

Our groups had some good debates about crime and whether a crime against a person is worse than one against property, but by the end of this unit we all understood the possible consequences of crime and the impact of crime on victims.

Before I studied this unit I had very little idea what the courts did and no real interest in ever working in the legal system. Now I am very interested in looking at a career with the Crown Prosecution Service and I've got some work experience lined up later in the year! I'd really like to work with a lawyer, helping to prepare case files for trials in court.

Over to you!
- What areas of the law and its impacts on the individual might you find interesting?
- Have you ever been a victim of crime?
- Have you ever had to appear in court?
- How could you prepare yourself for the assessment activities?

Key terms

Crime – a crime is an act (or a failure to act) which breaches the laws of the society and can result in punishment. The definition of crime changes over time as society changes and develops, although some acts, such as murder, would be seen as crimes in most societies.

Stated Case – Case stated is a form of appeal. A decision made by a Magistrates' Court may be appealed within 21 days if the defendant believes there has been a misinterpretation of the law.

Decided Case – A decided legal case is one where the decision has been made and there is no appeal pending.

Legal interpretation – decision made on the meaning of the law within a court or tribunal setting.

Offence – an act that violates what is considered right or natural. It is punishable by the courts.

Today we have clearly defined behaviours that society has decided are crimes, and we have legislation to ensure that those who behave outside of the law can be charged with those **offences**, tried by the court system and punished for wrongdoing.

Law is not static – it changes over time as the values and morals of society change. Certain types of behaviour that were considered criminal by previous generations have now been legalised. For example, male homosexuality was legalised by the Sexual Offences Act of 1967. Prior to this time you could be convicted and given a prison sentence (or be forced to take female hormones) for being a male homosexual. Other crimes have come to be seen as more serious. For example, cannabis was a legal drug until it was reclassified by the Misuse of Drugs Act 1971. Some crimes such as internet pornography, theft of mobile phones and credit card fraud are twenty-first century crimes – they could not have existed until the relevant technology was developed!

Views on crime and the seriousness of crime are strongly influenced by religion and an individual's belief systems. As children we are strongly influenced by the values our families have about right and wrong and what is acceptable behaviour. When we begin our education we have to work within the rules that the school imposes on us. Some behaviours have become a crime because of their impact on society and communities.

Did you know?

Alan Turing was a mathematician and hero who helped to break the Second World War Nazi 'Enigma code' (which it is estimated reduced the length of the conflict by 2 years).

He committed suicide in 1954 after he was prosecuted for being gay. He had lost his job working for the government and was forced to take female hormones as part of his sentence.

Case study: Anti-social behaviour

In September 2009 a jury at the inquest into a mother who committed suicide and killed her daughter by setting fire to their parked car found that the deaths were due to the ongoing stress of anti-social behaviour carried out by neighbourhood children over a period of many years. It is alleged that the lack of action by the police and local council had contributed to the mother's stress. Fiona Pilkington called the police over 30 times about the abuse which included mocking her disabled child, ramming bikes into her car when it was parked in the drive, urinating in the garden, throwing eggs and stones at the windows of her house, lighting fires in the road outside her house. No prosecutions were brought and she eventually gave up bothering to report the abuse.

Now answer these questions:

1 What do you think about the issues raised in this case?

2 What steps would you take to address the situation?

Anti-social behaviour has become an important issue in recent years and new measures such as anti-social behaviour orders (ASBOs) have been introduced to try to deal with offences such as shouting abuse at neighbours, graffiti, putting rubbish through letterboxes, swearing at people in the street.

The impact of what can appear quite trivial crimes can be devastating to the victims, their friends and families. Feeling vulnerable and traumatised after such experiences is a normal response because crime leaves victims feeling that they have lost their security and sense of safety. Previously confident people may be frightened to leave their home, or to be on the street by themselves, even in daylight or in a busy area where there are other people.

The media plays an important role in highlighting certain crimes and campaigning for changes in sentencing and punishment of offenders. For example, the media played an important role in the call for the introduction of 'Megan's Law' in the UK and the campaign to increase sentences for those causing death on the roads (while misusing mobile phones or driving under the influence of drugs or alcohol).

Case study: Megan's Law

The Sex Offenders Register was set up under the Sex Offenders Act 1997 and contains the details of approximately 29,000 people who have been defined as sex offenders (have been cautioned, convicted or released from imprisonment for sex related offences). The police update and monitor the register based on court and prison records. The police can photograph those on the register and people like head teachers and youth leaders are told confidentially if a sex offender is in their locality. Failure to register can lead to imprisonment.

In America under 'Megan's Law' parents have the right to see photos of all convicted paedophiles. This is not the case in the UK, although everyone working with children and vulnerable adults has to undergo a Criminal Records Bureau check (CRB).

Now answer the following questions:

1 Find out why Megan's Law was introduced in the US.

2 Do you think the Sex Offenders Register is a good thing? Why?

3 Can you think of any possible downsides or problems with the Register? Think about such things as the rights of the offender.

4 Can you think of any other examples of high profile crimes that have led to changes in the law?

! Link

For more on anti-social behaviour see Unit 12 page 238.

Some graffiti can be considered as anti-social behaviour. What are your thoughts on this issue?

Did you know?

People aged 16 and over who regularly commit crime or anti-social behaviour while under the influence of alcohol could be served with a 'booze ASBO' and have conditions imposed to prevent them committing further offences. These conditions could include being banned from drinking in public places, being banned from certain pubs and bars and being prevented from entering designated areas. These orders last for up to 2 years and breaches can lead to a fine of up to £2500.

! Link

Consider the case of Stephen Lawrence (see page 166) and other cases explained in Unit 12 page 238 and also Unit 13 page 274.

Key term

Statute – a law made by Parliament (this is distinct from case law, which is made by judges).

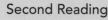

Legislation is introduced
(White and Green Papers)

⬇

Bill introduced in House of Commons or House of Lords, First Reading

⬇

Second Reading

⬇

Committee Stage

⬇

Report Stage

⬇

Third Reading

⬇

Passes to other Chamber

⬇

Royal Assent

⬇

Act of Parliament is implemented

Figure 11.1: How laws are made.

1.2 Legislation

What is legislation?

Our current legal system is based on common law and this is supplemented by legislation in the form of **statutes** created by acts of Parliament. Parliament is made up of Members of Parliament (MPs) who are voted in by ordinary people. They seek to represent the views of all citizens in the United Kingdom. The seat of Parliament in the UK is Westminster in London. It is made up of the House of Commons and the House of Lords.

In order for a law to be made or changed it has to pass through many different stages (see Figure 11.1). Most legislation starts as what is called a 'Green paper'. This is when the government wants to find out what individuals and groups think about a potential law. It can also start as a 'White paper'. This is based on intended government policy which can be outlined in a party's manifesto before an election or announced at the start of each session of Parliament in the 'Queen's speech'.

Once people have given their views on proposed laws a Bill is drafted. A Bill is an outline of intended law. Bills can be introduced into either the House of Commons or the House of Lords. A Bill must pass through many different stages in Parliament before it becomes law.

The first stage is known as the First Reading whereby the intended law is formally introduced. The Bill then has a Second Reading where it is debated by members of the House of Commons (MPs). If the proposed law is controversial there will be a vote after which the Bill will be sent to the Committee stage where it is examined in great detail by MPs representing all political parties. Following this the Bill moves to the Report Stage, where suggested changes from the Committee are discussed. The Bill then returns to the House for a Third Reading, where a final debate is held before the Bill progresses to the House of Lords. The Bill goes through a similar process here and, if accepted, it is passed and goes for Royal Assent or signature by the Queen. This is only a formality as the Queen cannot refuse to sign! The Bill now becomes an Act of Parliament. It then needs to be implemented (put into practice). Complicated Acts may be implemented in stages to allow time for everyone to prepare for the proposed changes.

Did you know?

Parliament at Westminster is made up of the House of Lords (members are not elected) and the elected House of Commons.

In September 2009 there were 645 MPs (Members of Parliament) of whom 126 were women.

You can visit Westminster (book your trip online!) or take a virtual tour through the Parliament website, available via Hotlinks (see page viii).

Assessment activity 11.1 BTEC **P1**

The legal system has developed over time from a system based on accepted behaviours in society to our current system which is supported by legislation.

1 *Discuss* how common law has evolved from community norms and customs to present day legislation. **P1**

Grading tips

To achieve **P1** you should explain the terms 'common law' and 'legislation'. *Discuss* means you need to present the important points, so you will need to highlight how the legal system in England and Wales developed over time and the influences on that development. You will also need to include the key points about the development of legislation.

Your tutor will suggest ways to present your evidence, but some points to consider are:

- Researching the internet using sites suggested by your tutor and government sites (these can be accessed through Hotlinks (see page viii).

- Using a timeline to show key events in the development of common law.

PLTS

Completing this assignment will help you develop your effective participator skills.

Functional skills

This assignment may also help you to develop your functional skills in English (and in ICT if you use a word processing program to produce your answer).

What is an offence?

The difference between a 'crime' and an 'offence' is sometimes explained as a crime involves a victim whereas an offence does not. So, for example, attacking someone with a weapon is a crime, but exceeding the speed limit while driving (but not causing accident or injury) may be defined as an offence.

In England and Wales crimes and offences are categorised by their seriousness and this determines the way they will be tried at court. The least serious offences are defined as **summary offences**. These carry a maximum sentence of six months in prison and/or a fine and are heard in the Magistrates' Court. The defendant does not have the right to ask for a trial by jury or to have the case transferred to the Crown Court.

Examples of summary offences are:

- driving while disqualified
- common assault
- public order offences
- fishing with a rod and line without a licence
- most motoring offences.

Defendants appearing in court (after they have been charged by the Crown Prosecution Service (CPS) will be asked to plead guilty or not guilty.

Key term

Summary offences – the least serious offences.

Link

For more information on the different types of court, see page 220.

203

A plea of guilty will lead the court to sentence and one of not guilty will lead to a trial to decide on guilt or innocence. Magistrates decide on guilt in the Magistrates' Courts and a jury decides in the Crown Court. Magistrates also decide on the sentence for cases heard by them, unless they think their powers to sentence do not reflect the seriousness of the offence, in which case they can commit the defendant to the Crown Court for sentencing. Sentences in the Crown Court are decided by the judge who hears the case.

Appeals in criminal courts

Once the court has made a decision (about guilt or about the sentence) the defendant may consider an appeal. Defendants have a right of appeal from the Magistrates' Court to the Crown Court. If they pleaded guilty they can appeal against sentence only. If not guilty, they can appeal against both conviction and sentence. Notice of appeal must be given to the court and to the CPS within 21 days of the hearing. The decision of the Crown Court on appeal is final unless there has been an error in interpreting the law, the court has acted beyond its powers, or failed to exercise its power.

Where the case has been heard in the Crown Court (other than on appeal) the defendant can give notice of appeal to the Court of Appeal (Criminal Division) within 28 days of the decision. The notice must state the grounds for the appeal. The CPS can also refer serious cases to the Court of Appeal where they consider the Crown Court sentence was 'unduly lenient', in which case the sentence may be increased.

There is a limited right of appeal to the Supreme Court (which took over from the House of Lords as the highest court in the land in October 2009) but only on a point of law of 'general public importance'.

PLTS

Completing this assignment will help you develop your reflective learner, creative thinker and effective participator skills.

Functional skills

This assignment may also help you to develop your functional skills in ICT if you use a word processing program to produce your poster.

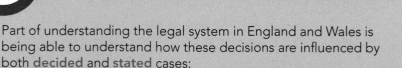

BTEC Assessment activity 11.2 (P2)

Part of understanding the legal system in England and Wales is being able to understand how these decisions are influenced by both **decided** and **stated** cases:

Produce a wall poster which:

1 *Explains* how decided and stated cases give direction to current cases being tried in court. (P2)

Grading tips

To achieve (P2) you should explain what decided cases and stated cases are and how these cases are used by the judiciary to help them reach decisions in cases currently being heard by the courts.

2 The codes of practice set out by the Police and Criminal Evidence Act 1984 and subsequent amendments which apply to the rights of offenders throughout the judicial process

2.1 Police powers

Activity: Police powers v human rights

The police have a wide range of powers that they use as part of their work to stop crime and protect law-abiding people. It is important that the police have these powers but it is also vital that the police use their powers lawfully.

Why do the police have these powers?

Aren't they a breach of human rights?

In order for the police to carry out their jobs effectively, they need to have certain powers. The Police and Criminal Evidence Act 1984 (**PACE**) sets out police powers, including powers to stop, search, arrest and hold in custody.

The most commonly used police power is the one that enables police to stop and search suspected people and vehicles. Stop and search is used if a police officer suspects that a person or vehicle is carrying stolen goods or offensive weapons.

Section 60 of PACE enables the police to search people in a specific area at a specific time if they believe that there is the possibility of serious violence or that a person is carrying a dangerous object or offensive weapon.

Section 44 of the Terrorism Act 2000 gives the police the power to search people for equipment that could be used to commit a terrorist act. Police can search anybody anywhere under this law, and they do not need reasonable suspicion to do so. It is under this law that police conduct random searches in train and tube stations. This power aims to deter terrorist activity.

Key term

PACE – the Police and Criminal Evidence Act 1984 sets out in a professional code of practice the rules by which the police must behave during the stop and search, arrest, detention, investigation, identification and interviewing of suspects.

Key terms

Warrant – a written order of the court that gives a law enforcement officer powers to act e.g. an arrest warrant gives the police the power to arrest the person named on the warrant.

Caution – a warning given to someone who has committed a minor offence but has not been charged.

Did you know?

The Ministry of Justice statistics on Race and the Criminal Justice System (2008) identified that:

- compared to the general UK population, Black people are 8 times more likely to be stopped and searched than White people, and Asian people are 2 times more likely

- London has the largest number of Black residents, and over 79% of Black people stopped and searched in the period were in the Metropolitan Police area.

A witness can use a mobile phone to record or report suspicious behaviour. A photo can subsequently be used to identify a suspect. Do you think this violates an individual's human rights?

The Serious Organised Crime and Police Act 2005 gave police enhanced powers and rationalised power of arrest for all offences.

If an individual refuses to be stopped, the police can use reasonable force to both stop and detain them so they can conduct a search. The police must have reason to suspect the individual (except in cases of suspected terrorism). Individuals can be arrested and taken into custody with or without a **warrant** for arrest. This will be issued if an individual is suspected of committing a serious offence such as murder, but the police can also take individuals into custody without a warrant to take fingerprints or if they have 'reasonable grounds' to suspect they have committed an offence.

If the police have 'reasonable suspicion' that you have been involved in an offence they can stop, question and search you and your vehicle. If the police do stop a member of the public they must give reasons. If the police search you without reasonable justification then a complaint can be made against them. The identity of any suspect must be confirmed (using details such as full name, date of birth, address). Other means of identification of a suspect may be:

- by witnesses (using photo or video identification or an identification parade)
- fingerprint identification (to establish identify or presence at a crime scene)
- footwear impressions to match with those at a crime scene
- DNA profile for proving identity or for comparing with crime scene evidence
- photographing suspects to record and check identity
- searching and examining detained suspects to find identifying marks such as birth marks or tattoos.

Under the PACE Code police officers stopping a suspect must record a first description of the suspect, their identity (or description of the person stopped if they refuse to give their name) and the grounds the police have to suspect that an indictable offence (an offence that can be taken before a crown court and jury) has been committed.

The PACE Code ensures that photos, fingerprints and samples are only taken, used and kept for legitimate purposes within the law.

Before being questioned by a police officer at the time of arrest, a suspect must be **cautioned**. If someone has voluntarily gone to the police station (not under arrest) to help the police with their enquiries they should also be cautioned, but they are free to leave at any time.

The caution should be repeated before any interview takes place, before a video or tape recording of an interview commences, before being arrested for any additional charges the police may bring and before the police charge a suspect with an offence.

What are my rights if I am arrested?

Before arresting you the police must have grounds for doing so. Some grounds may be:

- you are suspected of an indictable offence
- you have refused to identify yourself or give your address
- you are a danger to others
- you are in danger from others.

If you are arrested and taken to a police station the police must ask:

- Do you need medical attention or treatment?
- Are you a young person aged under 18? If so you need to have an appropriate adult (for example a parent or social worker) with you.
- Are you at risk of self-harm?

While detained you have the following rights:

- to be treated well. If the court later suspects you were not treated well, evidence such as confessions may be discounted. This means you have a right not to be physically, mentally or verbally abused. These rights are included in the Human Rights Act:
  - Article 3 (prohibition of torture, inhuman or degrading treatment)
  - Article 6 (the right to a fair trial)
  - Article 8 (the right to privacy)
- to let someone know that you have been detained. This is usually by a phone call, but could be by letter.
- to legal advice provided without charge and in private. You can request that you have legal advice prior to being questioned and you can ask that your lawyer be with you during any interview.
- to have any interview recorded. Any interviews with the police should be recorded.

Once in detention you also have certain rights. These are:

- to decent conditions during detention. Your cell must be clean, warm, lighted and ventilated and the bedding should be clean. You must have access to washing and toilet facilities. Meals and exercise should be provided

- to request to see a copy of the PACE Code

- not being detained for more than 24 hours without charge. In some circumstances this can be extended by the police to 36 hours or a magistrate can authorise up to a maximum 96 hours. Terror suspects can be held for up to 28 days without being charged if authorised by a judge.

Once charged you must be brought before the magistrate the next day (excluding Christmas Day, Good Friday or any Sunday) or bailed to appear at court at a given date.

Did you know?

The wording for a caution is:

You do not have to say anything. But it may harm your defence if you do not mention when questioned something which you later rely on in court. Anything you do say may be given in evidence.

Searches must be recorded and the following must always be recorded:

- name of the person searched, or if withheld, description
- self-defined ethnic background of person searched
- time, place and date of first detaining the person
- reason for of the search and the grounds for making a search
- outcome, i.e. arrest or no further action.

Activity: Rights of the individual

1 Joash has been arrested by the police on suspicion of stealing a mobile phone from a boy in the street. Joash is 15.

What rights does Joash have while in police custody before being charged?

2 The police decide to charge Joash.

What rights does Joash have once he has been charged?

Key terms

Bail – the temporary release of a suspect who has been charged. Being bailed is being released from custody awaiting appearance in court (for trial or sentence), sometimes on payment of a sum of money as security that you will appear.

Remand – the detention of a suspect before appearing at court for trial or sentencing (either in custody or on bail).

Prosecution – the lawyer representing the state who is putting the case against the accused to the court.

Defence – lawyers representing the defendant (accused) before the court.

Grievous bodily harm – unlawful and malicious wounding or assault inflicting serious harm on another (if convicted offence carries the possibility of a life sentence).

Common assault – unlawful wounding which results in a minor injury such as skin grazes or scratches, minor bruises, a 'black eye'.

Generally speaking, it is the extent of injury which results from the wounding that distinguishes these charges.

Bail

The police can **bail** you, without charge, to return to the station at a set date and time while they continue their investigation. Once you have been charged, the police must release you on bail unless:

- there is doubt about your identity and residence
- there is a need to protect you or someone else involved in the case
- the police believe you will fail to attend court
- the police fear you may intimidate witnesses.

The courts can also grant bail. Generally bail will be granted unless the courts suspect you will commit further offences; fail to appear as required at a court hearing; interfere with witnesses.

Bail can be granted with or without conditions. An example of a bail condition is that you report to a police station at regular intervals, that you keep to a curfew, that you keep away from certain places or people, or that you live at a certain address. The **prosecution** will oppose granting bail if you are charged with a serious offence.

If the court decides to **remand** a young person (particularly if charged with a serious offence) it must explain why and may remand:

- on conditional bail
- on unconditional bail
- to local authority accommodation
- in custody (secure remand).

Case study: Bail lottery

Is the granting of bail a lottery? Investigations showed that the chances of bail often depend on the geographic location of the court where the case is heard.

Who receives bail and why is sometimes controversial. Look at the examples below:

- A policeman accused of killing his wife was bailed. On release, he murdered his wife's mother and killed himself.

- A man was kicked to death by a teenage boy just hours after the boy was released on bail following another assault.

- A boy accused of pouring petrol over another young person and threatening to set him on fire was released on bail.

- A man accused of stealing some meat from a supermarket was remanded in custody pending trial for theft.

- A man charged with stealing a watch and gloves worth £90 was remanded in custody pending trial for theft.

- A man who admitted making racist remarks to a police officer while drunk was remanded in custody while awaiting sentence.

- One man convicted of assault and grievous bodily harm was released on bail pending sentence while a man appearing before a different court accused of assault with an iron bar was remanded in custody.

Now answer the following questions:

1 Think about these different examples. What do you think of each example of bail decisions? Were they fair? Could withholding bail have prevented any of these crimes?

2 What criteria do you think the police and the courts should apply when deciding on bail?

3 A defendant can apply for bail when charged with any offence. The only exception is that bail cannot be granted in cases of murder or rape or where the defendant has a previous conviction for such an offence. Do you think this is right? Explain your answer.

BTEC Assessment activity 11.3

The police in the UK have a range of powers to stop, search, arrest and detain suspects. Those suspected of an offence have rights under the PACE Code, including a presumed right to bail (except where specific concerns exist about the suspect).

In this assessment activity you will be looking at both sides of this – powers and rights!

Produce a booklet, to answer the tasks below, which identifies, analyses and justifies the powers of the police, describes the rights the PACE Code gives to suspects and explains when bail can be refused:

1 *Identify* the powers available to the police to deal with suspects. **P3**

2 *Analyse* the powers available to police dealing with a suspect. **M1**

3 *Justify* the use of police powers when dealing with suspects. **D1**

4 *Describe* the rights afforded to a person held in police custody before and after charge. **P5**

5 *Explain* when bail can be refused after charge for both adult and juvenile offenders. **M2**

Grading tips

P3, **M2** and **D1** are linked grading criteria. If you write a clear description identifying the main powers the police have you will achieve **P3**. To achieve **M1** you will have to *analyse* those powers. This means you will need to examine those powers in detail in order to highlight the essential points and how this contributes to the overall use by the police of the powers given to them by society.

For **D1** you will need to go a stage further and justify why the police have the powers they do. You will need to present a reasoned case, support your opinions and include a conclusion based on your views.

To achieve **P5** you should *describe* the rights that a suspect has while being detained and questioned by the police and after they are charged.

To achieve **M2** you will need to explain what bail is and on what grounds it may be refused after a defendant has been charged.

You may choose to present your findings in a range of ways, for example a frequently asked questions sheet, information leaflets, an audio/video presentation for a TV/radio broadcast.

3 The powers given and the points to prove to support a successful prosecution

3.1 Has an offence been committed?

The police need to establish an offence has been committed before they take further action. Sometimes this is straightforward. For example, if an intruder is found on a property or in possession of goods that are not their own it is very clear that they have committed an offence. At other times the evidence may not be so clear. Conflicting claims may be made, the police may need to collect evidence and witness statements to be clear of the facts and circumstances.

Activity: Has a crime been committed?

The police arrive at a property where the neighbours have reported seeing an intruder breaking and entering.

The police discover that the front window is smashed and it appears a man is on the premises. He has a suitcase in his hand when the police apprehend him.

What do you think? What evidence is there that a crime has been committed?

Sometimes individuals report an alleged crime because they want to get someone into trouble. Believe it or not, people have been known to wound themselves and blame someone else! Other people may report a crime for financial gain – to make an insurance or compensation claim. The police and the Criminal Prosecution Service need to be absolutely certain that an offence has occurred.

3.2 Evidence

Once the police have established a crime has been committed they will begin to gather evidence and put together a case file. Evidence may take the form of evidence from the crime scene (such as finger prints, DNA evidence) stolen property found in the accused's possession, **witness statements** from those at the scene or the victims of the crime and evidence like CCTV footage which proves the defendant was present at the scene or nearby.

Police will take statements from anyone who saw what happened. This is called a witness statement. Figure 11.2 shows all the information that must be recorded with a witness statement.

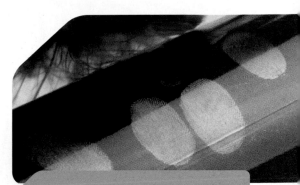

Police evidence may include fingerprints found at the scene of the crime. What other forms of evidence may the police use?

Key term

Witness statement – formal account of the facts relevant to the matter being investigated.

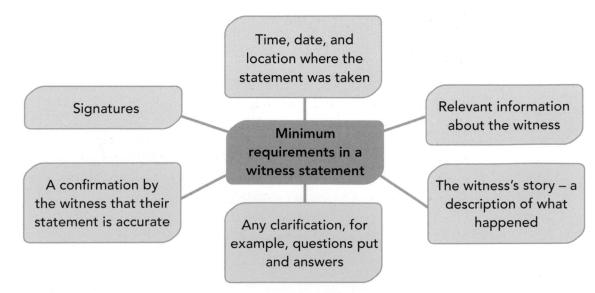

Minimum requirements in a witness statement
- Time, date, and location where the statement was taken
- Signatures
- Relevant information about the witness
- A confirmation by the witness that their statement is accurate
- Any clarification, for example, questions put and answers
- The witness's story – a description of what happened

Figure 11.2: Have you ever had to make a witness statement?

Case study: Kidnap!

4 August 2009, Westminster Magistrates' Court

A woman was sentenced to a year's community service and ordered to pay costs of £50 after admitting she lied to the police.

She claimed she had been forced off a train, kidnapped, bundled into a car, made to take drugs and held for 3 hours.

Police spent two days investigating the allegation, but failed to find any evidence to support the claim from examination of video footage taken at the rail station where the woman claimed the incident had occurred.

The police issued a statement saying that such false allegations wasted police time and diverted police resources from investigating real crimes.

Now answer the following questions:

1 Why do you think a person would falsely report that a crime had occurred?

2 Should the police investigate all crime reports?

3 How can the police decide the facts of a reported case? What kind of evidence can they use?

Key term

Shadow charging – a voluntary scheme in which police and CPS work closely together from an early stage (before a charge is made) in a potential criminal prosecution to ensure the appropriate charge is laid and there is a realistic prospect of conviction. This ensures there are fewer abandoned prosecutions and a better deal for witnesses and victims.

Once the police have assembled their evidence (or sufficient evidence to think they can bring a charge) they will pass the file to the CPS. The CPS will provide guidance to the police regarding the charge and the case. The process where the CPS, the police, lawyers and investigators cooperate to ensure the charge is appropriate is called **shadow charging**.

The CPS will decide whether or not to prosecute and what charge to bring. They will initially base their decision on the quality of the evidence that the police have collected. For example, if there is CCTV and DNA evidence that places the accused at the crime scene then that will provide a good case to proceed. If there is no forensic evidence or the witnesses only saw the outline of the offender at night, the evidence will be easier for the defence to challenge. For the case to proceed to charge and court hearing the CPS need to address two questions: can the evidence be used in court and is it reliable?

Can the evidence be used in court?

Could the court discount some of the evidence? Evidence needs to be collected in accordance with certain rules. For example, if the suspect is not cautioned before questioning, or not allowed to consult a lawyer, then the evidence is likely to be judged inadmissible.

If this evidence is inadmissible, is there enough other evidence available for the CPS to believe there is a realistic prospect of the accused being convicted?

Is the evidence reliable?

- For example, if the evidence comes from a confession did the defendant understand the implications of their confession? What about the defendant's age, intelligence, understanding of English?

- How strong is the evidence of identification? If the defendant claims not to have been present, is the evidence strong enough to put them at the crime scene?

- If the defendant admits to being present but has a plausible explanation, will the court believe them? Could there be an innocent explanation?

- How reliable are the witnesses? Have they got a motive to get the defendant into trouble? Have they got previous convictions themselves?

- What explanation has the defendant given? Is a court likely to find it credible in the light of the evidence as a whole? Does it support an innocent explanation?

The job of the police and the prosecution is to bring evidence before the court that proves *beyond all reasonable doubt* the guilt of the defendant. In contrast, the job of the defence is to put doubts into the mind of the court so that a conviction is avoided!

Disclosure

Generally speaking, anyone accused of an offence has the right to know what evidence the police and CPS have against them so that they can be defended properly. The police and CPS must disclose evidence unless there is a good reason not to. The grounds for withholding evidence may be about confidentiality or sensitivity. For example, a witness to a crime will not want their address released in case the defendant or defendant's family may threaten or intimidate them. Evidence gathered during a case that is ongoing or a suspected terrorist case will probably not be disclosed.

The disclosure officer is a police employee (they could be a police officer or a civilian) who manages the disclosure process on behalf of the police and CPS and uses a process like the flowchart in Figure 11.3 to decide whether or not evidence collected by the police during the investigation should be disclosed to the defence.

Key terms

Either-way offences – may be tried in either the Magistrates' Court or the Crown Court and include theft, drugs offences and some offences of violence against the person, such as assault and wounding (not with intent – i.e. it was not planned in advance).

Indictable offences – must be tried by the Crown Court, although the case will start in the Magistrates' Court and the defendant will be committed to the Crown Court. Indictable offences include murder, rape and robbery.

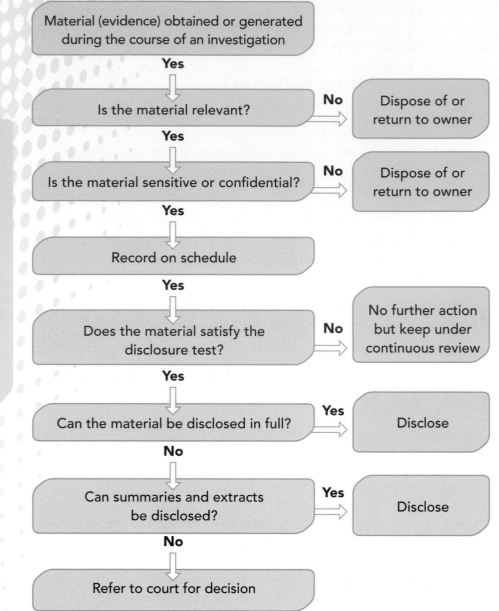

Material (evidence) obtained or generated during the course of an investigation

Yes

Is the material relevant? — **No** → Dispose of or return to owner

Yes

Is the material sensitive or confidential? — **No** → Dispose of or return to owner

Yes

Record on schedule

Yes

Does the material satisfy the disclosure test? — **No** → No further action but keep under continuous review

Yes

Can the material be disclosed in full? — **Yes** → Disclose

No

Can summaries and extracts be disclosed? — **Yes** → Disclose

No

Refer to court for decision

Figure 11.3: Flowchart of disclosure. Do you think the police should disclose all their evidence on a case? Why?

Activity: Mode of trial

Working in pairs

We have read of the three types of offences and where these would be tried. See how quickly you can copy and complete the table!

Offence	Examples	Where tried	Who decides guilt?	Who decides sentence?
Summary offence	1. 2. 3.		Magistrates	
Either-way offence	1. Shoplifting (theft) 2. 3.	Either Magistrates' Court or Crown Court		
Indictable offence	1. Murder 2. 3.	Starts in ... Committed to ...	Jury	

The CPS is governed by a set of codes to ensure decisions made about prosecutions of offenders are consistent and fair. The code aims to make sure that any decisions about whether to prosecute an offender uphold justice, the work of the police and other people who work in the justice and court system (or criminal justice system). It also aims to respect the rights of defendants, victims and witnesses. The main principles that underpin the code are: is there sufficient evidence for a successful prosecution and is proceeding with the prosecution in the public interest.

Prosecutions can be commenced by **summons** or by **charge**. Once a prosecution has started, the CPS will then decide whether to proceed with, alter or to drop the charges. They also have the power to take over private prosecutions and can then discontinue them. The CPS can direct the police on what further evidence or investigation is needed. They also have a duty to keep cases under review. A defendant and their solicitor can make representations to them at any stage.

Activity: In the public interest?

A defendant suspected of an armed robbery has been diagnosed with a terminal illness.

Should the prosecution continue?

Is the prosecution in the public interest?

Sentences of the courts

There are sentencing guidelines produced by the Sentencing Guidelines Council to help judges and magistrates decide on appropriate sentences. They must take into account the need to:

- protect society from crime
- punish those who offend
- rehabilitate those who offend
- reduce crime in society
- ensure offenders make reparation (amends) to the victims and society.

They also have to consider:

- how serious the crime is
- whether the offender has offended previously
- whether the offender genuinely regrets what they have done (remorse)
- time remanded in custody while awaiting trial.

Magistrates' Courts and Crown Courts have four sentencing options and these are financial, discharges, community sentences and **custodial sentences**. Courts can impose a mixture of these and can attach conditions to sentences.

Financial penalties. These include fines, compensation orders (where the victim is recompensed) and confiscation orders (where money and goods are seized).

Discharges. These sentences are imposed when the court decides that the type of offence and circumstance in which it was committed do

Key terms

Summons – is a legal document issued by a court requiring a defendant to appear in court.

Charge – a specific statement of grounds on which the defendant is being indicted.

Did you know?

The Sentencing Guidelines Council produce guidelines for use in all criminal courts. These can be accessed at their website, available via Hotlinks (see page viii). A distinct set of guidelines apply to Magistrates' Courts and Crown Courts.

Did you know?

Fines: 72 per cent of convicted offenders get fines.

Discharges (conditional and non conditional): 8 per cent get discharged.

Community sentences: 13 per cent get community sentences.

Prison: 7 per cent go to prison.

Key term

Custodial sentence – a prison sentence.

not justify a more severe sentence. The court is not ignoring the offence, as there is a conviction, but the sentence is mild (unless further offences take place). A discharge can be 'absolute' (which means it doesn't have conditions), or 'conditional' (on not committing another offence).

Community sentences. These are non-custodial sentences and involve the offender in programmes to help the community or programmes that will offer benefit to themselves. They can include the following:

- compulsory unpaid work for up to 300 hours. This involves work such as conservation, charity work, cleaning up graffiti that benefits the community
- programmes to address offending behaviour, for example anger management or domestic violence programmes
- participation in any specified activities, such as literacy classes. It can also involve prohibition from other activities, such as a ban on attending football matches if their offences relate to football hooliganism or violence
- a curfew that involves staying at an agreed location, being able to go out at set times and to predetermined locations and possibly being electronically tagged
- exclusion from specific areas
- a residence requirement to live in an agreed location
- mental health treatment (with the offender's agreement)
- drug rehabilitation for crime related to drug misuse
- alcohol treatment for alcohol abuse
- supervision by the Probation Service linked to specific programmes.
- attendance centre requirement (for under 25s) where the offender must address their offending behaviour in a group environment and give up their leisure time to do so.

Court orders

There is a range of orders the courts can impose. Some of the most common ones are shown in Table 11.1:

Table 11.1: Some common court orders imposed by the courts.

Order	Description
Anti-social behaviour order (ASBO)	can be given to anyone aged 10 or over for causing distress or harassment to someone or the community. They are civil orders but breaches could lead to a prison sentence of up to 5 years.
Acceptable behaviour contract	can be given to a young person (who is acting badly) and their parents/carers to agree a contract under which the offender agrees to stop their offending behaviour.
Curfew order	can be given to a young offender aged 16 plus.
Parenting orders	can be given to the parents of young people who offend; play truant; have received a child safety order, anti-social behaviour order or sexual offences prevention order.
Supervision order	requires offender to take part in activities including reparation to community or victim and programmes to address offending.
Reparation order	by agreement the offender and victim meet to discuss impact of the crime; could also involve community work.
Attendance centre order	requires offender to attend a centre run by police where activities include discipline, physical training, developing social skills.
Community punishment order	requires offenders aged 16–17 to carry out unpaid work for between 40–240 hours.
Drug treatment and testing order (DTTO)	involves treatment and regular testing for drug abuse.

Types of prison sentences

If a suspect is found guilty the courts have a range of sentencing options available. These depend on the type of offence, how serious it was, the circumstances in which the offence was committed and the legal maximum penalty available.

The judge or magistrate giving the sentence must consider a range of factors:

- punishment for the offender
- working to reduce crime overall
- rehabilitating the offender (so they don't commit further crimes)
- protecting the public (especially from violent offenders, drug dealers)
- getting the offender to make reparation (show they are sorry and repay society, maybe by doing voluntary work).

The sentence decided will reflect these factors.

Magistrates' and Crown Courts have different sentencing powers. More serious cases are sentenced in the Crown Court and less serious offences are sentenced in the Magistrates' Court. The maximum sentence the Magistrates' Courts can give is 6 months, but they can commit to Crown Court for sentencing if they think the sentence should be greater than 6 months.

When deciding upon the appropriate sentence courts have guidelines to assist them. The Sentencing Guidelines Council produce guidelines for use in all criminal courts. If the courts decide not to follow these guidelines they must give reasons.

Life sentences. Life sentences differ from fixed-term sentences in that offenders have no automatic right to release and only have a set minimum time in which to serve in custody. Even once released they are on 'licence' and could be recalled to prison for any breach of their licence.

Fixed-term sentence. The judge or magistrates set a tariff in the fixed-term sentence and after serving half the tariff, the offender can apply for release. If they reoffend or break the conditions of the early release they can be recalled.

Indeterminate sentencing. A minimum tariff for jail is set in indeterminate sentencing but the offender cannot be released until they have satisfied the criminal justice authorities that they are fit for release and have completed their agreed offending behaviour programmes.

Some sentences include time behind bars. What percentage of offenders go to prison?

Release on licence. If an offender is released before the full term of their sentence they are 'on licence' (which means they can be recalled if they breach the licence conditions imposed). While on licence the offender will be managed by the Probation Service and will be expected to live at an agreed address, obey any Curfew Orders, attend any appointments required by probation and, most importantly, not reoffend. A breach will result in recall to custody.

Breach of sentence conditions. If the sentence given by the court includes conditions (such as attending meetings with probation, or completing community service) a breach of those conditions will result in the offender being brought before the court again and further penalties may be imposed.

BTEC Assessment activity 11.4 P4

When the police collect evidence and the CPS put a prosecution case together for court they need to prove to the court, *beyond all reasonable doubt*, that the accused is the guilty party.

For this assessment activity you will need to select a piece of legislation against which the accused has been charged and identify the points that would need to be proved to convince the court of the guilt of the accused.

1 *Select* a piece of legislation and *identify* the points to prove beyond all reasonable doubt. P4

Grading tips

To achieve P4 you must first decide the breach of the law the accused might be charged with. You may, for example, have a defendant charged with shoplifting. Theft from a shop is an offence of theft under Section 1(1) of the Theft Act 1968.

Alternatively, you may decide to consider a defendant charged under Section 3, Misuse of Drugs Act 1971 who is accused of being in possession of cannabis.

Have a look at the local newspaper reports for cases brought before the courts in the last few weeks and see what the defendants were charged with.

Once you have selected the offence you want to use to base your answer on be sure to get agreement from your tutor. You will need to be clear that the legislation chosen will allow you to cover the P4 criteria fully.

You will then need to *identify* all the points the prosecution would need to prove to the court to ensure the court could convict.

Think about :

- identification
- witnesses
- physical evidence
- the facts of the case
- the motivation of the offender.

Include these in your answer.

PLTS

Completing this assignment will help you develop your independent enquirer, creative thinker and self-manager skills.

Functional skills

This assignment may also help you to develop your functional skills in English and ICT (if you use a word processing program to produce your answer).

4 The role of the prosecution, the defence and the courts

Activity: Who are they?

Think of the people you might see at a court hearing and their roles.

Write down five of the people you might see and what their roles are in the hearing.

Discuss your findings in small groups. How many different roles did you identify altogether?

Which of these people are employed by the court?

4.1 Who's who in court?

The Crown Prosecution Service (CPS)

The CPS is the government department responsible for prosecuting criminal cases investigated by the police in England and Wales. It was set up in 1986 (before which the police both prepared and prosecuted cases at court) to be an independent body to review cases presented by the police to see if they should proceed.

In court the role of the CPS is to bring offenders to justice through fair and impartial presentation of the case at the court hearing. **Barristers** and **solicitors** are used by the CPS for initial hearings. A Barrister is usually used to prosecute complex cases or cases in the Crown Court.

The defence

An individual suspected of a crime has the right to be represented by a lawyer when being questioned by the police and when preparing their defence if charged. Defence lawyers are independent of the court and the CPS and will plead the case where a defendant is claiming innocence and will try to mitigate (or explain) the circumstances where the defendant pleads guilty.

The defence lawyer will ensure evidence against the defendant is disclosed before the court hearing, will access any records from time in custody (including police interview transcripts) and represent the defendant at the court hearing. In cases where a guilty verdict could result in imprisonment, the lawyer's fees may be funded by the state (via legal aid) depending on the means or income of the defendant.

Key terms

Barristers and solicitors are both legally qualified but undertake slightly different roles in the criminal justice process.

Barrister – a lawyer who practises as an advocate for a defendant, especially in the Crown Court. Barristers often only become involved in cases once representation in court is required by the defendant. They are rarely employed by defendants directly, but are employed via the defendant's solicitor.

Solicitor – a lawyer who deals with legal matters and legal documents. Solicitors traditionally deal with any legal matter but do not usually represent their clients in court (except for Magistrates' Courts).

Did you know?

Criminal prosecutions can also be brought by some other government bodies. These include:

- UK Financial Services Authority (FSA) for financial offences
- Health and Safety Executive (HSE) for breaches of health and safety legislation
- Her Majesty's Revenue and Customs (HMRC) for tax and revenue offences
- Department of Work and Pensions (DWP) for benefit fraud.

In addition the RSPCA takes private prosecutions against people breaking laws passed to protect animals from cruelty.

Generally defence lawyers who appear in the magistrates courts are solicitors and those appearing in the crown court are barristers.

The Court

Magistrates' Court

Criminal cases are usually brought by the CPS and all criminal charges are initially heard in the Magistrates' Courts. About 95 per cent of cases are completed in the Magistrates' Courts. For young people (aged 10 to 18) cases are brought in Youth Courts (which are specialist Magistrates' Courts). Most court hearings are open to the public – so justice can be seen to be done. Youth Courts and Family Courts are always 'closed' or private hearings. Some adult criminal courts may be held 'in camera' (in private) because of issues such as national security or because the police are still investigating matters linked to the case and they do not want the evidence heard by the public. Court hearings may also be closed to protect the identity of witnesses.

In a Magistrates' Court, cases are usually heard by lay magistrates. These are unpaid volunteers who are not legally qualified. They are assisted by a legally qualified advisor employed directly by the court. Usually three magistrates (a bench) hear the case jointly. The senior magistrate acts as the Bench Chairperson. Magistrates' Courts also employ District Judges (who must be professional lawyers) who sit alone.

Crown Court

Crown Court hearings are managed by a judge (who must be a professional lawyer). Guilt is decided by a jury made up of 12 adult citizens who decide whether a defendant is guilty or not. The jury's task is to decide whether a person is guilty *beyond reasonable doubt*. In the Magistrates' Court lawyers do not usually wear wigs and gowns, but in the Crown Court the judge, prosecution and defence lawyers all wear wigs and gowns. A lawyer appearing in Crown Court without a wig and gown could be in contempt of court! Recently the traditional wigs and gowns have been modernised (and are no longer required for civil and family court proceedings).

Appeals are heard by 'higher' courts than the original hearing – this has created the concept of a 'hierarchy' of criminal courts. The 'highest' criminal court is the Supreme Court of the United Kingdom. Some cases can be referred from the UK to the European Courts (the European Court of Justice and the European Court of Human Rights).

Witnesses

If you have witnessed a crime you should tell the police who will take a statement. They may ask you to come to court to give evidence and if they do you are obliged to turn up. You may be asked to be a witness for the prosecution or for the defence. If you give evidence in court you may be cross-examined by the lawyers for both the prosecution and the defence.

Witnesses who are frightened of the impact of giving evidence (thinking that they or their families may be threatened or injured) can ask to give evidence in private. Children and victims of crime may be allowed to give evidence by video link (so the magistrates or judge can see the witness but the defendant cannot).

Activity: Rights of the individual

Sam, who is 16, witnessed Joash, who is 15, going up to a boy in the street and stealing his phone.

If Sam comes forward as a witness what key features should be included in his statement to the police?

Can Sam be forced to give evidence against Joash in court?

Witnesses need to be competent which means they need to understand what is required of them and the need to tell the truth. A young child who can't understand the questions asked or the meaning of giving evidence under oath will probably not be competent as a witness.

Witnesses can be *compelled* or required to give evidence. A spouse cannot be forced to give evidence against their husband or wife. Failure to give evidence could result in the witness being charged with *contempt of court* which may result in a fine or even imprisonment. Lying to the court when giving evidence is also contempt of court, and can be punished.

Victims and witness can ask for support through Victim Support (a voluntary organisation). The Witness Service (which is part of Victim Support) provides advice about the court hearings, can arrange a visit to the court before the hearing and can provide someone to sit with you during the hearing itself. Anyone giving evidence in court must swear an oath or affirmation to tell the truth to the court.

Before giving evidence you will be allowed to refresh your memory by looking at the witness statement you made. If you are a prosecution witness the CPS lawyer will asks questions to establish you are reliable and show that your evidence supports the guilt of the accused. The defence lawyer will then cross-examine you and try to show that your evidence is improbable or unrealistic, that your story is inconsistent or that you are mistaken or untruthful.

Activity: Child witnesses

In May 2009 a man was convicted of rape after evidence was given by the victim, a four-year-old child. The victim gave evidence by video link.

The prosecution presented video evidence of the child being questioned about the crime. This evidence was then challenged by the defence. The child was cross-examined for 40 minutes by defence barristers and asked if she had 'told fibs'.

Should a child be cross-examined by lawyers? Should there be a time limit to how long a child has to give evidence? If a child is not cross-examined, how else can the court find out the truth?

Did you know?

These are some of the oaths that you may swear in court:

General Oath

I swear by Almighty God that I will faithfully try the defendant and give a true verdict according to the evidence.

Affirmation

I do solemnly, sincerely and truly declare and affirm that I will faithfully try the defendant and give a true verdict according to the evidence.

Other oaths

I swear by Allah that I will faithfully try the defendant and give a true verdict according to the evidence.

I swear by the Gita that I will faithfully try the defendant and give a true verdict according to the evidence.

A Bible or other religious book is not always used when swearing the oath in court.

221

BTEC Assessment activity 11.5 P6 P7 M3

Knowing 'who does what' in the criminal justice process is important.

The roles of the CPS, defence and courts are quite different but interlinked. Understanding how the disclosure of evidence operates is also important.

Produce a leaflet in which you cover the following tasks:

1 *Explain* the process of disclosure. **P6**

2 *Describe* the role of the CPS, Defence and the Courts. **P7**

3 *Analyse* the role of witnesses and their part in giving evidence in court. **M3**

Grading tips

P6 requires you to explain the process of disclosure. You will need to include information in your answer from both perspectives (the prosecution and the defence). It would be useful to see examples to explain what types of evidence would be disclosed in advance (such as witness statements or DNA matches between the defendant and evidence from the crime scene) and what types of evidence the prosecution may be reluctant to disclose (especially evidence that might be sensitive or confidential such as the address of a witness to the crime).

To achieve **P7** you should explain the roles of each of the three organisations listed.

Explain means that you should not only say who these are and what they do but you should also add examples.

Make a list of the role and work of each of the three categories.

When thinking about the role of the courts remember to include information on witnesses and how evidence is given.

For **M3** you will need to consider why witnesses are important, how witnesses may be intimidated by defendants and how the police and courts may need to protect witnesses to enable them to be confident to give their evidence.

PLTS

Completing this assignment will help you develop your independent enquirer, reflective learner and effective participator skills.

Functional skills

This assignment may also help you to develop your functional skills in English and ICT (if you use a word processing program to produce your leaflet).

Fiona Wallace
Police Officer

I work with a team of six other police officers in a special unit set up to deal with the threat from suspected terrorist crimes. Initially I was an officer on the beat and I learned all about the day-to-day work of the police in a busy inner city. While part of the job is fighting crime and arresting suspects, a lot of the work is about supporting the community and helping people, especially people such as those who have been victims of crime.

To be a police officer I had to complete a comprehensive training course which taught me how to:

- be a reassuring presence in the community
- protect the public from violence
- provide support for victims and witnesses
- investigate complex crimes
- use both modern technology and tried and tested policing methods in my work.

I also had to make sure I knew my legal powers and my duties under the PACE police codes.

A typical day

To be honest, there isn't one! Since I joined the special operations unit one of the things that is key to every day is fitness training. All of our team work out in the gym for at least an hour a day and we also practise tactics for operations, but a lot of the rest of the time is spent on investigations and intelligence gathering and a huge amount of paperwork! I would say my job is a complex mix of excitement, danger, caring and routine.

Although we have to be physically fit, most of the challenges police officers face while doing the job are mental and emotional rather than physical, requiring us to have an understanding of why people behave in the ways that they do, and using that knowledge to support policing skills.

The best thing about the job

- The best thing is knowing I make a difference. My job helps to keep society safe.
- Being part of a modern and professional organisation. All police officers are highly trained and skilled.
- Working with my colleagues as part of an efficient and effective team. Teamwork is a vital part of modern policing – we rely on our colleagues for our personal safety and support.
- Solving crime gives me a buzz – in many ways it's like a jigsaw puzzle and finding that final piece of evidence to ensure a suspect can be charged and convicted.

I have a great career which gives me the opportunity to make an impact on the quality of life in the community.

Think about it!

1. Is this a career that you would be interested in and why?
2. What would be interesting about the job?
3. What qualifications, fitness and training do you think you would need?

Just checking

1. Write out and complete the table (below) explaining what the terms mean.

Term	Meaning or definition
Common law	
Legislation or statute	
PACE Code of Practice	
Bail	
Crime or offence	
CPS	
Disclosure of evidence	
Witness	

edexcel :::

Assignment tips

- Plan your work. Before you start writing up any assignment plan out how you will research the topics and how you will present your answer. You may find a mind map, or spider diagram, helps you with this.

- Make your own glossary of key words and definitions as you go so that you have your own quick reference guide always to hand.

- Always use reliable websites and textbooks for your research. All public service organisations have websites which have useful information. There are some, available via Hotlinks on page x, that would be excellent starting points for finding out about the work of the courts and being a witness in court.

- Keep a note of all the references you use (the date you accessed a website, the page numbers of reference books you used) to help you when writing your bibliography.

Credit value: 10

12 Crime and its effects on society

A large number of public services play a vital role in how society deals with crime and how crime affects society. Public services such as the police, probation and prison services are responsible not only for catching the criminals and supporting the victims of crime but for making sure that crime figures are reduced and that offenders are managed effectively. Catching the criminal is only one part of the story. Crime needs to be managed effectively by taking measures to combat crime, to reduce public anxieties and fears about crime, to manage offenders and to punish offenders. When working in the public services it is important to understand crime and its effects on society and how to deal with the victims of crime in a sensitive and responsible way.

This unit will enable learners to acquire an understanding of the effects crime has on a victim and society as a whole. It will also help learners to identify service providers who offer support, crime prevention advice and reassurance to victims of crime. The second part of this unit explores crime reporting and recording systems used by the police and the guidelines set out in the current national crime reporting standards as well as researching crime investigation and detection techniques. In the final part of this unit learners will examine the judicial system and identify the options available to process and manage offenders – for example final warnings and reprimands, cautions, fixed penalty notices, prosecution – explaining the subsequent outcome.

Learning outcomes

After completing this unit you should:

1. understand the impact of criminal behaviour
2. be able to investigate a local crime reduction initiative
3. understand the methods used to report and record crime
4. know the options available to effectively manage offenders.

225

Assessment and grading criteria

This table shows you what you must do in order to achieve a pass, merit or distinction grade, and where you can find activities in this book to help you.

To achieve a **pass** grade the evidence must show that the learner is able to:	To achieve a **merit** grade the evidence must show that, in addition to the pass criteria, the learner is able to:	To achieve a **distinction** grade the evidence must show that, in addition to the pass and merit criteria, the learner is able to:
P1 Explain the role of the public services to assist and support victims of crime **Assessment activity 12.1 page 237**		
P2 Describe the impact of crime on society **Assessment activity 12.1 page 237**		
P3 Investigate a local crime reduction initiative **Assessment activity 12.2 page 243**	**M1** Analyse a local crime reduction initiative **Assessment activity 12.2 page 243**	**D1** Evaluate a local crime reduction initiative showing how it has reached relevant groups in the community and reduced the fear of crime **Assessment activity 12.2 page 243**
P4 Identify the process involved to report and record crime **Assessment activity 12.3 page 251**	**M2** Describe how the National Crime Recording Standards impacted nationally upon the police service and the effect on crime statistics **Assessment activity 12.3 page 251**	**D2** Evaluate the impact of national crime recording on crime reduction **Assessment activity 12.3 page 251**
P5 Describe the role of the Crime Scene Investigation Unit **Assessment activity 12.3 page 251**	**M3** Explain how crime scenes can be linked and offenders profiled **Assessment activity 12.3 page 251**	
P6 Explain how the National Intelligence Model and intelligence-led policing have led to new policing strategies **Assessment activity 12.3 page 251**		
P7 Describe the different ways the legal system manages offenders **Assessment activity 12.4 page 258**		

How you will be assessed

This unit will be assessed by an internal assignment that will be designed and marked by the staff at your centre. The assignment is designed to allow you to show your understanding of the learning outcomes for crime and its effect on society. Assignments can be quite varied and can take the form of:

- small group discussions
- posters
- leaflets
- reports
- booklets.

Ashley, 16, police role-play volunteer working with new recruits

This unit helped me to see that crime has a massive impact on society as well as how it impacts on individual people's lives. I really enjoyed looking at the organisations that exist to support victims of crime.

As a police volunteer I work with new recruits in training and understanding how crime can impact people has really helped me with this. It was good to explore a local crime initiative because I was able to see how these can really help people in the area that I live in. Another really interesting element was looking at the role of crime scene investigation. I watch loads of programmes like *CSI*, *CSI New York* and *CSI Miami* so it was really good to gain a bit more understanding about how this helps fight crime.

The bit that I enjoyed the most was looking at the different ways that offenders are managed. It was really interesting to find out about all the different types of sentences that there are and which organisations are involved in keeping an eye on offenders to make sure they do as they are told! It was especially interesting when we went on a visit to the Crown Court and got to sit in on several different court cases where offenders were sentenced. It was a great learning experience to see the judge give out the different types of sentences.

Over to you!

- What part of crime and its effects are you interested in?
- Would you like to work at catching criminals or supporting the victims of crime?
- Have you prepared yourself for tackling assessment tasks on the job role in the area of your choice?

1 The impact of criminal behaviour

Talk up

Is everyone a victim?

Think about your friends and family, the people who you know the best. Have any of them been victims of crime? It could be anything, a stolen car, burgled house or even a purse/wallet stolen.

Write down:

- what type of crime it was (car stolen, house burgled etc.)
- who it happened to (mum, dad, grandma etc.)
- how they felt about it (angry, frightened, upset etc.)
- what did they do about it? Did they report it to the police?

Working in pairs or small groups

Discuss your findings and compare these with each other to see if you can establish the most common factor in each area.

Key terms

Victim – a person who has been targeted in a crime.

Offender – a person who has committed a crime.

Did you know?

According to statistics published by the Home Office there are more than 66 burglaries every single day in England and Wales: 32 of these are house burglaries!

Crime has a massive impact on society. It can impact individuals in many different ways as well as affecting whole communities, minority groups and businesses. The impact can be emotional as in the case of a house break-in; the **victim** might feel very upset that very personal or valuable objects have been taken. The impact of crime may also be practical as in the case of a house break-in; there may have been a forced entry where a window is broken and the victim of crime is left to replace the window. This may cause the victim inconvenience as well as having a financial impact.

The role of the public services is to help and support the victim of crime, to prevent crime and to manage the **offenders**. In an attempt to reduce the impact of criminal behaviour on the victims of crime, public services and other agencies are involved in providing care and support. The victims of crime are can be wide-ranging and in some cases they are not always directly involved in the incident. The consequences of a crime can last a lifetime.

1.1 Who are the victims of crime?

All kinds of people can be vulnerable to crime for different reasons. In general terms we can categorise the victims of crime as individuals, minority groups, communities and businesses.

Businesses

This category can include any kind of premises run as a business such as a shop, pub, hotel, warehouse, factory or restaurant. Businesses can be victims of a wide variety of crime. Think about a small newsagent's shop. They could be the victims of a theft because a customer steals a bar of chocolate. An employee might steal cash from the till or steal some stock from the shop. They could also be victims because of vandalism or damage to the shop, or the victim of fraud if someone uses a stolen credit card to pay for goods. Businesses can suffer from crimes such as burglary, damage to vehicles, structural damage (such as vandalism or arson) and these can lead to disruption in trade, loss of business, low staff morale and increased insurance costs.

Activity: How is a business a victim of crime?

Working in pairs

Think about different types of businesses, such as a hotel, supermarket, warehouse, factory and so on. Draw out and complete a table like the one below and explain some of the different ways that businesses can be victims of crime.

Type of business	How might they be a victim of crime
Restaurant	1. Customer may leave without paying bill 2. Employee may steal food or money 3. Intruders may break in and vandalise the property so it is unable to open (lost business)
Hotel	
Supermarket	
Small shop	
Warehouse	
Factory	

Share your findings with your classmates to see how many different ways you can identify that a business could be a victim of crime.

Did you know?

What types of crime?

The figures below show the most common types of crime. They are taken from recorded crimes in England and Wales for 2007/2008:

Type of crime	Number of crimes
Burglary dwelling	279,129
Criminal damage to a vehicle	425,612
Dangerous driving	4,709
Harassment	210,038
Possession of cannabis	158,086
Possession of weapons	32,397
Racially aggravated harassment	26,495
Serious sexual crime	41,460
Serious wounding	15,094
Shoplifting	290,625
Theft from a person	101,660
Theft from vehicle	432,377
Theft of pedal cycle	103,999
Unauthorised taking of a vehicle	159,847
Other theft	526,994

Communities

A community can be defined as the nation as a whole, a town or city, a suburb or housing estate, a street or village, or a minority group, such as an ethnic group or religious group, or even your local scout group, community centre or football team. Any of these may have their equipment stolen or clubhouse burgled. A community is not a victim of crime in the same way as a business. For example, a business may

Activity: Communities and crime

Working in pairs

Think about the area that you live in. Does crime occur in your community? Does it make people think your community is a nice place to live? What do you think about your community? Why?

Have a discussion in your pairs about the points raised above and share your findings with the rest of your class.

You can look up the crime figures for your community by going to Upmystreet website (available via Hotlinks on page x) and entering your town name or your postcode.

lose all its stock and be unable to operate or open until the stock is replaced. This may have a financial impact on the owners and they may have to close down. A community may lose items but should be able to pull together as one to deal with the consequences much more easily. High crime rate affects the look of an area. For example, an estate with high levels of crime may look more neglected and run down and home and car insurance premiums may cost more in this area. If an area is neglected and run down, it will affect the price of property. This will in turn affect the type of people the area attracts to live there, the type and nature of businesses the area attracts and the quality of life that people have in the area.

Minority groups

A minority group is a smaller group in society. It has less power or control over their lives than the majority. A minority group does not necessarily mean a smaller percentage of the population. It refers to groups such as people living with disabilities, religious minorities, ethnic groups, economic minorities (such as those who are unemployed) or those with different sexual preferences. For example, asylum seekers and migrant workers are considered to be a minority group and police have found that they can often be the targets of harassment, victimisation and violence. Other kinds of people that are considered to be more vulnerable to crime are shown in Figure 12.1.

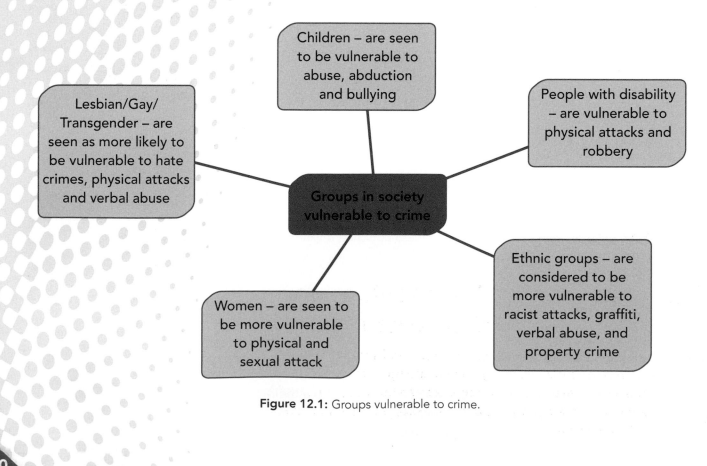

Figure 12.1: Groups vulnerable to crime.

Individuals

An individual can be the victim of crime. This may be the result of bad luck and being in the wrong place at the wrong time or the fact that some individuals are more vulnerable than others. All people can be vulnerable to crime but, for example, an elderly person can be more vulnerable to certain types of crime such mugging or burglary.

Activity: Victims of crime

Working in pairs

Individuals and minority groups can be the victims of crime. Different groups may be vulnerable to crime and affected by different types of crime for different reasons. Look at Figure 12.2 for the types of crime that might affect an elderly person.

Think about how each of these crimes might impact on an elderly person's life in terms of emotional and financial costs. Make a list of the possible impacts and then share these with the rest of the class and compare your lists.

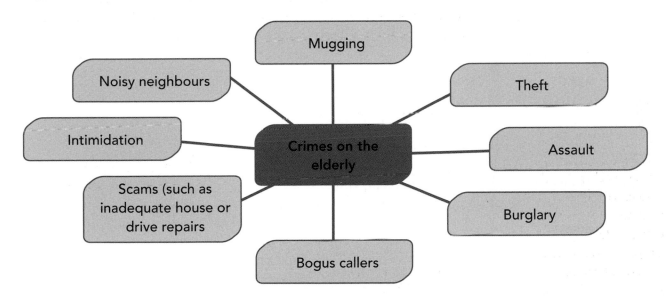

Figure 12.2: Impact of crimes on the elderly.

1.2 The role of public services to assist and support victims of crime

Understanding how crime can impact on people and society is very important in most public services. By understanding which members of society are most vulnerable, public services can think about how to protect them from crime but also how to offer support when they do become victims of crime.

Key term

Community orders – a range of punishments given to an offender to serve in the community.

Crime prevention is an important aspect of police work. What other methods can be used to alert the public?

There are a large number of organisations that exist both locally and nationally to assist and support victims of crime. A few examples are listed below.

Police Service. The police will respond to your call, investigate the crime as well as provide crime prevention advice. The Police Service role is one of rescue, crime prevention, crime investigation, crime detection, referral to victim support, acting as witness in court, providing advice and guidance as well as reassurance.

Probation Services. A probation officer may make assessments and recommendations about the risk posted by an individual offender to the courts. They manage and enforce **community orders**. Probation officers work with prisoners during and after their sentence to help with rehabilitation back into the community and to minimise reoffending. They work with offenders to change behaviours and reduce the risk of harm that they pose and work to reduce the impact of crime on the victim.

Prison Service. The Prison Service ensures that offenders of crime serve their punishment if a custodial sentence is given. A part of their job is to supervise offenders while they are serving their prison sentence. The job also involves working with offenders to make sure that they leave prison with skills and new attitudes and behaviours to be better able to contribute to society. This involves looking after them with humanity and helping them lead law-abiding and useful lives in custody and after release.

Victim Support. This is a registered charity which focuses on helping victims of crime in terms of emotional support and practical tasks, such as helping with insurance or compensation claims. It receives support from the police who refer victims to it and it receives funding from central government.

Witness Service. This ensures that the process of giving evidence in court is as comfortable an experience as possible. It was established in 1989 and is managed and organised by its parent charity Victim Support. There is a Witness Service in every Crown Court in England and Wales which provides information on courtroom procedure for witnesses and helps and reassures them.

Shelter for Abused Families. Agencies like this are designed to help break the cycle of domestic violence by providing facilities that allow women (but also men) the ability to make choices about their home life and give families the opportunity and support to get out of abusive environments.

Citizens Advice Bureau. The CAB began as an emergency measure during the Second World War and has now evolved into a much relied on national agency. It deals with queries mainly in relation to benefits, debt, consumer advice, legal issues, homelessness and immigration.

The Samaritans. Victims often experience significant emotional trauma in the aftermath of a crime committed against them. They may develop feelings of anxiety and depression, or more seriously post-traumatic stress disorder. The Samaritans is a voluntary organisation which operates a 24-hour service designed to help and support individuals who feel desperate or suicidal.

Criminal Injuries Compensation Scheme. This scheme gives compensation for personal injury, loss of earnings, medical expenses and so on. In some cases surviving dependents of a victim who died as a result of a crime may also be entitled to compensation.

Help the Aged. This is a charity that is designed to support older people from poverty, isolation and neglect including helping them if they have been victims of crime.

Survive. This is run as a not-for-profit organisation. It is designed to help raise the awareness of rape, but in particular it provides a support network of counsellors who can assist victims with reporting the crime to the police, getting medical treatment and support as well as talking through their ordeal with others in a safe, confidential environment.

Rape Crisis. This is a similar organisation to Survive. It is a registered charity to support the work of Rape Crisis centres in England and Wales and works to raise the awareness of the issues surrounding sexual violence in the wider community. Rape Crisis acknowledges all forms of sexual violence and so has a wider remit than Survive.

Link

Find out more about Help the Aged on page 169.

Activity: Agencies that support victims of crime

Working in pairs

Imagine the scene when Suky comes home from work at about 5:00 pm on a Friday evening. As she parks her car on the drive she notices that her garage door is slightly open. Knowing that it was definitely closed before she left for work she goes to investigate. On further inspection she sees there is still someone at the back of the garage. She is scared to go in but shouts to the person to get out. They rush past her on a bicycle knocking her to the ground. She is shaken up and has a nasty cut on her head. Her neighbour hearing all the noise rushes to help her and they go into the garage. They see that several items including her bicycle have been stolen. They also notice the person has entered the garage by breaking the lock on the garage. Suky has only just moved to the area and is unsure who could help her to deal with this.

Complete a table like this to explain the role of the different public services that could assist and support Suky.

Public service	How might they assist and support Suky?
Police Service	
Probation Services	
Prison Service	
Victim Support	
The Samaritans	
Citizens Advice Bureau	
Neighbourhood Watch	

Share your findings with your classmates to see if you all know how these services can support and assist victims of crime.

233

Key terms

Impact – (in victim support) the effect a crime has on a person.

Cost – (in victim support) the financial, physical and emotional costs of a crime.

Key term

Crime deterrence – the different strategies used to try to deter (stop) people from committing crime.

1.3 Impact and cost of crime

The **impact** and **cost** that crime has on both individuals and the community is huge. Crime impacts on society and individuals in both social and economic ways. The impact of crime on an individual can be emotional and financial. It can make people feel vulnerable and afraid. Crime also has a major impact on the victim's family.

Crime can also have a psychological effect. As you can imagine, attacks on a person, some burglaries and other crimes can and do leave lasting damage on the victims. These show as panic attacks, exhaustion, depression, flashbacks or nightmares and are called psychological impacts. An individual may also suffer longer-term psychological impacts, such as:

- many victims suffer a lack of confidence or are afraid to go out at night
- the quality of life of a victim is sometimes downgraded because they are worried and feel insecure and therefore won't go out after dark or alone
- the problem may be made worse by the fact that statistically once a person has become a victim they are more likely to be a repeat victim.

The impact and cost of crime can also be categorised in three ways:

Defensive cost. The defensive cost represents the financial cost of anticipating crimes, such as paying for burglar alarms, taking out insurance and paying for public services to be involved in **crime deterrence**.

Consequence. Crime has an emotional and psychological impact on individuals and their families and can have a financial impact because of the value of any property that might be stolen or damaged, or the time off work due to injury or medical costs.

Responding to crime. The cost of public services' response to crime is high. This includes the cost of the police response, the cost to the NHS when people are injured in crime and the cost for the criminal justice system in managing offenders.

Table 12.1 shows the estimated cost of crimes based on a Home Office report completed in 2000.

Did you know?

Most crimes go unreported. It is estimated that up to 60 per cent of crimes go unreported.

Activity: Financial cost of crime

Working in pairs

Look at Table 12.1. What are the most common crimes in terms of numbers? Are you surprised by any of these figures? Are there any categories of crime listed that you do not understand? Use the internet and other sources to make a glossary consisting of each category of crime used in the table.

Table 12.1: The estimated cost of crimes to the public services based on a Home Office report completed in 2000.

Offence category	Number of incidents (000s)	Total cost (£ billion)
Crimes against individuals and households		
Violence against the person	880	16.8
Homicide	1.1	1.2
Wounding (serious and slight)	880	15.6
Common assault	3200	1.7
Sexual offences	130	2.5
Robbery/Mugging	420	2.0
Burglary in a dwelling	1400	2.7
Theft (from a vehicle)	3500	3.1
Theft (not vehicle)	3800	1.3
Criminal damage	3000	1.5
Commercial and public sector victimisation		9.1
Forgery and fraud	9200	13.8
Traffic and non-notifiable offences		4.8
Total cost of crime (£ billion)		**59.9**

Crimes also have a major impact on local authorities, the Health Services and the Police Services. Most crime that occurs will have some kind of financial cost to the local authority, from the removal of graffiti or repair of broken windows to replacing damaged street lights or restoring roads. Many crimes leave visual scars on our streets, in our towns and city centres and we expect the local authority to replace, repair and remove all of these to leave our environment looking clean and feeling safe. Local authorities will budget for these types of costs in their financial plans that they put to central government, but ultimately it is the taxpayer who is footing the bill to keep our local areas clean and safe.

Many crimes require health service involvement. If someone is injured in a fight or incident they will attend the local hospital and receive medical treatment for the injuries they have sustained. Again, the cost of this treatment is free to the victim in most cases as it is covered by the National Health Service (NHS). The NHS is a service that is funded in part by taxpayers. Treatment for a victim of crime can be also short- or long-term depending on the situation and the injuries sustained. The medical treatment required can sometimes extend from the initial incident and can often be very costly. These are all costs that are associated with the initial crime indirectly. Taking all crimes into account, about one-third of all victims of crime have to see a doctor and 4 per cent are admitted to hospital.

Activity: Communities and crime

Think about the list of crimes shown below. These are examples of crimes that are categorised as anti-social behaviour. How do you think they impact on the public? Think about both the social and financial costs of these crimes on the individual as well as the community:

- drunkenness
- damage to property
- graffiti
- violence against an individual.

Did you know?

The cost of crime to households in England and Wales is an estimated £60 billion a year!

All crimes that are reported to the police have a financial implication on the Police Service. This can be the time taken for a police officer to respond to a call, the cost of providing police vehicles, even the cost of simple items such as the pens and note pads the police need to take a statement. A more serious crime that requires a full investigation from a team of officers, possibly including specialist officers, brings with it huge costs.

Since the introduction of the Crime and Disorder Act of 1998 (which will be discussed in greater detail later in this unit), agencies that support victims of crime as well as agencies that fight crime and deal with suspects have been urged to work together to try to reduce crime as a whole. There are several reasons for this such as:

- making communities safer for people to live in
- reducing the financial cost of crime on the taxpayer
- working as a team across the services will improve detection rates.

Agencies that support victims of crime, as you would expect, also have a financial cost. They are often required to deal with more and more victims, which impacts on the running costs of the agency. Some of these agencies are paid for through taxes while others are often charitable organisations who rely on volunteer workers and donations from the public to be able to continue providing their services.

Case study: Edith, a victim of crime

You have gained a summer work placement working as a volunteer in your local Citizens Advice Bureau (CAB) working alongside experienced advisers who give members of the public advice, support and guidance on a wide range of issue. Edith is a 78-year-old pensioner who lives alone since her husband passed away and has recently had her house broken into. She has been into the CAB for some support because she is quite frightened and not really sure what to do next.

You have been asked to create a leaflet that can be given out to customers that helps to explain the role of different public services to assist and support victims of crime.

You remember meeting Edith when she came into the office and really want to help her in any way you can, so you have decided to make a bright, colourful and easy-to-read leaflet for her to take away. This will explain some of the public services that might be able to help her as well as their contact details, so she can get in touch with them.

Now answer the following questions:

1 What type of support and advice will Edith be able to get from organisations like Victim Support and how can she contact them? You should give an explanation of what they can do to support Edith.

2 What other support could Edith get from the CAB? You need to think about how they could help her complete any insurance paperwork and so on.

3 How could organisations like the Samaritans help Edith?

4 Who and what is Neighbourhood Watch, could they help Edith in any way?

BTEC Assessment activity 12.1 P1 P2

Using the information you have gathered from the case study above, produce a number of informative posters that:

1 *Explain* the role of the public services to assist and support victims of crime. **P1**

The impact of crime is wide-ranging and it is important that everyone understands the range of costs both financial and psychological are considered. Produce a leaflet that:

2 *Describe* the impact of crime on society. **P2**

Grading tips

Remember that being a victim of crime is not the same for everyone and therefore some people might not need to access support from all the public services listed above. There are many other organisations that exist too. To maximise your success at **P1** look back at the activity where you helped Suky identify the support she might need from each of the public services.

A good way to show information on your posters for the financial elements of the impact of crime for **P2** is in the form of a table or chart.

PLTS

You will be able to develop your reflective learner skills when you consider how public services exist to support and assist victims of crime. As you consider the impact that crime has on society you will be able to develop your creative thinker skills.

Functional skills

Using a word processing program with images and tables will help develop your functional skills in ICT.

2 Investigate a local crime reduction initiative

Crime has a very high cost and impact on society. Although fighting crime and dealing with crime once it has occurred is important, of equal importance is the emphasis given to preventing crime and reducing the number of offences committed in the community. The police alone cannot be responsible for fighting and preventing crime. Preventing and reducing crime requires much more widespread involvement and support. Increasingly, it has been the role of local crime reduction **initiatives** which involve different agencies working together to deal with crime and social problems that affect a particular area.

Key term

Initiative – a venture to find a new and innovative way to do something, especially reduce and prevent crime.

2.1 Crime reduction initiatives

The Crime and Disorder Act 1998 created 376 crime and disorder reduction partnerships in England and Wales. The Act covers crimes such as:

- anti-social behaviour orders
- sex offender orders
- parenting orders
- child safety orders
- racially aggravated offences
- the aim of the youth justice system.

This legislation meant that local authorities, police and other agencies could work in partnership to develop and implement strategies to reduce this sort of crime and disorder (see Figure 12.3). The partnerships carry out an audit of crime and disorder every three years and publish a strategy for dealing with the problems it finds. The idea was that these strategies must reflect local needs and priorities which means different partnerships around the country will be tackling crime particular to their area.

Figure 12.3: Partnerships fighting crime. How do these partnerships work together to fight crime?

Dealing with offenders

As part of the Crime and Disorder Act of 1998 a system of anti-social behaviour orders were developed. They were designed to sit alongside the crime reduction initiatives as another way of supporting the Act by working with the public services as well as the community to find ways of reducing anti-social behaviour. Under the Act a wide range of measures were designed to address anti-social behaviour committed by adults and young people. These include:

Child Curfew Scheme. This scheme applies to unsupervised children under 16 and prohibits them from specified public places between 9.00 pm and 6.00 am. The police can remove children breaching their curfew and take them home or to a place of safety. In many cases social services are also involved.

Child Safety Orders. These are designed to protect children under 10 who are at risk of becoming involved in crime. They are issued if a child has previously breached a curfew. They are then put under the supervision of a social worker.

Truancy Orders. These address young people at risk of offending in the future (the importance of dealing with this early has been recognised).

Parenting Orders. These require a parent to control the behaviour of their children. These can be imposed by a magistrate when a child aged 10–17 is convicted of an offence or subject to an anti-social behaviour order (ASBO) . This means a parent may be convicted if a child fails to adhere to the order.

Reparation Orders. These require young offenders to make specific reparation either to the individual, the victim or the community. Orders such as these are for a maximum of three months and must have full consent of the victim. The orders are referred to a Youth Offender Panel who will produce a programme that will allow the offender to face up to the consequences of their behaviour.

Racially Aggravated Offences. The Act was also put in place to help prevent and deal with racially aggravated offences. This is a crime or offence that is motivated by hostility towards a member of a racial group or based upon someone's religion.

Activity: Orders and curfews

Working as a group

Look at the orders and curfews arising from the Crime and Disorder Act of 1998:

Do you think these orders would help to reduce crime and disorder? If not, why not?

Can you think of any other strategies that might work?

Discuss these in small groups then together as a class.

Did you know?

In April 1993 a young Black teenage boy named Stephen Lawrence was stabbed to death in South London as he waited for a bus. The subsequent police investigation revealed that the murder had a racist motive – Stephen was killed because he was Black. Although five people were arrested in connection with this crime, no one was ever convicted of his murder.

Link

Find out more about the Stephen Lawrence case on page 166.

Alongside the system of anti-social behaviour orders arising out of the Crime and Disorder Act of 1998 came the development of Safer Community Initiatives. These are more local initiatives that involve multi-agency partnerships intended to make areas safer and nicer places to live by beating crime and tackling drugs. Police, local authorities and key partnerships work together to deliver more coordinated services. These initiatives focus on anti-social behaviour and associated violence and criminal damage.

One of the biggest and most successful schemes has been Neighbourhood Watch. It is based on simple ideas and values that are shared by many people around the country.

Neighbourhood Watch

'Getting together with your neighbours to reduce local crime and disorder in the bid to make your neighbourhood a safe and better place to live, work and play.' The aim of Neighbourhood Watch is to:

- cut crime and the opportunities for crime and anti-social behaviour
- provide reassurance to local residents and reduce the fear of crime and anti-social behaviour
- encourage neighbourliness and closer communities
- improve the quality of life for local residents and tenants.

By:

- being a community-based organisation, involving residents and tenants who are working together
- working in partnership with the police, local authorities and other agencies to reduce crime and disorder
- sharing information and advice with the police and other agencies concerning crime and other incidents.

2.2 Crime prevention initiatives

A number of crime prevention initiatives in addition to those already covered have been introduced. The overall aim of these initiatives is to find new and innovative ways to reduce and prevent crime.

Secured by Design. This was established in 1989 and is owned by the Association of Chief Police Officers (ACPO). This is the corporate title for a group of national police projects focusing on the design and security for new and refurbished homes, commercial premises and car parks as well as the acknowledgement of quality security products and crime prevention projects.

Architectural Liaison Officers and Advisors. These are specialist crime prevention officers, trained at the Home Office Crime Reduction College, who deal with crime risk and designing crime advice for the built environment. In addition to physical security measures the officers will consider defensible space, access, crime and movement generators all of which can contribute to a reduction in crime and disorder.

Town planning. This focuses on the use, development and protection of land. Urban and rural planning is vital for the orderly expansion of new housing and industry into areas best suited for them. Town planning work in partnership with Secure by Design and the Architectural Liaison Officers in the planning and development for all land that is to be used in an environmentally, economically and socially responsible manner.

Social cost. This refers to the cost to society as a whole from an event, action, or policy change. It can include the setting up and management of a number of crime prevention activities as described above.

Did you know?

You can find out more about Secured by Design and Prison me! No way! Crime prevention initiatives by visiting ther respective websites, available via Hotlinks (see page viii).

In what ways would you like your community support officers to help you?

Neighbourhood renewal. This aims to improve the quality of life for those living in the most disadvantaged areas by tackling: poor job prospects; high crime levels; educational under-achievement; poor health; problems with housing and their local environment. Neighbourhood renewal harnesses the work of all government departments, local public services, the community and private and voluntary sectors to tackle deprivation and drive through improvements.

Police community support officers (PCSOs). A police community support officer works on the frontline of a local police force, providing a visible and reassuring presence on the streets and tackling the menace of anti-social behaviour. PCSOs have different roles in different forces, but they usually patrol a beat and interact with the public, while also offering assistance to police officers at crime scenes and major events.

'Prison me! No way!' Scheme. This was the first initiative of its kind aimed at young people aged between 12 and 17 years of age. Its purpose was to give a no-holds-barred insight from a young offender's perception of prison life inside Hull Prison. The scheme consisted of an information pack, a video as well as (in some areas) allowing the young people to see the living conditions within a prison. Its overall aim was to discourage vulnerable young people from making a mistake that could follow them for the rest of their lives.

Tackling Knives Action Programme. This programme was launched in June 2008 with ten police force areas in England and Wales (Essex, Greater Manchester, Lancashire, Merseyside, Metropolitan, Nottinghamshire, South Wales, Thames Valley, West Midlands, West Yorkshire) working to reduce the number of teenagers killed or seriously wounded by knives and to increase public confidence that our streets are safe. This has been done by the introduction of tough new guidance and hard work by the forces themselves, working side by side with local

Did you know?

The Respect Project is aimed at boys and girls in Y9 at school. They are nominated by their school to take part in activity days designed for students who might be struggling with the education system. It is designed to build self-confidence and self-esteem.

people to establish: fewer teenagers seriously wounded by knives; fewer young people carrying knives; fewer offenders getting off with a caution; more people going to prison with longer jail sentences.

Gun and knife amnesties. An **amnesty** introduced may typically last about five weeks and involves a plea by any police force across England and Wales for the public to hand in any guns and/or knives. Anyone can do this without fear of penalty or punishment over this period and so reduce the number of guns and knives on the streets. However, once the amnesty is over, tough action will be taken on those found armed with either knives or guns.

Key term

Amnesty – a period during which offenders are exempt from punishment.

Case study: Knife crime

During 2008 more than 70 teenagers were violently killed by stabbing in Britain. The deaths were concentrated in a handful of locations with London suffering the highest number of young victims. Other areas with multiple killings included Greater Manchester with five deaths; West Yorkshire, Merseyside and Strathclyde with four each and the West Midlands and South Yorkshire with three each.

More worryingly is the statistic that throughout 2007 and 2008 a total of 54 teenagers were stabbed to death in London, most of them belonging to ethnic minorities.

Working in pairs answer the following questions:

1 What other tactics do you think the police could take in an attempt to reduce knife crime?

2 What action can young people take to reduce the number of incidents where knives are present?

3 Who should be held accountable for crimes of this nature, particularly where the offender is underage?

Case study: Tackling Knives Action Programme

As a result of a recent campaign launched by the media and supported by the families of some of the victims of knife crime and the public, five key changes have been implemented:

In June 2008 the government launched the Tackling Knives Action Programme (TKAP) in 10 police areas.

- Several knife amnesties have been organised around the UK including an eight-week campaign in Glasgow which saw more than 60 blades a day handed in.

- In August 2008 draft guidelines were introduced, stating that all hospital staff should inform officers when knife victims are admitted.

- As part of the TKAP extra resources were given to the police to educate youths about the dangers of knife crime.

- In November 2008 an initiative to encourage schoolchildren to secretly text details of classmates with knives was launched by Crime Stoppers in 15 London boroughs.

Working as a class answer the following questions:

1 Do you think these five initiatives will have had a positive impact on knife crime?

2 Can you find out any statistics associated with knife crime to see if these initiatives have lead to a decline in knife crime?

Positive Futures Sport Lincs. This is a local crime prevention initiative aimed at reducing youth-related anti-social behaviour and crime and disorder within north-east Lincolnshire. The project is aimed at young people aged between 10 and 19 years who commit criminal-damage type offences. The Humberside Police Force, Humberside Police Youth Services, Sports Development, Grimsby Town Football in the Community all joined forces to initiate the 'Sport Lincs' project for north-east Lincolnshire.

This project has engaged the most disadvantaged and 'at risk' young people in the county in positive sporting activities that include football and street dance. The aim is to involve all community members, young people and victims in locations identified through police data as 'hotspots' in an attempt to set up weekly sporting activities to reduce youth-related anti-social behaviour, crime and disorder. Teams from these areas meet monthly to compete against each other at the Fairplay Football League. A number of benefits from the initiative have been seen including a reduction in anti-social behaviour, criminal damage and violence.

Link

Further details of this and other initiatives can be found at the Home Office crime reduction website, available via Hotlinks (see page viii).

BTEC Assessment activity 12.2 P3 M1 D1

Using a local crime prevention initiative like the one described above and your own personal research produce a poster that:

1 *Outlines* a local crime initiative. P3

To further extend your work you should write an extended report that:

2 *Analyses* the local crime reduction initiative. M1

3 *Evaluates* the local crime reduction initiative by showing how it has reached relevant groups in the community and reduced the fear if crime. D1

Grading tips

The internet is a good place to start with finding out about crime reduction initiatives in your area for P3.

To extend your work in M1 you could speak with local police representatives to see if they felt that the initiative has helped and what the actual benefits have been. You could also produce a short questionnaire that could be completed by the relevant groups in the community. Your questionnaire could incorporate detailed questions to see if the initiative has helped to reduce the fear of crime in the local area for D1. You could produce the questionnaire as a group (with support from your tutor) and then individually analyse and evaluate the results for your own report.

PLTS

As you consider a local crime initiative you will be developing your reflective learner skills. Analysing and evaluating the local crime initiative by Identifying questions to answer and problems to solve will give you the opportunity to develop your independent enquirer skills.

Functional skills

If you extend your report to include images and tables from the questionnaire you will develop your ICT functional skills.

3 The methods used to report and record crime

In all areas of society it is important that if a crime occurs it is reported to the police. All crimes that are recorded can then be categorised and investigated using a standardised system. Ensuring this is done accurately allows the police to compare crime statistics across the UK area forces and establish crime patterns. Recording crime highlights the volume of work police have to deal with and enables the police to work with other agencies to target specific crimes in certain areas and to implement crime reduction strategies more effectively.

3.1 National Crime Recording Standards (NCRS)

Since 2002, when the NCRS was introduced, all forces have used a nationwide system of reporting crime. This is now used to effectively and more accurately track both crimes and suspects. This standardised system has promoted a greater consistency between police forces across the country. It allows the comparison of crime figures across forces as well as the tracking of a suspect who might commit similar crimes in different areas.

As part of reporting and recording crime, it is vital that the process be victim orientated. A victim-orientated approach to crime reporting means that anyone reporting a crime can feel relaxed and not intimidated and that a victim is not put off making a formal report. It is particularly important to ensure all crime is recorded to be sure of catching criminals.

In order to ensure accuracy of reporting, statements should be taken from a number of people associated with the crime. This may be the victim, a witness or a third party who was not necessarily involved in the incident. These types of report fall into a two-tier system:

Crime report. A report by a victim or witness to say what has happened and if what has happened is a **notifiable** offence

Incident report. A report of a possible criminal act which cannot be confirmed, where there is no clear victim, or where the victim refuses to confirm that a crime took place.

All incidents reported to the police are recorded, whether they are a crime or not. An incident report, however, is not a record of a crime, and will not come into the recorded crime figures. An incident is recorded as a crime if (1) the circumstances as reported amount to a crime defined by law and (2) there is no credible evidence to the contrary. The NCRS will also record a crime even if the victim doesn't want anything to be done about it. From a statistical point of view it is important to record all crimes. It increases the chances of catching criminals.

Key term

Notifiable – describing something requiring official notification be given.

Crime recording process

There are a number of ways in which crime can be reported. These can depend on the urgency of the incident as well as the type of crime. The different ways to report crime are by:

- calling 999 for urgent crime, alternatively 112 can be used
- contacting the police in person
- phoning the local police on a non-urgent line
- phoning the local community safety unit
- reporting on the internet.

Are there any new ways of reporting a crime?

Activity: Ways to report crime

Undertake some internet research into your local police force and try to find out the different ways that your force has for members of the public to report crime.

Can it be described as an **auditable user-friendly system**?

Police forces are now looking at introducing more ways to report crime, including by text message. Another measure to help with recording and reporting crime is the Crime Management Unit initiative where a number of squads and units performing diverse functions come together. The officer in charge has responsibility for overseeing all crime-related matters, and in serious cases takes on the role of senior investigating officer, coordinating enquiries using divisional and departmental personnel as necessary. A director of intelligence performs a key role in promoting an intelligence-led approach to policing (see below) in order to make best use of resources.

Crimes are classified in a number of ways in the crime recording process. There are five main classifications:

- **Unreported crime.** A crime takes place but it is not reported to the police by the victim or anyone else.
- **Reported crime.** This is a crime that is reported to the police.
- **Unrecorded crime.** This is a crime that is reported to police but they have not written down the details.
- **Recorded crime.** This is a crime which is reported to the police, written down by the police and put on their computer.
- **Detected crime.** This is a crime where the culprit has been detained.

In order to ensure that crimes are recorded effectively and efficiently staff training is vital. In several forces dedicated officers have been appointed to ensure this process is carried out accurately and consistently.

Key term

Auditable user-friendly system – describes the many ways of reporting crime.

The impact of the NCRS on the Police Service has been varied and mostly positive. It has made available more reliable figures and statistics due to the consistency of crime recording. This allows forces and the government to get a better understanding of levels of crime across the country as well as the performance of different forces. It also helps researchers understand patterns of crime across the country more accurately and therefore plan future policing needs. It has meant that officers are paying more attention to the needs of the victims of crime, and this in turn has encouraged people to feel more confident about reporting a crime to the police. One negative aspect might be the increase in paperwork required, which can require additional time and sometimes special training.

Initially the impact of the NCRS on individual forces varied as they moved from their own individual system to a standardised one. The overall impact was to see an increase in total number of recorded crimes by 10 per cent. This apparent increase was put down to the introduction of a standardised system and the police believe that the underlying levels of crime actually committed have remained stable.

Activity: Crime figures

Undertake some internet research into your local police force and try to find out how crime figures for the crimes listed below have altered over the last three years:

- violence against someone
- robbery
- theft
- vehicle theft
- criminal damage.

Working as a class

Come together as a class to discuss your researched figures and suggest reasons for these.

Key term

Intelligence – (in reporting and recording crime) information about crimes and offenders.

3.2 National Intelligence Model (NIM)

The NIM is a code of practice governing the way the police use **intelligence**. It came into operation in January 2005 and the overall aim is that all police forces use the same ways of classifying and storing information so it can easily be shared and used by other forces. The NIM is primarily used for allocating police resources, to plan and work in cooperation with partnerships in the community and to manage performance and risks. It enables forces to standardise and coordinate the fight against crime at all levels.

As part of the NIM, it is important that there is cooperation across the police force and between different forces. A senior officer is usually given the responsibility of ensuring that cross-force coordination meetings are regularly held in order to ensure crime hotspots are identified and that the intelligence gathered can help officers to work more effectively.

Intelligence-led policing is central to the NIM strategy. It is a policing model that has emerged in recent years in which intelligence gathering is considered a priority in a police operation. It seeks to reduce the amount of police time spent responding to crime and increase the time used to target offenders. The police use surveillance, informants and intelligence to target **repeat criminals**. This enables officers to target these offenders as a result of the intelligence gathered. Analysis of where and when crimes occurred shows that a small number of offenders are responsible for a large number of crimes. This form of policing is an effective way of catching criminals in the act as well as preventing a crime from happening. Intelligence-led policing became a more significant practice globally following the terrorist attacks on the US on 11 September 2001 (usually referred to as 9/11).

NIM strategy involves classifying crimes as this helps towards tackling crime and implementing more effective crime reduction strategies. Crimes are classified into three areas:

- **Level 1** – local crime and anti-social behaviour. Usually the crimes, criminals and other problems are affecting a basic command unit or small force area. The scope of the crimes can be wide-ranging from low-value thefts to more serious crimes such as murder.
- **Level 2** – regional criminal activity usually requiring additional resources. This is usually the actions of a criminal or other specific problems affecting more than one basic command unit, neighbouring forces or a group of forces.
- **Level 3** – the most serious organised crime, usually operating on a national and international scale, requiring identification by proactive means and response primarily through targeting operations by dedicated units and a preventative response on a national basis.

By classifying crime in this way, forces are able to establish **crime trends**. For instance, they can look at Level 1 crime locally to assess problem areas that they can then focus their attention on and resolve.

As a result of the police using more intelligence-led policing, the Regulation of Investigatory Powers Act (RIPA) 2000 was introduced. This Act is designed to regulate a range of police investigatory powers and was introduced to ensure that policing and intelligence-gathering powers are used lawfully and in line with the European Convention on Human Rights. It ensures that anyone using covert techniques to gather intelligence and information gives proper consideration to whether their use is necessary and proportionate. RIPA regulates the following areas:

How do you feel about the increased use of CCTV?

Key terms

Repeat criminal – a person who commits crime over and over again.

Crime trend – an increase or decrease in crime over a period of time.

- to intercept (listen in) on phone calls or access emails and letters
- to have access to utility bills (such as a phone bill)
- to carry out surveillance (watch a person's movement in both public and private places)
- to use other forms of surveillance such as informants or under-cover officers
- to access data held on computers.

Case study: Cumbria Constabulary Policing Plan 2009–2012

The National Intelligence Model (NIM) is used to set and manage day-to-day priorities for operational policing. This plan sets out longer-term improvement priorities and organisational developments.

As part of NIM, strategic assessments are carried out which forecast patterns of crime and criminality in future. This analysis is used to set operational priorities.

The strategic assessment and operational priorities were a vital part of deciding on this Policing Plan and the strategic priorities.

NIM will continue to set day-to-day operational priorities at the front line.

This Policing Plan sits above it, shaping improvement and development priorities.

As you can see, the Cumbria Constabulary have targeted a number of priorities for operational policing by using the NIM.

Cumbria Constabulary	
NIM priority (October 2008)	**How this Policing Plan links to NIM**
Serious organised crime and criminality	We have set a target to manage how we disrupt and dismantle organised crime groups. We will improve our capacity and capability to do so.
Public protection	We will improve our arrangements to manage dangerous offenders, protect vulnerable adults and safeguard children.
Community priorities: • burglary • violent crime • anti-social behaviour • criminal damage • vehicle crime.	We have set a target to reduce the most serious kinds of violent crime. We will work to keep other crimes at their current low levels. We will focus, with our partners, on the problems which make communities feel they're not safe, like anti-social behaviour and criminal damage.
Terrorism/ extremism	We will continue our work to prevent terrorism and domestic extremism.
Roads policing	We will continue to support CRASH partnerships to make roads safer and reduce dangerous driving, achieving national targets by 2010.

Working in groups answer the following question:

Undertake some independent research into one of the operational strategies identified above and share your findings with the rest of your class.

3.3 Crime Scene Investigation (CSI)

When a crime occurs, the police and other agencies must gather as much evidence as possible if they want to solve the crime and arrest the offender. One way to do this is by investigating the **crime scene** using experts in forensic science.

Collecting evidence

Forensic science can be simply defined as the application of science to the law. Forensic science covers a number of key areas within the criminal investigation to guide the police towards arrest and conviction. At the crime scene the police are responsible for preserving life, preventing evidence and crime scene contamination, detaining suspects and witnesses, controlling the scene and examining the crime scene.

Forensic scientists are involved in searching for and examining physical traces which may have been left behind at a crime scene. These physical traces are then used to try to make a connection between someone suspected of committing a crime, the scene of the crime and the victim.

Physical evidence left behind at a crime scene commonly includes blood and other body fluids, hairs, textile fibres from clothing, materials used in buildings such as paint and glass, footwear and shoe prints, tool and tyre marks and flammable substances used to start fires. The scientist might visit the crime scene itself to search for evidence or might advise about the likely sequence of events that led up to the offence.

Other forensic scientists might be involved in the analysis of drugs, examining specimens from people thought to have taken drugs or thought to have been driving after drinking too much alcohol, or examining victims who may have been poisoned. Other forensic scientists specialise in firearms, explosives, or documents whose authenticity is in question.

One very important method of investigating a crime is through DNA analysis. DNA stands for deoxyribonucleic acid and is the genetic material contained in the cells of all living things. DNA carries the information that allows organisms to function, repair and reproduce themselves. Like fingerprints, DNA is unique to an individual and therefore a very powerful tool in the fight against crime. The traces of blood, hairs and other deposits of the human body found at crime scenes all contain DNA.

Key terms

Crime scene – the place where a crime has occurred or any place where evidence of a crime is found.

Forensic scientists – people (experts) who are trained in collecting, examining and processing evidence of crimes.

Did you know?

When someone is arrested a sample of their DNA is often collected and then a visual record kept on a national database. The national database only holds records of convicted criminals. Criminals have been convicted of a crime years after it was committed because of DNA evidence.

Figure 12.4: How can DNA be used to identify an individual?

Double helix structure of DNA — Cytosine — Guanine — Adenine — Thymine

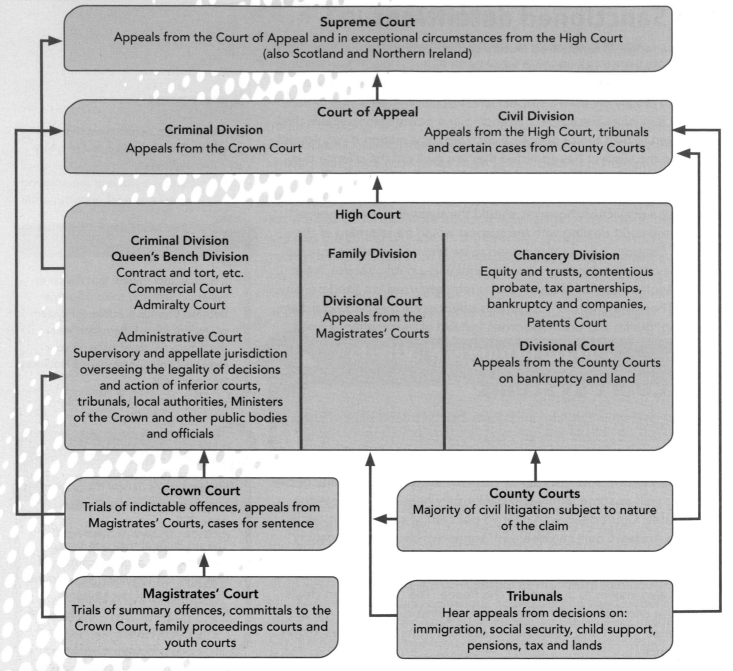

Figure 12.6: Flowchart of the court system. How does this link with the European Court?

Activity: The court system

Working in groups

Undertake some group research to find out more information about the court system and produce a presentation to share with your colleagues on the following:

- Civil Court
- Magistrates' Court
- Crown Court
- Court of Appeal
- Supreme Court
- European Court.

4.6 Penalties and sentencing

A wide range of penalties and sentences is used by the criminal justice system designed to punish offenders in various ways. Some of the most commonly used strategies are:

Community sentences. These can encompass a wide range of sentence styles to meet the needs of offenders in the community who have not been given a **custodial sentence**. Examples of these include:

- compulsory (unpaid) work
- participation in any specified activities
- programmes aimed at changing offending behaviour
- prohibition from certain activities
- curfew
- exclusion from certain areas
- residence requirement
- mental health treatment (with consent of the offender)
- drug treatment and testing (with consent of the offender)
- alcohol treatment (with consent of the offender).

Custodial sentences. For the most serious offences the court may impose a prison, or custodial, sentence. The length of sentence imposed by the court will be limited by the maximum penalty for that crime. A custodial sentence can only be imposed if:

- the offence is so serious that neither a fine nor a community sentence can be justified for the offence
- the offender refuses to comply with the requirements of a community order
- the offender is convicted of a specified sexual or violent offence and the court finds that the offender poses a risk of harm to the public.

The sentence imposed by the court represents the maximum amount of time that the offender will remain in custody.

Key terms

Custodial sentence – a sentence that involves some loss of freedom (this usually means imprisonment).

Non-custodial sentence – a sentence that does not involve some loss of freedom (not going to prison).

The Royal Courts of Justice, the Court of Appeal in Central London, presides over some of the most serious civil trials and family cases in the country. Where in the chain does this fit into our court system?

Activity: Penalties and sentencing

Working in groups

Undertake some research into other types of penalties used by the criminal justice system to manage offenders. Try to come up with your own definition of how these penalties are used:

- fines
- tagging
- bind over
- conditional discharge.

Working as a class

Bring your findings together on the board with your tutor so you can see the bigger picture of how different penalties and sentences are used by the criminal justice system.

Activity: Stacey, convicted of drug offences

Stacey is 18 years old and has already served time in a secure unit (when she was 13 years old). She is making £700 per week selling drugs for a dealer on the street but she spends almost all of it on drugs for herself. After arrest she told the police:

- I didn't have family so people on the streets were like my family.
- I didn't want to commit crime.
- I was 11 years old when I stopped living with my parents and I didn't see any other way to be able to look after myself.
- I am sorry for the things I've done.

Working as a class answer the following questions:

1   What type of sentencing do you think best suits Stacey and her situation and why?

2   Has Stacey been let down by the Criminal Justice System? Society as a whole? Try to explain your thoughts.

PLTS

When you discuss the different ways that the legal system manages offenders you will be developing your reflective learner skills. Considering how crime scenes can be linked and offenders profiles will give you the opportunity to develop your creative thinker skills.

Functional skills

If you extend your report to include images and tables you will develop your ICT functional skills.

BTEC Assessment activity 12.4 ⑦

1   Using what you have discussed in the activity above as well as your own personal research, produce a report that describes the different ways that the legal system manages offenders. **P7**

Grading tip

Think about all the different ways that offenders can be managed. Try to include all of these in your report to show a good understanding of all the sanctions that are available to the legal system in England and Wales.

WorkSpace

Melanie Tate
Prison Officer

During my six years working for the Prison Service I have worked in a number of areas within the prison. I have spent most of my time working on a wing. This is where prisoners eat, sleep and associate. I'm responsible for ensuring the wing delivers the essentials to people, such as access to medical care, exercise, association and education facilities. I and three of my colleagues, manage a team of 28 prison officers working on a rota system. They are responsible for ensuring the management of the wing and the service provided to the prisoners run smoothly. The rota system ensures that we have at least 8 prison officers managing the week for 24 hours per day 365 days per year.

A typical day

An average shift lasts about 8 hours but they do vary (days, nights etc). A day shift usually starts at 8:00 am and finishes at 6:00 pm and then a night shift will start at 6:00 pm and finish at 6:00 am. We work on a cycle of 2 day shifts, 2 night shifts then 4 rest days (days off), then we start all over again! As I said, the wing is staffed all year so this means we work Christmas and New Year plus Bank holidays … but between us we make sure we all get a fair share of days off at the important times of the year. Because we work this type of shift system we can get a good work–life balance. Thankfully, the team spirit among colleagues is excellent. I do interact with prisoners at all levels most of the day and you need to be able to adopt a good relationship with the prisoners. We offer 'care in custody' and although security is our predominant function, the ability to offer support to prisoners is essential!

The best thing about the job

As you can imagine prison life can be tough for both the staff and the prisoners so it is important to be able to switch off between shifts. It can also be upsetting to see someone who has recently been remanded in custody as it is often an emotional roller coaster for them so it's important that I help them through this.

During recent years the prison service has worked very hard to make sure it has employed prison officers from the wider community. This has helped to show equality of service to both the prisoners and society. It is really important that we are able to support all our prisoners in the best possible ways and this is an important step towards this. There are many female officers like myself who thoroughly enjoy working with prisoners and supporting them through their sentence as well as helping them with their rehabilitation. Overall, I am really glad that I chose a role in the prison service and would encourage people to give a career in the prison service some consideration in the future.

Think about it!

- What knowledge and skills do you think you might need to become a prison officer?
- What are the topics in this unit that will help you develop your knowledge and skills?

259

Just checking

1. I have just been mugged! Can you help me? Which organisations can I call upon to assist me? What are their roles?
2. On renewing contents insurance you see that your premium has gone up, why is this? Think about the impact crime has, both financially and emotionally, on society.
3. What is Sport Lincs? Can you outline this crime initiative?
4. Reporting crime is very important? Can you produce a list of the different ways you can do this?
5. Who are CSI? Can you describe their role?
6. It is important to deal with different types of offenders in different ways. Can you identify five more types of sentences that are given to offenders? Here is a clue: prison!

edexcel

Assignment tips

- Get on the internet – there's a wealth of information on many key areas in this unit. When looking for a local crime initiative access the Crimereduction website, available via Hotlinks (see page viii).

- Use the library as this will hold daily newspapers as well as specialist magazines such as *Police Review*.

- Think about the impact of crime on people that you know. Speak to your family; has anyone been a victim of crime? How did they feel? Are they more scared now?

- Watch the television! Programmes like *CSI* and other forensic crime dramas will be useful when you come to look at how crime scenes are linked and offenders profiled.

- Ask your tutor to arrange a court visit if possible; this will help you understand the different ways that offenders are managed. If this is not possible invite a guest speaker from the Probation Services.

13 Community and cultural awareness

It is important that people working in the public services understand what is meant by community and cultural awareness, both at a local and national level. Since the vast majority of public services work within a community setting: understanding how communities work, what problems they face and what kinds of people they are likely to be dealing with is an essential part of the knowledge you need in order to be able to do a good job. There are many costs and benefits to community life including the provision of facilities locally and nationally. You will be provided with opportunities to explore and research your local communities in order to find out what these costs and benefits are.

Diversity is another key element in our communities both locally and nationally. The public services have to work with a variety of people of all ages, genders, sexualities and cultural backgrounds in the course of their work. You will have opportunities to look at the diversity of our communities and their impact on the public services and their work. This will include ethnicity, religion, lifestyle choices and virtual cultures.

Many social problems arise in communities across the country, such as poverty, unemployment, racism, inequality, domestic abuse, substance abuse and bullying. These are some of the problems that the public services face in their daily work and it is important you understand them.

This unit will provide you with the opportunity to explore all of these issues in detail.

Learning outcomes

After completing this unit you should:

1. understand community and cultural awareness in the local and national community
2. know what is meant by the cost and benefits of living in a community
3. understand cultural diversity as an aspect of local and national community
4. be able to investigate the social and cultural problems that exist in a local community and national community.

Assessment and grading criteria

This table shows you what you must do in order to achieve a pass, merit or distinction grade, and where you can find activities in this book to help you.

To achieve a **pass** grade the evidence must show that the learner is able to:	To achieve a **merit** grade the evidence must show that, in addition to the pass criteria, the learner is able to:	To achieve a **distinction** grade the evidence must show that, in addition to the pass and merit criteria, the learner is able to:
P1 explain the differences between local and national communities **Assessment activity 13.1 page 272**	**M1** compare the awareness of community and cultural issues in local and national communities **Assessment activity 13.1 page 272**	**D1** evaluate the awareness of community and cultural issues in local and national communities **Assessment activity 13.1 page 272**
P2 discuss the awareness of community and cultural issues in local and national communities **Assessment activity 13.1 page 272**		
P3 describe the costs and benefits of living in a community **Assessment activity 13.2 page 277**		
P4 evaluate the positive and negative effects of cultural diversity **Assessment activity 13.3 page 284**	**M2** analyse the advantages and disadvantages of living in a culturally diverse community **Assessment activity 13.3 page 284**	
P5 investigate the categories of social problems in communities locally and across the UK **Assessment activity 13.4 page 290**	**M3** analyse the social and cultural problems that exist within communities in the UK **Assessment activity 13.4 page 290**	**D2** evaluate the social and cultural problems that exist in communities and across the UK **Assessment activity 13.4 page 290**
P6 explain the cultural problems in communities locally and across the UK **Assessment activity 13.4 page 290**		
P7 investigate the impact of social and cultural problems in the UK **Assessment activity 13.4 page 290**		

How you will be assessed

This unit will be assessed by an internal assignment that will be designed and marked by the staff at your centre. The assignment is designed to allow you to show your understanding of the learning outcomes for community and cultural awareness. These relate to what you should be able to do after completing this unit.

Assessments can be quite varied and can take the form of:

- reports
- leaflets
- presentations
- posters
- practical tasks
- case studies.

Jamille, 17, explores his community

This unit was really useful for me, it helped me understand what communities and cultures are and how they work. I hadn't really thought about my community at all. I didn't even know the people on my street, but now I see that if you are going to be a good public service officer then making contacts and relationships in your community is essential. You can't be a good police officer or social worker if you don't even know the people you are working for or how they have to live.

One of the things that I really enjoyed looking at was the section about social and cultural problems. We looked at lots of different problems communities and cultures can face and I recognised some of them are happening in my own community. Understanding why they happen and what could be done about it was really interesting and will help me when I apply to join a service.

The good thing about this unit is that it is very practical and there are lots of opportunities for research and going into your community to find out what is happening there. You can't just learn about community in a classroom – you actually have to go there as well. It was also good to be able to see how my small community compares with other communities and how it compares with the country as a whole. All of this is information which will be really useful to me when I apply to a service as it will show that I care about my community and I want to be able to serve it properly.

Over to you!
- What areas of community and culture might you find interesting?
- When was the last time you became involved in any community events?
- Do you think you know your own community well?
- What preparation could you do in your community to get ready for your assessments?

1 Community and cultural awareness in the local and national community

Talk up

What does community and cultural awareness mean to you?

Working as a group

Community and cultural awareness can mean different things to different people. In small groups, write down as many words or phrases as you can which describe what community and cultural awareness means to you. Once you have done this rank your list with 1 being the most important and so on.

Share your findings with the rest of your class. Did you come up with the same kind of things or was each group's list very different? Why do you think this is?

What type of area does this photo show? What issues do you think would affect a busy city compared with a small village? Do you think people in villages have a better sense of community than people in cities? Why might this be?

Community and cultural awareness is a category that covers important issues which impact on the day-to-day work of the public services. It involves looking at your understanding of what a community is and how you could make it better. It focuses on issues such as:

- What is a community?
- What are the advantages and disadvantages of living in a community?
- What problems do communities face?
- Who lives in communities?

An understanding of community and cultural awareness will make you appreciate where you live and the work of the public services in ensuring our communities are safe. What do we mean by community?

1.1 What is a community?

There are lots of ways of defining what a community is and there are certainly many examples of different types of community. You are probably a member of several different types of communities which have developed in different ways and are constantly changing, such as:

- **Geographical community**. This is the community you live in, your street or area. It is usually the place where you spend most of your time.

- **Virtual community**. This is the community you spend time with when you are online. They may be people you know in real life or people you only know by being connected to the internet such as a Facebook community or an online gaming community.

- **School/College community**. This is the community where you study, it is made up of all the staff and students. Each school or college can be very different from others even if they are very close geographically.

- **Workplace community**. This is the community where you work. Many places of employment have a very clear sense of community and a culture where people look after each other. The services in particular have a strong sense of community and a strong workplace culture.

- **Clubs or special interest communities**. This is where people get together to form a community based around a shared interest, such as books, photography or a sport.

Has your geographical community any similar features?

Some of these communities have existed for a long time and long before you joined them, for example your geographical community probably existed long before you joined it when you arrived there, but special interest groups can be started by one person and can develop to include lots of different individuals who share the same interests as the original member. These communities can be local or national and in the case of virtual communities they can also be international.

A community is therefore a group of people who may live in the same area or have common work or social interests that bond them together. Humans have always lived together in groups which were originally based around family bonds. These grew into small tribes and eventually into small communities. As more and more people were born or joined, communities became larger leading to towns and eventually cities. So communities are not static, they develop and change over time and in response to different circumstances.

Activity: Your communities

Which communities are you a member of? Write down a list of all the different communities you play a part in, such as school, work, sports, online or geographical. How many different communities do you belong to? Which ones do you consider to be the most important and why? What have learners in your class found? Do their groups differ from yours?

1.2 What is culture?

Culture is not the same as a community. There can be many different cultures within the same community. Culture can be defined as a shared set of values, behaviour or beliefs, it can include shared music and humour and sometimes a shared ethnic or national background. The public services come into contact with lots of different cultures on a daily basis and it is important that they understand and value different cultures if they are going to deal effectively with members of the public.

Cultures may be very different from each other or may share common aspects such as religion or ethnic origin. For example, British and French cultures can be quite different, but both are mainly Christian and both are mainly from a European ethnic background.

People from different cultural backgrounds will often come together in places of worship or at community venues and events to share aspects of their culture such as food, music or religion. Cultures may have their own leaders. A leader often acts as the spokesperson for their culture in wider society.

Different cultures often have their own set of norms and values. These are measures of what is considered normal in that culture, for example **arranged marriages** are normal in some cultures and very unusual in others. In some cultures children work from a very young age and in some cultures you cannot work until you are a young adult. In some cultures drinking alcohol is accepted and in others it is frowned upon. As you can see, what is normal and accepted varies from culture to culture. This is not a particular problem as many people have different ideas on what is acceptable and what isn't, but problems can arise when cultures clash and one culture views a certain behaviour as right and another culture views it as wrong. This can happen particularly with subcultures. Subcultures are group of people from a mainstream culture that have differing views on what is normal and accepted. Consider the case study below:

Key term

Arranged marriage – a marriage planned and agreed by the families of the couple concerned.

Case study: Gang subcultures

Jason is a member of the R8 crew in Nottinghamshire.

'I left school with no qualifications and I don't work, why should I? I get enough money from the social to keep me in fags and booze. I can knock about with my mates all day while other people are working – working's a mugs game. None of my mates work, we hang about all day, might do a bit of thieving if the opportunities are there and someone has been stupid enough to leave a window open in their house or something on the back seat of their car.

To be honest we make our own rules, I see how other people live but I've got no chance of living like that, I've got no qualifications and a criminal record so even if I wanted a job who would take me on? Besides I don't like being told what to do.

This is normal for me and for the people I know. This is how we grew up, it's what our big brothers did and some of our dads. I wouldn't even know what to do if I had to work like other people. I'm better off staying with what I know.'

Now answer the following questions:

1 How does Jason's view of what is normal and accepted in society differ from your own?

2 Explain how Jason's gang subculture is different from the mainstream culture in society.

3 How do people end up in subcultures such as this? What can the public services do to change the situation?

There are many benefits to understanding and being familiar with different cultures.

Table 13.1: Understanding cultures that are different from your own makes you appreciate and respect the way people behave.

Benefits	Explanation
Understanding people's motivations	Understanding people's cultures can help you understand why they may behave in certain ways or why they might do certain acts. This can help a public service officer get to the bottom of community issues.
Supporting communities	Someone who understands the culture or cultures in an area will be better able to help and support that community than someone who does not understand.
Appreciation of how other people live	Experiencing other people's cultures can give you an insight into how other people live, this could include food, personal relationships, music and so on. You can enrich your own life by finding out about the lives of others.
Respect for diversity	Many people assume the way their culture does something must be the best way. This is not necessarily true, just because something is different does not make it worse than any other option. Understanding different cultures can give you a respect for diversity and an appreciation that there are many different ways to live and behave.
Building community relationships	Understanding different cultures can help you in building community relationships. Some communities contain a lot of different cultures within them, if you understand and appreciate them you can help the community find common issues and respect for each other.

Cultural awareness

Cultural awareness, or the lack of it, can have a significant impact on our everyday lives and how we relate to individuals and groups. If we are culturally aware we will understand why people act and behave the way they do and we will be more accepting of diversity and welcome the benefits that different cultures can bring when they come together. If we are not culturally aware it may be easier for us to **stereotype** other individuals and groups or hold racist views that we don't challenge.

Cultural awareness makes us better citizens in our communities and helps us treat others how we would wish to be treated. All cultures should be respectful of others regardless of the differences between them. Disrespect between cultures can lead to tension, conflict and ultimately **social breakdown**.

Did you know?

Cultures can interlink and blend into one another over time. The Australian and US cultures are very similar to that in the UK because they are former British colonies. Now many cultures in Western nations are shared through our media and television programmes.

Key terms

Stereotype – this is where we think that all people who share the same characteristics are the same without any evidence to back the opinion up. For example, all redheads have a temper or all blondes are dumb.

Social breakdown – this is where communities do not work together, the sections of the community may be in direct conflict leading to violence.

Case study: The Oldham Riots, 2001

The riots in Oldham in May 2001 were considered to be the worst racially motivated riots seen in the UK for a long time. Oldham had once been a thriving mill town exporting cotton around the world. After the Second World War the UK government encouraged members of the Commonwealth, such as India, Bangladesh, Pakistan and Caribbean nations, to send workers to Britain to boost our economy and rebuild our towns. Many migrants such as these settled in Oldham due to its strong industrial heritage and availability of work.

Approximately 11 per cent of Oldham's population is of Asian descent with different languages, culture, religion and traditions. The area had become racially and culturally divided with Asian and White British cultures remaining distinct and very little interaction between the two groups.

There was a very high incidence of racially motivated assaults on both members of the White and Asian communities and a clear feeling on both sides of the cultural divide that the other culture was treated better by the police, media and local council.

The riots were the end result of decades of cultural separation and misunderstanding. On both sides people were attacked, property was destroyed and the police had to defend themselves from assaults by both the White and Asian community. The Ritchie Report (December 2001) into the riots blamed decades of segregation which had not been tackled by the authorities. It claimed that if communities were not encouraged to integrate and understand each other then worse violence could happen.

Now answer the following questions:

1 How might cultural awareness have helped the situation in Oldham?

2 What could be done in areas where different cultures do not mix and view each other with suspicion?

3 What is the impact on the public services of situations such as this?

Key terms

Cultural divide – this is the differences in the cultures living side-by-side in a community.

Segregation – this is the separation of people by race, culture or custom. Sometimes it happens in law such as in the southern states of the US prior to the 1960s and South Africa up to the 1990s and sometimes it is based on custom, tradition or choice.

Case studies such as the one above show how important it is for all members of society to be culturally aware and the possible consequences if they are not. If the public services such as the police or local council are perceived to be treating one cultural group more favourably than another then this can lead to conflict and violence. This is why it is so important that as individuals we respect the culture of others and they respect ours.

Local community

Local communities are generally the areas in which we live, they are geographical areas containing a variety of individuals and families who live close to one another. Local communities can have particular identities which make then different from another community just a few miles or even streets away. Local communities can be as small as your street or village or as large as a town. They are usually maintained by the local council who provide amenities which can be used and enjoyed by the residents of the communities.

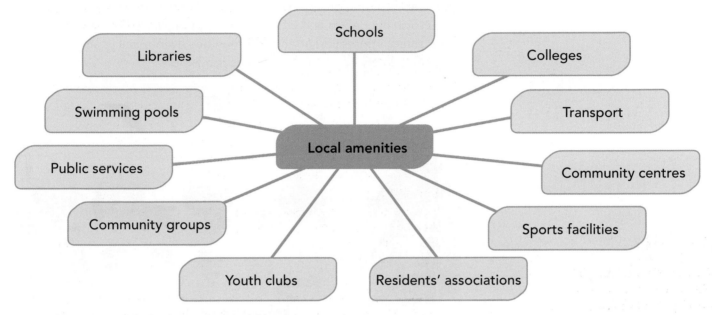

Figure 13.1 Can you think of any other useful local amenities?

The council provides a range of amenities for all ages and groups to enjoy, but like every other public service they operate on a budget and not all communities will have the same facilities. There are also many facilities in communities which exist independently of the council such as cadet groups run by the public services themselves and the scouts and guides. Churches, mosques, temples, synagogues and other places of worship can also provide services to the local community.

Different members of a community will have different needs, for example older members of the community may require community wardens, council-run meals-on-wheels services or home help while younger members may use recreation facilities such as bike tracks and youth clubs. Although the council may provide a great many services in an area, voluntary organisations will also provide some, such as Victim Support and Help the Aged. Residents can also band together to provide their own services by creating community groups, who usually have a specific role in the community such as Neighbourhood Watch.

National community

A national community is formed by all the citizens and services in a society. It is made up of all of the smaller local communities within it, such as rural and urban communities. Urban communities are those which inhabit large towns and cities such as Sheffield, London or Birmingham, whereas rural communities are much smaller and based in the countryside such as the Yorkshire Dales or the Scottish Highlands.

Activity: Your local community

Working individually

Look at Figure 13.1 and assess how many of these amenities your local community has. Are there any services in your community that aren't on the list? What services do you think are essential for your local area?

Working as a class

Discuss your answers with your classmates who may come from different areas. How do your local amenities compare? Is one area better than another?

Link

Find out more about Help the Aged on page 169.

Communities such as these often develop around the main industries based in the area when the communities were formed and the towns and villages grew, for example coal mining in South Yorkshire and Nottinghamshire, shipbuilding in the north-east and shipping in Liverpool and London. Communities can also develop from specific ethnic and cultural groups who worked or lived in areas, such as Chinatown in London and Little Germany in Bradford. These can have a long-lasting impression on the communities even many years after the original industry or cultural group has moved on.

What features show the cultural identity of this community?

Activity: British identity

Working as a group

In your opinion what are the characteristics on the UK that form a national identity? Is it the Union Jack, football teams or fish and chips?

In small groups, make a list of the things you can think of that seem characteristically British. Share your list with the rest of your group and compare your answers.

National identity

National identity describes the collection of characteristics that make a nation different from other nations. It is these shared characteristics that make people feel a patriotic attachment and personal affection towards their own nation. It is a special attachment to your country or state and a feeling that you belong because you share similar ethnic background, language, history and culture to the rest of the nation.

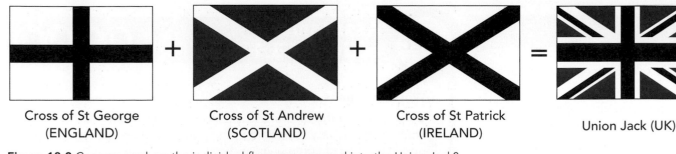

| Cross of St George (ENGLAND) | + | Cross of St Andrew (SCOTLAND) | + | Cross of St Patrick (IRELAND) | = | Union Jack (UK) |

Figure 13.2 Can you see how the individual flags were merged into the Union Jack?

Do you think Britain has a clear sense of identity?

Some countries have very clearly defined national identities and some nations do not. It has been argued that Britain does not have a clear sense of its identity and that no one can really define what 'Britishness' actually means. A survey on British social attitudes in 2007 found that only 44 per cent of the population would describe itself as British, the rest prefer to use Scottish, Welsh, Irish and English instead.

Having a strong sense of national identity has both positive and negative aspects to it. On a negative note it can be seen as quite exclusive and unwilling to accommodate people of other nations who live here. Also, it can be perceived as being associated with extreme right-wing parties such as the British National Party or the behaviour of football hooligans abroad who think that being British is a licence to assault other football fans. On a more positive note it can generate great pride when services are deployed abroad or a British institution is verbally attacked from outside as in August 2009 when US conservatives criticised our national health service (NHS) and thousands of bloggers in the UK and users of the Twitter service rushed to its defence.

Another aspect of being part of a larger national community is that you have a greater set of resources to draw from than if you were just tied to what was in your own local area. For example, in the event of a large scale **major incident** public services from many different areas could be deployed to provide additional support to the public services where the incident occurred. Part of belonging to a national community is understanding that the person who lives 200 miles away is every bit as important as the person next door and in the event of serious incidents, wars or crises we all belong to the same British community and we will pull together when needed.

Did you know?

The current look of the Union Jack dates from 1801 when the Kingdom of Ireland merged with the Kingdom of Great Britain. The Union Jack is actually made up of three different crosses, of St Andrew, St George and St Patrick, representing the nations of Scotland, England and Ireland. See Figure 13.2.

Key term

Major incident – a large scale emergency or disaster such as a terrorist attack or extensive flooding which requires all the services to work together in order to deal with the problem.

PLTS

Undertaking research for your presentation will give you the opportunity to develop your creative thinker and independent enquirer skills.

Functional skills

Preparing your presentation will develop your ICT functional skills and listening and and answering questions from your audience will develop your English functional skills.

BTEC Assessment activity 13.1

Working in pairs

Understanding the differences between local and national communities is very important in the public services as is an understanding of community and cultural issues. Research, prepare and present a 10-minute PowerPoint presentation with supporting notes in which you:

1 *Explain* the differences between local and national community. **P1**

2 *Discuss* the awareness of community and cultural issues in local and national communities. **P2**

3 *Compare* the awareness of community and cultural issues in local and national communities. **M1**

4 *Evaluate* the awareness of community and cultural issues in local and national communities. **D1**

Grading tips

For **P1** you need to research the differences between local and national communities and explain them in your presentation.

For **P2** you should consider what the most common community and cultural issues are and then present information on the awareness of those issues in society today.

To get **M1** your presentation should show comparisons between the awareness of local and national communities and for **D1** you should think about what problems communities are aware of and why and consider if these views need to be challenged.

2 The costs and benefits of living in a community

Living as part of community and participating in community life is not always an easy thing. It can be quite a challenge to live closely with all different types of people, many of whom may be very different from you. The differences between people in communities can lead to conflict which can be very difficult to resolve even if the public services are involved. Equally, sharing your life with others can be very rewarding in terms of making friends and having support when you need it. The costs/sacrifices and benefits of living in a geographical community are outlined below.

2.1 Costs/sacrifices

Personal investment

Living in a community takes a considerable personal investment from each person in terms of time and participation. Communities require people to know each other and take part in community activities, this can be very time-consuming and it is easy to ignore how important interacting with your community is when you have been at work or college all day and you are tired and want to rest. Even making conversation with neighbours in the street can seem like a chore at times. Personal relationships are at the heart of our communities and we must be prepared to give the time and effort to keeping the community clean, safe and friendly.

Activity: How well do you know your community?

Draw a map of your street with houses on. Colour-code the houses as follows:

- green – I know these people well
- orange – I know these people slightly
- blue – I don't know these people at all.

What is the largest colour on your map? What does this say about the community you live in and the efforts you have made to become involved in your community?

Accepting differences

Some people find it very difficult to tolerate differences in others and can be very rude and unpleasant about it. These differences can be large-scale differences such as race or religion, but in a community they can also be as simple as how neatly you keep your garden or the way you choose to dress. People who cannot accept differences can often be the focal point for trouble or nuisance in a community, making the lives of those around them miserable. As potential public service recruits you should remember that everyone has the right to live their lives as they wish as long as they do it within the law, this can require time and effort to accept for some people.

Community awareness

It is important to acknowledge that being aware of others around you and being sensitive to their needs is part of being a good community member. This can take effort and commitment as you have to know about others in your community. If you are ignorant about the needs and feelings of others you will be a poor community member and this can lead to conflict.

Community activities can bring together the people living in the area. What activities would you choose to bring a community together?

Key term

ASBO – an anti-social behaviour order is a court order that restricts what a person who has been found engaging in anti-social behaviour can do. ASBOs can restrict the areas you are allowed into and who you are allowed to see. If you break the conditions of an ASBO you can receive a custodial sentence.

What type of community facilities are available where you live?

Case study: Nuisance neighbours

The case of 67-year-old Rosemary Hill of Norfolk was reported in March 2008. Ms Hill received an anti-social behaviour order (ASBO) from Kings Lynn magistrates for poor conduct towards her neighbours. Her behaviour included:

- writing abusive letters
- slamming doors
- revving a chainsaw
- pointing security lights at the windows of another resident's home
- playing loud music.

Neighbours reported 69 incidents of such behaviour in a 6-month period.

Now answer the following questions:

1   Have you ever had to deal with nuisance neighbours?
2   Have you ever behaved in such a way that members of your community might see you as a nuisance?
3   What are the kinds of behaviour that will cause conflict in your community?

Community facilities

There is a cost to providing community facilities. As well as a financial cost there is a cost in the time and effort it takes to run the facilities, many of which are staffed by volunteers who give up their own time for their community. Community facilities are usually provided by the local council and they have a limited supply of money with which to do it. This can mean, in some areas, certain sections of the community are not provided for, such as elderly or young people. This can be a cost to living in a community which doesn't have amenities for you as you may have to travel a distance to a location where the facilities are available or do without certain facilities completely.

Community change

Another downside to living in a community is accepting that communities can and do change rapidly as a result of the economic situation in an area or political choices made at local and national level. These changes can harm a community, affecting house prices, youth behaviour and causing ethnic tension.

Case study: Mary's experience after the pit closed

'I've lived in a little village in South Yorkshire all my life, my dad and granddad were both miners, my brothers went down the mine to work when they were old enough and I married a miner. It was the main industry in the area for decades and I suppose we all thought it would last forever.

The situation changed dramatically in the early 1980s when the pits began to close down as it was cheaper for the government to pay for imported coal than it was to mine it from our own collieries. We fought for a long time to keep the pits open but looking back on it now we had no chance against the government.

We went from being a prosperous, clean and well-kept village to a destitute community with most of the men unemployed. This led to family break-ups, increased drinking and real poverty. Even now over 20 years later the effects are still there, the kids in the area have nothing to do so they get into trouble, there are no jobs in the area except for new call centres which the men round here aren't really suited for and schools which struggle to control the behaviour of their pupils. Everyone used to know everyone else, all the families worked together and pulled together, now you don't even know the people on your street. It feels like a hostile place not a home.

When the mining industry went so did our community and it's never really recovered.'

Now answer the following questions:

1 What are the disadvantages of having a community based around one industry?

2 How did the decision to close the mine impose costs on the local community?

3 Why did the community break down in this example?

4 What could have been done to help the community at the time of the pit closure and what could be done to help the area now?

2.2 Benefits

If there weren't any benefits to living in a community then there would be no reason for humans to live together at all. There are several main reasons why the majority of people choose to live closely to each other. The main reasons are highlighted below.

Social networks and support

Living as part of a community enables you to make social networks. These are groups of people who you know or become friends with who may offer you support in times of trouble. A social network can range from having very close personal ties with someone to the people you might nod to in the street. They all form part of a network of individuals you have contact with in your daily life. People are social animals, they like to have friends and get to know people so this is a benefit of living in a community.

Family and friendship

Many people live in the same community as their families and friends, this means they usually have sources of personal support and help very close at hand. People often rely on their family and friends for a whole range of needs, so having them close by is a benefit for most people. These personal ties to an area can be very important in providing a sense of belonging and providing you with the incentive needed to take part in your community and care for the people in it.

Community centres

Community centres are very valuable additions to any community. They act as a meeting place for residents and as a venue for all kinds of community events. These can include education classes, toddler groups, bingo and tea dances, which offer people who are often home all day, such as the elderly and new mothers, an opportunity to mix with other people and form community relationships.

Case study: Jane's new baby

'I've worked all my life since I was 18 and left college. That means that for most of my adult life I haven't really been a good community member, I wasn't there – I was at work all day. I've just had a baby girl and at first I was really happy and busy, but I started to miss the interaction and the company you get by going to work. I began to feel really lonely and a bit down in the dumps.

My health visitor suggested I go to the local parent and baby group or education classes at the community centre to get me out of the house a bit and it's been a lifesaver. I go out twice a week to the parents group and have made some new friends and I also go to a Spanish class once a week as they have a crèche on site and my daughter is looked after for an hour while I learn.

I still miss work and I'm looking forward to going back after my maternity leave, but I've discovered a whole new community of people that I didn't know existed and I'm going to make sure that even after I go back to work I stay a part of it.'

Now answer the following questions:

1 If you are at school or college all day do you know what is happening in your community during this time?

2 How do community centres benefit those who need to stay closer to home?

3 What happens to communities who don't use these facilities?

Local education

Many charitable organisations and local further education providers offer education classes in the local community. This helps bring education to those who cannot travel to the local college or aren't interested in taking formal classes. Education in the community helps bond people by sharing classes and increases the potential for getting back into work by improving job skills and confidence.

Communication

One benefit to living in a community and being an active member of it is that you are in constant communication with others. There are hundreds of people in your community and there is always someone to pass the time of day with. This can improve social skills and communication skills in active community members.

Sense of belonging

Being a part of a community can provide you with a sense of where you belong and a sense of your personal history. This can help people feel less lonely and provide them with confidence. It can help to make you feel part of an area if you know your family has lived there for a long time and has roots in the area. Also, being part of a community should help you feel less isolated and provide you with a sense of being 'home'.

A good community gives you the sense of belonging. Make a list of the factors that contribute to this feeling.

Caring for others

Taking care of others is a key benefit to living in a community, this could mean relying on your neighbours for some shopping or babysitting or having them keep an eye on your house or feed your pets when you are on holiday. Community members are normally the ones who will check that you are OK if your curtains haven't been opened or newspapers start to build up on your doorstep. Taking care of others and being taken care of yourself is one of the primary reasons people live together in communities. You are safer in a group than you are alone.

BTEC | **Assessment activity 13.2** | P3

Working as a group

In small groups, conduct some research on your local community and be prepared to take part in a discussion in which you:

1 *Describe* the costs and benefits to living in a community. P3

Grading tip

While you are researching your local community for P3 make a list of the positive and negative things you find about living there and make sure you raise them and describe them in your discussion.

PLTS

While you are considering the costs and benefits and weighing up what it is like to live in a community you are being a reflective learner. This can form evidence for part of your PLTS course.

Functional skills

As this is a discussion task you will be generating evidence towards the speaking and listening portion of your functional skills in English.

A view is held by some of the media and some political parties that the UK takes in too many people from ethnic minorities and that the White UK population is danger of being swamped by immigrants. The actual data shows this not to be true and that the UK is over 92 per cent White.

In comparison the population of the United States is 300 million and their ethnic minority population is 26 per cent, and in France the population is over 60 million and their ethnic minority population makes up 10 per cent of the whole.

Immigrants have been arriving in the UK for many years, it is not a recent phenomenon. Over the last thousand years we have seen immigrants from Ireland, the Huguenots in the sixteenth and seventeenth centuries and the Ashkenazi Jews in the late nineteenth century to name just a few. In the twentieth century immigration was from Commonwealth nations including the West Indies, India and Pakistan. Each cultural group brought with it its own traditions, professions, food and religion and each group has enriched British culture by its presence.

Traditional eastern cuisine in a night-time market in the Soho region of London, UK. Have you any strong cultural influences in your community?

Trends and lifestyles

Individuals and groups in the UK have a great deal of freedom to live how they wish as long as they do not break the law. This means they may choose which religion to worship (or not to have a religion), which language to speak, how to socialise, when and how to form personal relationships and how to live their lives. Although there may be a 'traditional' way to live you are not required to follow the tradition, you can choose an alternative path. For example, the majority of children are raised in families but an alternative, which briefly became popular in the 1960s and 70s, is in a commune. In a commune a group of people who are often unrelated live and work together collectively sharing money, work and childcare. The group becomes more important than the individuals within it and children may be raised collectively by all the adults in the group.

Other changes in lifestyle over the last 30 years include:

- the average age at which people marry is rising and the number of people who choose to marry is decreasing
- the average age for becoming a parent is rising
- the birth rate is declining
- church attendance is declining.

All of these lifestyle changes and trends make the lives we lead very different from those of our parents and grandparents.

Activity: Lifestyle changes

To show how lifestyles change over time, ask your parents or guardians the following questions about what they did when they were your age:

1 How did they spend their spare time?

2 Where did they socialise?

3 How much money did they have to spend?

4 When did they leave education?

5 How much freedom were they allowed?

Now ask the same questions of your grandparents and great grandparents, if you can. Compare their answers with your own answers to these questions. How does your lifestyle differ from your parents, grandparents and great grandparents?

Increasingly, virtual culture is becoming more important, particularly in those under the age of 25 years. This includes use of texting, instant messaging, social networking sites, online chat rooms, web forums and online games.

Online relationships and virtual cultures can be every bit as important to people as real life relationships and communities. It is very important when dealing with online communities that you take sensible precautions to protect yourself such as never giving out personal or private information and never meeting people who you speak to online unless you take a parent with you. You have no idea if the person you are chatting to is as they appear to be online, so don't take any chances. In addition, be aware that when you put personal or private details of your life on websites such as Facebook or Bebo you are making your life an open book. Do you really want your employers or tutors to see what you get up to? Or worse, do you want them to read what you say about them online?

Case study: Millie's online gaming community

'I have played World of Warcraft for over 4 years. Globally there are over 11 million players, but on my server there are only around 5,000 and of course they won't all be on all at the same time. I started playing at the same time as my husband did and we really enjoyed playing it together. I stayed with Warcraft even when he moved over to another online game.

What I like about Warcraft are the social relationships you can build up. I have made some really good friends who I now keep in touch with in real life as well. Since I started playing I've had a baby and the great thing is that I still get some social interaction even if I can't afford to have a babysitter and go out.

Lots of people think that relationships and online communities aren't as real as the ones in the outside world, I'd say they need to open their minds, there's more than one way to make friends and more than one community to be part of.'

Now answer the following questions:

1 Are you part of an online community?

2 How much time do you spend socialising with people online?

3 Why do you think many people are living their social lives online rather than in real life?

Did you know?

Only a quarter of the world's population have internet access with the lowest amount of users in Africa, Asia and the Middle East. This is likely to be a result of poverty or restrictive governments.

It is important to note that the internet and world wide web have opened up communications globally and people are able to interact with millions of others from hundreds of different nations if they wish, making cultural exchange easier and faster. It can also educate people in countries with heavy censorship about life in the wider global community, and provide a channel to spread information, for instance on the human rights abuses which some governments practise and would like to remain hidden. It is increasingly becoming the rallying point for campaigns to improve human rights as well as the environment. In 2008 Barack Obama's presidential campaign made extensive use of the internet to organise volunteers and donations for his campaign. In fact, it has been argued that without the internet he would not have been elected president.

There are many benefits to understanding and appreciating diverse cultures. It can open up a new world of experience in terms of cultural events, such as the festivals and ceremonies of other religions. You can gain an appreciation of new foods such as Indian, Chinese, Italian and North African, you can learn new languages which might open up new travel opportunities and you can make lots of new friends.

There are both positive and negative aspects of cultural diversity. These are illustrated in Table 13.3.

Table 13.3: The pluses and minuses of cultural diversity.

Positive	Negative
Exposure to new foods	People can be intolerant and racist
Learning new languages	Can be lack of integration in some areas
Meeting new people	Can cause distrust and misunderstanding
Good for the economy	Competition for government resources
Promotes understanding and harmony	Cultures can clash as what is accepted in one culture may not be accepted in another
New ideas and ways of doing things	

These positive and negative aspects of cultural diversity can apply equally whether in a local area such as a village or in a national setting. Overall cultural diversity has far more positive impacts on our communities and cultures than negative impacts. It is a fact that cultural diversity can be difficult to manage for many people and as a society we must contribute to educating people about the advantages and finding ways to overcome the negative impacts by promoting acceptance and appreciation.

3.1 Impact of cultural diversity on the public services

Cultural diversity can have a significant effect on the public services as they are required to make provisions that meet a variety of cultural needs. This can cover many aspects of a culture such as:

Providing information in a variety of languages. The public services have to provide all of their information in a number of community languages such as Arabic, Urdu and Chinese. Many services also have a bank of translators who can be called upon to help speakers of other languages understand the position they are in.

Cultural awareness and diversity training. The public services must understand the communities they work with. This isn't always about learning to speak another language, it is also about becoming familiar with the requirements of different religions so that care can be taken not to offend people without realising it. It is about understanding the culture of the people you work for so that you can show respect for the things that are important to them. This is why the public services put a great deal of time and money into training all officers on issues of diversity and cultural awareness.

Recruitment. It is important that the public services are representative of the communities that they serve. The more culturally diverse a community, the more culturally diverse the public services should be. The services spend time and effort in trying to recruit a diverse workforce so they can better serve their communities. Unfortunately, they don't always succeed in being fully representative, as shown in the figures for recruitment of ethnic minorities (see page 166).

Did you know?

On the Independent Police Complaints Commission (IPCC) website a leaflet on how to make a complaint against the police is available in 17 different languages.

Cultural diversity presents benefits and challenges to the public services.

Link

For more on recruitment of ethnic minorities into the public services, see Unit 6 page 166.

Accommodating different needs. The services need to be aware that individuals from different cultural backgrounds may have a variety of needs, such as special dietary requirements, and may need additional support educationally. For example, the Prison Service has prisoners who may require kosher or halal diets and may need prayer facilities which conform to the needs of their religion. In schools many children raised in households where English is not the first language may need additional support as they become bilingual.

BTEC Assessment activity 13.3

In order to show that you understand cultural diversity produce an A3 poster in which you:

1 *Illustrate* the positive and negative aspects of cultural diversity. **P4**

2 *Analyse* the advantages and disadvantages of living in a culturally diverse community. **M2**

Grading tip

The difference between **P4** and **M2** is in the level of detail that is required. To achieve **P4** make sure that you include on your poster as many positive and negative aspects to living in a culturally diverse community as you can and use images to illustrate your points. To get **M2** provide more detail on the good and bad points, perhaps you could support it with some of your own research from the communities local to you.

4 The social and cultural problems that exist in a local community and those that exist nationally

4.1 Social problems

Social problems are issues which cause the public concern and have a negative impact on the communities we live in. They cover a wide variety of issues such as gang behaviour, knife crime, anti-social behaviour or unemployment. Some social problems might be confined to local communities and some might be an issue for the whole nation. The scale and type of social problems can vary from community to community and they are often linked to wider problems in society, such as a poor economy, recession and high unemployment.

Poverty

A general definition for poverty is a state where people do not have enough food or money for their daily needs. There are several levels of poverty within this general definition.

Absolute poverty. This is a lack of the basic necessities needed in order to support human life such as food, water, shelter and heat. **Primary absolute poverty** is when an individual has no basic necessities at all. This occurred in the famine and drought in Ethiopia during the 1980s in which people starved to death by the millions. **Secondary absolute poverty** is when an individual has some basic necessities but they are not sufficient to keep them healthy and safe. This occurs in war-torn parts of the world where refugees cannot fulfil their needs. We rarely see absolute poverty in the UK as our welfare state takes care of most people who are in need.

Relative poverty. This is a level of poverty which leaves an individual unable to participate in the cultural and social life of a community. A survey reported in the *Sunday Times* showed that 50 per cent of people thought that a family was in poverty if they could not afford a phone, TV or washing machine. Clearly these families are not starving and they have access to health care and education but they are poor relative to others in their society.

The impact of poverty

Poverty is a major social problem across the world although there are differences in the types of poverty that each nation suffers. Poverty can have a substantial impact on the UK public services and communities in the following ways:

- cause possible increase in crime and violence leading to greater strain on the budgets and skills of the emergency services
- give rise to aid and humanitarian missions for the Armed Services abroad
- cause increased strain on the public services involved in social welfare
- cause businesses to close as people have less money to spend
- cause homeowners to lose their homes if they cannot pay rent or mortgages
- cause communities to look very run down, which can lead to other problems such as crime and anti-social behaviour.

More generally, poverty can affect your life chances. These are the opportunities you are given in life which often spring from your social background and social class. Reports show that children from poorer families are less likely to do well in school and more likely to engage in anti-social behaviour when they are older. Poverty can also affect how long you will live, particularly for babies and the elderly, the lower your income the higher is the average mortality rate.

This homeless person carries all his belongings in carrier bags.

Unemployment

There is a great deal of debate about how many people are actually unemployed. Current government figures put the number of people claiming Jobseeker's Allowance at around 1.64 million, but this is not necessarily the full picture. Although the government might claim that only 1.58 million people are actually unemployed these figures do not include people on any other benefits such as Income Support or Disability Living Allowance. The International Labour Organisation (ILO) put the figure for mid-2009 as 2.46 million unemployed.

Unemployment can have a tremendous impact on the individual causing depression, health problems and family breakdown and even leading, in some cases, to suicidal behaviour. Unemployed people have very low incomes, as state benefits are not meant to keep people in luxury but are meant to cover the basics only. This can have a negative impact on the lives of individuals, families and communities in terms of poor-quality housing and diet, which can have a negative effect on the health and well-being of children and elderly community members. The consequences to society are just as devastating and these consequences can have tremendous impact on the operation of the public services.

Racism and inequality

In conditions of economic depression and unemployment there is often an increase in **racist** attitudes as ethnic minority populations are scape-goated and blamed for the economic position of others. The same attitudes can be found against people with differing sexualities or against women in the workplace. This has direct implications for the public services in terms of dealing with incidents of **hate crime** and violence. **Racism** is very hard to get rid of. It is spread by ignorance and a lack of experience of populations of differing ethnic background. Often people pick up and don't question racist attitudes from older family members. The media has also played a part in perpetuating racist stereotypes. It is vitally important that the public services challenge these attitudes.

Mental illness

It has been estimated that about a quarter of the population may experience mental health problems at some point in their lives. This means that every day in the UK millions of people are suffering with mental health difficulties or know someone who is. Figure 13.4 illustrates some of the illnesses involved.

People are often very afraid of those who suffer with mental illness. They struggle to know how to deal with the sufferer or may actively avoid or fear them. A poll conducted by YouGov found that a third of people thought individuals with schizophrenia were likely to be violent, but the charity MIND, who deal with mental health awareness, note that you are more likely to be struck by lightning than be harmed by someone with a mental health problem. MIND also comments that people suffering from mental health problems often say that the shame and the way they are treated by others can be far worse than the illness itself. Individuals with mental health problems also need lots of support and care from their families, friends and loved ones as well as health and social services. This can be hard, especially for young people taking care of a parent of grandparent who has mental health issues.

Key terms

Racists – those people who treat other people unfairly based on their skin colour or ethnic background.

Hate crime – a crime where a criminal targets his or her victim based on their race, gender, sexuality or religion.

Racism – the belief that a different skin colour or religious belief make some people better than others.

Activity: Do you stereotype?

'Time to change' is a charity that aims to challenge the stigma faced by people with mental health problems. They have produced two short films about the issue which can be watched on their website, available via Hotlinks (see p viii).

Watch one or both of these films and consider how society views people with schizophrenia and compare this to the real situation. Are you guilty of stereotyping? What can you do to change your attitudes?

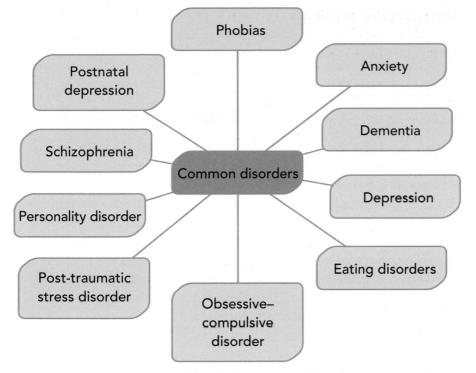

Figure 13.4: Examples of mental health illnesses. Are there any more examples you could add to the list?

 Case study: John's experience of PTSD

'My first tour of Afghanistan was OK, no one in my unit was hurt and although all of us would have rather been anywhere else than there, we did our job professionally and we were pleased to be in a position to assist the Afghan government with fighting the Taliban. I'd heard stories of other soldiers who had suffered from post-traumatic stress disorder (PTSD) and I hadn't paid that much attention to it. I suppose I was a bit ignorant if I'm honest. I never thought it would happen to me, I thought I was tougher than that.

Towards the end of my second tour we were out on a routine patrol in a small convoy when an improvised explosive device (IED) went off by the roadside and hit the vehicle in front of us. It was carnage, one lad had got severe injuries to his legs and chest and the lad in the back didn't make it. We got out and recovered the dead and injured and did our jobs – that's what the Army teaches you to do and it's what is expected of you by your colleagues.

It wasn't until a week or so later when we arrived home that things started to go wrong. I suppose I was too busy while we were on duty to think about it and I had my mates to talk to, but when I was

home I kept having flashbacks about the explosion and what I'd seen when we pulled the lads from the vehicle. I couldn't talk to my mum about it, she worries enough about me as it is and my mates at home wouldn't understand. I became really withdrawn and anxious and the flashbacks were awful, I could almost smell the burning and feel the blood. If it hadn't been for my dad I don't know what would have happened, he was a soldier before I was born and he had served in the Falklands in the early 1980s. He knew something was wrong straightaway and helped me sort myself out with the doctor and a counsellor. I started to feel better in a couple of weeks and I was able to return to my unit without any long-term problems.'

Now answer the following questions:

1 Why do you think it was difficult for John to talk about his experiences?

2 What help could the counsellor and doctor give him?

3 What other facilities can be offered to John to help him with his PSTD?

Domestic abuse

The charity Women's Aid defines domestic abuse as physical, sexual, psychological or financial violence that takes place within an intimate or family-type relationship. It can include a variety of behaviours including biting, kicking, punching, slapping, jealously, threats of suicide, withholding money, abuse of children and controlling behaviour.

A study by Walby and Allen (2004) found that 45 per cent of women and 26 per cent of men will have been a victim of interpersonal violence at some point in their lives. Domestic violence makes up about 20 per cent of all recorded violent crime and each year there are approximately 13 million separate incidents of violence or threats made against women by their partners or former partners. This places an enormous stress on the public services, for instance the police alone receive about 1,300 calls every day related to domestic violence. There is also the impact on the social services and education services who often have to deal with the after-effects of adults and children who are undergoing domestic abuse.

Substance abuse

Substance abuse is the use of any medication, drug or substance to produce mood-altering results. This may include illegal drugs such as cocaine, heroin, marijuana, but it can also include drugs which people are prescribed by their GP such as thyroxin and insulin. It also includes substances which are used recreationally such as alcohol and tobacco.

It can be difficult to get accurate information on substance abuse because many people will not tell the truth or their lifestyles are so dominated by the abuse that they may not know how much they use or when they use it. The British Crime Survey (2006) discovered that around 35 per cent of the population have tried drugs in their lifetime and about 7 per cent use them on a regular basis. There is no doubt that if binge drinking figures were included, the figure would rise sharply. Surveys have shown that 37 per cent of adults regularly exceed the recommended daily alcohol limits and 27 per cent drink three times a week or more. More worrying are the statistics for young people aged 11–15. It is estimated that 360,000 11–15-year-olds get drunk every week with serious consequences for the public services in terms of policing and NHS costs. The police and NHS casualty services are often stretched to breaking point over weekend periods when there are many drink-related violence and public order incidents. It is also worth noting that about half of all sexual assaults occur when victim, perpetrator or both have been drinking. There are also implications for the education and social services as there are strong links between drinking high levels of alcohol and youth offending, teenage pregnancy, truancy and exclusion from school.

Bullying

Bullying is defined as persistent unwelcome behaviour which a person experiences from another person or a group of people. It is not an isolated incident where someone is rude or unpleasant to you, it happens over an extended period of time and may happen frequently. Bullying can happen anywhere including schools, colleges, workplaces and in online communities – this is called cyberbullying.

The effects of bullying can be devastating to the individual and their families. It can cause a feeling of worthlessness and hopelessness and cause illnesses such as depression and anxiety. People who are bullied may become frightened to leave the house to attend school or work and may ultimately refuse to attend school leaving them with difficulties for the rest of their lives.

Activity: Bullying

Conduct some research into bullying. What type of behaviour is bullying? How is bullying online different from bullying in person? How many people are bullied? What can be done about bullies?

Put all your information together in a leaflet which you can give out to people in your school or college to help them cope if they are being bullied.

Compare this with your school or college policy on bullying. Are there any differences? Did you come up with any ideas which could be included in your school or college policy?

4.2 Cultural problems

As well as social problems many cultural problems can be found in local and national communities. Minority cultures can find it very difficult to exist alongside mainstream cultures without becoming diluted. This can be an issue when parents try to pass their cultural heritage on to their children. If their children have been raised in the mainstream culture they may not respect or accept their parents' ways and traditions. It can also become an issue in knowing your cultural identity as you will have been exposed to two very different cultures and may not know which one is right for you. Also, the culture of young people is usually different from the culture of older generations, this is natural as culture is not static and changes over time. The changes can include alterations to particular customs and traditions and changing values and morals.

Key terms

Cultural transmission – this is where you pass your culture on to the next generation. Changes in culture over time may lead to an inaccurate version of culture being transmitted.

Cultural alienation – this means that you are separated from the culture of your parents or the generation before you because you feel it has nothing to offer you or you prefer the customs and traditions of another culture.

Activity: Cultural identity

Can you think of things that make cultural identities different? List as many religions as you can and name two of their main customs or traditions.

289

Case study: Munita and her traditional parents

'My family are originally from Yemen, but they settled here when they got married 30 years ago. My sister and two brothers were born and raised in the UK. I'm the youngest of the four of us and about to start university. I really value my parents' culture, I've been back to Yemen on many occasions to see my grandparents and the rest of my family who still live there, but I also consider myself to be British, this has caused some problems at home.

I think the main problem is that my parents hold on to the culture they were raised in which was very traditional. What they don't realise is that their ideas of Yemeni culture are 30 years out of date. I've contacted my cousins and aunts in Yemen on a couple of occasions to have them explain to my dad that the things I want to do are acceptable in our culture because culture has moved on. My parents aren't just in a different culture from the mainstream British culture they are actually in a different culture from their own relatives at home in Yemen. It's

like they took a snapshot of Yemeni culture 30 years ago and haven't changed their views since.

It hard trying to keep a culture going in the face of everything you are bombarded with everyday, but I think my brothers, sister and I would be more willing to listen if my parents understood that culture is adaptable. I may have been born to Yemeni parents but my experience of being Yemeni needs to fit in with my experience of being British. I have to adapt and accommodate both cultures in a way that my parents didn't.'

Now answer the following questions:

1 Why do you think Munita's parents have ideas about their culture which may be out of date?

2 Should other cultures adapt and accommodate the mainstream British culture or should they try to preserve what makes them unique?

3 Why does culture change over time?

PLTS

By working as part of a team to produce your newspaper you may achieve evidence for the teamworking and effective participator aspects of your PLTS course.

Functional skills

Producing your newspaper may provide evidence of developing, presenting and communication information in your ICT functional skill.

BTEC Assessment activity 13.4 P5 P6 P7 M3 D2

Working as a group

In a group of no more than four, design and produce a newspaper or magazine which covers the issues of social and cultural problems in detail. You must:

1 *Report* on the categories of social problems in communities locally and across the UK. P5

2 *Report* on the cultural problems in communities locally and across the UK. P6

3 *Analyse* the social and cultural problems that exist within communities in the UK. M3

4 *Evaluate* the social and cultural problems that exist in communities across the UK. D2

5 *Investigate* the impact of social and cultural problems in the UK. P7

Grading tips

This assessment will require you to research the social and cultural problems which exist in communities locally and nationally and then write newspaper or magazine articles about them in order to pass. To get M3 your articles should be detailed and well balanced and for D2 you should show how these problems might be dealt with and use some of your own opinions to evaluate and draw conclusions.

Sarasa Dev

Police Community Support Officer

I work as a police community support officer (PCSO) for the local Police Service. I work full time in a busy city and support the regular police officers with their work in the community. We don't have the same powers as regular police officers but we are still a key part of keeping communities safe and trouble-free. PCSOs do a variety of work including:

- deal with minor offences
- offer early intervention to deter people from committing offences
- provide support for front-line policing
- conduct house-to-house enquiries
- guard crime scenes
- provide crime prevention advice.

A typical day

A typical day for me involves patrolling the streets and acting as a visible presence in certain areas to deter people from committing crime and reassuring other members of the community that they are safe. Dealing with anti-social behaviour is a big part of what I do and often this can be linked to alcohol and drugs abuse. Normally I would assess the situation and make a decision whether to deal with it myself or request support from my police officer colleagues. It's also really important to interact with the community which might mean popping in to the local school or having a chat with young people who are just hanging around. Building community relationships like this means it's much easier for people to trust us, and when they trust us they are more likely to tell us the problems the community has and then we can do something about it.

The best thing about the job

The best thing about being a PCSO is not being stuck in an office all day, I get out and about and speak to hundreds of people in a working week. Building relationships with people who often distrust the police is great as well, you can really see the atmosphere change and the community improves as a result. Making the community a better place to live and work is what it's all about after all.

Think about it!

1. What topics have you covered in this unit that might give you the background to be a good PCSO?
2. What knowledge and skills do you think you need to develop further if you want to be a PCSO in the future?

Just checking

1 What types of community are there?
2 What is culture?
3 What is the impact of poverty?
4 What are the benefits to living in a community?
5 What is the impact of cultural diversity on the services?

edexcel :::

Assignment tips

Getting the most from your assignments and aiming for the highest grades is not always easy. The tips below will help you in moving towards those merit and distinction grades.

• **Research and preparation.** This may sound very basic, but make sure you have read your assignment thoroughly and you understand exactly what you are being asked to do. Once you are clear about this then you can move on to your research. Doing your research well and using good sources of evidence is essential. Lots of students rely too much on the internet and not enough on other sources of information such as books, newspapers and journals. The internet is not always a good source of information, it is very easy to use information from American or Australian websites without noticing – but your tutor will notice. Always double-check the information you find, don't just accept it at face value. Good research and preparation is the key to getting those higher grades.

• **Primary research.** Primary research is a method of research where you go out and collect your information personally. A unit like 'Community and cultural awareness' lends itself to going out into the community and seeing for yourself how diverse it is and the kinds of social problems it faces. Reporting your first-hand findings will improve your understanding of community and culture and also help to improve your grades.

15 Expedition skills in public services

For many years the public services have used expeditions and outdoor activities in their recruitment, selection and training of personnel. Expeditions are physically, mentally and emotionally challenging, so completing an expedition is a test of character and endurance that marks you out as being different from others.

Expeditions in the public services are used to develop skills, qualities and attributes which the services see as essential for operational effectiveness, such as leadership, teamwork, self-reliance, confidence and problem solving. In addition the armed services require expedition skills themselves as there are many occasions where living in the field will be part of the job in the arena of combat.

This unit is very practical and covers the basics you will need to conduct a safe and successful expedition. It covers the equipment required for day and overnight expeditions and the planning required to conduct an expedition, ensuring that you take into account issues such as the weather, health and safety and first aid.

You will also examine route planning and explore some of the technical skills you might need while on your expedition such as grid references, bearings and escape routes. Another important skill covered in this unit is the reflection and evaluation required after your expedition, as judging whether you were successful, what went wrong and what went right is a key ability in improving your own skills and performance and the skill of your team.

Learning outcomes

After completing this unit you should:

1. know the correct equipment required for an expedition
2. understand the planning necessary for an expedition
3. be able to participate in an expedition
4. be able to review an expedition.

Assessment and grading criteria

This table shows you what you must do in order to achieve a pass, merit or distinction grade, and where you can find activities in this book to help you.

To achieve a **pass** grade the evidence must show that the learner is able to:	To achieve a **merit** grade the evidence must show that, in addition to the pass criteria, the learner is able to:	To achieve a **distinction** grade the evidence must show that, in addition to the pass and merit criteria, the learner is able
1 describe the equipment needed for an expedition **Assessment activity 15.1 page 306**		
2 describe the use of safety equipment **Assessment activity 15.1 page 306**	**M1** demonstrate the use of safety equipment **Assessment activity 15.1 page 306**	**D1** evaluate the purpose and function of all equipment required for a day and overnight expedition **Assessment activity 15.1 page 306**
3 explain the planning needed for an expedition **Assessment activity 15.2 page 313**	**M2** explain in detail safety and environmental considerations for an expedition **Assessment activity 15.2 page 313**	**D2** evaluate the planning of the expedition **Assessment activity 15.2 page 313**
4 produce a route for an expedition **Assessment activity 15.3 page 317**		
5 carry out an expedition identifying own roles and responsibilities **Assessment activity 15.3 page 317**	**M3** analyse the benefits of expeditions to the public services **Assessment activity 15.3 page 317**	
6 review individual performance from the expedition **Assessment activity 15.4 page 320**		
7 review team performance from the expedition. **Assessment activity 15.4 page 320**	**M4** assess the strengths, weaknesses and areas for improvement. **Assessment activity 15.4 page 320**	**D3** evaluate the expedition process from start to finish making recommendations. **Assessment activity 15.4 page 320**

How you will be assessed

This unit will be assessed by an internal assignment that will be designed and marked by the staff at your centre. The assignment is designed to allow you to show your understanding of the learning outcomes on expedition skills. These relate to what you should be able to do after completing this unit.

It is likely that you will be assessed for all of your pass criteria by means of a practical expedition with some written evaluation. However other methods may be used such as:

- portfolios of evidence
- learning journals
- blog entries
- video diaries.

Iris, 17, takes on an expedition

I was really dreading this unit. I'm not very fit and I was really worried about how I would cope with the physical side of the expedition, but I was with a great team and we all helped and supported each other. We got to negotiate our route with the tutor so we were able to choose something which all of us could manage. The route included an overnight stay at a campsite and it was the first time I had ever slept outdoors or in a tent.

My brother is in the army and I know he has to do a lot of expedition work both in this country and abroad. It gave me new respect for how hard he works and the skills which are needed in our armed services. For me the unit wasn't so much about doing an expedition but about finding out about my personal skills and qualities and what could be improved. I felt very different when we came back after the trip. I was more confident and felt I could rely on myself if I needed to.

One of the things that I really enjoyed looking at was the expedition equipment section. I had no idea about the variety of stuff that is available and I didn't even recognise what some of the stuff was. I've lived in a city all my life and there isn't much countryside near, so I guess I haven't had to deal with things like specialist boots and clothing that people who live in the countryside might have as part of their normal wardrobe. The best thing was learning about tents. Our tutor took us to a really big outdoor shop and they had a massive tent display. I had no idea that there were so many different types and designs.

The good thing about this unit is that it is very practical and there are lots of opportunities for getting out of the classroom and planning and practising your expedition. I know the expedition skills I've learned and the difference in my confidence will be useful whichever service I choose to join in the future.

Over to you

- What areas of expedition skills might you find interesting?
- Have you ever been on an expedition before?
- Do you have any fears or concerns about expeditions?
- What preparation could you do to get ready for your assessments?

1 The correct equipment required for an expedition

About expeditions

Expeditions can be unfamiliar to many people. Write down a list of what concerns you most about going on an expedition and what you think you might be best at.

Share your findings with the rest of your class. Did you come up with the same kind of things or was each person's list very different? Why do you think this is?

Did you know?

In 1860 an expedition led by Robert O'Hara Burke and William John Wills set off to discover a route from Melbourne in the south of Australia to the Gulf of Carpentaria in the north, a distance of over 2,500 km. As part of their 20 tonnes of equipment they took a Chinese gong, an oak table with chairs and a stationery cabinet.

Having the correct equipment for any task is essential if you are going to be successful, and this is especially true of expeditions. Not having the right equipment might not only be the difference between success or failure but also the difference between life and death.

The equipment that you take on an expedition will keep you warm, dry, comfortable and fed. If you choose the wrong equipment, at best you will be uncomfortable and at the worst you will be placing yourself and your colleagues in danger.

Expeditions are not just about walking, they can also involve cycling, use of boats, 4 x 4 vehicles or any other methods of transport. An expedition is simply any journey that has a clear and defined purpose. The kind of expedition you may be required to do by your tutor could include any or all of these methods of transport, but by far the most common and simplest is a walking expedition.

1.1 Day expedition

A day expedition is a one-day journey only. However, even if you are out only for one day you need to take sufficient equipment and resources with you to last for the whole day and some in reserve, in case you are delayed by bad weather or an injured party member.

Personal equipment

The choice of what to take with you is often based on experience of previous expeditions, the time of year, the predicted weather and the country you are conducting your expedition in. For example, an expedition to the far north of Europe may require thermals but a safari expedition in Central Africa would not. In order to decide what to take with you, you need to know the following things:

- where you are going
- the time of year you are going
- how long you are going for

- the equipment carried by other people
- the abilities and skills of your colleagues.

There will be some things you will take on every expedition such as suitable footwear, clothing, food and water, but some things may be optional based on the type of expedition and where you are going. Here are some of the most common expedition items you are likely to encounter and why it might be useful to take them with you.

Layering system

The key to being prepared for outdoor expeditions is having enough clothing so that you can mix and match items depending on the weather conditions, adding or removing layers of clothing as the weather changes. This is called **layering**. The 'base layer' sits next to the skin, then you have one or more 'insulating or thermal layers' which provide more or less warmth depending on how many insulating layers you need. Finally, you have the outermost layer called the 'protective layer' that protects you against wind and moisture.

Layers must be lightweight as you may have to carry them for many miles, they should be fast drying in case you are caught in rain showers and they should have **wicking** properties. Wicking is a term used for a fabric that can transport sweat from your body to the outside of the fabric to leave you dryer and more comfortable.

When you pack for your expedition you should be sure that you have enough clothing with you to be able to layer up or down several times during the day as the weather changes. It is often cooler in the morning and evening and you may require several layers at these points but it may warm up during the day and you might spend the middle part of the day in just a T-shirt and trousers or shorts. The weather in the UK can be unpredictable and you should take enough so that even if you are caught in a torrential downpour you have spare clothing to make up your layering system. You may also need to layer up and down based on your level of activity, you will sweat more and feel warmer going up a hill as you are more physically active, this means you will need fewer layers. When you get to the top of the hill and take a quick break or have a lunch stop your level of activity will decrease and you may need more layers to keep you warm.

Jackets. If you go to any outdoor shop you will see hundreds of choices of jacket of various lengths and with any number of zips, pockets, fillings and hoods. Jackets can range in price from as little as £10 all the way up to several hundreds of pounds. The key isn't to buy the most expensive jacket you can afford, it is to get the jacket which does just what you need it to do which is keep you warm and dry where you are going. A £500 jacket that will keep you snug in Antarctica would be overkill for a summer day trip to the Peak District and a waste of your (or your parents') hard earned money.

Trousers. Tracksuit bottoms or normal casual trousers are fine for short walks of most level, but on an extended expedition with lots of ups and downs these might irritate or chafe you in unexpected places and

Key terms

Layering – the practice of wearing several layers of clothes, especially for extreme climates.

Wicking – the movement of moisture away from the body to the outside of a fabric which helps keep you warmer and dryer. Not all materials wick so it makes sense to choose expedition or sports clothes that do.

Did you know?

The first person to arrive at the South Pole, Roald Amundsen in 1911, had clothing for his expedition team made out of reindeer and sealskins. He felt that the best way to keep his team warm and safe was to use the materials that the native people who lived all year round in the Arctic Circle used. Most of the explorers at the time were wearing woollen clothing, but once wet it would freeze solid.

are slow to dry. Most serious walkers wear synthetic walking trousers because they are light, quick drying and have lots of pockets and clips for other pieces of equipment. Many can also be zipped off to form three-quarter length trousers or shorts helping you keep cool or warm depending on the weather and how hard you are working. These can be bought from most outdoor shops. Jeans should be avoided when on expedition as they restrict movement and get very heavy and take a long time to dry when wet.

You can also take overtrousers which are made of a waterproof material and go over your walking trousers, this helps keep you dry and protected from the wind if the weather is really bad.

Socks. On a day walking expedition your socks are going to be very important. Inexperienced hikers often forget the importance of having the right socks but the wrong ones can cause you pain and discomfort and may mean you may have to abandon your expedition.

If you are walking some distance then a two sock layering system is best. This involves a thin synthetic liner sock as the layer next to your foot which will wick moisture and sweat away from your skin and a wool/nylon hiking sock over the top. Wool is water resistant so it helps your feet keep dry, and having dry feet is really important since wet feet are more likely to get blisters. Wearing two socks in a layering system means that any friction between your boots and your foot is reduced, since friction causes blisters this is another added benefit.

Thermals. Thermal garments are designed to help you manage your temperature and can form the insulating layer in the layering system described earlier. Merino wool is a popular choice for thermal garments, fleeces are also commonly used.

Fleeces. A fleece is a term used to describe the coat of certain animals such as sheep or alpaca. These coats were often turned into very warm garments used as expedition clothing in the past. However, the term fleece in expeditions today refers to a garment made from synthetic fibres that is designed to mimic the best aspects of natural fabrics, such as wool, and minimise their drawbacks. Fleece jackets are often used as part of the layering system and fleece hats and gloves are also very common.

Hats. A large proportion of your body heat is lost through your head. This is fine in normal conditions as it helps us regulate our body temperature keeping us at the right level of warmth to be able to do our normal daily activities. However, on a cold day on a windy moor the heat loss can cause us to be far colder than is necessary. A hat will prevent heat loss through the head and in warm climates or in the UK summer a hat will also help protect you from sunburn and heatstroke.

There is a variety of headgear ranging from headbands, which just cover the ears, to full balaclavas, which cover the entire head and neck. It is a sensible idea to take a couple of different sorts of headgear with you so you can choose the most suitable one for the conditions you are faced with.

Did you know?

A blister is a bubble of fluid underneath the top layer of skin. The fluid is called serum and blisters are normally caused through friction or extreme temperatures. Blisters can vary in size and be excruciatingly painful. The skin over the top of a blister acts as a natural barrier to prevent infection and most blisters will heal naturally if left alone.

Any sports shop will have a supply of balaclavas, hats, headbands and other headgear.

Gloves. In cold conditions the blood in the body moves away from the extremities and the skin's surface to keep the vital organs warm, this is called vasoconstriction. When this happens we lose some movement and **dexterity** in our fingers and toes very quickly. Since we rely on our hands and fingers for much of our survival this can be a serious problem. A good pair of gloves or mittens can help maintain finger temperature and dexterity allowing you to complete activities such as putting up tents and cooking food that become very difficult with cold unresponsive fingers.

Waterproofs. In the UK we have a lot of rain so good-quality waterproofs are an essential part of your expedition kit. Generally, your waterproofs will consist of a jacket and overtrousers which are designed to fit comfortably over your other layers and will have taped seams to prevent water leaking in and will be **breathable**.

Other personal items

Footwear. Your footwear is arguably the most important part of your expedition equipment, it keeps your feet comfortable, safe and dry. The wrong footwear choice can cause blisters and considerable pain making it difficult to complete your journey. In addition, the wrong type of footwear can compromise your safety by making slipping or tripping more of a hazard.

There are several types of possible footwear you could choose depending on the terrain you will be covering:

- **Walking boots** – these are boots which are designed specifically with walking in mind. They have a tough moulded sole which provides a solid grip in most terrain and they provide ankle support to avoid injuries on steep slopes. You can get different types of walking boot depending on where you are walking and at what time of year. Walking boot manufacturers describe their boots in terms of seasons.

  - A one season boot is flexible and usually used on easy path walking or long stretches of road, they are not suitable for difficult terrain or very wet weather.

  - Two season boots can be made of soft leather, suede or stretch and waterproof fabric and are useful on a variety of different terrains but have limited use in very rocky or uneven surfaces because the only have minimal ankle support.

  - Three season boots have a stiffer sole for more uneven ground and better ankle support and can be used for easy winter walking if required.

  - Four season boots are for the most challenging terrain and winter walking and climbing, they can be very rigid and quite uncomfortable for summer walking.

- **Walking shoes** – these are a much lighter alternative to boots which can be used in good weather on easy terrain.

- **Trainers** – these are useful for urban walks on paths and pavements, they can also be used in dry conditions for low level countryside

Key terms

Dexterity – the skill and control you have in your hands. It is about coordinating your fingers in fine movements such as tying knots or typing. Dexterity can be lost in cold temperatures making even simple tasks such as opening a bar of chocolate very difficult.

Breathable – describes textiles that are designed to be waterproof but allow the two-way flow of air.

walks on clear paths. They are often a suitable choice for low level summer day expeditions. They should not be used routinely on multi-day expeditions as they are not waterproof and do not offer the foot the protection of boots. In wet conditions they can be incredibly slippery leading to injuries.

- **Walking sandals** – these are specially designed sandals for summer walking. They have solid soles and a reasonable grip, but are not all waterproof and offer no protection from sharp stones or brambles. Many walkers use these as camp shoes only and do not use them for expeditions.

Activity: Which shoe for you?

Look at the type of footwear in Figure 15.1. Which type is going to be the most suitable for the following activities:

- walking to school or college
- climbing a hill in snowy conditions
- walking through a valley after a rainstorm
- relaxing at your campsite?

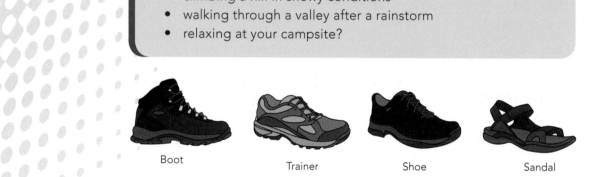

| Boot | Trainer | Shoe | Sandal |

Figure 15.1: There is a huge range of walking gear available. Be sure you choose appropriately for your expedition.

Gaiters. Gaiters are a type of protective equipment for your lower legs and calves which usually clip or tie on to your boots and end at the knee. They can be particularly useful in muddy conditions or if you are walking through low level grass or heather which might scratch your legs or stick to the fabric in your socks or trousers and cause you irritation. They can also help protect your legs from insect bites.

Walking poles. Walking poles make travelling over uneven ground easier as they provide additional points of contact with the ground. This can be particularly useful in places where loss of footing might be a problem such as muddy ground or river crossings. The poles are best used in pairs and can be lengthened for downhill walking and shortened for uphill walking.

Map and compass. A map is the most important navigational tool you have when you go out on an expedition. It is your means of following the route, finding your way home and locating yourself when you get lost. You can get lots of different types of maps such as street maps, political maps, geographical maps and world maps. Maps are two dimensional representations of the ground when viewed from above.

Remember

The maps you are most likely to come into contact with on your expedition are Ordnance Survey maps. The Ordnance Survey is a government department which is responsible for mapping the country, they produce maps in different scales showing more or less detail depending on your needs.

A compass is a magnetic tool which always points North. Once you know where North is you can work out which direction you are travelling in. There are several types of compass but the one you need for expeditions is called a base plate compass, shown in the photograph:

A compass also allows you to measure distances on maps, take grid references, take bearings and set your map to the right direction.

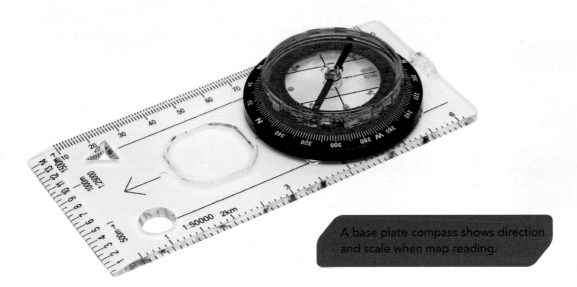

A base plate compass shows direction and scale when map reading.

Torch. A torch is essential when there is a possibility that you may be out after dark or there is a possibility you may be delayed. You cannot read a map, use a compass or see where you are going in the dark without a torch so it is an essential piece of kit unless you can guarantee being back from your expedition in daylight.

If you are responsible for navigating then a head torch is the only practical option as it allows you to point the torch directly where you are looking and keep your hands free to use the map and compass as well as allowing you to light your path. Hand-held torches are fine if you are not using a map and compass and just need to light your way. It is also important to check you have new batteries or carry spare ones with you.

Rucksack. Rucksacks or backpacks are the best way of carrying the equipment and supplies you need while walking. This is because they are designed to sit comfortably on the back and leave the hands and arms free for other tasks. Most rucksacks are made from very lightweight material which is essential for carrying over long distances and are mostly showerproof, in case of bad weather,

Rucksacks come in different sizes, the smallest is called a day sack and you may already have one of these for school or college. Most day sacks just have shoulder straps and contain no metal frame so are more flexible than larger rucksacks, perfect for carrying your waterproofs and some lunch, but not much else. Some day sacks have a hip belt and can be used for day expeditions. Larger rucksacks contain rigid frames and in addition to shoulder straps they will have a hip belt and possibly a chest strap. They also come in specialised shapes for women and children.

Rucksacks come in different sizes which are measured in litres. A small day sack may be around 20 litres, a short day expedition might require something in the region of 35–55 litres and for longer camping expeditions something closer to 60–80 litres might be more appropriate.

Activity: Expedition equipment

What equipment might you need for your expedition? How much of this equipment do you already have and what can you borrow from your school/college or classmates?

Start writing a list of what you need and tick off what you already have. Make a plan for how you will get the rest. Show your list and plan to your tutor so it can be double-checked.

1.2 Overnight expedition

On an overnight expedition you should take some additional equipment to ensure you have a place to sleep and sufficient food to keep your energy levels up. Table 15.1 lists the additional equipment you might need for an overnight stay.

Table 15.1: Additional equipment for an overnight expedition.

Equipment	Description
Spare clothing	If you are staying away from home for more than one day it makes sense to take sufficient suitable clothing to change into for as long as you are going to be out and about. Clean clothes to change into at the end of a wet day are very important.
Towel	You will need to wash and keep yourself hygienic and clean while out on expedition – you will feel better if you do and your tent mates will thank you for it. You can get lightweight camping towels which are very absorbent and don't take up much space, they also have the added bonus of being able to be folded up into a pillow or used as an extra blanket if they are dry.
Tent	The type of tent you take on an expedition will depend on where you will be camping and whether you have to carry your tent with you. If your tent is being carried to a campsite by a support vehicle then weight will not really matter and you can choose something with plenty of space. If you are carrying your tent to a remote area then the tent will have to be lightweight. The size of your tent depends entirely on how many people are planning to share it, remember in wet weather your rucksacks and gear will have to be accommodated inside the tent as well.

Table 15.1: (Cont.)

Equipment	Description
Toiletries	You will need a basic toiletry bag when you go on an overnight expedition including soap, toothbrush, toothpaste and whatever else you might need for your personal care. Do not bring your entire bathroom from home or a full make-up bag, it will not be necessary. Bring small travel-sized bottles or tubes and wrap them in a plastic bag to protect your bag and other gear from leaks or spills.
Sleeping bag	Even in the height of summer in the UK you will still need a sleeping bag. They are graded similarly to boots based on 'seasons' – each season matches different weather conditions. The type of sleeping bag you will need will vary depending on the time of year you are going on the expedition, where you will be sleeping (higher altitudes require warmer sleeping bags as it gets colder the higher you go) and what you are sleeping on. There are two main types of sleeping bag: caravan bags which are rectangular quilted bags with long zips down one or two sides and mummy sleeping bags which are shaped to fit the body and are built for expeditions and backpacking as they are lighter and can be packed into a rucksack easily.
Sleeping mat	Sleeping on the ground is not a pleasant experience, it is usually cold, damp and uneven. You can lose a lot of your body heat very quickly if you do not use a sleeping mat. There are several types of sleeping mat you could choose from each with different advantages and disadvantages but one most commonly used by students is a roll mat. Roll mats are rectangular pieces of foam which you put under your sleeping bag, they provide a layer of insulation between you and the ground, they are waterproof and roll up tightly for strapping to your rucksack. They have the advantage of being a relatively inexpensive piece of kit.
Stove	You will need to cook or warm the food you take on expedition, for this you will need a stove. A good stove should be stable on the ground, have protection from the wind and have an adjustable flame so food can be cooked correctly. Stoves come in many different varieties and use different sorts of fuel, the most common types used among school or scout groups is the meths-burning Trangia because it is stable and very simple to use. Cooking should be done outdoors where possible. Tents are often made from material that burns easily. Do not take risks – **it is not safe to cook in a tent**.
Food	You need to carry food on expedition that is high in energy, such as carbohydrates, easy to cook and easy to carry. Good things to carry are sandwiches, cereal bars, biscuits, fruit, nuts. You can also buy pre-prepared camping food in bags that only require heating in boiling water. You should also take plenty of water to drink, particularly if you are **'wild camping'** where there may not be a source of fresh water available.
Sanitation	If you are going on an expedition where you don't expect to encounter many toilets then a small plastic trowel can be useful as well as a toilet roll or toilet wipes. Wrap each of these in a plastic bag to keep them dry. For women having a period while you are on an expedition can be a nuisance as it may not be easy or convenient to change your sanitary protection without access to a toilet. It is not recommended that you keep tampons in for extended lengths of time, but there are products such as menstrual cups, which are suitable for backpacking. Taking some wet wipes and antibacterial hand gel can also help if you have limited access to hand washing facilities. Tissues are also a useful thing to have handy.

Case study: Steven makes a meal of stew

'We went on a three-day expedition as the assessment for the expedition skills unit for my BTEC First in Public Services. We were split into tent groups who would share the carrying of the heavier gear like the tent and food and sleeping bags. There were three lads in my group and my job was to organise and carry the food for the entire expedition. So in my rucksack I had all of my clothes, toiletries and personal gear that I needed plus three days worth of food for my group. I really struggled on the first day. It shouldn't have been a hard walk, we had actually done part of it as a practice but I hadn't carried my rucksack then.

We were the last group into camp and I was exhausted. The weight of the rucksack had left me with swollen and sore shoulders. It was my responsibility to cook the food as well, so while the other guys set the tent and camp up I got out the meal for the first night. I had planned to make a stew, so I had tins of potatoes, carrots, peas and meatballs in gravy which I put into one of my mum's pans on the little stove we brought.

It was only when everything went quiet that I looked around and noticed everyone was staring at me trying not to laugh. The tutor came over and couldn't believe I had brought tins of food rather than lightweight food! The pans were really heavy too. She made me tip my rucksack out and saw I had another six tins in there for the following night's dinner.

I hadn't realised how much a few tins can weigh when you have to carry them for 10 km. I was allowed to put the food in the safety vehicle for transport to the next day's camp, but the tutor wasn't pleased and my group weren't shy about telling me what they thought.

Still, one good thing to come of it was that I've never carried tins of food in a rucksack since.'

Now answer the following questions:

1 Why was Steven so exhausted at the end of the day?

2 What could Steven have done before he set off to test the weight of his rucksack?

3 What would have been better types of food to carry?

Activity: Expedition food

A typical 24-hour army ration pack might contain the following items:

- an oatmeal block
- corn beef hash (boil in the bag)
- chicken and pasta (boil in the bag)
- chocolate pudding (instant)
- chocolate bars or a bar of Kendal Mint Cake
- biscuits, brown (malted and hard, pack of six)
- biscuits, fruit-filled (malted hard garibaldi-like, pack of six)
- cheese, processed, or meat paté
- Tea, instant, white, 4 x sachets
- coffee, instant, 2 x 5 grams sachets
- sugar, quick dissolving, 8 x 10 grams sachets
- drinking chocolate mix, 1 sachet
- vegetable stock drink mix, 1 x sachet
- instant soup (varying flavours), 2 x sachets
- beverage whitener (non-dairy creamer), 2 x sachets
- gum, chewing, 5 sticks
- sweets, boiled, 1 pack assorted flavours
- fruit drink mix, (enough for 1 litre of drink)
- tissues, paper (individual pack)
- waterproof matches (10) and striker (1)
- water purification tablets (6)

1 Why do you think so much food is needed for a soldier in a 24-hour period?

2 Would you be happy to eat this menu?

3 What kinds of things might improve the menu for you?

Look again at the 24-hour ration pack on page 304. Use the items to devise your own meal plan for the day. Research your chosen items to find their calorific value and the total number of calories you would consume in a day. Is this enough to sustain you on an expedition?

1.3 Safety equipment

Safety equipment should be carried on any expedition. You should carry certain items yourself and other larger items, such as a stretcher, may be transported in an accompanying vehicle.

First aid kit. You should carry a small personal first aid kit for yourself. This would normally contain the following items:

- plasters
- blister kit
- tweezers
- your personal medication, such as asthma inhalers or antihistamines for allergies
- painkillers such as paracetamol
- bandages and small wound dressings
- scissors and tape.
- sterile wipes.

Key term

Wild camping – camping in the countryside not at a campsite. This needs to be done carefully so that you do not cause problems for livestock or farmers.

Remember

Your tutor or group leader will not be able to give you painkillers so if you know you are prone to aches and pains it makes sense to take your own in a personal first aid kit, as long as you are not allergic to them.

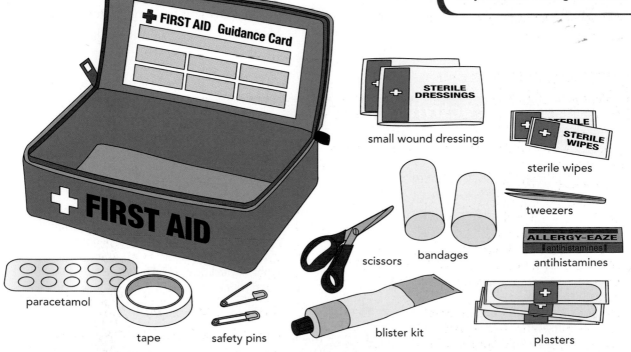

Figure 15.2 Recommended contents of a personal first aid kit. Is there anything extra you would carry?

Survival/Bivvy bag. The most common type of survival bag used for student groups is a bright orange plastic bag which covers you from feet to head and is used if you unexpectedly have to spend the night outdoors without your camping gear. It can also be used to keep a casualty warm if you have to wait for rescue. Each member of the group should carry one and they are normally very cheap to buy. You should ensure that you have ventilation at the top of your survival bag so you don't suffocate.

Whistle. You will need to take a whistle with you in case you get lost and have to be found. The emergency signal is 6 blasts on your whistle or 6 flashes on your torch. A mobile phone will not always alert people if you need help as coverage in remote areas can be poor and signals can be blocked by hills and mountains.

Flares. Flares are a signalling device which can be used in remote areas to help a rescue team locate you in case of an emergency. They can be quite expensive and are more likely to be carried by your expedition leader than you.

Emergency rations. It is always sensible to take more food than you think you will need in case you get lost or have to spend an additional night on expedition that you didn't plan for. It is better to have too much than too little.

Sun cream. Although in the UK we are not known for our sunny climate it is still possible to get sunburned very easily particularly if you have fair skin. It is sensible to take some sun cream to protect you from burning.

Insect repellent. Some insects and ticks can give you quite nasty bites which can be uncomfortable, itchy and become infected. Taking some insect repellent is a sensible precaution against being bitten.

Remember

You could add some additional water, sandwiches, cereal bars or chocolate to what you would normally carry.

Assessment activity 15.1

P1 P2 M1 D1

Understanding the equipment you need for an expedition is one of the key elements to a successful journey. Create a leaflet which details the equipment you will need and be sure you:

1 *Describe* the equipment needed for an expedition. **P1**

2 *Describe* the use of safety equipment. **P2**

3 *Demonstrate* the use of safety equipment. **M1**

4 *Evaluate* the purpose and function of all equipment required for a day and overnight expedition. **D1**

Grading tips

In order to get **P1** think about all the equipment you would need for a one day expedition and describe it. For **M1** explain the purpose and job of the equipment you would need if you were on an overnight expedition, for **D1** say why you would take each piece of kit, what are your reasons for including it?

Activity: Sample kit list

A sample kit list for a day expedition might look like this:

- rucksack
- survival bag
- waterproofs
- map and compass
- boots
- torch
- food and drink
- whistle
- hat and gloves
- spare clothing
- first aid kit/sanitary supplies
- sunglasses and sun cream.

1 Can you think of anything else you might want to take?

2 What kit would you add if you were staying overnight?

3 If you were on a multi-day expedition what kit could be shared among your group?

2 Understand the planning necessary for an expedition

Planning is essential if your expedition is going to be safe and successful. You will be required to think very carefully about a whole range of issues, such as your possible route, your group and their individual abilities and strengths and the weather.

Did you know?

If you want to know more about the work of Mountain Rescue or make a donation to this public service then you can find out more on their website, available via Hotlinks (see page viii).

Case study: Cairngorm Mountain Rescue

In 2004 the Cairngorm Mountain Rescue Team were called to rescue a party of schoolgirls and their teacher who had become lost after reaching the top of Meall a' Bhuachaille in Scotland. The party were wearing skirts and trainers and most had no waterproofs apart from some bin liners and plastic sheets wrapped around them. The ratio of 39 pupils to one teacher was inadequate and went against safety guidance issued to schools and colleges about excursions and expeditions.

Rescue leader John Allen commented to BBC Radio that, 'It is one of the worst, if not the worst, cases that I have come across of a group being ill-prepared going on to the mountains.'

Now answer the following questions:

1 If the group had not been rescued from the mountain what would have happened to them?

2 What planning should they have done to ensure their safety?

3 Who is responsible for the safety of school pupils on expeditions?

2.1 Planning a day expedition

Aims and objectives

An aim is a reason why you are going on the expedition and objective is what you hope to have achieved by completing it, for example:

Aim: To practice my map-work and navigation skills

Objective: By the end of the expedition I will be able to set a map and take compass bearings.

Once you know why you are going on an expedition (aim) and what you are hoping to get out of it (objective) it will be easier to decide where and when to go. If you are inexperienced at expeditions then going to Scotland or Wales in winter would be a foolish move as the terrain, navigation and weather conditions would be above your level of skill. A more suitable destination might be a summer expedition to the Peak District or the North Yorkshire Moors. So you can see that having clear aims and objectives are an essential part of the planning process.

Individual and group ability

It is essential to know your own abilities and those of your party if you are going to choose a route that is challenging but not impossible. This includes issues such as navigational skills, fitness levels, disabilities or illnesses. If all the group has to complete the expedition but some party members have low fitness levels then choosing a route which is very strenuous is setting them up for failure. The experience of your team is also a key factor; if all of you have completed several expeditions in the past then this might influence your choice of route and length of journey. If some party members have never been on an expedition before, it might be best to choose something easier for them to begin with.

Destination

Your destination depends on a number of factors, such as:

- How much money do you have?
- How large is your group?
- How fit is your group?
- How experienced is your group?
- How well equipped is your group?

A walking expedition to Kilimanjaro in Tanzania may sound wonderful, but if your party cannot spare the several thousand pounds each for the costs of the expedition then you may have to set your sights a bit lower. The destination you choose should be a compromise between all these factors ensuring a safe and achievable destination suitable for the abilities and wallets of all party members.

Transport

Transport for your expedition needs to be booked well in advance, this may include a coach to take you to the start point of your journey and pick you up again at the end. For other types of expedition it may include cycles or boats. You cannot leave booking transport to the last minute, particularly with larger groups, as you may be stranded.

Cost

On the surface, an expedition seems like a very cheap way of travelling. After all, you are supplying your own food, accommodation and using your own legs for transport. However, once you have factored in campsite costs, transport costs and payment for specialist walking leaders the costs can add up. You need to plan carefully to ensure that all of your party members can afford the expedition and make adjustments if they cannot.

Time

You need to plan your expedition to fit in the time you have got. A 50-mile hike is not going to happen in the six or seven hour time window of a school or college day. Think carefully about the amount of time you have and what you could reasonably fit into it given the abilities of your team members. It is also important to consider that the route you choose can affect the time it takes to complete it. Flat walking on a clear path will take less time that an uphill walk with lots of tricky navigation. It will be essential for you to take a watch with you so that you can keep track of your progress.

Transport arrangements need to account for all the required equipment. What precautions can you take to ensure all members of the group and the necessary equipment are transported comfortably?

Equipment

We have already discussed equipment at length. It is crucial that you plan to take with you all the things you will need for a safe and successful day.

Route plan

In order to avoid potential hazards your route needs to be planned well in advance. Preparing a route plan allows you to estimate the amount of time you will need and balance this against the amount of time you actually have and the weather conditions you might face. A route plan can also be left with other people so that they can contact the emergency services if the party is delayed. A route plan will also look at escape routes in case you need to return urgently to base or other inhabited area quickly. All of your expedition group should have a copy of the route plan and be familiar with it, this means that someone can take over if the group leader is injured or the group gets split up.

> **! Link**
>
> Find out more about suitable items to take on an expedition. Look at the kit list on page 307.

Health and safety/Risk assessments

The health and safety of your expedition group is not just the responsibility of the walking group leader – it is the responsibility of **every** party member. You will be relying on each other when you are on an expedition and you must behave sensibly and responsibly. Even the best walking leader can do very little to protect you if you choose to behave like a fool. The health and safety of the party can be jeopardised by things such as:

- not paying attention to instructions
- not obeying instructions
- using alcohol or drugs
- failure to disclose medical conditions such as asthma
- horseplay
- not bringing the right equipment.

Health and safety is managed through risk assessments. **Risk** assessments are estimates of the risks of certain activities and the **control measures** that can be put into place to minimise the risk. All of your planned activities will require a full risk assessment which all party members are familiar with and anything that is not planned should either be avoided or a dynamic risk assessment made at the time. A dynamic risk assessment is an on-the-spot consideration of the risk factors of the activity. If the risk is too high and you cannot put control measures in place then you should not do the activity.

Key terms

Hazard – anything which may cause harm, such as chemicals, working at heights, river crossings or fire.

Risk – the chance that someone might be harmed from a hazard.

Control measure – These are the preventative measures you put into place to try to make sure that the hazard doesn't cause a high risk. For example a control measure on a busy road is a zebra crossing, control measures when abseiling are a safety harness and a helmet.

Activity: Risk assessment

The Health and Safety Executive is the government department responsible for making sure health and safety legislation and risk assessments are followed and that business and organisations take all reasonable steps to protect people. They recommend five steps to risk assessment:

Step 1
Identify the **hazards**.

Step 2
Decide who might be harmed and how.

Step 3
Evaluate the risks and decide on precautions.

Step 4
Record your findings and implement them.

Step 5
Review your assessment and update if necessary.

Part of your expedition route requires you and your party to cross a river. Produce a risk assessment based on the five factors above.

First aid

Minor injuries such as small cuts, bruises, aches and strains can happen frequently on expeditions and it is your responsibility to plan for your own safety. Taking a personal first aid kit is essential, but if you are responsible for a group you may need to take a walking leader's first aid kit as well.

Weather forecasts

If you are going on an expedition your plan might need to be weather dependent. This means the weather may dictate some of your choices such as your route and your footwear. You will need to know where to find reliable weather information. You can get weather forecasts through the following:

Make plans for several of your group to take a first aid qualification. Have you contacted your local ambulance service or a nearby charity to enquire about first aid courses?

- telephone/fax
- television
- internet
- newspapers
- posted bulletins
- radio.

Good planning will allow you to deal with whichever type of weather you are faced with during your expedition.

Permission

During your planning process it is important to make sure that if you are planning to cross any private land you have consent from the landowner. If you do not then you and your party could be prosecuted for trespass.

Consent forms

Your planning process should include obtaining consent from your party members to go on the expedition; for under 18-year-olds this consent must come from a parent or guardian. The consent form should highlight enough detail about what you are planning to do and where you are planning to go that the person signing the form understands what is involved. Consent forms normally also include consent for medical treatment if the need arises.

Countryside Code

The Countryside Code is based around five key points:

1 'Be Safe', plan ahead and follow any signs.
2 Leave gates and property as you find them.
3 Protect plants and animals and take your litter home.
4 Keep dogs under close control.
5 Consider other people.

During the planning process of your expedition you should ensure all your party members are familiar with the code and able to follow it.

Did you know?

You can find out more about the Countryside Code at the Natural England website, available via Hotlinks (see page viii).

Did you know?

You can find a list of campsites in the UK via Hotlinks (see page viii).

2.2 Planning an overnight expedition

Planning for an overnight expedition is very similar to the plans you would make for a day expedition. Many of the considerations you need to account for, such as the weather, will be identical. There are some factors though that you will need to plan for over and above those you would include on a day expedition, see Table 5.2

Table 15.2: Planning for an overnight expedition.

Overnight planning	Description
Location	Ensuring you end up in a sensible location at the end of your day's walking or cycling is essential. Finishing a journey halfway up a mountain or in the middle of nowhere is less than practical. Plan to end your journey at the location where you want to spend the night.
Accommodation	Planning your accommodation in advance is very important. For overnight expeditions you will need to book suitable accommodation, this could be a hotel, youth hostel or campsite. It is likely you will be camping so be aware that campsites can quickly get fully booked, especially at peak times, and if you don't plan ahead you may be left without accommodation. Some campsites won't take groups of young people and some won't take single sex parties. You need to check on prices, the reputation and the cleanliness of the site. It makes sense to go out and check it in person if you can, that way there are no unpleasant surprises when you arrive.
Tent group	If you are camping overnight it is likely that you will be sharing a tent with others. This is sensible for several reasons, first you can share the weight of the tent between the group while you are walking, second when you arrive exhausted at the campsite there are lots of willing hands to help you set up and if it is particularly cold the tent will be full of warm bodies generating heat to share. If you have the option to choose your own tent group make sure you choose people who you get along with. Sharing a very small space with difficult people can be a challenge.
Menus	Depending on how long your expedition lasts for you may want to plan a menu. On a one- or two-night expedition this isn't so important but on a longer trip you will want to plan your menu so that you have a variety of foods and are not eating the same meals every night.
Hygiene	On a day expedition you may only need to wash your hands, but on a longer trip you will need to pay attention to your personal hygiene and the cleanliness of your camp. Make sure you keep yourself clean, no one wants to share a tent with someone who hasn't washed after a long day on the hills. Equally, your camp should be clean and tidy to prevent countryside animals from scouting round your camp for food you have left lying around. Always prepare your food in a hygienic manner – a case of diarrhoea while on expedition is no one's idea of fun. It is important to wash up pans, plates and cutlery as soon as you have used them; waking up to the washing up is not pleasant!

Assessment activity 15.2   P3 M2 D2

PLTS

By contributing to the planning of the expedition you will be developing your effective participator skills.

You need to be able to prove that you have contributed to the planning of your expedition and you know how correct planning is conducted. Complete the following tasks:

1   Keep a log of all of your planning activity including any meetings so you can use it to explain the planning needed for an expedition. P3

2   Produce a written report that explains in detail safety and environmental considerations for an expedition M2 and also evaluates the planning of the expedition you are going to undertake. D2

Grading tips

Make sure you log all the planning you do both individually and as a team and in your report fully explain why planning is so important and what kinds of things need to be planned for.

3 Plan and carry out the route for an expedition

This outcome is very practical and the best way to learn the skills covered by it is by carrying them out. It is likely that your expedition skills tutor will arrange several practical sessions for you on topics such as:

- navigation skills
- route planning
- grid references
- bearings
- escape routes
- camp craft
- cooking.

Case study: Damien's practical experience

'I'm a very practical learner, I'd much rather be out doing something than in a classroom. I really struggled with understanding navigation skills and all the other things you have to know before you go on an expedition. My tutor had gone through the basics loads of times in class but it wasn't until I actually got out into the countryside and started to be able to do tasks practically that I actually got the hang of it all.

I really think there are some things you need to learn by doing them – for me navigation was one of them.'

Now answer the following questions:

1   Do you learn better by doing?

2   Why do some skills need to be taught outside the classroom?

3   What plans does your class have for some practical sessions?

It is likely that most of these skills will be taught to you by your tutor in a practical way and so they will only be covered briefly here.

3.1 Route planning

The equipment you need to plan a route has already been mentioned, it includes:

- map
- compass
- route card
- watch.

A good route card is essential as it will put all your careful planning on one document and enable you to measure your progress against the card several times a day. You can then make adjustments if you are going slower or faster than you had anticipated.

Figure 15.3 shows what a route card might look like.

Destination: Bleaklow Stones   **Date:** 21/6/10

Party members: I M Lost, H Elp, May Day, O Ops

Speed: 4 km/hr, + 1 min/10 m climbed   **Emergency contact number:** 0123 456 789

From	To	Distance	Rests	Time taken (a)	Height climbed	Time taken (b)	Height lost	Direction	Time (a+b)	Description	Escape routes
Cairn, Nether Moor 147873	Druid's Stone 134874	1300m	0	19.5	140m	14	0	278	33.5	From flat head uphill to stone on 2nd footpath	Lady Booth Brook to YHA
Druid's Stone 134874	Spot height, Hartshorn 115877	2400m	0	36	60m	6	30m	W	42	Carry on along footpath, at Upper Tor head up to high ground	Ollerbrook Clough to Vale of Edale
Spot height, Hartshorn 115877	Ford, Blackden Rind 115883	650m	0	9.75	10m	1	30m	012	10.75	Follow bearing across plateau to footpath	Golden Clough to Grindsbrook Booth

Figure 15.3: Have you seen a route card before?

As you can see, a good route card will contain information such as:

- destination – this is where you are intending to go
- date – when you are intending to go
- times – the times it will take you to complete specific legs of your journey and the total time of your journey overall
- leg – your journey broken down into easily manageable sections called legs
- distances – the distance overall and the distances of each leg usually measured in metres or kilometres
- height gained or lost – so you can look at whether you will be going up or downhill
- rest stops – you may want to break after a long uphill climb or for lunch
- escape routes – this is a quick way down from the hill or back where you came from in case of emergency or poor weather.
- direction – the direction of travel for each leg; this can be a bearing or sometimes a more simple direction , such as north east
- features – notable points on the landscape, such as rivers, roads, railway tracks; being aware of these will help you kept to your route.

Route cards can also contain grid references and **bearings**, these are things best learned practically.

Activity: Compass bearings

There are some excellent web-based compass exercises that allow you to work out compass bearings try the activities on the Geography fieldwork website, available via Hotlinks (see page viii).

Use this site or another like it to practise your skills if you don't have access to a map and compass at home.

Key term

Bearing – a bearing is a measurement of direction between two points. It is usually given either a direction such as 'the hikers proceeded on a north-easterly bearing' or a number based on the degrees of a compass 'the ship travelled on a bearing of 36 degrees'.

Remember

A useful reminder for compass bearings is 'go along the corridor and up the stairs!'

Grid references

You will normally find grid references on a route card for your start destinations, including the start of each leg. The Ordnance Survey created the National Grid so that places in the UK could be plotted on a map easily. The National Grid divides the entire country into 100 km grid squares, each grid square is given a two letter reference. These 100 km grid squares are further divided into 10 km grid squares as shown in Figure 15.4. The smaller square is labelled TL63 because the larger square has the TL reference and the smaller square is 6 across in an easterly direction and 3 up in a northerly direction. These are called **Eastings** and **Northings**. You always measure across in an easterly direction first and then a northerly direction.

Key terms

Eastings – references in an easterly direction on the National Grid to show the position of a landmark or place.

Northings – references in an northerly direction on the National Grid to show the position of a landmark or place.

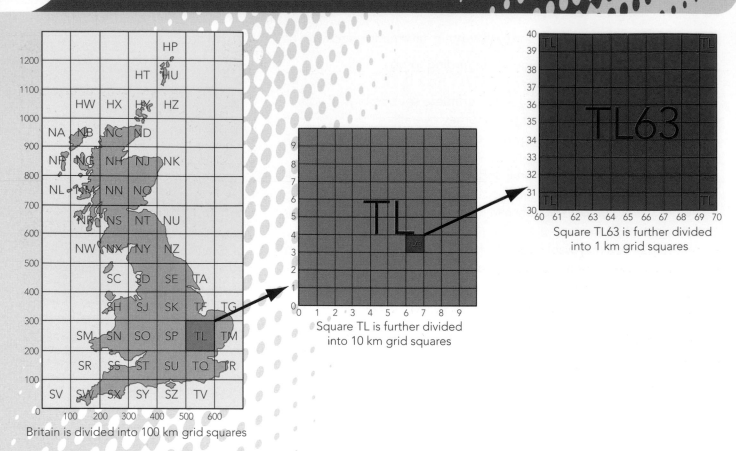

Figure 15.4: Use the National Grid to determine a six-figure reference.

Britain is divided into 100 km grid squares

Square TL is further divided into 10 km grid squares

Square TL63 is further divided into 1 km grid squares

The grid references you will use when walking are usually six-figure references. Look at the example in Figure 15.5.

Case study: Worked example

If you want to find the six-figure grid reference for the church you go along in an easterly direction to the start of the square that it is in, which is 63 and then divide the 63 square into tenths – the church sits about 5 tenths of the way along giving an Easterly reference of 635.

You then look at the northerly direction, the church sits above the 32 line of the square so the first two digits are 32. Divide the 32 square into tenths and you will see the church sits above the halfway mark at about 7 tenths. This gives you a Northerly reference of 327.

Your full six-figure grid reference for the church is therefore 635 327

What would be the six-figure reference for the telephone?

Do some examples from real OS maps.

Figure 15.5: An example of six-figure grid reference TL 635 327 (this six-figure grid reference is determined by estimating the eastings and northings to one tenth of the grid interval).

Northings

Eastings →

3.2 Day expedition

There are many tasks you will need to demonstrate in order to pass this part of your expedition skills unit including:

- navigating your planned route
- using your map and compass
- identifying different types of terrain
- your individual and group strengths
- teamwork
- communication
- applying the countryside code
- making minimal impact on the environment.

3.3 Overnight expedition

For an overnight expedition you will also need to demonstrate:

- setting up your camp
- cooking food
- taking down your camp
- listening to weather information
- good camp craft.

These are practical skills which will be taught to you by your tutor who will give you time to practise these skills before you undertake your expedition.

Practice putting your tent up several times before you set off on your expedition. Have you tried doing this in the rain?

Assessment activity 15.3 P4 P5 M3

For this assessment you should produce a route plan for your expedition **P4** and carry out the expedition identifying your own roles and responsibilities **P5**. Your route plan should be written according to normal conventions, but your expedition and the identification of roles is a practical activity. In addition write a 250 word report which analyses the benefits of expeditions to the public services. **M3**

PLTS

Taking part in an expedition will be developing you teamworking skills.

4 Be able to review an expedition

Once you have completed your expedition you need to be able to review it to see what was satisfactory and what you could do better next time. This enables you to continually improve as the things you learn can be applied to the next expedition and the things that didn't go so well can be altered and made more effective. The public services routinely evaluate their expeditions since they are often designed with a specific mission in mind. If the mission fails then the services need to know why so they can avoid those mistakes in the future.

4.1 Evaluation

The factors you may want to evaluate after your expedition are shown in Table 15.3.

Table 15.3: Expedition factors to evaluate.

Factors	Evaluation
Aims and objectives	You will want to assess whether you achieved what you actually set out to do. If the purpose of your expedition was to learn more about the countryside, did you actually do this? If the purpose was to test your navigation skills, did you achieve it?
Travel	Were the travel arrangements suitable? Did you choose the right transport, was it big enough, was it comfortable and safe enough? Would you use the transport company again? Would you plan for different transport next time?
Accommodation	Was your accommodation clean and safe, was it what you expected? Would you choose somewhere different next time?
Value for money	Did the expedition provide value for money for the participants? Was it too expensive? Could you have charged a little more and had a better campsite or more instructors?
Group strengths	What were the strengths and weaknesses of your group, what can you do about these if you are in the same group next time? What have you learned from the experience of working in a group?
Individual strengths	What were your own individual strengths? Where do you need to improve? What steps can you take to improve your skills and abilities for next time?

One of the key aspects of an evaluation is making clear recommendations about what can be improved for the next time. These recommendations are not just so you and your group can improve, but also so that following groups such as next year's BTEC First group can learn from your mistakes.

Case study: Charlotte's expedition review

'We had to do a full review of our BTEC First in Public Services expedition last year. It had been a really poor expedition for my group, our planning had gone quite badly because none of us would give up the time to meet and discuss things properly so we just ended up doing whatever was easiest, which turned out to be a 5 mile walk to a nearby campsite.

The walk was really boring, it was all flat and with clear paths so we didn't get a chance to try out many of the skills we had practised and we arrived at the campsite mid-afternoon and had nothing to do for the rest of the day. We ended up messing about on the campsite and being told off by the owners and some of the other campers, worse than that they told our tutor when she came to assess us.

We failed the expedition and had to re-do it. I was so angry with myself and the group for the time we wasted. I made sure that I sorted the group out so we got it right the second time. It meant I had to be a bit bossy and some of my teammates didn't like it, but I didn't care, I wasn't going to fail a second time because we couldn't get our act together.

Now answer the following questions:

1 What went wrong in the planning process for this expedition?

2 What went wrong during the expedition?

3 What do you think Charlotte did to improve the expedition for the second attempt?

4.2 Benefits of expeditions

There are plenty of good reasons to go on an expedition and you will find that you see great personal benefits from completing one – no matter how hard it might seem at the time.

Skill development

You will develop some specific skills such as map reading and compass use, which will be useful in many situations.

Communication

Your communication skills will be improved as you discuss and plan with your team and participate in the expedition. You will have to communicate in order to arrive safely, set up your camp and share tasks fairly.

Teamwork and cooperation

Teamwork is an essential part of any expedition. You will be relying on others and they will be relying on you. Effective teamwork can make the difference between success and failure.

Self-confidence

Being self-reliant in the outdoors can be a great boost to your confidence. You will have cooked for yourself, slept outdoors in an unfamiliar environment, overcome physical challenges, like hill walking, and made efforts to get to know people and get on with them. All of these things can improve your confidence.

Problem solving

The entire process of planning your expedition will have been a problem-solving exercise, before you even set off. However, you will also come across problems to solve while you are on the expedition such as what to do if the ground is too boggy, what to do if a pole for your tent is missing, what to do if one of your party twists their ankle. You do not have the option of walking away from these problems, you must find a way round them – a solution. Problem-solving skills are looked for by all the public services as an essential quality in their new recruits.

Physical benefits

Carrying all your gear in a rucksack over difficult or challenging terrain can have real physical benefits. You will be increasing your heart rate and improving your fitness. It may also kick start you into becoming fitter so that you cope better when you go on an expedition.

Planning

As we have already discussed planning is a key part of expeditions and you will have done lots of planning for yours. These planning skills are transferable, this means that you can use them in other parts of your life such as organising your assignments or your social and family life.

BTEC Assessment activity 15.4 P6 P7 M4 D3

Reviewing your performance after an expedition is very important if you are going to learn from it. Maintain a journal in which you:

1 *Review* individual P6 and team performance P7 from the expedition.

2 *Assess* strengths, weaknesses and areas for improvement. M4

3 *Evaluate* the expedition from start to finish making recommendations. D3

Grading tips

You should start keeping your journal from the very first time you sit down and start your planning. It should include a frank assessment of how well you and your team did in terms of strengths and weaknesses and contain several recommendations for future improvement.

PLTS

Evaluating your expedition means you have had the opportunity to develop your self-manager and reflective thinker skills.

Geoff Wates

Walking Group Leader

I work as a Walking Group Leader at an outdoor residential centre in the Lake District. The centre does all kinds of outdoor activities such as canoeing, kayaking, abseiling, caving and hiking. We see many different groups from small schoolchildren to pensioners and everything in between so we need to be able to adjust what we do to match the groups we are responsible for.

It's my job to ensure that walking groups are well prepared, well equipped and safe on their journey. I do this by spending the day before they set off on an expedition with the group going through all the basics and ensuring everyone has everything they need and is comfortable with the route.

A typical day

A typical day out on the hill involves an early start. We aim to get walking straight after breakfast because if the route is a long one we may need the full day to complete it. Once we are away from the centre and into the countryside I nominate one person to navigate for each of the legs of the journey and then I'll monitor them and check their understanding of the map or correct their compass work if they are not doing it right. It doesn't help people to learn if I do the navigating, they need to learn and practise those skills themselves. I am responsible for safety throughout the trip and the group always gets a health and safety briefing before we set off which I reinforce all the way around the route if any hazards crop up.

The best thing about the job

It's great to go out into the countryside several times a week, I'm not one to sit in an office. Being able to teach people practical skills in the fantastic Derbyshire countryside is the perfect job for me.

Think about it!

1. What topics have you covered in this unit that might give you the background to be a good walking group leader?
2. What knowledge and skills do you think you need to develop further if you want to be a walking group leader or outdoor specialist in the future?

Just checking

1. What equipment would you take on a day expedition?
2. What additional equipment might you need for an overnight stay?
3. What kinds of foods are good for expeditions?
4. What is a bearing?
5. What should a personal first aid kit contain?

edexcel :::

Assignment tips

- If you are required to keep a learning diary or a journal then be sure to record your work in a way that cannot be lost or mislaid. It might seem better to have a dedicated notebook for this, but what if you lose it? A better way might be to create a blog or electronic journal so that you always have a back-up if you need it.

- It is easy to think that practical tasks are going to be easier to pass than written tasks. This is not the case. You will need to practise your skills before you are assessed, you cannot just jump in and hope for the best. This may include planning and practising in your own time as well as class time. It is also likely that you will be photographed or videoed so you should be prepared for this.

17 Attending emergency incidents in public services

Working in a public service may seem glamorous and exciting but it can also be very dangerous; the uniformed public services have to respond to a variety of emergency incidents, including fires, road traffic collisions and terrorist attacks.

In order to respond effectively to emergency incidents, the public services need to understand the different types of incidents, their causes and the best way to deal with them. They need to have established procedures and the training and equipment to deal with a wide range of incidents. This involves working with other agencies and taking into account a range of safety legislation. The public services also have a large role to play in preventing incidents.

This unit will develop your understanding of the different types and causes of emergency incidents, and the role played by the public services in responding to them, as well as preventing them from occurring in the first place.

Learning outcomes

After completing this unit you should be able to:

1. know the causes of different types of domestic and leisure fire and emergency incidents
2. know the need for fire and accident safety legislation
3. understand domestic and leisure fire and incident prevention measures
4. be able to review the practical work undertaken by the public and emergency services in dealing with fires and incidents.

Assessment and grading criteria

This table shows you what you must do in order to achieve a pass, merit or distinction grade, and where you can find activities in this book to help you.

To achieve a **pass** grade the evidence must show that the learner is able to:	To achieve a **merit** grade the evidence must show that, in addition to the pass criteria, the learner is able to:	To achieve a **distinction** grade the evidence must show that, in addition to the pass and merit criteria, the learner is able to:
P1 identify causes of different domestic and leisure fire and emergency incidents **Assessment activity 17.1 page 333**		
P2 describe the need for fire and incident safety legislation **Assessment activity 17.2 page 341**	**M1** analyse the causes of domestic and leisure fire incidents, referring to appropriate safety legislation **Assessment activity 17.2 page 341**	**D1** compare domestic and leisure fire and emergency incidents making suggestions as to how they could be prevented **Assessment activity 17.2 page 341**
P3 explain how incidents can be prevented **Assessment activity 17.3 page 350**	**M2** compare fire and incident prevention methods **Assessment activity 17.3 page 350**	
P4 explain how fires can be prevented **Assessment activity 17.3 page 350**		
P5 review the practical work undertaken by public services when dealing with an emergency incident scenario **Assessment activity 17.4 page 354**	**M3** analyse the practical work undertaken by public services when dealing with an emergency incident scenario **Assessment activity 17.4 page 354**	**D2** evaluate the practical work undertaken by public services when dealing with an emergency incident scenario **Assessment activity 17.4 page 354**
P6 review the work of the fire service when dealing with a fire incident **Assessment activity 17.4 page 354**		

How you will be assessed

This unit will be assessed by an internal assignment that will be designed and marked by the staff at your centre. The assignment is designed to allow you to show your understanding of the learning outcomes for attending emergency incidents. These relate to what you should be able to do after completing this unit. Your assessments might include some of the following:

- portfolios of evidence
- wall displays
- learning journals
- video diaries
- role plays
- presentations
- leaflets
- reports.

Katie, 17, gets firefighting experience

Before I studied this unit I wasn't sure which uniformed service I wanted to join but I fancied joining the Police Service because my uncle's in the force and I think it's a really worthwhile job. Now I'm not so sure because I've become interested in joining the Fire Service and I really enjoyed learning about all the things that a firefighter does but I'm not sure that I could cope with some of the difficult situations they have to deal with.

We went to see the firefighters training at their training school and I was well impressed with how they work together and just seem to know what to do but I know they train hard to get to that standard. I didn't realise that they had to study all those different laws and rules, and all about different fires. I suppose they need to know all that if you think about it. And some of the equipment they use looks so heavy so I know I'll have to keep fit and build myself up so I can use the equipment properly.

I would really like a career where I can help people and dealing with some of those emergencies would be very rewarding and I'd feel very proud but I'm not sure about all the terrible sights that you must see. I've spoken to some firefighters and they say that some parts of their job are sad but you have to get on with it and not let it bother you.

Over to you!
- Do you think you would be able to remain calm in an emergency when people are injured and suffering?
- Do you think you would have the courage to enter a smoke-filled room or collapsed building to rescue people, while at the same time looking out for the safety of your colleagues and team members?
- Would you be able to advise the owner of a sports ground on health and safety issues?

1 The causes of different types of domestic and leisure fire and emergency incidents

Talk up

Can you deal with difficult situations?

If you are considering a career in the emergency or public services you should begin to think about your potential and what qualities are needed to be able to deal with extraordinary and difficult situations.

Did you know?

An emergency is defined as:

an event or situation which threatens serious damage to human welfare, or

an event or situation which threatens serious damage to the environment, or

war or terrorism, which threatens serious damage to security.

Activity: Witnessing an incident

Have you ever witnessed a domestic or leisure activity emergency incident?

Excluding fires, can you think of four domestic and four leisure activity emergency incidents?

1.1 Incidents

An incident is the general term for an event or occurrence and includes accidents, fires, disasters and road traffic collisions.

Major incident. Some incidents occur on a large scale and call for the attendance of all the emergency services and other organisations, or they may need to rely heavily on a particular emergency service, which might stretch the resources of that service. Incidents that fall into this group are called 'major incidents'.

Domestic incident. This is one that happens in or around the home and these may occur more often than you think. For example, a faulty gas fire can give off poisonous fumes (carbon monoxide) which could easily kill. Another example would be a faulty electrical appliance, like a kettle, that could give a severe electric shock.

Leisure activity incident. This might take place anywhere, indoors or outdoors, where someone is pursuing a leisure interest. For example, there was a crash on the Big Dipper at Blackpool Pleasure Beach in 2009, where 21 people were rescued and taken to hospital. Another example of a leisure activity incident could be where a group of skiers get caught in an avalanche and become buried and trapped by snow and rocks.

Workplace incident. Besides domestic and leisure activity incidents, there are thousands of serious incidents in the workplace each year. Some occupations are more dangerous, like working underground or at great heights, for example. In November 2009, a man was rushed to hospital after falling from the top of some scaffolding when a bus collided with it. The man suffered facial and leg injuries.

Accidents in the workplace not only cause pain and suffering to victims and their families, they also have a drastic effect on the economy.

Types of incidents

There are several different types (sometimes called categories, which are based on the causes) of incidents, including the following:

Human error. These are incidents that result from an act of carelessness, incompetence of neglect. For example, failure to carry out routine safety checks and report faults on aircraft could lead to serious accidents.

Natural causes. These include such things as earthquakes, tsunamis, floods and drought. They are classed as having natural causes because they are the result of a natural event. For example, earthquakes are caused by the collision of tectonic plates that move deep within the earth.

Hostile acts (human causes). These can range from acts of terrorism, or civil unrest, to vandalism or other forms of ant-social behaviour. A hostile act is one that is unfriendly or aggressive. For example, the destruction of the Twin Towers in New York in the United States on 11 September 2001, was as a result of terrorism and was a hostile act.

Technological failure. These are where the failure of technology or science has played a part in causing the incident, like the failure of an electrical component in an aircraft crash, for example.

Health-related causes. These are incidents where a virus may be the cause of an **epidemic** or **pandemic**, such as avian flu or swine flu.

Chemical causes. These occur from the reaction of different materials in chemical production. The reaction may produce too much energy in the form of heat, which could lead to an explosion causing serious injury, or death, to operators in a chemical plant, as well as to the general public.

Key terms

Epidemic – the spread of a disease throughout a community and is normally contained within that area.

Pandemic – the spread of disease over a much larger area, possibly an entire country or even the world.

Activity: Pandemics

Why should a flu pandemic be classed as an emergency incident?

Other than flu, can you think of any other causes of pandemics?

1.2 Roles of and cooperation between public and emergency services in dealing with incidents

You often hear the term 'public services' and 'emergency services' but do you know the difference? 'Public services' is the general term for all the services that belong to the public sector and includes such services as a local authority, HM Coastguard, NHS, Neighbourhood Watch, as well as the Police, Fire and Ambulance Services. The Police, Fire and Ambulance Services, as well as being public services, are also known as the 'emergency services' because they are usually the first services that respond to and deal with emergency incidents, though several other public services also attend many emergency incidents.

The police fire and ambulance services attend a road traffic incident. Can you identify the roles for each service in this incident?

Roles

While all the public services have different roles and responsibilities during the normal course of their duty, they each have specific roles when dealing with emergency incidents, especially major incidents. Regardless of an agency's specific roles and responsibilities, they all share common objectives when dealing with major incidents. These include:

- saving life and lessening suffering at the scene
- protecting property
- preventing the escalation of a disaster
- protecting the environment
- sharing information between all agencies involved in the incident
- protecting and preserving the scene
- contributing to debriefing and subsequent investigation and inquiries into the incident
- restoring normality
- maintaining normal services where possible
- providing whatever resources are necessary for the recovery from the incident.

These roles are not necessarily the routine roles of the services but a major incident is a non-routine event because, fortunately, they do not occur on a daily basis.

Emergency services

The following grid lists the duties of the emergency services when attending emergency incidents.

Table 17.1: Roles of the emergency services at major incidents.

Police	Fire	Ambulance
Provide and update control room with clear information	Fight fires in a fire situation	Provide emergency aid and triage
Directing and diverting traffic	Minimise risk of fire by removing combustible materials or using foam	Resuscitate where necessary
Ensure access and exit routes are clear	Advise other services on health and safety at the scene	Establish casualty loading point
Cordon off the immediate area	Search for and rescue of casualties using specialist equipment	Establish casualty clearing area
Control crowds, sightseers and onlookers	Identifying hazardous substances	Transport casualties to designated hospitals
Obtain witness statements	Diluting or neutralising harmful chemicals	Order medical resources where necessary
Coordinate other services	Establishing decontamination units	
Preserve the scene for evidence	Assisting in salvage operations	
Collate and distribute casualty information	Providing first aid at the scene	
Identify dead on behalf of HM Coroner	Using pumping apparatus for removal of water	
Inform and warn the public through media	Investigate the cause in case of fire	
Investigate the cause		

Local authorities

Local authority emergency planning teams play an important role at major incidents and their role is threefold.

- First, they have to ensure that the responding services have enough resources to deal with the incident. For example, if heavy lifting equipment is required at the scene of say, a train crash, it is normally the duty of the local authority to arrange for the lifting equipment to be brought to the scene.
- Second, in some incidents where evacuation has taken place, in severe flooding for example, the local authority is responsible for providing rest and reception centres, or temporary accommodation, which might be private accommodation or makeshift, temporary accommodation in schools, leisure centres or village halls.
- Finally, because emergency incidents can often bring disruption to the community, it is important for normality to be restored as quickly as possible and normal services, such as social care and catering services for those who are reliant upon them, are maintained.

Emergency incidents, especially those on a large scale, are a source of great concern for all victims, but friends, relatives and loved ones will also feel anxious, particularly if they have heard about the incident on the news. Therefore, it is vital that there is a contact number so friends and relatives can find out the information they require, and this is usually provided by the local authority.

Highways Agency

Some road traffic collisions on our major roads are extremely serious in terms of personal injury, road congestion and traffic disruption, often requiring main roads to be closed for hours at a time. The Highways Agency is responsible for managing traffic on all motorways and 'A' class roads in England. So where an incident is likely to cause serious disruption on the major roads then the Highways Agency should be contacted. This agency can inform road users of problems on the major roads through their call centre, internet or matrix system, which you often see on illuminated traffic signs on motorways. The Highways Agency also has the technical capability to close roads and divert traffic quickly.

Congestion is monitored and managed through the Regional and National Traffic Control Centres (run by the Highways Agency), with detailed information readily available to the public.

> ## Key term
>
> **Local authority** – an elected governing body that looks after a town and its citizens; like a miniature government. Local authorities provide several services, such as education, emptying bins, maintaining roads and making local laws for the good of the town's people. They also have a duty to look after their citizens in cases of emergency by providing temporary accommodation if necessary.

> ## Key term
>
> **Highways Agency** – a branch of the Department of Transport responsible for managing traffic and dealing with congestion and traffic problems on the motorways and other main roads in England.

Activity: Other agencies involved in major incidents

Besides the agencies just mentioned, can you think of three more agencies that might be required to respond to an emergency incident?

What type of incidents might they be?

Cooperation

In an incident the emergency services and local authorities are known as Category 1 responders, while other services, such as the Highways Agency, gas, water and electricity companies, are known as Category 2 responders. Category 1 responders are legally bound to cooperate with Category 2 responders and other agencies at emergency incidents.

How do the emergency services, other public services and agencies know what to do when dealing with:

* a road traffic collision involving several vehicles on a motorway?
* a fire at a large chemical factory?
* a train collision?
* a terrorist bomb in a shopping complex?

The answer is quite simple: they practise. The emergency services and other services hold emergency planning meetings where they discuss approaches to different scenarios within their area. These are known as Local Resilience Forums and the emergency services must attend a forum at least once every six months where they cooperate with other personnel in both preparing for and responding to emergencies. Preparation is done by assessing local risks and deciding how best to deal with them, sharing information, joint training and exercises with agencies, such as utilities (gas, water and electric) companies, local authorities and any other agencies that might be involved in attending emergency incidents. By participating in emergency planning, the public services are able to produce multi-agency plans and agreements, and coordinate multi-agency exercises and training events.

Emergency exercises can take lots of different forms and may range from an evacuation exercise, using only a few services, to a full-scale simulation of, say, a terrorist incident, using several public services and agencies.

Who does what?

For the public services to work effectively there must be a system whereby each individual of a particular service knows what to do. This is done through a **chain of command**, which follows a set procedure at emergency incidents and consists of the following three levels:

* operational (also known as (bronze))
* tactical (also known as silver)
* strategic (also known as gold).

Operational command consists of teams of personnel at the immediate scene of an incident, and could involve such things as firefighting, rescuing trapped victims from wreckage, and ambulance personnel treating the injured, and so on. An inner cordon is established around the incident to prevent unauthorised access to the disaster site while operational personnel carry out their work.

Activity: Support services

Carry out some research from the Red Cross website (available via Hotlinks, on page viii) and, in your own words, write a couple of paragraphs about the British Red Cross Fire and Emergency support service.

Key term

Chain of command – a set procedure for emergency incidents where a strict system of communication is followed.

Tactical command consists of a member from each of the emergency services who takes charge of the scene and forms a link between operational and tactical command. Tactical command, unlike operational command, is not directly involved in the hands-on approach but is normally established further away from the scene, in an outer cordon, possibly in mobile units designated as special operations rooms.

Strategic command is comprised of senior officers from the emergency services and other organisations as required. Their role is to form a strategy, or plan, to deal with the incident and to support tactical and operational commands. Gold command, as it is more often called, is located away from the incident, possibly at a police station or council building. However, if the incident can be resolved by operational and tactical command, there may be no need for strategic command.

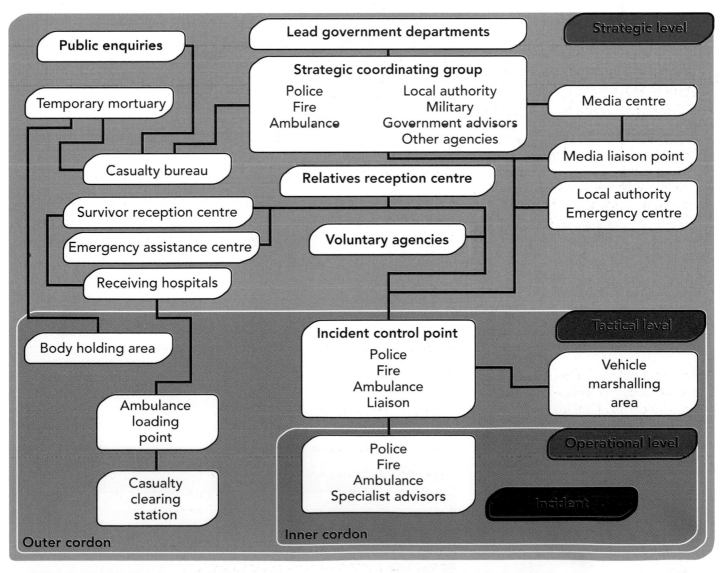

Figure 17.1: The three levels in the chain of command.

1.3 Domestic and leisure activity fires

At the beginning of this unit we looked at domestic and leisure activity incidents but now we are going to look specifically at fires.

A domestic fire is one that occurs in or around the home whereas a leisure activity fire is one that occurs at, say, an amusement park or local recreation centre. Both domestic and leisure activity fires are extremely dangerous in that they can both claim lives. Leisure activity fires can often claim more lives due to the nature of circumstances of where they occur. Fires, wherever they are, can be started accidentally or deliberately.

Types and causes of fires

Fires in the UK are classified into six types or classes depending on the cause or the material affected:

Class A – these are fires that involve solid substances, such as paper, wood and coal

Class B – these are fires that involve flammable liquids, such as petrol and once the liquid reaches a certain temperature, the substance will burn

Class C – these are fires that involve flammable gases, such as butane

Class D – these are fires that involve metals (yes, metals: steel wool is very flammable)

Class E – these fires involve electrical equipment and electrical equipment will have a continuous heat source whenever the electricity supply is on

Class F – these fires involve cooking fat and oil, which will burn once the oil reaches a certain temperature

Classifying fires

The reason that fires are classified in this way is because each class of fire involves a different technique to extinguish it. For example, a wood fire will be extinguished differently from a chip pan fire, which will be extinguished differently from a fire involving electrical equipment. You will see how different extinguishers are used to deal with different classes of fires later on in the unit (see page 350).

(see page 350)

Did you know?

Do you know the correct term for deliberately setting fire to property?

Activity: Class of fire

Working as a group

Consider the different classes of fires and have a group discussion as to how you would extinguish each one.

Activity: Classifying fires

Look at the types of fires above and think of three where they could apply to leisure activity fires and three domestic fires.

What could be the causes of those fires?

Chemistry of combustion

Combustion is the term given for the chemical reaction between certain elements, namely, fuel, oxygen and heat. In other words, it is a fire, though a fire can only occur if the three elements of fuel, oxygen and heat are present. If one of those elements is missing, then there will be no combustion (or fire), or if combustion is already in progress, then taking away one of the elements will cause combustion to stop. Fuel comes in a variety of **flammable** (capable of burning) materials, which can be in solid, liquid or gas form and some materials are more flammable than others.

To begin its combustion, most fires must have a source of ignition or heat, which can come from things like a lighted cigarette, a match, a spark, and so on. However, some fires can be ignited simply by a substance coming into contact with air.

Fire analysis triangle

The triangle in Figure 17.2 shows the necessary elements of fuel, heat and oxygen that combine for combustion to take place.

Role of the Fire Service in dealing with fires

The primary role of the Fire Service is to save lives and property but firefighters must also ensure the safety of themselves and their colleagues. When attending the scene of a fire, the service must assess what type of fire it is, who and what is at risk and how best to deal with it. This is known as a dynamic risk assessment, which will guide the fire service in the best approach to dealing with the fire, including the need for evacuation, extra fire engines and any specialist equipment that might be required to deal with the fire.

> ## Key terms
>
> **Flammable** – easily set on fire.
>
> **Non-flammable** – not easily set on fire.

> **Did you know?**
>
> Anything is capable of burning if it becomes hot enough.

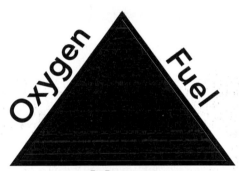

Figure 17.2: Fire analysis triangle.

Firefighters need to determine the cause of a fire in order to put it out effectively. What are the likely causes of this fire?

BTEC **Assessment activity 17.1** **P1**

As a member of the emergency services, it is extremely important that you understand the causes of different types of fire incidents. Regardless of which service you belong to, you ought to understand the particular natures of different classes of fires. The fire service will need to know what type of a fire it is in order to extinguish it quickly and safely.

Address the following task in the form of a wall display:

1 *Identify* causes of different domestic and leisure fire incidents. **P1**

Grading tip

P1 requires you to recognise the causes of different fires in the home and at leisure activities. It would be a good idea to give examples of different classes of fires and say how they are caused. You might like to illustrate your examples on the poster.

2 The need for fire and incident safety legislation

2.1 Incident safety legislation

Working in the emergency services often involves a certain amount of risk and danger, so for their own protection, and that of the public, the emergency services have to assess the risks and make decisions based on an evaluation of those risks. It is not only the risk that the emergency services have to consider, though, they also have to comply with health and safety law, which can have an impact on the way they carry out their duties.

Health and safety legislation governs, amongst other things, the health and safety in workplaces and of employees while at work. It places a responsibility on employers and employees to exercise a duty of care to others. While this type of legislation has lots of advantages in terms of safeguarding employees, it can also have disadvantages, and some would say that health and safety considerations have gone mad by imposing ridiculous rules.

Health and Safety Executive

The Health and Safety Executive (HSE) is a public body, sponsored by the Works and Pensions Department, and the enforcing authority that ensures health and safety in the workplace is adhered to. This means that the HSE can bring about prosecutions if employers, employees and contractors break health and safety regulations in the workplace or while carrying out working activities. Health and safety in the workplace is governed by several laws but the most common law is the Health and Safety at Work Act 1974 (HASAWA).

Organisational procedures in the workplace

HASAWA sets basic rules and regulations to be followed by employees, employers and contractors to help ensure a safe workplace. (HASAWA is an enabling Act, which means that further health and safety regulations can be added to the Act without having to pass through Parliament.) Some of those rules include:

- protecting others against risks to health or safety in connection with the activities of persons at work
- controlling the keeping, use and possession of dangerous substances
- ensuring the activities of employers do not endanger anybody, and providing information, in certain circumstances, to the public about any potential hazards

Did you know?

Firefighters in some areas are not allowed to use stepladders to install smoke alarms in people's homes because this is a contravention of the Health and Safety Executive Work at Height Regulations 2005.

In most fire stations, firefighters do not use poles anymore because of the health and safety risk.

- no one shall intentionally or recklessly interfere with or misuse anything provided in the interests of health, safety and welfare
- employees should take reasonable care for the health and safety of themselves and others who may be affected by their acts or omissions at work.

First aid at work legislation

Many people are taken ill or have accidents at work, even though their job might not be particularly dangerous, and some accidents can lead to death. To ensure employees receive immediate care and attention in the event of accident or illness at work, employers have to provide adequate first-aid cover, which means appropriate equipment, facilities and trained first aiders. This is required under the Health and Safety (First Aid) Regulations 1981, and applies to all workplaces, though there is no requirement to provide first aid to non-employees. Failure to provide adequate first-aid cover could mean that the employer is prosecuted by the HSE.

Activity: Safety provision

Schools and colleges have to provide adequate first aid to people who work there but do they have to provide first aid to students?

Ask someone at your school or college and find out their first-aid provisions.

How do Police and Fire Service authorities provide adequate first-aid cover to their employees when they are attending an emergency incident?

Using the internet, or visit a local police station or fire station, research the first-aid provision for police officers and firefighters when they are attending an emergency situation.

'Adequate' and 'appropriate' simply means what is suitable for a particular place of work. For example, what might be suitable for an office might not be suitable for a chemical factory. It is the duty of the employer to carry out an assessment of the first aid requirements to see what is suitable, taking into account the nature of the work normally carried out.

Did you know?

The Health and Safety at Work Act 1974 is an Act to make further provision for securing the health, safety and welfare of persons at work, for protecting others against risks to health or safety in connection with the activities of persons at work, for controlling the keeping and use and preventing the unlawful acquisition, possession and use of dangerous substances, and for controlling certain emissions into the atmosphere; to make further provision with respect to the employment medical advisory service; to amend the law relating to building regulations, and the Building (Scotland) Act 1959; and for connected purposes.

Did you know?

When it became law in 1974, HASAWA did not apply to police officers or their working environment, but the Police (Health and Safety) Act 1997 made it compulsory for all police officers to follow the health and safety laws.

HASAWA 1974 classed police officers as 'office holders' and not employees, which meant they were exempt from health and safety regulations. However, the new legislation amended the definition to include police officers, police cadets and special constables.

Sports ground legislation

For over a hundred years there have been many serious accidents at football stadiums in the UK and in Europe, resulting in the deaths of hundreds of people and hundreds of others receiving serious injuries. Even since the early 1970s at least 219 people have died in tragic circumstances at football grounds, including 96 at the Hillsborough Disaster of 1989.

Case study: The Hillsborough Disaster 1989

On Saturday 15 April 1989, 96 football fans were crushed to death in an overcrowding incident at the Sheffield Wednesday football ground in Hillsborough, Sheffield.

At 3.00 pm on that date, Liverpool Football Club was due to play Nottingham Forest in the semi-final of the FA Cup, at the neutral Sheffield Wednesday football ground. Shortly before 3.00 pm, a few thousand Liverpool fans were trying to enter the stadium through the turnstiles at the Leppings Lane end of the ground. The volume of fans at that time was so great that the turnstiles could not cope and it was feared that they might be crushed. Consequently, a request was made to the officer in charge of the game, Chief Superintendent Duckenfield, to open Gate C, a large concertina-style gate at the Leppings Lane end, so that fans could gain access to the ground without being crushed. The order was given for the gate to be opened and thousands of fans entered the ground and made their way through a tunnel that led to an enclosed area behind the goal.

As the fans surged forward into the crowded pens, those fans that were already in place were crushed against the perimeter fence. Confusion followed and some fans tried to climb over the fence to the safety of the pitch while others climbed up onto the stand above. Initially, the police believed a pitch invasion was taking place but it soon became evident that a tragedy was unfolding. Shortly after, the game was abandoned and the enormity of the tragedy was revealed.

Now answer the following questions:

1. With hindsight, what could have been done to prevent the amount of fans entering Leppings Lane?
2. Do you think Gate C should have been opened or remained shut? Explain.
3. Even though the gate was opened, what other precautions could have been taken?
4. If there was one main cause of this disaster, what would you say it was?
5. Was safety at the ground the responsibility of the football club or the police?
6. What lessons were learned from Hillsborough?

Activity: Contributing factors

Carry out some research into the Hillsborough Disaster by accessing the news websites on the internet, available via Hotlinks (see page viii). List six factors that you believe contributed to the disaster.

Following a tragic incident at the Ibrox Stadium in Glasgow, in 1971, in which 66 football fans were crushed and suffocated to death, with many more injured, the Safety of Sports Grounds Act 1975 was established for all sports grounds with a capacity for more than 10,000 spectators. This included football, cricket and rugby grounds and safety was implemented in the form of a safety certificate that was issued by local authorities. Unfortunately, this safety precaution was inadequate and failed to take into account the risk of fire, which happened at Valley Parade Football Ground, Bradford in 1985, where 56 people died as a result of burning. As a result of this the Fire Safety and Safety of Places of Sport Act 1987 was brought into force to cover all grounds with a capacity of 5,000 fans, but still tragedies occurred.

The latest legislation to cover sports grounds is the safety of Sports Grounds (Designation) Order 2000. It requires all sports grounds to be issued with a safety certificate, which can only be issued by meeting certain standards. Sports grounds are also covered by the Fire Safety and Safety of Places of Sport Act 1987.

Fire safety legislation

Besides protecting people who visit sports grounds, the law also tries to protect people from the risk of fire in certain premises, known as 'designated buildings'. These include such premises as:

- sleeping accommodation (in hotels and boarding houses that provide accommodation for more than six guests)
- institutions (such a hospitals, schools and colleges)
- places of entertainment and recreation
- other places where members of the public have access
- places of work (but these are also covered by extra legislation).

As these premises are designated buildings they require a fire certificate from the fire authority under the Fire Precautions Act 1971. However, before the application for a fire certificate is granted, the fire authority must be satisfied that in case of fire there must be:

- an escape route
- firefighting equipment
- a way of warning people in the premises of fire.

A fire certificate will specify the particular use of the premises and it must be kept in the building for which it was granted. The certificate will specify what to do in case of fire, and it may limit the number of persons who may be in the premises at any one time.

Once a fire certificate has been granted, the fire authority has the right to inspect the premises to ensure there have been no changes to the layout of the premises or that fire regulations are not being broken. If the owner of the premises wishes to make any structural alterations, then they have to notify the fire authority, which will review the fire certificate and make any necessary recommendations to the owner or occupier. If these recommendations are carried out then the fire authority may issue a new certificate.

Activity: Fire as a factor

Carry our some research into the Bradford City FC fire by accessing the news websites on the internet, available via Hotlinks (see page viii).

What faults or problems were there with the football ground?

Poster of instructions in case of fire in the workplace. Would you include any other instructions?

Fire Precautions (Workplace) 1997 (as amended)

We have already looked at health and safety in the workplace, but this legislation deals solely with the risk of fires in the workplace. All the previous legislation relating to fires in the workplace was replaced by the Regulatory Reform (Fire Safety) Order 2005 (FSO), which came into effect in 2006.

This legislation, like that relating to designated buildings, requires that all places of work must have a fire certificate with the extra regulation that the owner must:

- carry out a fire risk assessment of the workplace
- identify the significant findings and detail anyone who might be especially at risk
- monitor and review the risk assessment and revise as appropriate
- inform staff of the risks
- plan for an emergency
- nominate persons to assist
- provide and maintain necessary fire precautions to safeguard those in the workplace
- provide information, instruction and training to employees about the fire precautions.

Interestingly enough, these regulations do not apply to the following (which have their own set of regulations):

- construction sites
- means of transport
- mineshafts
- merchant ships
- offshore installations or open farm/forestry land.

Gas and electrical safety regulations

Gas and electricity, including gas and electrical appliances, can be extremely dangerous. Not only is there an obvious high risk of fire and explosions, gas appliances can give off the poisonous gas carbon monoxide (CO), and electricity can deliver fatal electrical shocks.

To protect the public from the danger of death or severe injury from gas-related and electricity-related incidents there are two pieces of legislation:

- Gas Safety (Installation and Use) Regulations 1998
- Electrical Equipment (Safety) Regulations 1994.

The legislation relating to gas places responsibility on installers, landlords and gas suppliers to prevent injury to the public from either carbon monoxide (CO) poisoning or fire and explosion. To ensure the safety of gas and gas appliances, installation of gas and appliances can only be carried out by a Council for Registered Gas Installers (CORGI) engineer.

The legislation relating to electricity safety is covered by the Electrical Equipment (Safety) Regulations 1994, which are designed to protect the public when using a range of electrical equipment with a high voltage. In the case of private homes, the regulations are enforced by local authority trading standards, while the HSE enforce the regulations in the workplace.

The regulations cover the use and installation of such electrical appliances as:

- cookers
- kettles
- toasters
- electric blankets
- washing machines
- immersion heaters.

Unlike the gas safety regulations, the electricity regulations do not have a council or register for electrical installers, though electrical work should be carried out by a qualified electrical engineer.

HAZCHEM

HAZCHEM is an abbreviation of the term hazardous chemicals but generally refers to the HAZCHEM System and is concerned with the transport of hazardous chemicals and dangerous goods by road, rail and sea. Where an incident involving hazardous chemicals occurs, the consequences can be extremely dangerous to both the public and to the environment, and since it is always the emergency services that have to respond to the incident, it is vital that they know what type of dangerous substance they are dealing with. Therefore, any vehicle that transports hazardous substances must display a **hazchem plate**. This is compulsory under the Carriage of Dangerous Goods and Use of Transportable Pressure Equipment Regulations 2004.

> **Did you know?**
>
> You cannot simply take an electric kettle to work and plug it into the socket to make a hot drink.
>
> You must first have it tested because the Electricity at Work Regulations 1989 say that all electrical equipment in the workplace must be checked at regular intervals.

> **Key term**
>
> **Hazchem plate** – a display of a coded system that immediately informs the emergency services, through an Emergency Action Code (EAC), how to deal with hazardous substances that are carried in vehicles.

Emergency Action Code The EAC number tells the Fire Service which fire suppressant to use while the letter tells them which equipment to wear, if there will be a violent reaction and how to dispose of the substance	**Warning symbol indicates the danger of the substance presents**
United Nations Identification Number that identifies the dangerous substance. These are assigned by the United Nations Committee of Experts on the Transport of Dangerous Goods	
Telephone number if specialist advice is required	**Company name or badge**

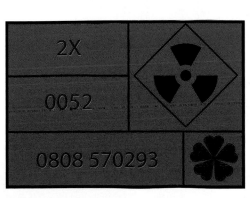

Figure 17.3: HAZCHEM plate and explanation. What can you tell about this substance?

Table 17.2: Key to numbers and letters of Emergency Action Code.

Number	Suppressant	Letter	Violent reaction (V)	Equipment (Liquid tight suit (LTS), Breathing apparatus (BA))	Disposal (dilute or contain)
1	Coarse water spray	P	V	LTS	Dilute
2	Fine water spray	R		LTS	Dilute
3	Foam	S	V	BA	Dilute
4	Dry agent	T		BA	Dilute
		W	V	LTS	Contain
		X		LTS	Contain
		Y	V	BA	Contain
		Z		BA	Contain

Note: There may be a second letter 'E' in the EAC and this indicates that the incident presents a threat to the public beyond the immediate vicinity. In this case, the public may need to be evacuated or warned to stay indoors with doors and windows closed.

The Control of Substances Hazardous to Health Regulations 2002 (COSHH)

COSHH is designed to protect employees from hazardous substances that are stored or used in the workplace. These include oils, bleaches, paint, solvents and any by-products emitted from burning, as well as biological agents. The regulations require exposure to hazardous substances to be prevented or adequately controlled so that the health of workers and others exposed to them is not threatened.

If there is an incident involving hazardous substances at a place of work, the emergency services would have to respond. What would you expect to find in the workplace where dangerous substances are stored?

The Reporting of Injuries, Diseases and Dangerous Occurrences Regulations 1995 (RIDDOR)

RIDDOR enables the HSE and local authorities to identify risks in the workplace by placing a legal obligation on employers, the self-employed and any people in control of premises to report:

- work-related deaths
- major injuries or injuries lasting more than three days (including fractured limbs, loss of sight, electric shock, burns)
- work-related diseases (including lung disease, skin disease and infections)
- dangerous occurrences (including explosions, failure of breathing apparatus).

Near misses must also be reported under the regulations. A 'near miss' is when something happens but, luckily, it did not result in injury or death, though it could have done. This is classed as a dangerous occurrence and must be reported under RIDDOR.

BTEC Assessment activity 17.2 ② ① ①

If you are to be effective in your job as a public service officer, you must understand the relevant legislation so that you can advise members of the public in health and safety, thereby making the community a safer place. Address the tasks in the form of a presentation in which you:

1 *Explain* the need for fire and incident safety legislation. ②

2 *Analyse* the causes of domestic and leisure fire incidents, referring to appropriate safety legislation. ①

3 *Compare* domestic and leisure fire incidents making suggestions as to how they could be prevented. ①

Grading tips

② simply requires you to say why there is a need for fire and incident laws. You could make this interesting by giving examples of real cases or by using your imagination to think of scenarios. For ① you need to look at the causes, or possible causes, of the fires in as much detail as possible and relate it to relevant legislation, saying how it would break a law or how the law could prevent such a fire or incident. You might like to refer back to what you did for ② for part of this. ① is a comparison of the different causes of domestic and leisure fires and incidents, making some suggestions as to how they could be prevented.

It would help with ① and ① if you reflected on your research into the Hillsborough Disaster and the Bradford City FC Disaster and presented your findings.

3 Domestic and leisure fire and incident prevention measures

3.1 Accident prevention

While the emergency services are highly trained in responding to, and dealing with, emergency incidents, it is an unfortunate fact that the violent nature of some serious incidents, fires and road traffic collisions, for example, cause severe injury or death before the emergency services arrive at the scene. Because not all incidents end with a positive outcome, it would be far better if they did not happen in the first place. The public services understand the consequences of domestic and leisure incidents and that is why they are involved with fire and incident prevention.

Police Services

Road traffic collisions, especially those caused by speed or reckless driving can be very serious or even fatal. Part of the Police Service's role is to ensure that people keep within the law of the land and this can help with the prevention of accidents. For example, it is the duty of the police to ensure that drivers don't break the speed limit because that could lead to serious injury or worse. However, it is not only speeding and breaking the rules of the road that cause accidents; quite often it may be something about the condition of the driver or the vehicle that leads to a serious collision.

Activity: Rules of the road

Think of three rules of the road that, if broken, might lead to a collision.

Think of three things that could affect the condition of the driver of a motor vehicle.

Think of three faults on a motor vehicle that could lead to a collision.

Can you think of three rules for drivers of heavy goods vehicles and buses that could be dangerous if they are broken?

Working in pairs

Design a safety campaign poster that you would like to be shown on TV and in the press, which you believe would reduce road accidents.

Case study: Selby Train Crash 2001

Shortly after 6.00 am on Wednesday 28 February 2001, a Land Rover towing a trailer carrying another vehicle was being driven along the M62 motorway in North Yorkshire near Selby. For no apparent reason, the Land Rover veered off the motorway and careered down the embankment, coming to rest on the East Coast main railway line. The driver managed to get out of the vehicle and as he was speaking to the emergency services on his mobile phone the Land Rover was struck by the Newcastle to London train with over 100 passengers on board. The train remained upright for a short distance until it collided with a freight train, carrying approximately 1,000 tonnes of coal, travelling in the opposite direction.

Ten people died as a result of the accident and many more were seriously injured. It was alleged that the driver of the Land Rover, Gary Hart, fell asleep at the wheel but he strongly denied the allegation. At his subsequent trial he was sentenced to five years imprisonment for unlawful killing.

When the vehicle left the motorway it narrowly missed some crash barriers which were protecting a bridge over the railway line. The barriers were inspected by the HSE and found to be adequate. A report by the HSE described the accident as 'wholly exceptional'

and the railway industry could have done nothing more to prevent the accident. A chief inspector of railways said: *'It's clear that the chain of events that led to this catastrophe were determined by sheer chance.'*

It emerged on 13 February 2010, that a brake fault had been found on Mr. Hart's trailer, which meant that, according to road safety experts, the vehicle he was driving and the trailer he was towing would have been impossible to control.

Now answer the following questions:

The report from the HSE about the accident being exceptional, together with the chief inspector's comments about chance determining the events leading to the accident tend to suggest that accidents will happen no matter what we do to try to prevent them.

1   What are your views on this?

2   Could the Selby train crash have been prevented? How?

3   In view of the latest evidence, what do you think caused the accident?

Local authorities

We have already mentioned that local authorities have a role to play in dealing with emergency incidents (see page 329), but like the accident services, they are also actively involved in emergency prevention.

As previously mentioned, local authorities are Category 1 responders and under the Civil Contingencies Act 2004 (CCA) they are bound to cooperate with other organisations in trying to prevent major incidents, as well as having an obligation to protect the people of their area from harm or injury. You should understand that not all emergency incidents turn into disasters and by careful planning many disasters can be prevented. The CCA outlines six duties of Category 1 responders, with the seventh specifically for local authorities, which serve to prevent incidents turning into disasters:

Risk assessments. These should be carried out so that proper measures can be put in place. This would include things with potential risk to the public, such as amusement parks, public events, hazardous chemical sites and so on.

Emergency planning. This should include training and exercises to test the efficiency of responding organisations.

Communicating. Informing and educating the public to spread public awareness and understanding so that the public know what to do should an emergency situation arise.

Cooperation. Maintain cooperation by having regular meetings with other agencies and organisations that may be involved with emergency planning.

Sharing information. The necessary information must be available to all agencies and organisations to allow an efficient response to any incident.

Business continuity. This means that the organisations to which Category 1 responders belong can still provide normal services during an emergency incident.

Promotion of business continuity within the community. This means that the local communities not affected directly by an emergency can still expect normal services.

Many local authorities provide leaflets with advice for the public on how to cope with an emergency situation, as well as having websites containing public information.

Fire Services

Like the Police Service, the Fire Service is committed to saving lives and property and the dangerous nature of their work, together with their rigorous training, makes them expert in the field of accident prevention, especially fire prevention. All Fire Services have dedicated teams of firefighters that work in the community giving advice and information on how to prevent a variety of potentially dangerous accidents, and what to do should an accident occur. The accidents may involve:

- chip pans
- barbecues
- bonfires
- fireworks
- car fires.

However, fires are not the only type of accidents that the Fire Service tries to prevent; they also advise on the dangers of swimming in lakes and rivers, the safe storage of fuels and how to reduce the risk of carbon monoxide poisoning (the toxic fumes given off by faulty gas burners). Furthermore, the Fire Service gives vital information on what you should do in the case of flooding.

Activity: Water as a factor

We cannot always prevent flooding but we can prevent it from causing unnecessary hardship and turning into a disaster by taking certain precautions. See if you can think of six precautionary measures that would prevent flooding from turning into a disaster.

Bonfires are a potential cause of dangerous fires. Do you take precautions to avoid accidents on Bonfire Night?

RoSPA

RoSPA stands for the Royal Society for the Prevention of Accidents, which is a registered charity whose sole aim is to promote safety and prevent accidents in all areas, including the workplace, the home, roads, schools and leisure activities (including at or near water). The society provides information, advice and training to numerous industries and organisations with the intention of bringing about safety culture.

RoSPA also promotes safety in the home for disadvantaged children under five, who, according to statistics, are more prone to injury than less disadvantaged children.

One of RoSPA's aims is to educate young people about the risks in leisure safety and to provide children with the skills to be able to assess risks in their daily lives for themselves. This can prepare them with the necessary life skills to keep them safe in adulthood. RoSPA believes that children should be exposed to a certain amount of risk as part of their natural development.

Remember

Emergencies cannot always be prevented but they can be prevented from turning into disasters by taking the correct course of action.

Media and TV

The press, radio and television play an important part in accident prevention by communicating with the public at large. The media advertise topical campaigns at different times of year on behalf of the emergency services and other safety organisations, including RoSPA. For example, as the year approaches Bonfire Night, we often see, hear and read about campaigns warning of the dangers of fireworks and how to enjoy them safely. Similarly, around Christmas time, we see several reminders about drinking and driving.

Media agencies are also involved in the preparation and prevention of major emergencies because they communicate the information supplied by Category 1 responders under the Civil Contingencies Act (2004) to warn the public of potential emergencies. Communicating with the public has two aims:

- to warn of any potential or current emergencies
- to provide information and advice, including how they will be responded to in an emergency.

The press, radio and television need to release factual information to warn, inform and advise the public but without causing alarm.

Motor sport safety

Motor sports, such as car rallies and motorcycle racing, have a certain risk attached to them for those taking part, but there is also a risk to employees and spectators, especially where there are large crowds.

The HSE and local authorities offer guidance to motor sport organisers to reduce the risk of accidents. Organisers have to take these factors into account:

- course and track design
- type of fuel and fuel storage
- vehicle safety
- spectator safety
- protective clothing
- adequate firefighting resources
- paddock safety
- noise and manual handling.

Did you know?

The health and safety of Formula 1 motor sport is under the control of the Federation Internationale Automobiles.

Activity: Safety for event organisers

Consider the list of factors for motor sport safety. Can you think of any other considerations when organising an event?

Sports venues

With all sporting and leisure venues, a significant risk is the size of the crowd and how they behave, since they all behave differently at different types of events. As we saw in the Hillsborough Disaster 1989 case study, large crowds and poor crowd management can lead to crushing, injury and even death.

Organisers of any event which attracts crowds should have a health and safety management system, including efficient communications and trained staff who can deal with potential crowding risks. All venues should have a risk assessment to decide if arrangements are adequate, as well as researching the type of visitor and likely crowd behaviour.

Activity: Assessing crowd behaviour

How might different venues affect different crowd behaviour?

Think of three different sports venue events and think about crowd behaviour that might pose a risk.

Seafaring and boating safety

Leisure activities include using boats, either on the sea or the inland waterways of Britain, like the Norfolk Broads, for example. If you have been on a cruise on the sea or an inland waterway during the last few years, then you will have had to comply with the following legislation:

1 The International Convention of the Safety of Life at Sea (SOLAS) Regulations 2002, which sets certain standards and safety regulations for using vessels at sea. These include such things as showing evidence of planning a journey and keeping on board a set of SOLAS life-saving signals.

2 Merchant Shipping Regulations 1999, which apply to all vessels over 45 feet long and include extra regulations, such as carrying a maritime radio, an approved life raft and buoyancy jackets for all on board.

3 Boat Safety Standards of 2002 and 2005, which apply to all boats with fitted engines, cooking, heating and other domestic appliances. Such boats which will need to pass an examination before they can be allowed to navigate the inland waterways.

Fire prevention and fire safety in the home

The Fire Service is involved in educating the public on fire safety in the home since lots of people are unaware that some basic precautions can prevent a disaster. Safety campaigns relating to fire safety are often advertised in the media, the Home Fire Risk Assessment is an example. This involves a home visit by a member of the Fire Service, free of charge to:

- identify and be aware of the potential fire risks within your home (including electrical plugs and sockets, wiring, smoking and the use of electric blankets)
- know what to do in order to reduce or prevent these risks (including correctly shutting doors and any repair work)
- put together an escape plan in case a fire does break out and ensure you have working smoke alarms.

The Fire Service also fits smoke alarms free of charge to those households that qualify. The Fire Precautions Act (1971) and Fire Precautions (Workplace) Regulations 1997 (amended in 1999) cover preventative legislation.

Leisure and commercial fire safety

The Regulatory Reform (Fire Safety) Order 2005 extended fire safety regulation beyond the workplace to include all non-domestic premises and includes:

- sleeping accommodation (including hotels, guest houses, hostels, care homes and residential training centres
- small and medium places of assembly (including clubs, restaurants, village halls, churches and other places of worship)
- large places of assembly (including shopping centres, sports stadia and cathedrals)
- theatres and cinemas (including concert halls)
- open air events (including theme parks, zoos, music concerts and fairgrounds).

The legislation makes it compulsory for owners or managers to:

- take general fire precautions
- complete a risk assessment
- apply the principles of fire prevention
- ensure adequate fire safety arrangements
- eliminate or reduce risks from dangerous substances
- ensure adequate firefighting and fire detection equipment
- ensure sufficient emergency routes and exits
- provide information to employees.

Case study: Tower block blaze, London 2009

On Friday 3 July 2009, fire swept through Lakanal House, a 12-storey block of flats in south-east London, killing six people, including a baby and two children.

A total of 18 fire engines and 100 firefighters were used to fight the fire, which started around tea time. About 30 people were rescued, with at least 20 of them being taken to hospital.

Fire investigation teams believed the fire was caused by a faulty portable television set on the ninth floor. Once it reached the stairwell it spread to other areas.

Now answer the following questions:

1 You might take precautions to prevent fire in your home but if you live in a block of flats how can you ensure that other people take precautions because a fire in one home can easily spread to another?

2 Should there be stricter monitoring of fire safety in the home? How could this be done?

3 How would you ensure better fire safety in tower blocks?

Buildings and their fire properties

While most modern buildings are constructed of fire retardant materials, concrete, bricks and mortar, for example, buildings contain many combustible materials, like, paper, carpets, curtains, and so on. Modern furniture, such as chairs and settees, are made from fire resistant materials, but many homes still contain older furniture that is made of highly combustible material. When a fire starts in buildings with several floors, it is very easy for the fire to take hold and spread quickly through a stairwell, especially if it is not contained by closing doors.

3.2 Accident prevention aids

Dry and wet risers

You might have wondered how firefighters deal with fires in high buildings. The Building (Minimum Standards) Regulations 2000 made it compulsory for buildings over a certain height to have dry risers and wet risers included in their construction. Dry risers are required on all buildings where any floor is 18 metres above the ground floor. These assist in tackling fires in tall buildings where firefighting is difficult.

A dry riser is a vertical pipe that is designed to distribute water to several floors of a building in the case of fire. The pipe, as you would expect, is dry and rises within a fire resistant shaft with an inlet box at the bottom, which has to be kept free of obstruction to allow fire engine access. Water from a fire engine can be pumped through the riser inlet to several floors above where a hose may be attached on each floor.

Wet risers are of a similar construction to dry risers except they are always full of water, which is under pressure from the mains or some other source so do not require water to be pumped from a fire engine. Buildings that are more than 60 metres high will have wet risers as part of their construction.

Extinguishers, smoke detectors and sprinklers

Fire extinguishers. These are an effective way of suppressing fires in the home or workplace. Remember that fire requires oxygen in order to maintain combustion but fire extinguishers distribute a coating of foam over a fire, which smothers it and deprives the fire of oxygen.

Most fire extinguishers are hand-held, with instructions clearly written on the extinguisher. A pin is attached to the handle which needs to be released before the extinguisher can be activated. By aiming the nozzle at the base of the fire and pressing down on the operating leaver, a foam discharge will deprive the fire of oxygen and extinguish it.

Smoke alarms (or **smoke detectors**). These can save a home and the lives of families. They are relatively small devices that are easily attached to the ceiling of premises and can detect smoke given off by

Do you know which class of fire each extinguisher is used for?

349

Remember

- Class A – remember that these are fires that involve solid substances, such as paper, wood and coal. Sometimes a dry chemical extinguisher would be more suitable than water for extinguishing a fire because they do not produce steam.

- Class E – remember that these fires involve electrical equipment that will have a continuous heat source whenever the electricity supply is on. This means that water is no good to extinguish the fire since it does not take away the heat source and could conduct electricity.

- Class F – remember that these fires involve cooking fat and oil, which will burn once the oil reaches a certain temperature. Again, water is ineffective to fight the fire as oil and fat are lighter than water and will float on water.

Activity: Putting fires out

Remind yourself of what these classes of fire are? If you have forgotten, now is the time to refresh your memory.

Why wouldn't you attempt to extinguish an electrical fire with water?

Why wouldn't you attempt to extinguish a chip pan with water?

fire. Once the smoke is detected a piercing alarm sounds, thus warning the householder of the presence of fire and allowing the premises to be evacuated before the fire takes hold. Some smoke alarms may be connected to several others so that once smoke is detected in one part of the premises the warning is relayed through other alarms.

Smoke alarms can be powered by battery or mains electricity, or a combination of both, and some incorporate emergency lighting.

According to the Fire Service, there are 140 fires a day in the home and many lives could be saved if people had a warning and were able to get out in time.

Fire sprinklers. These are devices that are normally fixed to the ceiling of premises and they release water droplets onto a fire once heat is detected through a heat-sensitive valve. The sprinkler is attached to a water pipe and the head of the sprinkler has a spinning component that enables the device to sprinkle water in a specific pattern over the fire.

Fire sprinklers may be fitted in the home and they are compulsory for some commercial premises.

Chemical systems

Chemical fire extinguishers. These can be either dry or wet systems. Wet chemical systems contain a chemical foam which can be used on fires where fat is the source of fuel, like chip pan fires. The foam extinguishes the flames and coats the oil to prevent it from reigniting.

Dry chemical extinguishers are suitable to extinguish Class A, Class E and Class F fires.

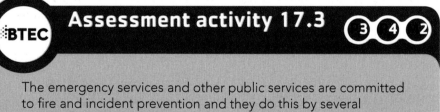

Assessment activity 17.3

The emergency services and other public services are committed to fire and incident prevention and they do this by several methods, including advertising through the media. In the form of a video diary, make sure you:

1 *Explain* how incidents can be prevented. **3**
2 *Explain* how fires can be prevented. **4**
3 *Compare* fire and incident prevention methods. **2**

Grading tips

3 and **4** require you to look in some detail at how incidents and fires can be prevented. You could explain the various types of prevention and how people are made aware of the dangers of not following safety guidelines. You could even explain about different safety campaigns. **2** is a comparison of the fire and prevention methods in which you could say how and why they are different.

4 Review the practical work undertaken by the public and emergency services in dealing with fires and incidents

4.1 Practical work undertaken by the public and emergency services

Police investigations

The Police Service normally coordinates the activities of other organisations at a major incident that is based on land. Their primary aim is the saving and protection of life in conjunction with other emergency services, as well as preserving the scene to safeguard evidence because it could be that criminal proceedings follow.

Where it is possible, the police will establish and protect inner and outer cordons to enable other responders to carry out their duties safely. The police, in conjunction with other agencies, for instance, the Highways Agency, will establish traffic cordons and diversions to keep traffic away from the scene.

It is also the duty of the police to take witness statements, control onlookers, safeguard a victim's personal property, gather evidence and oversee any criminal investigation. They also have responsibility for the identification of fatalities on behalf of HM Coroner.

Use of Scenes of Crimes Officers (SOCO)

Scene investigation

Every incident is a potential scene of crime and it is important to find the cause of an incident to see if criminal or negligence charges should be brought. The more a scene is protected during the incident, the better the likelihood of finding the cause. This is one reason why a cordon (or protective barrier) is placed around the immediate scene of an incident, but it is often difficult to preserve the scene intact if a rescue is necessary. All incidents of a suspicious nature are investigated by Scenes of Crime Officers (SOCO) and Forensic Science Officers, who gather and analyse evidence found at the scene to try to establish the cause. Scene investigation may also be investigated by the following:

- CID
- Fire Service
- forensic science
- Civil Aviation Authorities
- Health and Safety Executive.

In cases of explosions resulting from terrorist attacks, Scenes of Crime and Forensic Officers gather fragments of wreckage and reassemble

> **! Link**
>
> For more on crime see Unit 12, page 225.

them like a jigsaw puzzle in an effort to establish the cause. This was the case in the 1988 Lockerbie Air Disaster where wreckage was strewn for several miles over Dumfries and Galloway in Scotland.

When the scene of an incident has been investigated and there is sufficient evidence to suggest criminal intent or negligence, then proceedings are brought against the person or organisation responsible. This could mean, as with the case of the Lockerbie Air Disaster, that the people believed responsible are extradited to stand trial.

An inquest is held into all sudden, suspicious, and unnatural deaths by HM Coroner and if, during the course of the evidence, the coroner decides that there has been criminal negligence, then they can direct that a person be investigated and charged.

Role of the Ambulance Service

The specific aims of the Ambulance Service at an emergency incident are:

- Perform **triage** (assess the condition of casualties and attend to the most serious first).
- Establish a casualty loading area (a specific area at the incident where all casualties will be assembled prior to being taken to hospital).
- Transport casualties to designated hospitals (names of hospitals must be given to police coordinating officer so relatives can be informed).
- Order adequate medical resources (drugs, blood supplies and human resources if necessary).

Use of Army, Navy and RAF in emergency incidents

The military has a wide selection of vehicles, including helicopters, which may be available in an emergency for airlifting victims to safety or transporting them to hospital, as was the case in the 2004 Boscastle Floods, in Cornwall. In incidents such as flooding and foot and mouth outbreaks, the services of the Army prove particularly valuable, as well as responding to the reports of unexploded devices. However, military assistance to the civil community can never be guaranteed because of operational commitments, though where it is possible military assistance will be provided. Therefore, the military are not directly involved in planning for major incidents in the civilian community.

Mountain and Cave Rescue involvement in emergency incidents

Mountain and Cave Rescue organisations are voluntary public services and they provide their services free of charge. They are often called out to search for missing persons on the hills and in caves, as well as searching for people who may have disappeared in avalanches. Teams of rescuers are expert at rescuing people from dangerous rocks, using ropes and stretchers, in areas that are inaccessible by helicopter or other rescue vehicles.

Key term

Triage – assess the condition of casualties and attend to the most serious first.

4.2 Practical work undertaken by the Fire Service in dealing with fires and incidents

Fire Investigations Unit

All Fire Services have Fire Investigation Teams and some brigades have mobile Fire Investigation Units that can be driven to the scene of a fire to carry out the investigation. The unit is like a mobile office where interviews can be carried out and plans discussed relating to the investigation; CCTV footage can also be viewed.

The units contain specialised equipment, lighting and excavation tools that can allow investigation teams to work independently without having to rely on the presence of other resources that may be required for active operations.

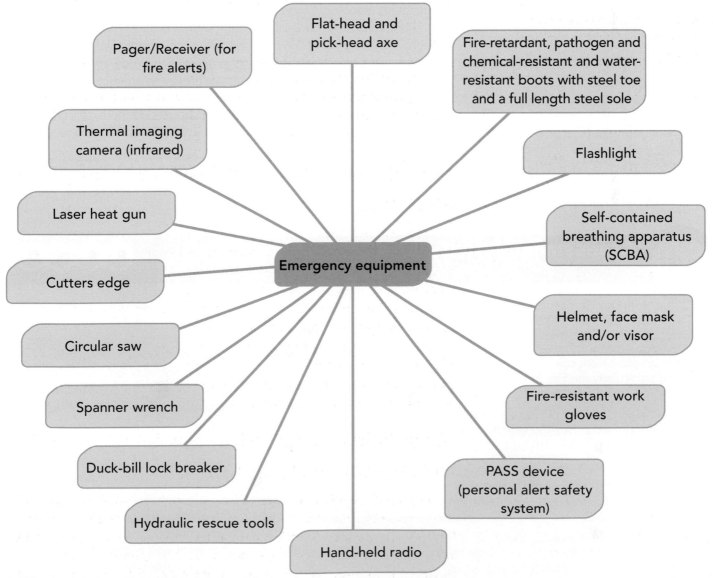

Figure 17.4: Emergency equipment carried by the Fire Service.

Activity: Working together

Cutting people from trapped vehicles requires exceptional teamwork. How good is your teamwork? What type of teamwork experience have you had? How could you improve your teamwork skills to ensure you are a valuable team member even when under pressure?

Firefighting and rescue equipment

Besides the standard fire engines (or fire tenders), some brigades have Incident Support Units (ISUs) that have been especially designed to deal with certain types of incidents. For example, Water/Ice Rescue Units are fully equipped with boats for rescues from deep water, and Heavy Rescue Units contain necessary cutting and lifting apparatus for incidents involving building collapse or large-scale road traffic accidents. Such apparatus consists of hydraulic cutters, spreads, rams, high pressure hoses and chains for stabilising vehicles. Furthermore, the Fire Service has Pollution Containment Units for dealing with chemical or hazardous material incidents. Figure 17.4 shows some of the emergency equipment carried by the Fire Service.

Rescues and road traffic collisions

Firefighters are highly trained in all types of rescues, including collapsed buildings, burning buildings, floods and road traffic collisions.

For incidents involving dangerous chemicals, the service has direct access to a computer system, called Chemdata, which contains data on thousands of chemicals and trade name products, including essential information for emergency response, such as physical properties, hazards, containment, decontamination, basic first aid, protective measures and action in the event of fire. This means they can ensure members of the public receive the proper care when coming into contact with dangerous chemicals, and they can make the Ambulance Service aware of what care victims may require.

Where there is a road traffic collision that leaves victims trapped in vehicles, the Fire Service are very skilful at cutting trapped victims from wreckage, while working closely with paramedics who may be administering immediate and vital first aid.

BTEC Assessment activity 17.4

A range of practical work is undertaken by the public services, including dealing with road traffic collisions and major incidents. You need to show that you understand the practical work carried out by the public services, and particularly the Fire Service when dealing with a fire incident. In the form of a written report make sure you:

1 *Review* the practical work undertaken by public services when dealing with an emergency incident scenario. **P5**

2 *Review* the work of the Fire Service when dealing with a fire incident. **P6**

3 *Analyse* the practical work undertaken by public services when dealing with an emergency incident scenario. **M3**

4 *Evaluate* the practical work undertaken by public services when dealing with an emergency incident scenario. **D2**

Grading tips:

For **P5** it would be a good idea to assess the work undertaken by a range of public services at a major incident, and for **M3** you need to break down the roles into more detail and give more of an explanation.

For **P6** you could assess the practical work undertaken by the Fire Service at a fire incident scenario. **D2** requires an evaluation of the practical work of the public services in general when dealing with an emergency incident scenario, which you could do in the form of a case study and say what went well and what didn't go so well. At the end of this you should give a balanced conclusion.

Dean Goddard
Firefighter

I've been a qualified firefighter for four years now and I think it's a great career. The training was quite tough and I don't just mean the physical side because there is a lot of theory to get through, which meant I had to do a fair bit of private studying during the evenings and weekends. You've got to know the law and all about different hazards or you can't advise people on safety and prevention. After all, our job is not just about fighting fires; we're responsible for fire and incident prevention and we deal with lots of other things, like rescuing animals, chemical spillages and cutting casualties from road traffic collisions.

A typical shift

Well, we work day and night shifts and they are unpredictable because you just never know what will happen. We all have our routine days, where we inspect, clean and maintain our equipment ready for the next job, and we have practice drills and train with new equipment. But if we get a shout (emergency call) we have to leave whatever we're doing and set off. You never know what to expect: the temperatures can be extreme, too, really hot or very cold, you might be using BA (breathing apparatus) in a smoke-filled room or your cutting gear to release someone who might be trapped after a collision; you might even have to rescue people from floods, like we did a couple of years ago. Like I say, you just never know what will happen.

The best thing about the job

First, there is great job satisfaction from helping to save lives and people's property. There's no finer feeling than rescuing someone from a dangerous situation and seeing the look on their faces when they're safe, but sometimes that is only a small part of the job.

Next there is the teamwork and comradeship that you get from doing the job; it can be very demanding and physical and you have to trust and depend on each other. Having said that, there are lots of times when you have to use your initiative and be able to solve problems quickly and decisively because a life could depend on it.

Finally, it makes you feel proud that you're doing a worthwhile job in the community.

Think about it!

1. What topics have you covered in this unit that might give you the background to become a member of the emergency services?
2. What knowledge and skills do you think you need to develop further if you want to become a member of the emergency services?

355

Just checking

1. Give four causes, with examples, of emergency incidents.
2. What is meant by 'combustion'?
3. What is the Highways Agency responsible for?
4. What three things are needed for fire?
5. What are the three levels of command at an emergency incident?
6. What do HSE, HASAWA, COSHH and RIDDOR stand for?
7. What is a Hazchem plate?
8. What does RoSPA stand for?
9. Is there any legislation that covers canoeing on a river?
10. How does a smoke alarm work?
11. Why do SOCO visit the scene of an emergency incident?
12. Which service would you call upon if you were dealing with a party of schoolchildren who were trapped in a cave?

edexcel

Assignment tips

- This unit gives you the basic outline of how emergency incidents are responded to by the emergency services. It would be a good idea to carry out your own research into any fire or emergency incident that you have heard about on television or read about in the press. When you carry out the research, see if you can apply the principles you have learned in this unit, especially the roles and responsibilities of the services and the level of command and control sequence (operational, tactical and strategic). You could read about them in the past editions of newspapers, which may be kept in your library. Your tutor or librarian should be able to help so don't be afraid to ask. Researching a topic for yourself gives you a greater insight into a subject, as well as giving you a better chance of achieving the higher grades in your assignment.

- Any of the services outlined in this unit require certain qualities of character and because of this they have quite demanding selection and recruitment procedures. Some of those qualities are teamwork, problem solving and working with others, which are excellent skills to have in any career, but especially in the emergency services. How could you develop these qualities? Can you make the right decision when under pressure? How could you practise and develop such a thing? Critical thinking would be a good thing to practise, whereby you are faced with a problem (sometimes called a dilemma) and decide which would be the best solution, if indeed there is a best solution. Senior officers are often faced with difficult decisions in life-threatening situations but how do they decide which course of action is best? Some people believe that the correct course of action is one that brings about the greatest good for the greatest number, or one that brings about the least amount of suffering. Does that mean, then, that it is acceptable to let a few people die as long as there are more who survive?

20 Volunteering in public services

You may well be tempted to ask the question, 'Why should anyone give up their time to carry out work without getting paid?'

Once you have completed this unit you will know the answer to that question and clearly understand the benefits of volunteering to both the individuals who volunteer and to society.

Volunteers play a vital part in many public services either by direct involvement (for example, as special constables with the police), or by working with organisations such as St John Ambulance (which provide invaluable back up to public services especially in times of emergency) or the RNLI (which can be regarded as an emergency service in its own right).

As part of your study you will be expected to take part in some form of voluntary work in an area that interests you. This could be by organising a one-off event for charity or by carrying out voluntary work for a period of time. You will need to investigate how to apply for voluntary work, carry out any planning involved and devote sufficient time to the volunteering activity to gain the knowledge and experience necessary to achieve the learning outcomes for the unit.

Learning outcomes

After completing this unit you should be able to:

1. understand the importance of volunteering in public services
2. know the different types of voluntary work available
3. understand the skills required for voluntary work
4. be able to undertake voluntary work.

Assessment and grading criteria

This table shows you what you must do in order to achieve a pass, merit or distinction grade, and where you can find activities in this book to help you.

To achieve a **pass** grade the evidence must show that the learner is able to:	To achieve a **merit** grade the evidence must show that, in addition to the pass criteria, the learner is able to:	To achieve a **distinction** grade the evidence must show that, in addition to the pass and merit criteria, the learner is able to:
1 explain why volunteering is important in the public services **Assessment activity 20.1, page 365**	**M1** analyse the importance of volunteering in the public service sector **Assessment activity 20.1, page 365**	**D1** evaluate the importance of volunteering in the public service sector **Assessment activity 20.1, page 365**
2 discuss the benefits to be gained from volunteering **Assessment activity 20.1, page 365**		
3 identify the different types of voluntary work available **Assessment activity 20.2, page 372**	**M2** compare and contrast the different types of voluntary work available **Assessment activity 20.2, page 372**	**D2** appraise the different types of voluntary work available **Assessment activity 20.2, page 372**
4 demonstrate skills required for voluntary work **Assessment activity 20.4, page 486**	**M3** explain in detail the skills required for voluntary work **Assessment activity 20.3, page 377**	
5 carry out voluntary work **Assessment activity 20.4, page 486**		

How you will be assessed

This unit will be assessed by internal assignments that will be designed and marked by the staff at your centre. It may be subject to sampling by your centre's External Verifier as part of Edexcel's ongoing quality assurance procedures. The assignment is designed to allow you to show your understanding of the learning outcomes for volunteering. These relate to what you should be able to do after completing this unit.

Your assessment could be in the form of:

- activity logs and diaries
- presentations
- tutor observations
- witness statements (from people like your supervisor when you are volunteering)
- case studies
- practical tasks
- leaflets
- posters
- written assignments.

Sarbjit, 17, studying Public Services

'This unit helped me to understand what volunteering is and why people do it.

When our tutor first introduced this unit and said that as part of it we would have to take part as a volunteer I thought 'no way!' After all, I've got a busy social life and with college work to do and fitness training to make sure I can pass the army entry test, I didn't want to find time for doing unpaid work! We discussed in class how we could organise our time to fit in a voluntary activity each week (in the evenings or at weekends), but I couldn't see it working for me.

Now I have completed the unit I realise how wrong I was. Not only did I really enjoy taking part in a conservation project during the Easter holidays, but I've signed up to go back in the summer for another two weeks! Giving up a block of time worked for me because it was like having a (working) holiday and because we were residential, all the volunteers really got to know each other well and develop as a goal-oriented team.

I really want to join the army and called in to talk about how to apply last week. When I spoke to the army recruitment officer she asked me if I had any work experience. I explained I hadn't had paid work experience but that I'd been on the two-week conservation project as a volunteer. It turns out this is just the sort of thing the army are looking for and I was advised to include all the details on my application! She said any voluntary work is seen as showing a positive attitude and commitment when applications are looked at.

The other great thing about volunteering was meeting new people and working with them as a team. Normally I mix with my family or my mates from school and college, but while I was doing the conservation project I was working with a real mixture of people aged 16 to 70, male and female, White, Black and Asian, unemployed and even a lawyer! I made a lot of friends and we all met up last week to share our photos and talk about our experience. Six of us have signed up for the summer project too.

I found out about the conservation project at the mockin4life website (available via Hotlinks on page viii). I had to apply formally to take part and explain why I wanted to volunteer and what I could contribute. Going through that process made me think carefully about my skills and helped me be more confident about completing my army application form.'

Over to you!

- What volunteering activity appeals to you?
- Could you spare a few hours every week or would you rather devote a block of time to volunteering?
- Have you got any spare weekends?
- Do you want to do something locally or further afield?
- Could your class organise a voluntary activity to raise money for a charity?
- Could you put together a voluntary project to improve your local environment?

1 The importance of volunteering in public services

What motivates you to give up your time and work for no pay?

Reasons for volunteering may include:

- making a contribution
- developing new skills
- working in teams
- gaining useful work experience
- meeting new people.

Can you think of any other reasons?

What would motivate you?

1.1 What do we mean by the term 'volunteer'?

One definition of a volunteer is an individual working on behalf of other people and not motivated by money or material reward.

Volunteers may undertake all sorts of roles. They may:

- give up a regular block of time each week, for example volunteering to help with a youth club or Brownie pack
- undertake a volunteering project during their holiday, as Sarbjit described on page 359
- undertake fundraising for an event such as 'Comic Relief'
- raise sponsorship money to support a school or college project
- do work in the UK or overseas during a gap year between school and college
- be part of a public service or **third sector** organisation and volunteer on a regular basis (such as St John Ambulance, Army Cadets, Special Constable)
- work for an employer who **seconds staff** to take part in voluntary projects as part of their work role (for example, police officers are seconded to the Prince's Trust and the Home Office supports staff by giving employees 5 days paid annual leave each year to take part in voluntary work)
- represent a **private sector** organisation that has decided to put some of their profit into helping those in need (for example, Marks & Spencer have a policy of matching charitable fundraising that that their staff do out of working hours).

Key terms

Public sector – the part of the economy that is controlled by the government or state.

Private sector – the part of the economy that is not directly controlled by the government or state.

Third sector – the part of the economy that includes charitable and voluntary organisations.

1.2 The importance of volunteering

Volunteers are important to both public services and to charitable organisations for the following reasons:

- They provide expertise free of charge for both charities and public services that the organisation would otherwise have to pay for.
- They give up their time to undertake a whole range of activities that public and third sector organisations need to fulfil.
- Volunteers provide extra help to public service and third sector organisations and their paid personnel and free up time that the paid staff can use in other ways. For example, reserve forces also provide a valuable back up to the full time armed forces. Personnel and units from the Territorial Army (TA) and Royal Air Force Reserve (RAFVR) have been active in Afghanistan and Iraq.
- Volunteers bring fresh ideas to organisations and new ways of looking at things!
- They help public services when responding to emergencies when it is vital that as many competent people as possible can offer assistance. Many public service organisations rely on their own volunteers or voluntary organisations to support them during an emergency.
- The Fire Service also calls on part-time or retained firefighters. In many parts of the UK there are no full-time employed firefighters so retained firefighters are vital to the service. Retained firefighters are on call 24 hours a day (and most have other full-time jobs) but they drop everything else when the incident call comes in.
- Volunteers help forge closer links between public services and local communities. For example, the Special Constabulary is made up of members of the public who volunteer to help the police in their local community.
- Public services may look favourably on people who have been volunteers with them when recruiting for full-time positions (for example, some Police and Fire Services favour people who have been in their cadet forces).
- Volunteers can help charities with raising funds and donations and publicising the work of the voluntary organisation. The RNLI relies on over 40,000 volunteers to help with fundraising as well as working on lifeboats at stations and on the beaches.

Why are volunteers important to organisations? Let's look at a range of organisations and consider the benefits of volunteers from their point of view. Charities (or **third sector** organisations) rely on fundraising for most of their activities. They need to keep their costs to a minimum and rely heavily on people not only making financial contributions but also giving up their time to provide necessary expertise. Each voluntary organisation will need different skills sets but most will need people to:

- help raise funds
- carry out office tasks
- deal with phone enquires
- help with ICT
- help with volunteer recruitment
- help with training volunteers.

Did you know?

In England and Wales the Fire Service employ 33,000 firefighters and have a further 12,000 retained firefighters available to call on.

Did you know?

A Home Office survey in England and Wales in 2003 found more than 20 million people were actively involved in a volunteering activity, 11 million of them at least once a month.

Their activities included organising events, being members of committees, religious and educational activities, sporting activities, practical activities (providing help to others, such as housebound neighbours) and fundraising for a range of organisations.

Did you know?

There are over 15,000 Special Constables serving with police forces across the UK.

Key term

Second staff – an employer or organisation arranges for members of their staff to work for a period of time in another organisation as a volunteer. They are still employed and paid by the organisation which has seconded them.

- The benefits to the police from volunteering are:
- It increases police capacity, leading to better performance and achievement of goals.
- It allows full-time personnel to get on with core police activities and improve response times to emergencies.
- It encourages more participation from the local community and builds community relationships.
- It offers police access to an extensive pool of skills, talents, experience and local knowledge.
- It attracts a diverse range of people, more reflective of the local community.
- By volunteering individuals gain a better understanding of the work the police do.

Let's look generally at the benefits of voluntary work for those involved as shown in Table 20.1.

Table 20.1: Benefits for those involved in voluntary work.

Benefits to students	Benefits to school or college	Benefits to the community
<ul><li>Good on their CV</li><li>Strengthens job and college applications</li><li>Offers the chance to show good citizenship</li><li>Opportunities to communicate with a broad range of people</li><li>Develops organisation skills</li><li>Builds a social network with other students</li></ul>	<ul><li>Boosts the profile of the school or college</li><li>Good publicity</li><li>Shows community engagement</li><li>Makes links with other organisations outside school/college</li><li>Students develop skills which may boost their achievement</li></ul>	<ul><li>Meets a need or solves a problem</li><li>Raises funds</li><li>Gets vital work done voluntarily</li><li>Builds links across different organisations</li></ul>

Case study: Citizens Advice Bureau (CAB)

The CAB was founded during the Second World War and provides free advice, which is confidential and impartial, to anyone who asks for it. Advice covers both rights and responsibilities. There are 448 branches (each of which is an independent registered charity). Last year between the CAB's 428 branches dealt with over 6 million problems for nearly 2 million people!

Table 20.2: Some of the roles CAB volunteers undertake.

Role	Job description
Adviser	Trained for interviewing people, negotiating with others on their behalf, making phone calls and drafting letters. May represent clients at tribunals or in court. (If you are a law graduate and train as a CAB Adviser it cuts 6 months off your solicitor's training contract!)
Receptionist	Dealing with clients face to face, managing the waiting area, answering the phone, proving information leaflets.
Campaigner	Researching and writing reports. Identifying common issues from clients to campaign on. Campaigning in the media.
Peer Education Worker	Promoting the work of the CAB to students in youth clubs, colleges and schools. Providing advice services for young people.
Fundraiser	Producing promotional materials for distribution. Tailoring national campaigns to local needs. Helping with fundraising events. Completing applications for funding grants. Giving presentations to support funding applications.
Volunteer recruitment	Real human resources (HR) role; producing recruitment leaflets and posters; running open days for potential recruits; giving talks and staff information stands; keeping the website up to date with vacancies; dealing with enquiries from potential volunteers.
IT Support	Helping the CAB use their ICT effectively. IT trouble-shooting. Web designing. IT training for volunteers

Now answer the following questions:

1 Discuss these volunteering roles.

2 Were you surprised at the range of roles available?

3 Do any of these roles appeal to you?

1.3 What are the benefits of volunteering?

Gaining new life skills

Voluntary organisations do recruit people who already have skills that contribute to their organisation as paid employees. Additionally, they also look to recruit those with the potential to develop the skills required on an unpaid basis. Voluntary organisations provide training opportunities, often ones that can benefit the volunteer, such as those describe in the CAB case study. If you research voluntary organisations through their websites, one of the key things you will find is information and details about the training they provide for their volunteers, much of which helps volunteers to develop their interpersonal and work-related skills.

Developing existing skills

If you already have specific skills, you may be able to use and develop those skills working as a volunteer. For example, if you are already a good swimmer, you could develop that skill working with the Royal Life Saving Society UK and train as a life saver. If you are a first aider you could volunteer with St John Ambulance. Someone with expertise in recruitment and selection could develop those skills by becoming a recruiter for a charity on a voluntary basis.

Diversity awareness

Voluntary organisations adhere to equal opportunities in volunteering policy. This means that their volunteers can be recruited from any background and will be trained within a framework of positive values, fair treatment and challenging discrimination. Volunteering will give you the opportunity to work with a very diverse range of people, quite possibly people you wouldn't otherwise have met.

Did you know?

Organisations in the UK usually have equal opportunities policies as they have to work within the equal opportunities laws and this applies to voluntary organisations too.

This means that voluntary organisations must not discriminate against anyone on grounds of age, gender, race, religion, disability or sexual orientation.

The criteria for appointing an individual to a role in a voluntary organisation should be their ability to carry out the role required after suitable training and support (if necessary, with reasonable adjustments such as being provided with documents in larger print if visually impaired).

Case study: Volunteering with a disability – Jo's story

'When I finished college I found it difficult to get a job. While I was doing my college course I'd been involved in fundraising for a group of disabled children to have a holiday in Disneyland. I decided to get more involved as a volunteer to give me the opportunity to develop my skills and have useful experience to add to my CV!

I approached a local children's charity. They were really interested as I'd just completed a BTEC National (IT Practitioners) which had given me skills in designing databases and websites! The charity was looking for help with improving their website and wanted to improve their ICT so my volunteering really worked out well for both me and the charity!

Part of the work I do for the charity is helping young people use IT and helping adapt IT systems for disabled users. That gave me a chance to work with young children and it's totally changed my career direction.

I'm now working in a primary school as a classroom assistant, with responsibility for managing the school's IT. I'd never have thought of this career without having done the volunteering!

At my interview the head teacher asked me what skills I could bring to the classroom assistant's role and I could honestly give a whole list of examples including experience of working with young people, being reliable, responsible, turning up on time and loads more, as well as my technical IT abilities.'

BTEC Assessment activity 20.1 P1 P2 M1 D1

1 Create an article for a Public Services journal which *explains* why volunteering is so important in the public sector. P1, M1, D1

2 Give a talk to the rest of the group encouraging them to become involved in volunteering and listing the benefits of this for them as individuals, and for organisations. You will need to *discuss* the benefits to be gained from volunteering. This means you will have to show you understand what the benefits are and you will need to present the key (or most important) points. P2

Grading tips

M1/P1/D1 are linked grading criteria. You do not have to do extra work for M1 and D1, but you do have to ensure your work not only explains but also analyses and evaluates.

To achieve P1 you should *explain* why volunteering is important to the public services in your leaflet. Make sure you use some real examples to illustrate your answer.

To achieve P2 you will have to *analyse*. This means you will need to examine in detail why volunteering is important to public services, highlighting the essential points. For D1 you will need to go a stage further and *evaluate*. This means you will need to present a reasoned case and give reasons to support your opinions. You will need to include a conclusion based on your views.

PLTS

Undertaking the assessment activity will develop your independent enquirer, reflective learner and creative thinker skills.

Functional skills

The work on this assessment activity will give you the opportunity to develop your English functional skills. If you use a word processor and include facts and figures you will also develop your ICT and numeracy functional skills.

2 The different types of voluntary work available

As a volunteer you have a vast range of activities to select from! Everyone will be able to find a voluntary activity that appeals to their particular interests, skills and availability.

Some ideas are listed below but this list is not exhaustive. If you have a specific interest then research the voluntary activities that might support that interest.

Conservation projects

People are becoming increasingly aware of the environment and the need to take actions to conserve their environment. Opportunities exist to undertake one-off environmental projects or to work on a regular basis with a conservation organisation. Volunteers may take part in activities such as building dry stone walls, replanting hedgerows, litter collection, tree planting and gardening.

Big Issue magazine is sold on the street to raise money for the homeless. The sellers wear an official green waistcoat, a vendor's badge, and an identification tag. Do you know of any other charities for the homeless?

> ### Did you know?
>
> Students in a college in Croydon took part in a pledge to help their local community.
>
> They designed a replica Olympic torch and passed it from class to class as each completed their chosen community project.
>
> Projects included gardening and shopping for the elderly, litter collection, and cleaning graffiti from bus shelters.
>
> Agricultural students in the south-west have recently used their skills to help the local National Trust with replanting gardens in a National Trust property.

Helping the homeless and disadvantaged

There are a number of charities that provide shelter, food and clothes for homeless people. Some of these operate internationally while others are UK-based. Two well-known examples are the Salvation Army and St Martin-in-the-Fields (Trafalgar Square, London).

- The Salvation Army provides both hostels and soup kitchens for the homeless and their volunteers undertake all sorts of roles from cooking and distributing food to providing a listening ear and giving first aid and medical attention.

- St Martin's is best known for its annual Christmas appeal but it provides a day and night centre all year round which not only provides food and shelter but also offers careers advice and skills training. It helps homeless people who are newly arrived in London, long-term homeless, and people leaving the armed forces and prison.

Activity: Find out about a homeless charity

Research a charity of interest to you that supports the homeless with food, clothes and shelter.

Does this charity operate locally, nationally or internationally?

Does it focus on a specific group (such as young people, ex-offenders)?

What voluntary roles are there that you could help with?

How much time does the charity ask their volunteers to commit?

Helping with clubs and groups

Youth clubs rely heavily on volunteer workers for support, as do organisations like lunch clubs for the elderly or for refugees. The roles that volunteers undertake may be practical ones like cooking or providing activities or they may be behind the scenes, like fundraising, paperwork, answering the phone. If you have a special Interest, for example if you are good at football or dancing, you may want to use that skill to help out at a club for younger children and encourage them to build their own skills. If you are a good listener you may decide to help at a club for the elderly, listening to their stories and experiences.

Helping with fundraising

Voluntary organisations generally operate as charities and rely largely on donations for their funds (although many are able to access funds from government and from organisations like the National Lottery for specific projects). Fundraising takes a number of forms.

- Charity shops are to be found on all high streets and give us an opportunity to donate unwanted clothes, toys, books and presents that can be sold to raise money to help others. Charities are always looking for volunteers to staff their shops and working in a charity shop allows you to develop skills such as dealing with customers, handling stock and money, as well as working as part of a team. Many charities sponsor their shop volunteers to achieve qualifications in retail and customer service, so giving them the opportunity to apply for paid work in the retail sector.

- Much of the fundraising activity is still street and door-to-door collections. A local authority permit is required for any collection made in the street or in a public place or door to door. Collectors must wear a badge and carry a certificate of authority from the charity they are collecting for. The police should be notified of charitable collections or events scheduled to take place in the street. Those collecting must be aged at least 16 years and collection boxes must be sealed.
- Charities need people to work in their offices for tasks such as addressing letters and sending out emails as part of their attempt to encourage the public to donate.
- If you have design skills these might be useful in tailoring any fundraising to the needs of your local community, helping to produce leaflets, posters and flyers to put through people's letter boxes.
- Your class could undertake a specific project to raise funds for a chosen charity by organising a fundraising event – we will look at this in more detail later (see page 383).

Helping as a first aider

Both the Red Cross and St John Ambulance recruit volunteers to help with providing medical assistance. This may be emergency care during a civil contingency or disaster, working alongside the emergency services or providing support at events such as football matches and other large public events.

St John Ambulance provides first aid support at the events such as the London Marathon and the Wimbledon Lawn Tennis Championships. In addition to the first-aid activities they offer health-based community support programmes.

The Red Cross recruits volunteers for emergency response and first aid, charity shops and fundraising. They also need volunteers to support migrants trying to trace their families, and to support with patient transport. Some of the Red Cross volunteers offer support and care for the elderly and vulnerable in their own homes.

Emergency relief work

Volunteering for emergency relief work may involve supporting UK-based public services or it may involve helping internationally. Disasters such as the earthquake in Haiti in 2010 brought both public services and volunteers from all over the world to help with the rescue, provide emergency shelter, food and clothing and to stay on to help with reconstruction in the areas that had been devastated by the flooding.

Did you know?

Face-to-face fundraising tends to attract younger givers, such as people in their 20s and 30s.

Many of them will be giving a gift to charity for the first time.

Did you know?

The Special Constabulary is a part-time volunteer Police Force. The 'specials' support regular officers by patrolling alone or with another special or regular police officer, either on foot or in a car. They are issued with the same kit (baton, handcuffs, CS spray) as a regular police officer.

International voluntary service

Organisations such as VSO (Voluntary Service Overseas) and CWW (Challenges World Wide) offer the opportunity for volunteers of all ages to make a contribution overseas. Many students leaving school see this as a great opportunity to make a difference during a gap year, before going on to college, while professional people may take a year out from work to use their skills (maybe as a healthcare professional, engineer or teacher) to help people in an economy less developed than our own.

Cadets

All the armed forces have cadet sections (Army, RAF, Navy and Marines) and these provide young people with training and the opportunity to take part in a range of activities. Other organisations have cadet forces, too. St John Ambulance run a cadet scheme. Some fire and rescue services and police forces offer cadet schemes. Check with your local Fire Service and Police Force to see what they offer.

The Metropolitan Police in London have a large cadet force with a number of branches and offer young people opportunities to get involved with:

- community policing initiatives such as leaflet distribution, test purchase of illegal items such as knives, alcohol, fireworks
- London triathlon
- physical activities and residential camps
- drills and inspections
- parades such as Remembrance Day and Trooping the Colour.

Did you know?

The Territorial Army (TA) is made up of over 30,000 volunteers. They meet regularly and commit to a minimum of 40 days training a year, as well as taking an active role in supporting the cadet organisations.

These sea cadets offer voluntary support to their local community. Can you make a list of the voluntary work they could undertake?

There are many ways you can help sick, elderly and vulnerable people. Can you suggest some that are not offered by the well-known charities?

Did you know?

Find out more about Age Concern on page 169.

Did you know?

Opportunities for volunteering to work with animal charities both in the UK and internationally include:

- working with endangered species and helping return them to the wild
- feeding wolves and orphaned fox cubs
- returning strays to their colonies once neutered
- monitoring wild dolphins
- nursing sick and injured animals.

Supporting sick, elderly and vulnerable people

Some hospitals have schemes (often organised through charities like Age Concern) which provide volunteers to visit people in hospital. Some patients may not have any relatives or anyone living close by who can visit them. Volunteers may read to them or maybe play cards. There are also charities which put art into hospitals (believing that a brighter environment may help recovery).

The WRVS provides cafes at venues like hospitals (they also provide refreshments for prison visitors). The WRVS also provides 'meals on wheels', a library book collection and delivery service and drivers to help those with mobility problems to get around.

Closer to home, you may want to think about helping a sick or elderly neighbour by doing shopping for them, collecting library books or talking their pet for a walk!

Charity fundraising events

There are all sorts of ways you can become involved in charity fundraising. It may be that your school or college support a specific charity and you hold events such as sponsored silences, dress down days or book reading events to help raise funds. Many schools and colleges get involved in big events such as Red Nose Day and Children in Need. You could also take part in a run or other sporting event and look for sponsorship for your chosen charity.

Animal charities

There are hundreds of animal charities registered in the UK including ones to support wild animals and birds, ferrets, guinea pigs, donkeys, horses, dogs and cats! Support for these charities may be through fundraising or it may be more practical, like volunteering to help at a local animal refuge and feed, groom and care for the animals. Volunteers also get involved in rescue (for example when animals have been ill-treated or when they have been caught up in a disaster, like a fire or a flood). Some animal charities are also involved in trying to ensure endangered species are protected, that they are bred and in many cases returned to the wild (and their natural habitat).

Mountain and Cave Rescue (MR and CR)

MR mainly works with a range of public services and other voluntary organisations to rescue people injured or stranded on mountains. It also performs many other functions as the list below demonstrates. All its personnel are highly trained volunteers and the emergency public services rely on those volunteers for the expertise they provide. MR is organised into regional teams and it also has specialist teams that use trained dogs to help with search and rescue. The MR:

- has 3500 volunteers
- is available 24/7, 365 days a year
- is available no matter what the weather is
- helps police in missing persons searches
- helps police in preserving crime scenes and finding evidence
- searches snowbound roads for stranded motorists
- helps the Ambulance Service in accessing areas cut off from normal access
- provides assistance in emergencies (like the Grayrigg, Cumbria Train Crash in 2007)
- rescues people trapped by flooding
- helps the Fire Service put out moorland fires.

CR operates in a similar way to rescue cavers.

Royal National Lifeboat Institute (RNLI)

The RNLI provides a life saving service all day and every day for the UK and Republic of Ireland. Most of their personnel are volunteers who give their time to rescue others, often putting themselves in danger.

The RNLI works closely with the emergency public services and the Coastguard (MCA) who coordinate rescues on the coast and at sea.

The RNLI undertake rescue work both on beaches and at sea and in support of flood rescue (both in the UK and internationally).

The RNLI works closely with other charities such as Mountain Rescue and the Royal Life Saving Society UK (who aim to safeguard lives in, on and near water and undertake lifeguard and life saving training).

Other volunteering roles with the RNLI

As well as crews for lifeboats the RNLI has volunteers who act as:

- lifeguards (protecting beaches)
- shore helpers (run the lifeboat station, assist with lifeboat launch and recovery)
- fundraisers (raising money to keep the service operational, shaking collection boxes on the streets)
- trustees (bring expertise, experience and knowledge to support operational and financial management).

The RNLI also gets support from a range of celebrities including sports men and women involved in water sports and those from the worlds of music, art, entertainment and business.

Did you know?

- In 2008 the RNLI rescued 8,000 people (or 21 each day of that year!)
- RNLI lifeguards patrol over 100 beaches and in 2008 helped 10,000 people.
- Flood Rescue teams are on 24-hour standby at all times.
- The RNLI works hard to educate the public so they don't take unneeded risks.
- The RNLI has 7,600 operational volunteers and a further 35,000 shore-based volunteers who carry out a range of support roles.
- RNLI income comes from legacies, fundraising and sales of merchandise.
- Spending is mainly on rescue, education and lifeboats and equipment.
- In 2008 the RNLI raised £170 million.

BTEC Assessment activity 20.2 (P3) (M2) (D2)

To evidence the linked criteria of **P3**, **M2**, **D2** you should produce a wall poster and handouts. Carry out the research with the aim of displaying the poster in the classroom and in which you:

1 *Identify* the different types of voluntary work available. **P3**

2 Provide additional supporting notes for **M1** and **D2**.

Grading tips

To achieve **P3** you should make sure you include information about a range of different volunteering situations (the relevant unit content to help you is conservation projects, shelters for homeless, clubs, fundraising and charity shops, Red Cross, St John Ambulance, Mountain Rescue, emergency relief work, VSO, Cadets, visiting sick and elderly, charity fundraising events, animal sanctuaries and many others).

To achieve **M2** you will need to *compare and contrast* those opportunities. That means that you will need to identify differences and similarities between those opportunities. For **D2** you will need to *appraise* (which means you will have to evaluate those opportunities according to their value or merit) and draw some conclusions.

3 The skills required for voluntary work

3.1 General qualities and skills for voluntary work

What are the qualities and skills required for working in a high street charity shop?

There is a range of very general skills that a voluntary organisation would expect a volunteer to possess. These are not skills that you train for but are intuitive skills that generally people have. These skills are important to a charity as they want volunteers to have a good attitude, to positively represent their organisation and to provide support to people that they are helping. For example, if you are working as a volunteer to collect donations, it would be expected that you are honest and that any money that you collect is given to the charity. Commitment is another important quality. This means that if you promise to do something then you carry this through and perform the promise. A charity may have organised an event around a certain number of people turning up. If people commit to the event but do not turn up it leaves the charity in a difficult situation.

Activity: Skills for voluntary roles

The table shows some skills that may be required in voluntary roles. Draw up and complete the table then check your ideas with the rest of the class. If you find any of the words difficult, then you can look up their meaning in a dictionary.

How might those skills and qualities be useful in paid work too?

Did you add any more to the list?

General skill or quality	Explanation of the skills/quality	How it might help, examples
honesty		
commitment		
reliability		
cheerfulness		
empathy		
reliability		
dedication		
punctuality		
confidentiality		
non-judgemental		

Communication skills

Communication skills can be very important in voluntary work (see Table 20.3). They may be useful in a practical sense (like making phone calls or writing letters on behalf of a client or the voluntary organisation). Being able to communicate visually may be useful when designing publicity materials and posters. Presentation skills may be useful if you are trying to fundraise or promote the voluntary organisation at events.

Table 20.3: Situations where communication skills might be useful.

Skill	How it might be used by a volunteer	Plus points	Things to think about
Letter writing Formal record, using set layout	Internally or externally To inform someone (e.g. of an appointment or event) To request information	Record that can be used as evidence of the communication	House style Good spelling, grammar, punctuation No confirmation of receipt
Email composition	Written message sent via computer Internally and externally To inform someone To request information To fundraise	Quick Inexpensive Can send to lots of people at the same time Can be printed and/or stored if needed	Language must be clear and unambiguous Can easily send to the wrong audience Not everyone has email accounts
Active listening	Listening to colleagues Listening to manager Listening to client	Active listening shows you are engaging with someone and care about their views and feelings	Superficial listening suggests you are not really interested and you may miss key information
Oral communication	Used in face-to-face situations or on the phone	Generally a two-way exchange Can communicate not just information but also use tone to engage others	No written record Must be clear and unambiguous
Presentation skills	Useful when communicating both internally and externally	Can use audio visual media to support your words Can be interactive	Need to know your audience and tailor the presentation to meet their needs
Giving and receiving instruction	In a range of situations including emergency response situations	Passes information to those who need it	Must be clear and unambiguous Must be audible Generally not subject to questioning May need to debrief after the event

Link

There are many other ways that communication skills may be required in voluntary work and you will have reviewed communication skills when you were studying Unit 1 (page 22) so remember to link back into your work for that section.

Teamworking skills

Why do we need teamworking skills to volunteer? If we think about the RNLI, which we discussed earlier, we can see that there are a number of teams involved in their work.

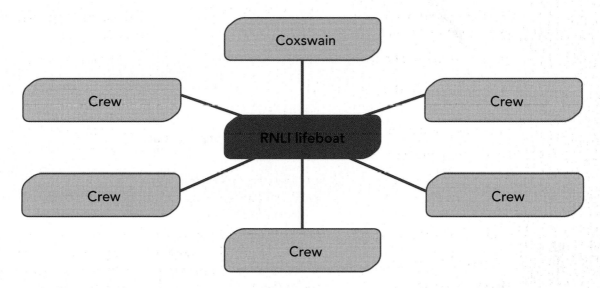

Figure 20.1: Members of the RNLI lifeboats

For the rescue the team needs to be made up of highly trained and skilled crew and managed by the coxswain. Back on shore the lifeboat crew depend on having a mechanic to keep their vessel seaworthy and volunteers to launch and recover the boat and run the lifeboat station.

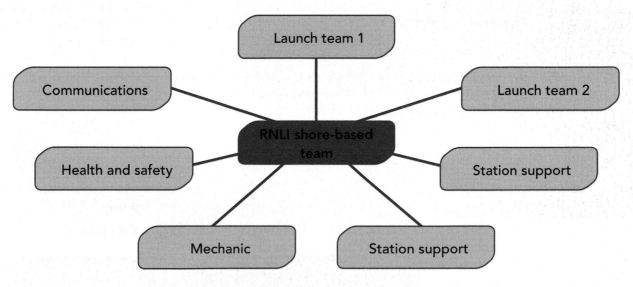

Figure 20.2: Members of the RNLI's shore team

For all of this to happen, RNLI needs a much bigger team of people like fundraisers, publicity and media personnel, people to deal with recruitment of personnel, people skilled in managing the finances of the organisation.

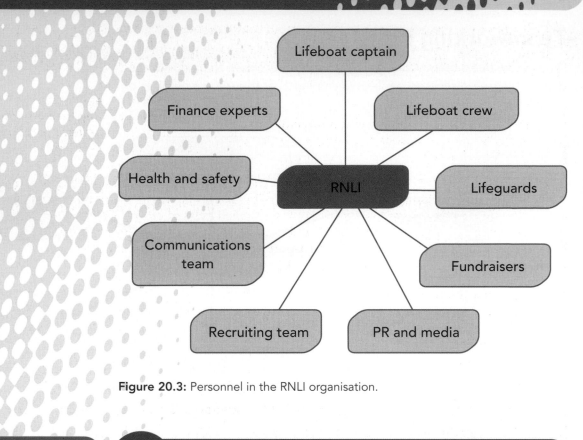

Figure 20.3: Personnel in the RNLI organisation.

Activity: What qualities are needed to be an effective team member?

Look back to Unit 1 where we looked at the importance of team work in the public services. What are the qualities needed to be an effective team member? For example:

- knowing the goals of the team
- making a positive contribution.

Think about one of the charities that we have looked at, such as the St John Ambulance. Why might these skills be important to that charity? Why might the ability to follow orders be needed?

You studied teamwork skills in public services in Unit 1 so look back to that section for more ideas.

Specific skills or abilities required

Some types of voluntary work require specific skills in addition to the teamworking and communications skills and the other qualities discussed above. Some examples of specific skills are being a capable seaman for the RNLI, mountaineering skills for the Mountain and Cave Rescue, first aid for St John Ambulance and the Red Cross, and being able to drive to deliver meals on wheels.

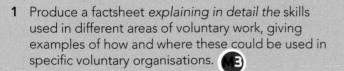

Activity: Specific skills for specific organisations

Working in pairs

Think about the organisations that we have looked at so far. What organisations might require the specific skills listed below?

What charity are you interested in? Can you research and find out if they are interested in any specific skills or expertise? Are these skills covered in the table below? If not, add them in.

Matching skills to charities	
Specific skill or expertise	**Explanation**
Driving	Needed to deliver meals on wheels or to take the elderly shopping as transport is a vital part of these activities
Cooking	
General computer skills	
Web design	
Design/publicity materials	
Physical fitness	
Coaching skills	
Seamanship skills	For RNLI to undertake rescue both at sea and on rivers inland
Drill and parade	
First aid	For St John Ambulance and Red Cross as these organisations provide emergency medical aid
Sign language	
Legal knowledge	
General office skills	

BTEC Assessment activity 20.3 M3

1 Produce a factsheet *explaining in detail the* skills used in different areas of voluntary work, giving examples of how and where these could be used in specific voluntary organisations. M3

Grading tips

To achieve M3 you will need to *explain in detail* the skills that might be involved in voluntary roles.

One way to approach this would be to select three different voluntary organisations, research the types of volunteer roles they have and the skills, qualities and expertise required for each of those volunteer roles and produce your factsheet in sections, one for each organisation, showing the general skills and qualities, communication skills, teamwork skills and specific skills required for the volunteer roles in each of the chosen organisations.

To help you prepare for the next part of this unit, where you will be applying for and undertaking a volunteering role, you may decide to focus your research and your assignment on voluntary organisations that you have a personal interest in.

4 Undertake voluntary work

For you to be really motivated in a voluntary role you need to select an activity and/or a voluntary organisation which really interests you.

We are going to look in general at identifying a voluntary role to apply for and how you can match your skills and interest to that role and complete an application process. This section of this unit will link back into your study of Units 2 and 3, Exploring careers in the public services where you consider the application process for a public service.

We will also look at organising a fundraising event and how you plan and undertake that for real as a class project that will help you to generate relevant evidence.

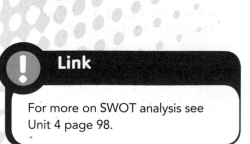

Did you know?

A survey by a major charity found that the motivation given by people to volunteer was:

- useful training for a future career (36%)
- making a difference (27%)
- helping others (23%)
- trying out something new (18%)
- looks good on the CV (17%).

Link

For more on SWOT analysis see Unit 4 page 98.

4.1 Applying for voluntary work

Identifying suitable work which matches my skills and interests

A good way to identify this is to undertake a personal analysis of your own skills using a technique called a SWOT analysis – Strengths, Weaknesses, Opportunities and Threats. A SWOT analysis can help you to focus your activities into areas where you are strong and where the greatest opportunities lie.

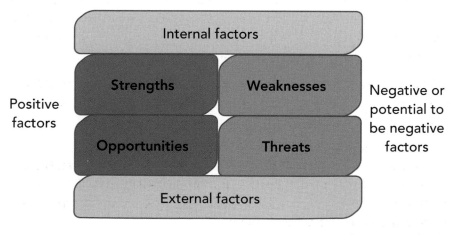

Figure 20.4: Opportunities and threats used in SWOT analysis.

Table 20.4: Analysis of skills.

Strengths	Weaknesses (development needs)
• What am I good at? • What skills and talents do I have? • What fitness levels have I achieved? • What's good about my personality? • What have I achieved in exams or school? • Who do I know who can help me succeed? • What experience have I had? (e.g. working with children, in a shop)	• What could I improve? (e.g. fitness, timekeeping) • What skills do I need to develop? • What's not so good about my achievements? • What aspects of my personality could be developed? (e.g. could I be more confident and less self-conscious)
Opportunities	**Threats**
• What opportunities do I have to undertake voluntary work? • What opportunities do I have for my future career? • What educational opportunities do I have? • What opportunities do I have to improve my fitness, skills and qualifications?	• What could hold me back? • What obstacles or problems might get in my way? • Could any of my weaknesses (development needs) make me unsuitable as a volunteer?

Applying for suitable work which matches my skills and interests

There are a number of ways of applying for any role (both paid employment and voluntary work). Let's look at each in turn.

Face to face

You are walking along the high street and go past a charity shop. In the window you spot a poster (see Figure 20.5). This has got you interested – the shop is an outlet for a charity you support and 2 hours a week is possible. You decide to go in and speak to Sally.

What information should you have to hand? There are some ideas listed here. You may wish to add others of your own. You will certainly need to be able to provide:

- personal details such as name, address, date of birth
- details of your availability (so you may need your class timetable or list of football fixtures that your team are playing)
- references who can be contacted (for example a tutor at school or college, a faith leader who knows you)
- when you will be able to start
- previous relevant experience.

What questions will you want to ask? It will be helpful for you to get answers to these questions:

- Hours of work/times
- What training is provided?
- When do you need to start?

> **! Link**
>
> This section will support the work you have undertaken while studying Units 2 and 3 (see pages 37–82).

Figure 20.5: Poster for volunteers. Is this the sort of work that appeals to you?

- What responsibilities does the role involve?
- Do you need to complete an application form?
- Do you need to provide references?

What will you need to think about in terms of making the right impression on Sally? You can rehearse what you might say with a friend. It helps to hear your reasons out loud. Think about the following:

- appearance and presentation (if you have just come out of the college gym and look a bit dishevelled or scruffy it may be best to come back later!)
- being polite and confident when you enter the shop to enquire
- explaining sensibly why you have decided to apply
- explaining your interest in that particular charity (you may have a question you would like to ask them)
- speaking clearly, making eye contact.

In most organisations, although you may apply face to face initially, you will also be required to complete an application form and may need to attend for an interview.

Applying by phone, phone interviews

In this example, if Sally was not in the shop when you called in, you may offer to phone back later to speak to her. If you see the vacancy advertised in the press you may need to phone to apply.

The information you will need to have to hand will be similar whether you are applying in person or by phone and the questions you need to ask will also be similar, although if you are applying by phone you may need to make a follow up face-to-face interview appointment.

Some organisations use telephone interviews rather than face-to-face interviews. It is a good idea to pre-book a time if you are having a phone interview so you can make sure you are somewhere quiet and you have the information you might need to hand.

Online applications

It is very common for organisations to use internet-based forms for applications. Generally they include all the same questions as a paper application form would, so if you decide to make an online application, make sure you have all the required details to hand before you begin!

Unlike paper applications, you can't really practise with an online application so it may be a good idea to wait until you have a printer available to print off the filled in application to check it before sending. In any case, it is good practice to keep a printout (to remind you of the information you provided before you attend for interview).

Application forms

Application forms allow information to be presented in a consistent format so making it easier to collect information from different applicants in a logical way and making it possible to compare different applicants and judge them against the skills and qualities required for the role.

Typically, an application form includes questions on:

* basic personal details
* work experience
* education and work-relevant training
* references.

There may also be questions specific to the role being recruited (so if a charity wants to recruit a driver they will need to know if the applicant can already drive).

Application forms should be completed carefully in line with the stated requirements (for example, completed in black pen if specified).

It is a good idea to photocopy the application form and practise filling it in. Ask someone (ideally your tutor) to check this for you before you complete and send off the final version.

Even if a covering letter is not requested with an application form it is good practice to include a short cover letter as a courtesy.

Activity: Form filling

Complete an application form as provided by your teacher (or one you have requested from your chosen voluntary organisation) and an equal opportunities monitoring form.

Keep a copy of your completed forms as part of your evidence for **P4**, **P5**.

(It may also provide evidence for your functional skills in English).

Application through interview gives you the best opportunity to put yourself forward. How would you prepare yourself for a job interview?

Supporting statements

Most organisations will expect you to provide a supporting statement either in the application letter or as part of the application form.

This is a very important part of the application process and you need to give it careful thought. On the application form it may ask you to explain:

* why you are interested in the volunteering opportunity and what you would like to gain by volunteering
* what knowledge, skills and experience you have which you feel are relevant to being a volunteer.

It may ask for some real examples to be used to illustrate your comments. This is a good general guide to writing a supporting statement so keep it in mind when producing your own statement.

Make your fundraising fun for all concerned. Which charity would you choose to support?

Letters of application

Some organisations ask you to send a letter of application. They may also ask for a CV and an application form to be completed, so what you include will vary.

The letter should be set out in business style with your address and contact details, the organisation's contact details and information such as where you saw the vacancy, why you are applying, what you can bring to the role. Be careful not to duplicate information supplied on your CV or application form, but check that everything that is required is clearly presented.

Some organisations ask for a handwritten letter. This may be to check that your handwriting is legible (and if your chosen volunteering role may require you to handwrite file notes, messages and so on, so this is very important). If the organisation asks for a handwritten letter (or application form) make sure you comply!

Other things to consider

It is important that, if you agree to undertake a volunteering role, you carry out that commitment and are punctual and reliable. Before you decide what will work for you think about:

- How will I get to the location/premises?
- If I need public transport does it run on the days and times I need it?
- Who will pay my fares?
- If I need to get a lift, do I have someone reliable to take me?
- Will my commitment to the volunteering clash with other commitments (like school and college work, clubs and sports teams)?
- Do I want to go on a regular basis or for a block of time in the holidays?

4.2 Undertake voluntary work

To complete this unit you must be involved in some form of voluntary work. This could be in a one-off event for charity or carrying out voluntary work for a period of time.

Fundraising

If it is for a specific charitable event (like Children in Need or Comic Relief) then it is worth contacting those organisations for a pack which helps you in deciding what to do and how to manage the process.

If it is to help a local group (like a new sports strip for a local youth club's football team or fundraising for a local hospice) then you need to talk to them.

Deciding on the event

A good approach is to undertake an 'A2Z brainstorm' keeping in mind that what you decide on must be feasible in the time you have available and the venues you can use.

Activity: Recording your skills and participation

Working in pairs

To achieve **P4** and **P5** you will need to provide evidence of the relevant skills you demonstrated and your participation in the activity.

One way of doing this is to keep a log or diary.

You should also keep copies of any emails you send, a copy of your CV and any phone calls that you made.

You should ask your tutor to complete an observation record and ask other group members to give feedback on your involvement and the skills you demonstrated.

An example of a log is given below.

Log/Diary to show skills used in job application				
Date	**Who was involved**	**What we did**	**Skills I demonstrated**	**Evidence**
9 October	Me, Joe Rav, Monty	Brainstormed ideas. Decided on a staff car washing day to raise money for the local children's Hospice. Decided on roles.	Teamwork Communication	Notes of our meeting
14 October	All 4 of us and our tutor	Agreed the date and got it approved by the head teacher. Discussed publicity. Identified resources needed and drew up a budget and I volunteered to try to get sponsorship and buy the gear.	Numeracy (for my functional skills) Organisation skills Negotiation skills	Budget Resources list Notes of meeting Draft publicity materials Email confirming date from the head teacher
16 October	Me and Rav	Printed off the leaflets and posters we had designed and put them on display. Left leaflets in all the teachers mail boxes and also emailed them. Put leaflets in the school office, gave to kitchen staff, put on 6th form notice boards.	Teamwork Design and ICT skills More negotiation!	Copies of publicity materials and emails sent to staff
20 October	Me	Negotiated a donation from my auntie to pay for the buckets, sponges and car wash liquid.	More negotiation skills!	Till receipt for all my purchases
23 October	All of us plus 3 friends	Washed 30 cars. Collected the money.	Car washing skills Money handling Teamwork	Photos of us all at work
29 October	All 4 of us	Went to the Hospice to give them the money. Met some of the kids in the Hospice and the staff.	Communication skills	Copy of the cheque for £120 plus lots of photos

PLTS

Completing this assessment activity will give you the opportunity to develop your independent enquirer, creative thinker, reflective learner, team worker, self-manager and effective participator skills.

Functional skills

This assessment activity may help you to develop your functional skills in English (and in ICT if you word process your answer). If you produce a budget that will develop your functional skills in mathematics.

BTEC Assessment activity 20.4

1 For this assessment you need to produce evidence that you have carried out a volunteering activity and also demonstrated relevant skills in that role. This evidence may be in the form of a logbook or diary supported with photos, copies of publicity materials, application letters, video, supervisor's report **P4**, **P5**

Grading tips

To achieve **P4** you will need to *identify* the skills you have demonstrated while undertaking a voluntary role and *produce evidence* that supports your claim to have demonstrated those skills. Try to include in your portfolio of evidence the general skills and qualities you demonstrated, communication and team work skills and any specific skills that the role required (such as ICT to design publicity and posters).

To achieve **P5** you will need to carry out some voluntary work and produce evidence to prove that you have done so.

Make sure you clearly evidence the type of voluntary activity you undertook and the outcomes (for example, if you were fundraising, what was the total that you raised?).

If you undertook a voluntary activity on an ongoing basis (like joining the cadets or working in a charity shop) log that activity and the things you did on different occasions and get someone to sign your log as a witness to what you did (the charity shop manager, the cadet's instructor).

This portfolio will be useful evidence if you later apply for a job or another college course so put it together with thought and care, include an index, personal information, a reflective statement identifying what you think are your achievements.

Petra Marsh
WRVS volunteer

I work with a team of other volunteers in the WRVS cafe in our local hospital. I help with baking produce to sell (largely cakes and biscuits); making meals, teas and coffees; serving customers; clearing and cleaning tables; washing up; clearing away when the cafe stops serving and even mopping the floors!

A typical day

We work on a shift system (we sign up 2 weeks ahead to say when we are available) so what I do each day depends a bit on who is working in the team with me. As I've been a volunteer here for 3 years now, I sometimes take the supervisor's role and organise the others, although, to be fair, the other volunteers don't really need supervising!

If I'm on a morning shift I come in early and help with baking the cakes and biscuits and the snack we serve (like jacket potatoes).

Often one of the volunteers will bring some flowers in (from their garden or some they have bought). If so I'll make flower arrangements for the tables.

The best things about the job

The cafe meets a real need – people who are visiting sick relatives do need food! But it's more than that. The cafe gives people a little breathing space away from the stress of watching a friend or relative who is poorly. We volunteers are always ready to chat if one of our customers wants us to, but we also know when to leave people to their own thoughts.

I left college 3 years ago and I didn't get a job straight away. I was feeling really sorry for myself and a friend of my mother's suggested I volunteer to help at the WRVS cafe. I thought it was a daft idea and for older people but once I got involved I realised how volunteering can really make a difference. Our work supports what the hospital staff are doing and provides a vital service.

I've since got a job in an office, which I like, but to be honest, in some ways I prefer the bustle of the cafe and working with different volunteers on different shifts.

My long-term ambition is to have my own cafe now – I'd love to run my own business. But it won't stop me volunteering – I get too much fun from it!

Think about it!

1. What areas have you covered in this unit that provide you with the background knowledge and skills you could use as a volunteer?

2. What further skills might you need to develop? For example, you might need to improve your ICT skills or written communication skills.

3. Which organisations are you going to explore in more detail in preparation for your volunteering activity?

4. What can you and the other students in your class do to support fundraising or make a positive contribution to your local community?

Just checking

1. Complete the table below explaining the terms.

Term	Meaning or definition
Volunteer	
Third sector organisation	
Fundraising	
Community work	
Conservation project	
Communication skills	
Personal statement	

2. Name three benefits volunteering may bring to each of the following:

- public services
- voluntary organisations
- individual volunteers
- your school or college
- your community.

edexcel

Assignment tips

- Build up your portfolio of evidence for **P4** and **P5** as you go, including as wide a range of evidence as possible (which will also be useful for your PLTS).

- Always check the unit content when writing up assignment work. Use it as a checklist to ensure you have covered everything you need to.

- Check the meanings of the verbs (like *explain*, *identify*, *analyse*) in the grading grid and make sure you do what the verb asks!

- Check your work through before you hand it in. You are not being assessed for your BTEC Public Services on your spelling and grammar, but you are for functional skills!

Glossary

Act – a piece of law which is created by the government and passed by Parliament. All of the public services are governed by acts that set out their roles, purpose and responsibilities.

Amnesty – a period during which offenders are exempt from punishment.

Appeal – The decision of a court can be challenged by appeal against that decision. There are rules which set out both grounds on which appeals can be made and to which tribunal the appeal can be addressed.

ASBO – an anti-social behaviour order is a court order that restricts what a person who has been found engaging in anti-social behaviour can do.

Bail – the temporary release of a suspect who has been charged. Being bailed is being released from custody awaiting appearance in court (for trial or sentence), sometimes on payment of a sum of money as security that you will indeed appear.

Barrister – a lawyer who practises as an advocate for a defendant, especially in the Crown Court.

Capitalism – a system of running a country where wealth and the ways or producing wealth (such as factories or industry) are owned by private individuals.

Caution – a warning given to someone who has committed a minor offence but has not been charged. You are cautioned when a police officer gives you a caution.

Census – the Census in England and Wales is a large household survey which is sent out once every 10 years and monitors all aspects of a population including how many of us there are, our religion or ethnic status and our household income and gender.

Charge – specific statement of grounds on which defendant is being indicted

Civil law – civil legal systems (in countries such as Scotland and France) are based on codes which set out rights and duties that are considered fundamental to society. In English law civil law means not criminal law, such as marriage and property ownership.

Common law – this covers the law and rules of interpretation that have been developed by judges based on cases brought before them and the decisions they have made.

Communism – a system of running a country where wealth and the ways of producing wealth are owned by the state on behalf of all its citizens.

Community orders – a range of punishments given to an offender to serve in the community.

Control measure – the preventative measures you put into place to try to make sure that the hazard doesn't cause a high risk.

Conviction – a formal decision by a judge or jury that someone is guilty of a criminal offence.

Crime – a crime is an act (or a failure to act) which breaches the laws of the society and can result in punishment.

Crime deterrence – the different strategies used to try to deter (stop) people from committing crime.

Crime scene – the place where a crime has occurred or any place where evidence of a crime is found.

Crime trend – an increase or decrease in crime over a period of time.

Criminal law – the area of British law that deals with crimes and their punishment.

Criminal record – a list of someone's crimes.

Defence – lawyers representing the defendant (accused) before the court.

Discipline – a system of rules of conduct or method of practice.

Disclosure – this means telling defence lawyers all the evidence which has been collected about an alleged offence.

Diversity – the differences between people or groups, such as gender or religion.

Either-way offences – may be tried in either the Magistrates' Court or the Crown Court and include theft, drugs offences and some offences of violence against the person, such as assault and wounding (not with intent – i.e. it was not planned in advance).

Final Warning – (in the UK) this is a warning given by the police to young offenders for offences which may be more serious than those for which a reprimand is given, or it may be that the offence is minor but the young person has already received a reprimand and therefore is suitable for a Final Warning.

Glossary

Fit for purpose – this means it is in a suitable format, is written clearly and accurately and is relevant to the situation.

Forensic scientists – people (experts) who are trained in collecting, examining and processing evidence of crimes.

Hate crime — a crime where a criminal targets his or her victim based on their race, gender, sexuality or religion.

Indictable offences – must be tried by the Crown Court, although the case will start in the Magistrates' Court and the defendant will be committed to the Crown Court. Indictable offences include murder, rape and robbery.

Leadership – when a person takes charge or control of a situation and gives instructions to others to complete.

Legal interpretation – decision made on the meaning of the law within a court or tribunal setting.

Major incident – a large-scale emergency or disaster such as a terrorist incident or extensive flooding which requires all the services to work together in order to deal with the problem.

Morale – the confidence within a team, the team spirit, the willingness to succeed and support each other.

Multi-cultural – about a society where individuals and groups from different cultural or racial backgrounds can exist peacefully, side by side.

Offence – an act punishable by the courts.

Offender – a person who has committed a crime.

Offender profiling – building a mental picture and understanding of an offender.

PACE – the Police and Criminal Evidence Act 1984 sets out in a code of practice the rules by which the police must behave during the stop and search, arrest, detention, investigation, identification and interviewing of suspects.

Prejudice – a negative way of thinking about a person or group of people based on personal opinions rather than evidence.

Private sector – the part of the economy that is not directly controlled by the government or state.

Prosecution – the lawyer representing the state who is putting the case against the accused to the court.

Public sector – the part of the economy that is controlled by the government or state.

Racism – the belief that a different skin colour or religious belief make some people better than others.

Racists – those people who treat other people unfairly based on their skin colour or ethnic background.

Remand – the detention of a suspect before appearing at court for trial or sentencing (either in custody or on bail).

Reprimand – (in the UK) anybody above the age of 10 years can receive a reprimand. It is a formal verbal warning given by a police officer to a young person who admits they are guilty of a minor first offence.

Risk – the chance that someone might be harmed from a hazard.

Segregation – this is the separation of people by race, culture or custom. Sometimes it happens in law such as in the southern states of the US prior to the 1960s and South Africa up to the 1990s and sometimes it is based on custom, tradition or choice.

Sentence – the punishment that is given to a person who is found guilty by a criminal court.

Social breakdown – this is where communities do not work together, the sections of the community may be in direct conflict leading to violence.

Solicitor – a lawyer who deals with legal matters and legal documents. Solicitors traditionally deal with any legal matter but do not usually represent their clients in court (except for Magistrates' Courts).

Statute – a law made by Parliament (this is distinct from case law, which is made by judges).

Summary offences – the least serious offences.

Summons – a legal document issued by a court requiring a defendant to appear in court.

Suspect – someone thought to be guilty of an offence or crime.

Third sector – the part of the economy that includes charitable and voluntary organisations.

Triage – assess the condition of casualties and attend to the most serious first.

Victim – a person who has been targeted in a crime.

Warrant – a written order of the court that gives a law enforcement officer powers to act, e.g. an arrest warrant gives the police the power to arrest the person named on the warrant.

Witness statement – formal account of the facts relevant to the matter being investigated.

Index

Credits

I would like to thank the following people:

From Pearson Education: Amanda Hamilton, Lewis Birchon, Alexandra Clayton and Priscilla Goldby whose editing, patience and support have been invaluable.

From Dearne Valley College: A big thank you to the entire public services team for their humour, patience and resilience in the face of the challenging FE sector and having me as a boss, John Vause, Barry Pinches, Paul Meares, Charlotte Baker, Boris Lockyer, Kelly Ellery, Nick Lawton, Mick Blythe, Jean Tinnion and Debbie. Thanks also to my boss Julie – you are one in a million.

From the Services: Lance Corporal Kelly Stevens 38 Signals, South Yorkshire Police, South Yorkshire Fire and Rescue Service, South Yorkshire Ambulance Service.

To my family, Ben, India, Sam and Genevieve who make every day brighter. And to Jin who started me on this path.

DG

The authors and publisher would like to thank the following individuals and organisations for permission to reproduce photographs:

p.1 Photodisc/Life File/Nigel Shuttleworth, **p.3** YinYang/iStockphoto, **p.5** and **p.291** Janine Wiedel Photolibrary/Alamy, **p.8** Mark Rose/iStockphoto, **p.10** NDP/Alamy **p.15** and **p.179** Andreas Gradin/Shutterstock, **p.19** Kevin Britland/Shutterstock, **p.24** and **p.365** Erwin Wodicka/Shutterstock, **p.26** Photodisc/Keith Brofsky, **p.28** and **p.261** Kumar Sriskandan/Alamy, **p.29** Shaun Lowe/iStockphoto, **p.30** Sonia Birch, **p.34**, **p.131** and **p.152** Stefan Hamilton, **p.37** Steven Harrison/Alamy, **p.38** TopFoto.co.uk, **p.39**, **p.85**, **p.177**, **p.193**, **p.197** and **p.325** Pearson Education Ltd/Studio 8/ Clark Wiseman, **p.41** and **p.343** Richard Crampton/Rex Features, **p.44** Kevin Britland/Shutterstock, **p.47**, **p.321** and **p.369** Pearson Education Ltd/MindStudio, **p.58** and **p.141** TopFoto.co.uk, **p.63** Kelly Stevens/Debra Gray, **p.65** Yellow Dog Productions/Getty Images, **p.67**, **p.81**, **p.181**, **p.190**, **p.240**, **p.265**, **p.295**, **p.370**, **p.372** and **p.382** Pearson Education Ltd/Jules Selmes, **p.71** Ray Tang/Rex Features, **p.83** Inspirestock Inc./Alamy, **p.86** and **p.103** Photolibrary, **p.94** Adam Gregor/Shutterstock, **p.86** and **p.355** Stefan Hamilton, **p.105** David Sacks/Getty Images, **p.107** Pearson Education Ltd/Gareth Boden, **p.119** Medical-on-Line/Alamy, **p.120** Photodisc/Getty Images, **p.128** Pearson Education Ltd/Tudor Photography, **p.129** Photodisc/ Jeff Maloney, **p.130** Photodisc/Photolink, **p.135** Getty Images, **p.139** Michael Grecco/Getty Images, **p.143** JinYoung Lee/Shutterstock, **p.147** AFP/ Getty Images, **p.148** Graham Jepson/Alamy, **p.151** Photodisc, **p.157** Image Source, **p.159** Photodisc/Getty Images, **p.173** Digital Vision/Rob van Petten, **p.175** BLOOM image/Getty Images, **p.188** Photodisc/Jack Hollingsworth,

p.191 My Media Quest/Shutterstock, **p.195** Toby Melville/Reuters/Corbis, **p.201** KPT Power Photos, **p.202** www.imagesource.com , **p.206** Pearson Education Ltd/Gareth Boden, **p.211** and **p.225** Jim Varney/Science Photo Library, **p.212** Pearson Education Ltd/Debbie Rowe, **p.217** Corbis, **p.221** Rim Light/Photolink/Photodisc, **p.223** Dave Bartruff/Corbis, **p.227** Janine Wiedel Photolibrary/Alamy, **p.232**, **p.241**, **p.247**, **p.271**, **p.283**, **p.285** and **p.366** Pearson Education Ltd/Naki Kouyioumtzis, **p.257** Peter Evans, **p.259** Image Source Black/Alamy, **p.263** Naluwan/Shutterstock, **p.264** Gregory Wrona/Alamy, **p.270** Stephen Finn/Shutterstock, **p.273** Chris Parker, **p.274** Roy Lawe/Alamy, **p.277** and **p.317** Photodisc, **p.280** Kevin Foy/Alamy, **p.293** Jupiterimages/Getty Images, **p.297** The Illustrated London News Picture Library, **p.298** Pearson Education Ltd/Martin Sookias, **p.301** Terekhov Igor/Shutterstock, **p.302** Imagestate/John Foxx Collection, **p.306** Pearson Education Ltd/Rob Judges, **p.309** Photodisc/Photolink, **p.311** Mark Boulton, **p.317** Tandem/Shutterstock, **p.323** Phanie Agency/Rex Features, **p.328** NDP/Alamy. **p.333** Creatas, **p.338** and **p.349** Pearson Education Ltd/David Sanderson, **p.345** Pearson Education Ltd/Debbie Rowe, **p.357** Stockbyte/ Getty Images, **p.359** Art Directors & TRIP/Alamy, **p.381** Pearson Education Ltd/Lord and Leverett, **p.387** Ekaterina Monakhova/iStockphoto.

The authors and publisher would like to thank the following for permission to reproduce copyright material:

p.12 South Yorkshire Police, **p.42** West Yorkshire Police, **p.45** Merseyside Fire and Rescue Service, **p.51** HM Prison Service, **p.53** HM Revenue and Customs, **p.70** National Health Service, **p.245** Surrey Police, **p.248** Cumbria Police, **p.253** Crown Prosecution Service

p.166 Macpherson Report (The Stephen Lawrence Inquiry, 1999), **p.165** Ministry of Defence Hansard (HC Debate, 12 May 2009, c179w), **p. 235** **Table 12.1** Total cost estimates of crime by type (Home Office 2000), **p.279** **Table 13.2** Population of the UK by ethnic group, UK Census 2001: Crown Copyright data and information is reproduced under the terms of Click-Use Licence (C2010000590).

Texts cited in this book are as follows:

Roe, S and Man, L, Drug misuse declared: Findings from the British Crime Survey (Home Office Statistical Bulletin, 2005–6)

Walby, S and Allen, J, Domestic violence, sexual assault and stalking: Findings from the British Crime Survey (Home Office Research, 2004)

Every effort has been made to contact copyright holders of material reproduced in this book. Any omissions will be rectified in subsequent printings if notice is given to the publishers.